Also by Tim Palmer

*The Heart of America: Our Landscape, Our Future*

*America by Rivers*

*The Columbia*

*Lifelines: The Case for River Conservation*

*Yosemite: The Promise of Wildness*

*The Wild and Scenic Rivers of America*

*California's Threatened Environment: Restoring the Dream*

*The Snake River: Window to the West*

*The Sierra Nevada: A Mountain Journey*

*Endangered Rivers and the Conservation Movement*

*Youghiogheny: Appalachian River*

*Stanislaus: The Struggle for a River*

*Rivers of Pennsylvania*

# Pacific High

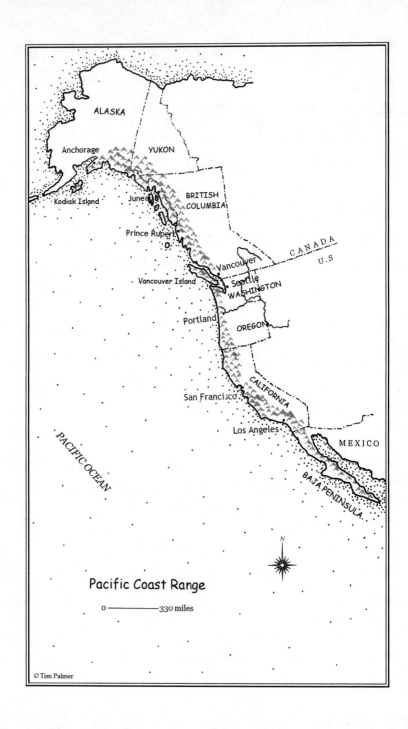

ALASKA

Anchorage

YUKON

Kodiak Island

Juneau

BRITISH
COLUMBIA

Prince Rupert

CANADA

U.S

Vancouver

Seattle

Vancouver Island

WASHINGTON

Portland

OREGON

CALIFORNIA

San Francisco

Los Angeles

MEXICO

PACIFIC OCEAN

BAJA PENINSULA

N

Pacific Coast Range

0 ——————— 330 miles

© Tim Palmer

# PACIFIC HIGH

*Adventures in the Coast Ranges*

*from Baja to Alaska*

## Tim Palmer

ISLAND PRESS

*Washington · Covelo · London*

## To Ann

A *Shearwater Book*
*Published by Island Press*

Copyright © 2002 Tim Palmer

All rights reserved under International and Pan-American Copyright
Conventions. No part of this book may be reproduced in any form or by
any means without permission in writing from the publisher: Island Press,
Suite 300, 1718 Connecticut Avenue, N.W., Washington, DC 20009

Shearwater Books is a trademark of The Center for Resource Economics.

The Coast Range sketch on page 1 is by Ann Vileisis.
Maps are by Tim Palmer and Ann Vileisis.

*Library of Congress Cataloging-in-Publication Data*
Palmer, Tim, 1948–
  Pacific high : adventures in the coast ranges from Baja to Alaska /
Tim Palmer.
      p.  cm.
Includes bibliographical references (p.   ).
  ISBN 1-55963-649-1  (hardcover : alk. paper)
  1. Coast Ranges—Description and travel. 2. Pacific Coast (U.S.)—
Description and travel. 3. United States—Description and travel.
4. Mountains—Pacific Coast (U.S.) 5. Palmer, Tim, 1948—Journeys—
Coast Ranges.  I. Title.
  F851 .P23 2002
  917.904'33—dc21                                              2002005689

British Cataloguing-in-Publication Data available.
Printed on recycled, acid-free paper

Manufactured in the United States of America
09  08  07  06  05  04  03  02      8  7  6  5  4  3  2  1

# Contents

## Prologue: Between the Sea and the Sky

On the first of January, at dawn, with winter rain pounding on the windshield, we set out on a journey of nine months from Baja to Kodiak, a tour of North America's coastal mountains high above the Pacific.

We began with a sense of discovery, allowing ourselves to wander where impulse would take us. I foresaw little of the path ahead, but, trying to understand the world, I would explore, identify, interview, read, photograph, dig in the dirt, and climb to the next horizon, all the time searching, all the time hunting, hunting. I wanted to see for myself, to learn by doing, to realize what was happening by being there. But mostly, my wife, Ann, and I looked forward to simply delighting ourselves day after day in new and extraordinary places.

Exceptional by any measure, America's longest nearly continuous mountain mass stretches for 3,600 miles as a marathoner crow might wing his way from the southern Baja Peninsula in Mexico to Kodiak Island in Alaska. Within this reach, 740 miles lie in Baja, 790 in California, 290 in Oregon, 150 in Washington, 530 in British Columbia, and 1,130 in Alaska. It's like driving from San Francisco to Miami and then up the Atlantic coast to Philadelphia and having it *all* be mountains.

Though I knew that hills and steep slopes rise up behind Los Angeles, and in San Francisco, and from the rugged seashore almost anywhere along the Pacific, my awareness of the Coast Range as a continuous chain of mountains with its own identity was vague at best. I think this is the case with most people, including those who live along the way. Yet all I had to do to grasp the bigger picture was look at a relief map of the continent. Right away the darkly shaded slope at the border of our western ocean popped out as the boldest, most continuously definable feature anywhere to be found. In that moment when my eye followed the crescendo course of the mountains up the Pacific coast, the concept for our trip was born.

Most often known by the familiar names of its subranges — Santa Monica, Olympic, Saint Elias, and many more — this collection of mountains is usually referred to in the plural: the Pacific Coast Ranges. But after traveling the whole way, southeast to northwest, I now recognize the mountains' continuity and so use the singular: the Pacific Coast Range. Along this length measuring the whole sunset edge of North America, the subranges link together like the ends of interwoven ropes. For Ann and me, the months ahead and the revealing stories of adventure and belonging would be linked in the same way.

If the West Coast were only a matter of soil meeting sea, it could be a New Jersey, a Louisiana, a Bangladesh. But the land here at the Pacific shore is rugged and uplifted. The mountains give the place its character and a certain magnetism that has attracted pilgrims and pioneers, refugees and escapees, seekers of opportunity, beauty, and love.

For generation after generation, people have packed up and headed west, and beyond the seaward slant of the Coast Range, you can't go any farther. So here they stayed. Others emigrated from the south, still others from the west, across the water. Some thirty-six million people now live on North America's Pacific edge, most of them in seven large cities within sight of the mountain country I would explore. Here where high expectations collide with capricious reality, the continental plates also collide, setting off earthquakes that rupture the earth into some of the world's most dramatic scenery.

The legendary storms of the Pacific mercilessly hammer this shoreline, and the mountains force clouds up over ridgelines and summits, agitating the weather even more. Rainforests, snowfields, and glaciers result, and the rivers carve valleys and canyons unlike any others on earth—spectacular landforms that I could only begin to picture from what showed on the maps.

Nature thrives here in ever changing arrays of life. Consider the ancient trees, the whales' migrations, the cry of eagles, the bugling of elk. Yet nature is also under attack here as viciously as anywhere, maybe more. Just look at the clearcutting, the oil spills, the smog, the engines of urban growth. I knew that the prognosis was grim for much of what I cared deeply about, and the more I learned about the problems, the more I was inclined toward despair. Yet having hope is essential, so I aimed to search out special people who seemed connected to their native or adopted ground—people who loved their place and strived for better stewardship. I wanted to see what they were doing to face the future in uncertain, troubled times.

Starting out, my mind and spirit were open to the mystery of foreign cultures, the spareness of aridity, the tension of seismicity, the heat of fire, the exuberance of the vast, the abundance of rot and rebirth, the kindness of strangers, the indomitable rules of climate, the triumph of life, the limits of the earth. I wanted to see it all, Mexico through Alaska, an idea at once challenging and playful.

It excited Ann as well. An adventurous soul, she had been leading educational wilderness trips for Outward Bound when we met on a river in Idaho six years before. Immediately we knew we had much in common and much to hold us tightly together. After a youth spent in New England, the Rockies had become her adopted home, but the draw of the Pacific, and the unknown, pulled on her as they did on me. "I love mountains, and I love the ocean," she said. "So, sure, I'd love to see it all."

Ann was writing a book that had demanded her attention for three years. Work remained, but she ached to cut loose. And this was the year to do the trip, we both agreed. We had no children of our own, no mortgage to burden us, no rent coming due the first of the month, no home to tend except for our well-equipped van and the big, round earth under our feet. Ann's manuscript was easily portable, and in another year she would start a new book with a challenging plan for research. Plus, our van had already clocked 90,000 miles, and with an eye on reliability, I hesitated to sojourn to the distant deserts in Mexico or the far North once it topped the 100,000 mark. "Can you finish your book while we travel?" I asked my wife.

"I'll be jealous of you having fun while I'm sitting and writing," she answered honestly, "but let's give it a try. If I work as we go, I should be done before we hit Alaska."

With the critical spousal go-ahead, my heart began to leap at the possibilities before us.

With great care we loaded the van. When I had bought it seven years before, I customized the well-windowed rig by raising the roof so I could stand up inside. Behind the driver's seat, alongside a long window, I built a table for writing, cooking, and other work or projects. Wired under the hood, an extra battery powered two lights and a computer for typing. Crawling underneath, I bolted a propane tank to the chassis to fuel a miniature furnace inside. Our two canoes and kayak lay lashed to the roof rack, and a whitewater raft hid, rolled up, inside. Cross-country skis and a mountain bike rounded out our fleet. We carried clothes for all seasons and a full complement of kitchen gear. Plus books, lots of books. Maxing out the van for this trip, we added an extra six-gallon water jug and several crates of nonperishable food. I stocked up on fuel for the Coleman stove and filled the propane tank for cold mornings, long sieges of bitter dampness, and the possibility of snow.

The whole setup was comfortable, efficient, and satisfying in both physical and metaphysical ways. In it, we own and consume little but see and experience much.

I was all puffed up with feelings of freedom and self-sufficiency and motivated by the promise of the open road. The words of Henry David Thoreau, written so long ago, inspired me still: "Rise free from care before dawn, and seek adventures. Let the noon find thee by other lakes, and the night overtake thee everywhere at home."

# PACIFIC HIGH

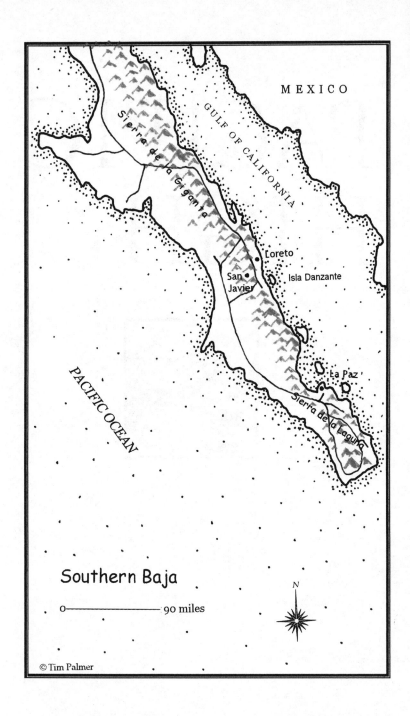

MEXICO

GULF OF CALIFORNIA

Sierra de la Gigante

Loreto

San Javier

Isla Danzante

La Paz

Sierra de la Laguna

PACIFIC OCEAN

Southern Baja

0 ——————— 90 miles

N

© Tim Palmer

chapter

# 1 | *Into Baja*

$F$IRST LIGHT began to etch the rocky eastern horizon, and a rooster crowed for about the hundredth time since it had begun waking me up at three A.M. Soon it would be light enough for me to evade the chain-link cholla and other spiny cacti—no casual challenge on my route to the top of the mountain.

Crawling out of bed while Ann still dozed in the cozy back of our Ford van, I drew in a deep breath of anticipation. At times like this—at the beginning—life is full of wonder, and the sharpened edge of the unknown quickens my heart. The deep blue behind the morning stars promised a clear day, a day full of possibilities. The empty space out there somehow drew me to it. Nothing diminished my eagerness to get out and see what was around me, to learn what I could about this part of the earth. After dressing warmly and grabbing my camera pack and water bottle, I was on the way, aiming to meet the sunrise at the summit.

Except for the roosters' machismo calls, the village of San Javier, six hundred miles south of the border on the Baja Peninsula of Mexico, lay still and silent. The surrounding dry mesas stood boldly in black as the day began to glow behind them, refracted light just beginning to reveal important details that tell stories on the ground.

At the edge of the one-lane dirt road, cobbles and sharp-sided stones had accumulated from both directions: some raked off by road graders, others thrown out of people's gardens, each an effort to bring human order to a harsh and resistant land. I left the road and struck out cross-country.

The gray, unshadowed light began to glow on the swollen, pleated skin of the cardón — cacti up to forty feet tall with bold trunks pointing toward the heavens. Their stubby arms jutted out or curved up, a signpost of the Sonoran Desert in Mexico. A close relative to the saguaro cactus of old TV westerns, these charismatic cacti seemed to welcome me, but underfoot and too close for comfort lurked pincushions, protruding nails, spiked trip wires, and the snakepit twinings of curled cacti with nasty barbs ready to pierce me at the slightest misstep.

Where I walked there was no trail, so I tried to be careful, and wondered, Is growing old a matter of becoming ever more cautious? I hoped not. I was forty-eight that winter and still felt the reckless indomitability of youth. Like many fools, I failed to recognize myself as middle-aged, though I had been so for some time. I didn't really like being careful, but out in that desert, greater knowledge definitely bred greater care.

This morning my yearning had to do with beginnings. I wanted to be on the first mountaintop of my Coast Range exploration for the opening moment of the day.

Beginnings are fragile things, promising, portentous, consequential, painful. But my goal seemed simple enough at face value: I wanted to stand on top of the mountain for sunrise. Deep into Baja, I wanted to sense the beginning of the day, of the trip, and of the mountains that run nearly nonstop through Alaska. By climbing to a high point of ground, I hoped to sense the power of the place, to feel its life and its history in my bones, to imagine its future, and mainly to belong there in some satisfying way. If I didn't feel all those emotions today, maybe I would on some other mountain before the end of our Baja adventure. And I knew that some of my grander ambitions would have to wait for their own good time during the nine months to come.

The arid slopes opened a bit more enticingly, and with soil and stone crunching underfoot, I moved up quickly into the spreading light. I found a goat path along the ridge. After twisting around the clutches of catclaw acacia, scrambling over basaltic rocks, and breathing heavily as I broke into a heavy sweat, I set foot on top of the mountain just before the fireball of sun pierced the horizon.

Propped against a rock and resting there after my prickly climb, I happily soaked in the scene of roughcut mesas while the light seeped down the east-facing mountainside next to me. In shades of brown, it was not a colorful mountain range, nor shapely in the sense of having sharp peaks or undulant and sensuous forms. Rather, I looked at a vast desert topography populated by domestic goats, a white cross propped on the next mountain, and a black flurry of vultures.

Though I couldn't see the ocean, this was part of the greater Coast Range. The Baja Peninsula, seven hundred forty miles long, seventy miles wide on average, is the third-longest peninsula in the world behind the Malay in Southeast Asia and the Antarctic, but it's the skinniest and most peninsular of the group. Mountains form the backbone of Baja, a seismically shifting, volcanically active land. Here, in the largest subrange, aptly named Sierra de la Giganta — Mountains of the Giantess — the view was typical, with harsh, dry country everywhere evident.

The fiery sphere of sun was doing its incandescent job, and with a dusty shine down below it illuminated the dome of a church, a three-story stone bastion of faith built by Indians long ago at the direction of Spanish missionaries. I tried to imagine those people, who had lived all their lives in wholly adequate houses of stick or thatch, suddenly confronting orders to cut, quarry, and haul rocks that might have weighed a ton in order to build this smooth-walled, high-roofed mission for the worship of a brand-new god.

Three centuries later it still stands as the centerpiece of the village of San Javier, made up of thirty houses or so from this vulture's-eye view. The church is considered a healing mission, so icons of body parts, such as little painted arms and legs and hearts made of wood, are left there in hopes of *milagros* — miracles.

Beyond the mission, the town's ditch system outlined small fields of onions with a border of green. The modest irrigation network was also built by Indians under the supervision of Spanish missionaries.

One of the oldest irrigation systems in Baja, it predates by far any-thing now functioning in the United States. A canopy of olive trees planted by the padres lined the main waterway.

The town was waking, and even from eight hundred feet above I could hear the cry of babies, the murmur of women's voices, a single, gruff shout of a man, the tinkling of a goat's bell, the crow of a roos-ter still at it, and always, always the barking of dogs. The sounds built as the minutes passed — now the chopping of wood, the laughter of children, the cranking of a reluctant pickup, the rattling bounce of a capable truck on the washboarded road — all told, an audio micro-cosm of humanity on the earth.

The sun now beamed on the whole village, heating it up in a pro-cess that wouldn't quit for many hours. Even there — way out there — the new light glinted off a bright red sign that advertised Tecate beer.

I descended quickly, making tracks back to the van, where Ann had prepared a breakfast of oatmeal. Not just any oatmeal, and cer-tainly not the soggy mush of minute oats, her recipe included organic apples, raisins, walnuts, cinnamon, and nutmeg. As in all matters of food, Ann takes a healthful breakfast seriously.

"What did you see?" she asked.

"The sun and the mountains," I synopsized, following with only the briefest elaboration. "Tell me about what you wrote," I countered, knowing that she was refining the last chapter of her book about the history of America's wetlands, worlds away from the aridity we faced at this end of the coastal mountains.

"I had time to read over only a page or two. But look, let's catch up later. Trudi's due here any minute now. How's this for lunch?" Ann displayed a hunk of cheese, an apple, and two slabs of bread we had made in a covered skillet on our stove. Having consulted a phrase book, she made an irresistible offer with a tilt of her head: "Te gustaría almorzar conmigo hoy?" Would you like to join me for lunch today?

Because Ann grasped only a bit of Spanish and I knew none at all, I required the help of Trudi Angell. But even if I were bilingual from birth, I still would have needed Trudi's help for what I wanted to do in the Mexican mountains.

With a name of circumstantial elegance, this woman had come to Catholic Baja in 1976. Quickly it became a part of her. Slowly she became a part of it. In Trudi, I knew I had found not only the guide I needed to help me learn about this foreign place but also the exact kind of person I was hoping to meet on my journey — one who loves where she is on this earth and lives with deliberate care for her place.

"I was twenty," Trudi recapped, straining back through many good years as we bounced over a washboard road in her veteran truck. Ann and I had left the van at a site where we could camp for the night and crowded onto the front seat along with Olivia, Trudi's delightful only child. "My boyfriend back then taught ocean kayaking and led trips out of Mulegé. He worked for NOLS — the National Outdoor Leadership School." NOLS offers courses in outdoor skills and trains people to become teachers for outdoor programs.

To skip the intervening quarter century for the time being, let me just say that Trudi and her partner, Douglas Knapp, now ran trips of their own in a business called Las Parras Tours. Knowing of my interest in the remote mountains of Baja's interior, she had agreed to take Ann and me on a three-day excursion to get the flavor of the Sierra de la Giganta and to see people on the way. "Here's our first stop," Trudi said, stepping on the brake and allowing our dust to overtake us. "Rancho los Dolores."

The house was adobe brick and could have been ancient. An outdoor kitchen enjoyed the shade of a thatched roof and the privacy of walls made by weaving sticks together. Trudi and a prancing Olivia were greeted by hugs from Maria Luisa Veliz, Maria's mother, and her mother-in-law, who was quite old and wrapped tightly in a dark shawl. They all stationed themselves near the *hornilla,* a clay-bottomed wood-burning stove that smelled delicious with warming tortillas.

The women's dresses — beautiful florals — were spotlessly clean, there in a smoke-puffing kitchen with a floor made of dirt. Was this how they always dressed? Or were they spruced up for us? Some things — a lot of things — you just don't ask.

They welcomed Ann and me with smiles and did not hesitate in their animated Spanish conversation with Trudi. They gave her a bag of homegrown oranges and grapefruit. They chatted about the fields, the weather, the road, whatever. Trudi offered Ann and me an abbreviated running commentary, leaving out most of the news but still giving us the gist of their everyday chat.

That was fine, but all the while I couldn't help but wonder how their lives in these remote mountains related to the larger world. How was the civilization out there pressing in on them? Not knowing how to get a grip on my question, I finally asked Trudi to inquire, "How have your lives changed in recent years?"

Suddenly they all fell silent. They had to think about this. Eventually, haltingly, a consensus was reached and cautiously expressed. "We used to be very poor. We had no cars at all. Now we are wealthy in comparison."

That was it. I could see how these good-spirited women felt. They liked their cars, of course. We all do. But I wondered: As the commercial culture tentacled out to these people, what was happening to their land? How were the changes affecting their families?

Leaving the women and their conversation, I wandered alone into a patchwork of fields ranging from very small to an acre. Several men —fathers, sons, and grandsons—hoed weeds, thinned onions, and tinkered with irrigation flows from a gravity system that diverted water out of a spring, shunted it through a concrete sluiceway two feet wide, ran it into a cement cistern plugged with a hand-carved block of wood, and then dropped it into a stone-lined ditch feeding the furrows of the irrigated fields. This system—from gravity flow to wooden plug—struck me as appropriate technology. It had survived continuous use for several hundred years. Unlike the salt-poisoned, selenium-laced, leached-white soil and noxious weedlots now common in big western irrigation systems and factory fields elsewhere in Baja and in California, the plots that these men tended looked good. They looked as if they could produce for another few centuries, maybe forever.

For all its differences, the workday scene reminded me of generations-old photos of subsistence farming by my own ancestors in the Appalachian Mountains. The men wielded long-handled hoes and broad-bladed scythes, all hand tools. The midwinter light at those lower latitudes rubbed a golden cast into everything it touched.

Old Enrique Veliz, with a thick, white mustache, white shirt, black pants, and soil-covered sandals, smiled at his family and leaned on his hoe.

"Enrique, podría tomar tu foto?" May I take your picture? It was one Spanish phrase I had been able to memorize.

"Sí. No es problema."

"Your garden, it's beautiful," I offered in English with a sweep of my hand and a smile.

"Sí." He nodded. I wanted to know more about how he did it.

"Do you rotate your corn and onions year by year?"

"Sí."

"And how do you fertilize the fields?"

"Sí."

I waited a moment in quiet appreciation of my welcome. "Gracias," I offered, and retreated toward the house and the women.

I was impressed by these rural Mexicans' friendliness, a manner I noticed perhaps because of unfriendliness I'd encountered elsewhere. As I walked back, it occurred to me that they probably didn't even think about it. It was simply the way they were. Well, at least so long as Ann and I showed up with Trudi Angell.

With this window to life in the mountains of Baja cracking open a bit, we reboarded the truck and rolled on a little farther.

"So, your boyfriend worked as a kayak instructor and guide," I said to Trudi.

"Yes. I signed up as a student, and we paddled on Conception Bay. I loved the water. I loved the place."

As with most people, it was the sea, not the mountains, that had drawn Trudi Angell to Baja.

"I went home to Calistoga, California, but couldn't get Baja out of my mind, so I bought a Klepper—a kayak you can take apart and fold up for shipping. When I came back in 1978, NOLS needed help. I bounced around in the desert looking for watering holes and campsites, scouting out trips for them. After that I ran logistics for a few years, driving the truck and dropping off water and food. It was a good introduction to the land. And to the need for water. The best part came at the end of the season, when a few of us loaded the kayaks and took a six-week trip of our own.

"Then, in the winter of 1983, I thumbtacked five-by-seven cards up at the recreation equipment co-op in Berkeley. The cards said, 'Kayaking in Baja.' People called, so I gathered up a few more Kleppers and started doing trips for a hundred dollars a person. My partner and I rented a place, and in 1984 we ran seven trips, some of them all the way from Mulegé to Loreto. I guided everybody myself. Now we offer sea kayaking, whale watching, mountain biking, tours to missions and cave paintings, and mule-riding expeditions into the mountains."

Wondering why Trudi liked Baja so much when brilliant watery green mountains such as the Sierra Nevada beckoned so much closer to home, I asked, "What do you like about it here?"

Her eyes and face came alive, and she did not hesitate. "The openness. The wildness. Riding on a mule in the desert and discovering an oasis is a wonderful feeling. And I like the people. Especially in the mountains. The older people are part of the land here. We'll run into a cowboy dressed up in the traditional garb of a deerskin *cuera* — a wraparound leather jacket — and I feel like I'm transported back a hundred years. You can't get that feeling in the United States, certainly not in California."

"And you like living in Loreto?"

"Yes, but our dream is to move up to the mountains. It's one of many dreams you have when you're out here. In Loreto, it's nice, and the people are good. But it's changing. The great landgrab has started, with big business rearing its head."

I immediately pictured the posh resorts of travel magazine ads. "And this isn't the style?" I gestured to her truck and to the dusty route ahead of us.

"No. People are using the word *ecotourism,* but they don't know what it means. Uncontrolled fishing is depleting the Gulf of California. Roads are opening up remote areas. The whole package is an awful intrusion, and the tourists don't get much out of it. I know because I've seen that business; I've seen how it operates. The big resorts bring in their own vans to bus clients back and forth, so the tourists don't meet the people or see the land. Now they're talking about opening casinos. But no one needs this place to play slots and blackjack. They could do that in Tijuana."

"Tell me, Trudi," I said, shifting the subject as we hit a rut in the road, "how do you know all these farmers and ranchers up here?"

"It's taken years, but once they understand what I'm doing, it's easy. Once they get to know you, they're quite friendly."

Trudi omitted that her reputation preceded her. When I arrived in Loreto and inquired as to her whereabouts, an English-speaking shop owner had said, "Sí. Sure I know her. She's famous. You just go down here and take a right and cross the dry wash and take another right," and so forth. Explaining some of the referred-to fame, another friend had told me that Trudi hires Mexicans to lead her tours. She uses local taxi drivers for her shuttles. She drives local people to the hospital when nobody else can. She loans money to local families so they can start small businesses. She does what very few gringos do when they go to Mexico.

For dinner we visited Guillermo and Bili Bastida. It was difficult to tell where home ended and restaurant began. The comfortable outdoor patio accommodated us and a few other people, including ninety-nine-year-old Loreto de los Santos and her eighty-four-year-old brother, Priciliano.

With Trudi's help I engaged Guillermo and the older man in a discussion of range conditions. Though I've never worked as a buckaroo, grasslands have long interested me. After all, along with deserts they account for over half the land in North America and are what most of life — human and otherwise — depends upon in arid country such as Baja.

To put it bluntly, the grazing conditions looked pitiful. I had seen almost no grasses or forbs but rather cacti, thorny shrubs such as acacia, weeds spiny enough to kill a cow, and lots of mesquite. This coarse, thorny shrub ruthlessly invades deserts when grazing wipes out native grasses and when groundwater tables drop owing to the abuse of soil and streams. Mountain people around the world typically turn to raising goats when the range becomes too depleted for cows. And goats were what everyone here raised.

"Are there fewer grasses now?" I asked.

A long and animated discussion ensued. Trudi followed the volley but reported no score. After several minutes the talk slowed a bit and I asked what they had concluded. Trudi simply reported, "There is less grass now, but they think it's because it used to rain more." Their response seemed to be suspiciously reliant on the role of God. I could tell they were having trouble with the topic I had raised.

By way of explanation Trudi said, "Change, over time, is something they just don't think much about. They think about today. Tomorrow, *mañana,* will take care of itself."

*Mañana* means more than just "tomorrow." It loosely describes an outlook on life that runs deep in Mexican culture. It means "We can deal with it tomorrow" or "Tomorrow will come regardless." One hears the word *mañana* often in Mexico.

Along the same line but in a slightly more hopeful vein, people here are also fond of saying, "Si Dios quiere." God willing.

As longtime Mexico correspondent Alan Riding explained in his illuminating portrait *Distant Neighbors,* "the future is viewed with fatalism, and as a result, the idea of planning seems unnatural." By extension of this personal philosophy, the health of the land simply exists. Its future will simply happen.

I tried to ask my question in a different way, and Guillermo, who worked as a farmer, not a rancher, reflected that there used to be more cows where there were now goats, and that a vine with yellow trumpet flowers tended to take over whenever the grasses were grazed off.

Trudi turned to me and said, "I would love to have seen the range-lands before cattle and goats, but that would mean going back three hundred years, before the Spanish. Once I rode around to the top of a box canyon where cows couldn't go. The grasses grew thickly there even when everyplace else was dried out."

"Is there any effort to improve the range? To cut back on grazing and give native plants a chance to recover?"

Trudi answered that during more extreme droughts, ranchers do their best to cull the herds and sell off stock before large-scale loss. They'll pull cows off the range and give them a feed concentrate just to keep them alive until the desert plants sprout again. But in terms of any systematic effort to restore grasslands or improve the range, there was nothing to report.

Changing the subject, Trudi mentioned that Bili for years had grown plants used by naturopathic doctors in the United States. Her own little cottage industry supplied herbs that wouldn't grow in the North. Her fifteen-year-old daughter lived in Loreto so she could attend high school, and she wanted to go to the university in La Paz to study medicine. Her son didn't like to study and worked here with his father.

"Do most of the young people leave the mountains?"

"Many do," Trudi answered. "The population of San Javier is about the same as it was a hundred years ago."

Catching our drift, Bili offered, "In the city, it's very difficult for young people. They want to have a car. They want to own all those things. They think they'll get rich quick but are not prepared, so they cannot earn money. They become disillusioned, and some return to help on the farms. They are happier when they come back." Yet according to Trudi, few actually do return.

This arid land — any land — can support only a limited number of people. In these mountains, which have been settled since the seventeenth century, when colonizing missionaries arrived, and by local Indians nine thousand years before that, there's not enough water or land for more children to live on. So if there are more than two children per family, they pretty much have to go to the cities. Otherwise — and this has been happening for a long time — the pie of resources is divided into smaller and smaller pieces, pieces too small for a family's livelihood.

"Big families have been the norm," Trudi explained. "Four or five children are common, and up to twelve is not uncommon. Sometimes I'm asked, 'Don't you want more children so it will be happier?'"

Trudi pointed out that children here not only are considered the source of happiness but also supply labor and social security for the parents. Everyone seems to think that having lots of children is encouraged by the Catholic church. But more important, according to some knowledgeable observers, plentiful offspring are considered proof of male machismo. Furthermore, Mexican people have had an obsession with increasing their population ever since the Spanish invasion, when up to 90 percent of local populations were killed by soldiers or smallpox that the soldiers and missionaries brought over. The die-off spawned a durable cultural imperative to replace the lost people, and as with many aspects of Mexican culture, the past remains the present. The momentum continued on and on, with little change or consideration of the future.

Here in the mountains of Baja, the result was plainly evident. Even though the place is sparsely populated, water supplies and arable acreage are used to the hilt; the land is full. Children move to the cities. But at that point, a lot of new problems have only begun. In the cities, where nobody expects to live off the land, overpopulation is harder to recognize. People can survive even though their numbers exceed any reasonable standard involving the supplies of land and water, the economic welfare of mass numbers of citizens, the personal freedoms that are sacrificed in overpopulated places, and the most basic qualities of life that many Americans consider essential.

The lesson I took from the harsh hillsides around San Javier was that the ability of the land to support people is limited, and the many ways we have of avoiding that reality are delusions for which we will someday pay.

That night we camped at an unfinished cement-block shell that Trudi was fixing up with high hopes of a mountain home. In the morning, we all got ready to ride on mules to some remote ranches in the mountains.

We drove to Rancho Viejo, a goat farm, where we met Agapito, a stocky man with powerful features and dark skin, one of few local people with a good sample of local Cochimi Indian blood. He showed us to our mules. Raul de los Santos, the ranch caretaker, would be our guide. Trudi and Olivia mounted without hesitation and handled their mules as capably as cowgirls in Montana. Ann and I had ridden horses only once in a while over the years. But we each swung a leg up, and away we went.

Our route followed a dirt road deeper into the mountains. The mules walked and occasionally trotted. Following Raul, we veered off the road and onto a trail that cut back and forth across a dry wash. The land was exceedingly arid, with rock, dust, and cacti. The mesquite snagged at our pantlegs and at the mules' bellies.

"You can see why nobody hikes here," Trudi explained as she rode beside me. "It really is mule country. Plus, the only water is at the ranches. If you're camping, you have to stay there."

We stopped at the inviting home of Juan Bautista Romero and his wife, Chari. In their thirties, this couple, along with their three children, managed to live off an unaccommodating land and do it in good style.

Potted flowers brightened the patio. Separating an outdoor kitchen from the house and yard were beautiful screens woven from *cariso,* a wetland reed. Juan had picked the stems and then crushed, split, and pulled them open by hand. Once they were dried, he wove them into five-foot-tall panels. Strips of the inner wood of the cardón were used as lath along one wall of the house. The well, hand dug and four feet in diameter, never went dry, fed by the sparse and seasonal rainfall. Bolted to the side of the house was a two- by three-foot solar panel, the only new thing in sight. The first appliance that got powered was a fluorescent light. Second was a radio.

Juan and Chari grow onions and cows. Each cow needs two hundred or more acres of land. For comparison, that figure drops to one acre or less in temperate climates of the eastern United States. With cows and goats grazing heavily, there is little vegetation left for wildlife. Nevertheless, Juan shoots a deer occasionally, as most ranchers do, though rules supposedly restrict hunting to December and January. Raul added that he once guided hunting trips for bighorn sheep, but now there are few sheep left.

The ranchers chop wood for construction materials and for fires, though government regulations recognize the slow growth rate of trees in this desert and theoretically restrict cutting. Raul had recently attended a meeting held by officials who tried to explain the rules, but he suspected that people do what they want anyway. "They have their regulations; we live our lives" seemed to be the operative slogan.

After saddling up we departed again, the sun cooking us as we bounced along, but we were served cool drinks of water at three different ranches. Dirt or stone floors were kept clean by the women, and hand-dug wells provided surprisingly dependable water. Inside, pictures of Jesus appeared. Pinups more commonly decorated outbuildings or workshops.

Though the people seemed well aware of contemporary Baja, the ranches were resoundingly remote, and the people lived a good life that drew heavily on heritage. Yet, Trudi said, "Many of the old ways are being lost. Before the road was drivable, everybody rode on horseback and stopped for visits on their way through. Now, people just zoom by in a hurry."

Late in the afternoon, at the end of the ride, we returned to Rancho Viejo, handed our mounts over to Raul and Agapito, and strolled around, awaiting an aromatic dinner that Angelina — Raul's wife — was busily preparing.

In the American West, it's impolite to ask how much stock a rancher raises. You might as well ask how much money he makes. So on my own I counted fifty goats in a pen. And others ranged wild. Without prying too much, I learned from Raul that a herd of forty goats could modestly support a family. The goats might go for forty dollars each when sold for meat, but primarily they are milked for goat cheese. The ranchers make the cheese and sell it to stores or to roving distributors.

Singing the praises of goats, Raul said: "They drink little water. They eat rough forage and don't need grass. In dry years you just cut off the tops of trees for them to eat. And if you lose one, it's not like losing a cow, which costs a lot of money." The goats might stray five miles into the mountains. They are rounded up with dogs and on foot because the country into which they disappear is too rugged for horses.

At a dinner table long enough for many ranch hands, Angelina's roasted goat tasted a lot like the rabbits my mother once cooked by a generations-old family recipe after I had plugged the quick little bunnies with my shotgun out back. Both had a delicious wild flavor. Along with the goat, we ate homemade tortillas just moments off the griddle and beans refried in lard.

As I chewed on the last bit of goat gristle because it tasted so good, some people from town arrived in a sport utility vehicle, made a friendly round of conversation with the people at Rancho Viejo, and negotiated a price for a goat. Raul polished off his dinner, headed over to the goat pen, strung a young animal up by a rear leg, and slit its throat, to the great joy of the dogs, which lapped up the blood from the rocks.

While I rode in the truck back to Loreto, with Ann following behind in the van, Trudi said, "I don't know how long that kind of life will last. In some form it'll last quite a while, but the changes are coming. The government is saying that more land can be cleared for farming if they put in big wells farther down the canyon. But many of us fear that might take the groundwater away from these people. Near the city of Constitución they drilled a lot of new wells to serve what the Japanese and Mexican governments call 'joint ventures' to open up new farms. In the process they've ruined family wells, and now some of the new farms are already being closed down because the water didn't last. Nature's way of serving generation after generation here could be ruined almost overnight."

It sounded all too familiar. But keeping the mountain people's lifestyle alive is Trudi's passion.

"There are ways of using the land well and helping these people," she explained. "I'd like to set up a fund for local families to open bed-and-breakfasts and pursue other opportunities that take advantage of the place simply as it is. Anybody willing to come and visit Baja on its own terms can have a great experience. If I can play even a small role in keeping these mountains the way they are, I'll be pleased."

A QUICK GLANCE at a three-dimensional map of the Baja Peninsula shows that mountains run with scarcely a break the whole way. Mountains everywhere are built by seismic or volcanic forces, and both have performed spectacularly here, where the southern end of the Coast Range is flooded on both sides by salt water.

Rising as seven distinct but interconnecting blocks, the Baja mountains are called the Peninsular Ranges and align north–south. They generally surge abruptly on their east side while sloping more gradually to the west, much like the profile of a breaking wave approaching from the Pacific Ocean. Various smaller ranges, volcanic in origin, pop up here and there above the desert plains.

Seismic rift is what made Baja and what separates it from mainland Mexico. Opening up the Gulf of California, this earthquake-induced parting of the lands began twelve million years ago and continues today. As the seafloor beneath the Gulf of California spreads apart, Baja drifts northwestward two inches per year on roughly the same shear line that becomes California's familiar San Andreas Fault. In some millions of years, the mountains where we rode with Trudi will parade past what remains of California on their way to the big train wreck of rock and dirt that's piling up at the northern limits of today's Coast Range in Alaska.

But for the time being, Baja lies at the same latitude as Florida, and at fifty-five thousand square miles it's roughly the same in area, though longer, skinnier, and profoundly mountainous, whereas Florida is just as seriously flat. For another comparative grasp of this foreign land, Baja California is one-third the size of Alta California, the United States' California. The length of the two are comparable, but at Baja the sea fronts on both sides instead of on only one, which causes it to have two times the ocean frontage—three thousand miles, counting the jigsaw cutouts of bays and inlets. Unlike that of Alta California, the quiddity of Baja is wild, generally lacking in cities, military bases, nuclear power plants, and roads.

Considering all that, one might think the ecosystems and nature of Baja would be in good shape, but owing to even limited population growth in such a spare land and to a lack of regulatory effectiveness, they're not. For example, few of the bighorn sheep that once grazed from end to end remain. Native riparian life has been lost because the groundwater has been depleted. The winter refuge of the gray whales is threatened by salt mines. On and on it goes.

Because this mountainous land rises next to the ocean, one might expect it to be stormy and rainy. But rainfall is rare, and here's why. Sunlight, of course, shines directly on the Tropics and heats air the most at equatorial latitudes. Being lighter, that air rises and cools as it gains elevation. Quickly it reaches the dew point, at which it can no longer hold abundant moisture, and rain falls out to water the jungles of tropical latitudes. As it reaches a high elevation in the atmosphere —by now cool and dry—this air has to go somewhere when additional warm air rises up underneath it. Picture a ceiling fan pushing air straight up. So winds peel out to the north and south from the equatorial latitudes, falling back to the earth as they go, creating permanent high-pressure systems as they descend. These force other weather systems away and create nearly rainproof zones. That's why the earth's great deserts occur where they do, in two belts between 15 and 30 degrees latitude both north and south of the equator. Baja lies between 23 and 31 degrees north of it.

The limited rainfall splits into two distinct seasons — winter and summer — with most coming early in the year. This dual season is partly a quirk of winter storms imported from the Pacific and partly one of tropical storms that blow up from the south, bringing monsoons, or *chubascos*. Even in the desert, humidity during those dog days becomes unbearable to Americans.

The dual seasons of rainfall make the Sonoran Desert — covering most of Baja and a significant lobe of the American Southwest — the richest of all continental deserts in diversity of vegetation. Twenty-five hundred species of plants grow here.

All native life survives with splendid adaptations to local conditions. For example, through transpiration, leaves normally lose a lot of water, so paloverde trees carry out photosynthesis by tapping chlorophyll in their green bark and stems. The cardón cactus, living for two hundred years, can double its weight with stored water as its trunk swells, flattening the accordion-like pleats.

As a showpiece of Baja botany, occurring in the northern third of the peninsula, the *cirio* may rank as the strangest tree on the globe. Like a great inverted green carrot stick, it rises up to fifty feet high, with only the tiniest leaves, a mere fuzz, clinging to the trunk.

The elephant tree is my favorite, growing with a white, fleshy trunk and branches that remain fat for most of their length but then bluntly taper down to nothing, a stout little dwarf of a tree shaped to reduce evaporative loss. Incredibly, it has no thorns. Fifty species of acacia, five species of mesquite, plus ocotillos, cacti, and many other Baja plants, do have thorns — adaptations to discourage browsers here, where food is at a premium. Yet for all its harshness, the winter and summer rains can turn the land to dazzling green.

Emphatically desert, Baja receives an average of only six inches of rain a year. But being colder, higher elevations get more, making the mountains crucial to both natural habitat and people's existence. The peninsula's two streams that flow year-round to the ocean — only *two* in the length of California — draw their water from the mountains. Likewise, groundwater, on which people and agriculture everywhere depend, seeps down from the peaks.

Though you'd never believe it from the dusty barrens below, the north-facing slopes high in the Sierra San Pedro Mártir of northern Baja support pinyon pine, juniper, live oak, Jeffrey pine, lodgepole pine, sugar pine, incense cedar, white fir, and quaking aspen — a forest that could have been transplanted from California's Sierra Nevada. Even in the far south, summits of the Sierra de la Laguna can get forty inches of precipitation, the same as New York. But this life-affirming gift of moisture comes only to the limited acreage of mountaintops.

All these natural processes relate intimately to the way people live. Mexico ranks eleventh worldwide in population, but few of those people reside in Baja. Distinctly separated from the mainland by a ninety-mile-wide sea, by history, by economy, and by politics, people here prefer to call themselves Bajacalifornios. Sixty-three percent of them reside in the three northern cities of Tijuana, Mexicali, and Ensenada. Outside those, population density averages one person per ten square miles — low by any standard. The United States, by comparison, houses seventy people per square mile. In Baja's desert there is simply not enough water to supply a large population. Per capita income is far above the average in Mexico owing to tourism; this sunny vacationland just happens to lie at Americans' doorstep. More than fifty million people per year visit.

In fact, Ann and I found that tourism was a hopping business in Loreto — the first permanent settlement of the Spanish in Baja and its capital for more than a century. Walking the streets, I said "Buenos días" to older men and "Hola" to younger men. Most answered in kind or politely, reciprocally, said "Good morning." With potted flowers in front of shops, the mid-January atmosphere held a balmy tropical fragrance that triggered a near-autonomic response to breathe deeply and sigh, especially when I thought about our usual winter digs in the frigid mountains of western Wyoming.

A seashore town, Loreto vulnerably and opportunistically fronts the Gulf of California. But looking west on any number of streets, I saw that the mountains loomed powerfully behind, outside, above.

One peak, El Pilón de las Parras, was sharpened as perfectly as a child's schematic of a volcano and seemed to rise from the neighborhoods. In the Third World foreground, tiny cement-block houses crowded together, with children pattering at the edges of dirt streets.

It just so happened that Tiffany Bingham — an old college friend of Ann's — was in Baja because she guided sailing trips for NOLS. So we met in Loreto, strolled the streets, and took in a collective eyeful. Shop owners proudly displayed their wares. Outdoor restaurants featured fish tacos fashioned from the day's catch. The grocery store stocked truckloads of juicy local melons.

In a prominent restaurant we sat down for lunch. Paranoid about pollution in Mexico, I ordered bottled water. Sure enough, it came in a bottle, but the grooves in the screw-top cap were embedded with dirt as black as on the lunch box of a mechanic, obviously the result of opening and closing, opening and closing. Now that I think about it, the bottle was less likely to have been washed at all than the water glass Tiffany drank out of. While guidebooks advise avoiding tap water, many travelers don't worry. Baja's water is much better than that of mainland Mexico.

After lunch, with Tiff as security, I tried out a little Spanish, though I never had what school counselors called an aptitude for foreign languages.

"Buenos días. Tienes bonitas cosas en venta." You have nice things to sell. I had memorized this for the day in town.

"Gracias. Puedo ayudar en encontrar algo?"

"Perdón," I answered, quickly stumped. "El español no comprende," I said, which seemed clear enough to me.

The shop owner chuckled.

Tiff said, "Good try, Tim, but what you said was "The Spanish man doesn't understand.""

I tried again: "El español no sabe nada." I knew that pidgin Spanish was as good as I'd ever do, but I thought I had made a reasonable second try.

Tiffany smiled at the man apologetically. "Forget it, Tim. Now you said 'The Spanish man, he does not know nothing.' I think maybe you'd better let me do the talking."

When we wandered the streets as a threesome, young Mexican

men unerringly noticed that there was an extra woman in our ensemble. They seemed to think that Ann was the available gringa, probably because, being five feet, ten, she stands an inch and three-quarters taller than me. Regarding this height difference, I have no problem. But the interested looks of the men fired me up. Even the Irish have machismo. So I wrapped an arm possessively around my wife and immediately noticed that the leering stares shifted to Tiff.

"It's all quite harmless in this situation," she said. "Though when I'm alone, it feels different. Men smile, wave, hail me from across the street, whistle as they drive by, stop to talk, and try not to let me go."

Later that evening I decided to look up an old friend, Guy Bonnivier, who by circumstances unknown had come to town. I knew this only because he had dropped by to say hi to Trudi, one of those amazing coincidences that make the enormous world seem small.

For some years the director of the Idaho chapter of The Nature Conservancy, Guy is one of many people whose relationship to Baja might be called an addiction. Every winter he leaves the snow behind and comes down for a while. Like others, he's drawn not by the mountains but by the sea.

"Have a beer," Guy offered in the kitchen of the house he had rented for a few weeks. We popped our cans and propped our feet up for a chat.

"So what brings you to Baja this time, Guy?"

He paused, seeming to evaluate my interest. And I must have passed.

"Let me go to the beginning," he began, settling quickly into a mission of explanation. "When I first started coming here, in the 1970s, there was not a better sea on earth. The fish were thick, dolphins everywhere. The Gulf of California was a paradise."

Fish populations had plummeted, victimized by the enthusiasm of sport anglers, who had been coming down ever since the 1,050-mile road was paved. "They fill their coolers with six hundred pounds of fish and go home," Guy explained. "Even worse are the Japanese factory ships. They comb the seafloor of the Gulf by dragging nets. It's called trawling, but being a Pennsylvania boy, you'd recognize it as strip mining." The required permits from the Mexican government are said to be a bureaucratic formality when the decisions are properly lubricated.

"I suspect you're not here just to enjoy what's left of the place," I commented. I had a hunch that this professional conservationist was on a busman's holiday.

Between sips of Tecate, Guy shared his plans with me. "I'm helping to set up a way for the local people to take control of their waters. With Pronatura — an environmental group based in Mexico City — we're trying to fund and train Bajacalifornio wardens so they can patrol their waters. There's still time to save something of real value down here. And policing for illegal fishing is just the first step."

As Guy described it, conservation in Baja means trying to get a grip on the direct overkilling of fish. But another initiative has established several nature preserves, such as a park in the Sierra San Pedro Mártir. And since the 1970s, Baja law has forbidden structures within twenty meters of the high-tide line. Unfortunately, enforcement is subject to the shifting winds of politics, to limited regulatory ability, and to corruption that's so widespread it's considered perfectly normal. As Mexico expert Alan Riding explained, "The concept of commonweal barely exists and community approaches to shared problems are rare. . . . Mexicans regard the environment as a free and renewable resource rather than one that requires careful protection and preservation."

"New roads, land development, resorts — they're all big problems needing attention," Guy summed up. While efforts were under way to better care for the seacoast and the fishery, he confirmed that little was being done for the mountains of Baja. "Enjoy this place while you can. I know you have your boats with you — you should make a point of getting out on the water. Even if it's mountains you want to see, traveling by water is the easiest way to do it."

TAKING MY friend's advice, Ann, Tiff, and I loaded up my Mad River Explorer canoe for a different kind of mountain tour. Western grebes, California gulls, and brown pelicans kept us company as we sorted colorful stacks of gear and food on the beach.

We had cottoned to this idea of seeing the Coast Range of Baja by boat. After all, the mountains are bordered by the Pacific and its inlets the whole way north. For most of that distance, a vicious surf would prevent us from canoeing or kayaking, but here in the tranquil sea along the eastern side of the Baja Peninsula we could safely launch.

Tiffany and I waded the canoe into the waves while Ann wiggled into her river kayak and lurched off like a seal leaving the beach. No one recommends open canoes for travel here, but I knew we'd be fine as long as the wind and sea stayed reasonably calm.

Ahead lay three miles of open water to Isla Danzante, an alluring mountainous island jagging up out of the Gulf. To me, symbolically, it became the place where the Coast Range begins, a mountain starkly emerging from the ocean.

Though many people still call it the Sea of Cortés, the Mexican government officially renamed this water body the Gulf of California in the early 1900s, not wanting to name anything so beautiful after the conquistador Hernán Cortés, who had murdered, butchered, and burned his way across the country, making it to Baja in 1535.

In no time we were paddling in the midst of fifty dolphins. Blue-footed boobies, magnificent frigate birds, and double-crested cormorants soared overhead. A fat sea lion with smooth, furry skin surfaced, bared an intimidating flash of dagger-sharp teeth, and hissed with what I swear was contempt.

Then something else surfaced. "What *was* that?" I asked Tiff.

"I don't know."

We stared, fascinated, at this mystery of the deep, awaiting its reappearance. Finally, breaking the water again with an ancient face, it surfaced, reptilian in stoic expression as water drained from its sentient eyes. A broad, armored back floated free of the depths. It was a tortuga, or sea turtle, four feet long.

"They're rare," Tiff said. "That's the first one I've ever seen."

Commanding a price of thousands of pesos or hundreds of dollars, the tortuga is killed by many Mexican fishermen, even though all five species are nearly extinct and officially protected. When I talked about this issue later with a young Mexican fisherman named Blas, his eyes lit up just at the word *tortuga*. He acknowledged the regulations, saying, "Yes, the government gives us a lot of problems." Knowing an unfolding tragedy when she saw one, Trudi Angell had bought living sea turtles at a discount from Mexican fishermen for the sole purpose of setting them free.

Out on the island we camped on a sandy beach and felt fortunate for the most basic of hygienic conditions: we were free of the feces and toilet paper that epidemically afflict roadside beaches and fish camps along both the Gulf and Pacific sides of Baja. For camping at remote beaches without facilities, the official policy of groups such as NOLS is to defecate as far below the high-tide line as possible, burn your paper, and let the waves take the rest away. Given the limited amount of use at sites such as our island, this works. The ocean dilutes effectively and decomposes the waste far better than dry sand does.

Happily, we camped alone in sweet serenity and sunny isolation. We snorkeled in the chill sea of winter, opening our masked eyes to underwater wonders. We walked the length of our beach, and as I turned an oyster shell in my hand, I reflected on the billions upon billions of shells whose calcium carbonate was required to make even one foot of the limestone later thrust up by earthquakes into mountains from here to Alaska. The tiniest ocean creatures and the mightiest Coast Range peaks are related in this intimate, life-giving way.

A small octopus pulsed through our embayment. Jellyfish like colorless gelatin pizzas blobbed in the waves. Ospreys snagged their talons on some of the five hundred species of fish that still live in the Gulf. Lobster-red crabs sneaking around the rocks at our camp were among the three thousand species of Gulf-dwelling invertebrates. All this remaining richness owes to extraordinary geography: the Gulf plunges to ten-thousand-foot seismic depths in some places and barely oozes over shallow mudflats in others. Water remains marginally fresh at the Gulf's upper end, where the nominal remains of the Colorado River enter, but then it becomes 30 percent more saline than the oceans, owing to evaporation and muted flushing action by the sea. This varied spectrum of habitat contributes to the diversity of life.

We basked in sunsets glowing above the dark profile of the Sierra de la Giganta, a forbidding western horizon of volcanic dikes, plugs, and sky-high lava flows. Close up, rocks of the Giganta looked pink or lavender — gorgeous pastel layers tinted by the chemistry of the ash that settled into the rock when it hardened. I imagined that this view, today, must look something like the Central Valley of California or the inland basins of Nevada in the geologic past when they, too, contained inland seas bordered by mountains.

With the gift of ocean moisture, a layer of clouds streaked the Giganta's two-thousand-foot level while a thicker band hovered at its top. Fiery orange light streamed between the layers, colorfully illuminating both. I knew I would see the interplay of air, water, and land everywhere along this coastal chain of mountains, and here, at the start, the connections were artfully evident in every view.

Early the next morning I scrambled to the top of Danzante to catch sunrise over the Gulf. A blue sea of tranquility surrounded me amid enormous reaches of land and water, with no sign of humanity anywhere. To the northeast, the larger profile of Isla del Carmen rose out of the sea like an enchanted isle, numinous in the day's early light. Biologists say that thirty Gulf islands have prime scientific importance, some with plants and animals found nowhere else. One island rises 4,324 feet.

On our last night there, a special surprise awaited. The surf suddenly stopped my eye, not for the waves' size but for their shine, their sparkle—far brighter than just the reflection of moonlight. The water flashed like a fluorescent strobe as the tiny waves lapped ashore. Each break of foam sparkled with the unexpected bioluminescence of microscopic life. Wading into the alive water, I scooped up handfuls of the organic brew, and it continued to glitter in my palms for long seconds, as fascinating a light show as the stars overhead.

Gazing up into them, Tiff pointed out the North Star, which I never would have recognized because the dipper wasn't attached. At that point in its rotation around Polaris, the dipper lay entirely hidden under the horizon line—we were that far south. Tiff, the sailor, cued off the *W* in Cassiopeia to find the North Star. Beneath it—in the direction we would travel for nine months—the mountains of Baja rose in faded gray light. I tried to imagine what we would see there.

ON THE NEXT morning our return trip to the peninsula began quietly, as so many adventures do. Tiffany wanted to test her hand with Ann's kayak, so Ann joined me in the canoe. Because the tide was draining the channel, we had to cut a sharper angle toward a point of land to the north, making the crossing longer. And then the wind began — El Norte, the infamous bellows of swell-inducing winter air, with a fetch running six hundred miles toward the international border near the head of the Gulf.

Mere scratches roughened the water at first. Then the texture resembled peaked-up meringue on top of a lemon pie. Then it grew to swells, then swells with small waves on the sides, then waves with thinly breaking tops. Who knew what would come next. One badly breaking wave could overtop the sides of the canoe and swamp us. Another could knock Tiffany over. I wasn't sure how well she could roll to re-right herself, and there was no point in asking now. This seemed to be the first threatening moment of our Coast Range odyssey.

Taking at least one precaution, I had inserted air bags — durable nylon sacks blown full of air and wedged into the ends of the canoe — so that if we were swamped we would float high and have a chance to bail the boat. But we had no protection from the cold January water, which would quickly induce hypothermia even in Baja. We had brought our wet suits but hadn't bothered to wear them because it was hot when we departed the island, in retrospect a foolish choice.

I kept one eye on the point of land, constantly adjusting the boat's angle to compensate for the onslaught of wind and tide and hoping, ever hoping, we'd make it safely to a sheltered cove at the base of the Sierra de la Giganta. My arms ached, but still the waves and wind came at us. To match them, I paddled harder and harder, having no choice.

Finally, when we gained the protection of a headland, the waves subsided and then settled to a friendly roll. Beneath a steep rise of cliffs, we happily ran aground on a beach that we could call home for a short while before starting north.

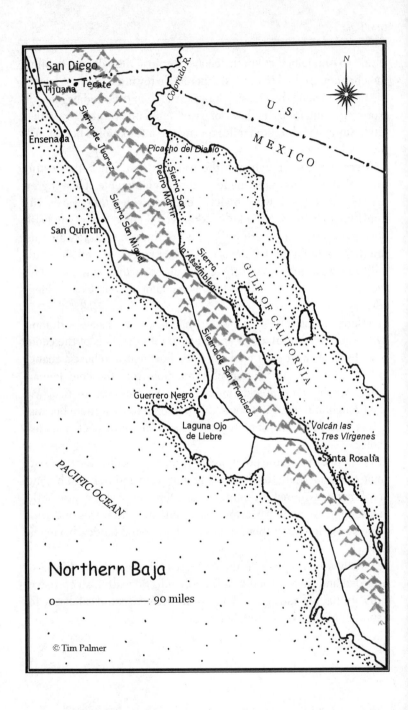

Northern Baja

0 ——————————— 90 miles

© Tim Palmer

# 2 The Volcán and the Mexican Desert

Having seen the beginning of the mountains as they rose out of the sea, I now searched for something big—a mountain impressive and tall and towering over the desert empire of Baja.

And then, there it was! Volcán las Tres Vírgenes. Less than half-way up the peninsula, south to north, the tallest volcano of the three-some topped out at 6,547 feet, more than a mile straight up from sea level. It last erupted in 1746, and geologists still consider it active.

A five-thousand-foot climb in a day? Sure, we could do it. We'd done it before. Without a heavy backpack the elevation gain posed no serious problem, so long as the route was easy going.

From the highway, the route looked like a clear shot up talus slopes—large piles of small rocks the whole way to the summit. Yet every mountaineer knows that distance hides obstacles, say, a twenty-foot cliff band that looks like a simple step up from so far away, or a gouged-out canyon lurking behind the first intermediary ridgeline. There's always something unforeseen. But that's the nature of adventure and discovery, and we just hoped the surprises wouldn't amount to much.

Humming along a dirt road as we searched for an approach to the mountain, we came to a geothermal power plant, sited at the base of the volcano because it was still steaming inside. A Mexican worker had just locked the gate. We had left Tiffany to her sailing in Loreto and were now on our own with nothing but a pocket Spanish dictionary. Ann quickly prepared, cobbling together a phrase or two.

"Perdón," she said. "Nos gustaría escalar la montaña." Excuse me. We would like to climb the mountain.

With a serious, discouraging demeanor, the young man pointed back out the road and said something like "No es aquí. Tienes que volver por la carretera y ir a la derecha." It's not here. Da-dah, da-dah, da-dah. The language barrier now called for mapping and pointing.

"Queremos escalar la montaña a pie," Ann tried, meaning to say, "We want to walk to the mountaintop." She pointed to the largest of the three cones.

"Sí," the man said understandingly. He again pointed back the way we had come.

I took out a paper and pen and drew our road as an arced line and the mountaintop as a pointed cone. Ann ran her finger across the road while asking something like, "Donde está el sendero a la cima?" Where is the trail to the mountaintop?

"Seis kilómetros," he responded, pointing again.

"Out to the six-kilometer sign?" I asked. He nodded. "Gracias, Señor." We had noticed the sign on the way in.

We retraced our route to the "6 K" sign and turned right on a two-track lane that dead-ended at a dilapidated corral, where we happened onto three mustachioed Mexicans wrestling a bony cow into the back of a sag-spring pickup truck with high sideboards. For a starving animal, the bovine put up impressive resistance, seeming to comprehend: it's here or the taco stand. Words painted on the pickup's door advertised a deli in Santa Rosalía where I would not now choose to eat. When the grunting, pulling, kicking, and stomping ended, we ventured over and asked, "Es esto el camino al volcán?" Is this the way to the volcano?

Their sidelong glances said it all: crazy gringos. I remembered what David Kallgren, director of NOLS, had told me. For years, local people had regarded with great suspicion any Americans who went hiking. "They thought we were looking for gold," he said. "Why else would we be out there?"

"Volcán?" the truck driver said with a sense of amazement that cut straight through the language barrier, now fortified with a cultural barrier. "Sí, es. Es muy difícil." For effect he shook his head and repeated, "Muy difícil." The other men both shook their heads in support.

They lurched away, leaving us with five misery-stricken cows. One could almost say the remains of cows. Around a stone and cement tub, locally called a *pila,* holding scummy water, the cattlemen/delimen had strung a fence to keep the stock out. I could only presume that the cows would otherwise drink the *pila* dry in a day or maybe an hour. One bony mother and calf were fenced in an adjacent pen and additionally tethered to ropes. The others roamed free among the cacti, though *free* isn't really the right word. The phrase *imprisonment by vegetation* popped into my mind. One cow's head was impaled by a cactus pad. Blood ran from the nose of the calf, which quivered all over. Like dartboards from bovine hell, all the cows were stuck with thorns and bellowed miserably. They constantly eyed the fence barricading them from the water. Taking in this sad spectacle, I could clearly see why the good people at Rancho Viejo were raising goats instead of cattle.

I have no soft spot for these inbred, range-ruining ungulates, but this was pathetic, and I climbed over the fence, dipped two buckets that I found lying on the ground into the *pila,* and carried them to the tethered cow and calf, which sucked the contents dry in a flash. The earth all around was beat to dust, the dried manure composed of twigs, thorns, and roughage I'd never thought possible in fecal matter of any form anywhere. A dozen vultures squatted in paloverde trees with what I took to be a keen interest in the quivering calf.

Beyond the corral, a disengaged, board-stiff cowhide stood propped in two dimensions against a mesquite tree, the peeled-off face of the beast pointing to a path that entered the mesquite and cactus forest and led in the direction of the Volcán. The raggedy, worm-eaten, desiccated skin pointed the way for us, an omen we might well have taken to heart. But trying to accept things at face value — whatever that was in this odd case — I didn't see the remains of this bad skinning job as anything to be worried about.

Exploring a short distance, we found the trail to be good, though wholly made of pulverized pumice and basalt, a lot like sand, which concerned us because loose sand makes walking difficult. And for us to climb five thousand feet and return before dark, everything would have to go like clockwork.

Before crawling into bed we packed lunch, matches, camera, sweaters, raincoats, three quarts of water each, and ski poles. We find the latter useful for arming our way uphill, for reducing shock on our knees coming downhill, and for catching ourselves when we teeter or stumble off balance. I packed a compass because I could see that a brush-covered flat of two miles stretched to the base of the mountain — before the scree even began — and if it got dark before we returned, we might wander in maddening circles on the vegetated flats, trying to find our way out.

Getting a leg up on the day, we departed at dawn. In no time, as our first setback, the cow path faded to nothing. From then on, the strategic route aimed for the peak while the tactical route exploited any small opening in the jungle of cactus, mesquite, and catclaw acacia. Virtually everything had the potential to rip our skin wide open. Slowed to the pace of a careful crawl, I found it difficult, in those weak moments, to appreciate the Sonoran Desert as the continent's most diverse in biota. What grew there was not nature's welcome mat, as plant life often seems to be, but rather a stern warning: Keep out.

And, of course, it always gets bad before it gets worse. In some places we had to step on cacti with our thick-soled hiking boots, which, fortunately, were the old-fashioned, all-leather style and tough enough to resist the sharp spines. We often had to sweep thorny branches aside. For some cacti, I wanted a machete, but my ski poles had to do. With them I could eliminate nothing, but they did enable me to push back prickly limbs to open up body-width passages, a new use for those straightforward tools designed for snow — the furthest thing from what nature dished up on the Volcán.

I called the sour pitahaya cactus "the snakepit" because it lay curled and intertangled in creepy prone masses blocking our route. Even more formidable, the catclaw acacia snagged our clothing and skin like a temperamental house cat, the branches quick to retaliate against our ski poles and swat at us like striking paws. We twisted and turned and detoured but still had our run-ins with a lot of lacerating plants. All the time I tried to keep one eye on the mountain for direction and one eye on the ground for rattlesnakes, whose habitat this surely was. Indeed, I had read that thirty-five species of snakes make their home in Baja and fully half are venomous, poor odds for the unsuspecting gringo. You can be bitten by six kinds of rattlesnake alone.

By far the worst, however, was the chain-link cholla. It grew to head height, with outer branches burnishing fist-sized pads, each bristling with spines surely crafted for our undoing. Though the plant's pattern of growth vaguely resembles a chain-link fence, this cholla acts more like a medieval war club. At the slightest, most imperceptible touch, the pads disconnect from their base and leap onto your tender body. Hence the other nickname for this species, jumping cactus. Worse, the pads don't just impale at the point of contact. Rather, they roll onto you, causing spines to pierce your skin at various angles, much as a carpenter anchors a board by angling the nails variably so the board doesn't work loose. The chain-link's motive is reproduction: it hitches a ride until it gets dropped off somewhere else, where it can readily sprout vegetatively just by falling on the ground, a scary prospect for the rest of the world.

To extract a chain-link pad, I pulled with one hand and my pierced skin peaked up sharply where each impaling spine, minutely barbed, refused to give up its grip on me. Some of the spines broke off because of the variable angles at which I had been skewered, leaving splinters I could feel but not see.

Amid these jumping cacti at the base of the Volcán, more than in any other place I've been, I could see how people develop an adversarial relationship with nature. I had always begrudged the North Dakota farmer who, once getting his tractor stuck in the mud, ever after spent his discretionary time digging, ditching, and draining the prairie wetlands. Or the Oregon logger who, after fighting a tangle of vine maple with the hazards of a chainsaw sabering at high rpm's, just wanted to cut everything down and get rid of it. Now I yearned for a bulldozed road or trail or even a cow path to get me out of there. Maybe it's enough just to say that the chain-link cholla is a serious deterrent to traveling off-trail in the vegetated realms of Baja. Places such as this, and others in the Coast Range where similar conclusions might be drawn, are just as well left alone.

Precious hours ticked by, and as we became more and more committed to the climb by nature of the struggle we had endured, our goal became harder and harder to achieve, leading us deeper and deeper into thorny entrapment — more committed, more entangled — viciously on and on, not unlike some of life's other struggles.

When the sight of the mountaintop distracted me for a second, a cholla embedded itself in my forearm with the sensation of multiple bee stings. This wasn't just the most difficult hike I had ever been on. This was five times as difficult.

We realized that, no fooling, we *had* to make it out by nightfall. Travel in the dark would be utterly impossible, and sitting out the chill night imprisoned by cactus spines would be no picnic. There would be no late-afternoon summiting. When it came time to turn around, we would *have* to turn around.

Looking up at the still-distant Volcán, even with my poor aptitude for foreign languages, I understood what *muy difícil* means in Spanish. And I understood why most people who go to Baja go to the sea, not to the mountains. And I understood why Trudi Angell traveled only on trails and only on mules. I understood a lot that I hadn't before. But I still wanted to reach the top of the Volcán. Now that I knew what was *here,* I wanted to see what was *there.*

After dripping a quart or two of sweat in the warming hours of the day, we began to ramp up out of the cactus maze and onto piles of lava, rusty brown with broken-bottle edges, scoriaceous and splattered onto the slope by the bomb-throwing volcano in centuries past. Walking on the tippy clinker called for balance, care, and luck. Falling on it would hurt, but compared with the cactus maze below, it was a welcome thoroughfare. We began to gain some elevation, rock by rock.

At noon, when we stopped on a flat boulder for lunch, Ann decided to drop out of the masochistic effort aimed at an ever receding summit.

I left her to tweeze splinters out of her body while I pressed on, puffing and sweating upward at a full aerobic pace, tramping on rocks the size of grapefruits that had not yet collectively found their angle of repose and so slid when I sought traction on them. Then came steep slopes covered by prickly weeds and billions of smaller stones that rolled like marbles atop the underlying lava. Mounting a ridgeline, I found myself on an incline of enduring steepness, where I trudged on and up. Mercifully I was spared stepping on a rattlesnake; one could have lurked anywhere in the mottled brown cover at my feet, fine habitat for mice and thus for any creature that eats mice.

Topping another ridgeline, I saw that eight hundred vertical feet remained, the summit finally looming approachably before me. After six hours of trench warfare, I could be there in another half hour.

But my time was up.

My goal, now so easily achievable, would have to go unrealized. Though my brain stopped climbing, my feet continued in their heedless, rebellious obsession. But eventually my mind and body came to terms. I sat down, either to cry or to drink from my water bottle, I wasn't sure which. Had I climbed in vain? I sat and stared because there was nothing else to do.

People have different reasons for climbing mountains, but I do it, quite simply, for the view of my world that the summits afford. I had never thought of it quite this way—never boiled it down this far—but I live to see. To simply see—and to see as much as possible—is one of my main goals in life.

Now, at this new vantage point, I looked to the south and admired

the furnace land of central Baja that stretched in ridge after inciner-
ated igneous ridge, a scene so elemental that it wouldn't have completely surprised me if a volcano had erupted while I watched.

To the east, the other volcanic peaks now rested below me, awesome cones in their own right, consecrated in rock rubble just like
where I sat. At their base, the Gulf of California made quite the sight,
deep and blue, waves in glittery herringbone, islands studding the
mirrory surface. And across the water, more than a hundred miles
away on the mainland of Mexico, the summit of a great mountain
shone as a snowcap, its crown rising from beyond the distant curva-
ture of the globe. I could see a part of the earth I had never seen and
would never see again. I had not climbed in vain.

Descending more quickly, I slid on loose pumice, joyfully skiing in
my boots, poling to keep my balance or to turn and dodge chunky
cannonballs of lava that had been shelled onto the slope. Rounding a
shoulder of the mountain, I finally saw the little speck of color that
signified Ann below, and on some gravelly pumice I made a beeline
for her.

Hoping to avoid some of the cactus hell we had suffered on the
approach, we descended by a different route, where we saw more
open ground in rock and grass. But as if the cactus route and this one
had engaged in some sneaky behind-the-scenes price-fixing, new
problems lay hidden, namely eight small canyons that intersected
our route. We hustled down and up their crumbling slopes, down
and up.

As daylight faded, on the last steep slope, on one of my last steep
steps, which is so often when things go hazardously wrong, a rock
rolled out from under me. Destabilized, other rocks to my rear sym-
pathetically broke loose. Instinctively I leapt out ahead of the slide
rather than be crunched in its midst. But once ahead, I had to stay
ahead. So I jumped down, springing off big stones at the toe of the
slope, where I hit the flats with a momentum that sent me sprawling
in the dust. But that was okay. It was dirt without cacti.

In this staggering, faltering, darkening finale I considered myself
lucky to have made it off the Volcán at all, and whenever a close call

happens — even face-down in the dirt — life itself tastes sweeter. I felt as though the mountain had sucked me in and now spit me out.

Ann, who had predictably been more careful in her descent and thus triggered no landslides or other problems of any sort, asked with some concern if I was all right.

As dusk began to roll in and the twilight hour pressed upon us like a drip of cold water creeping down my collar, we emerged onto a hoof-worn trail, and I have never in my life been so happy to see a crapped-upon cow path. By the time we got to the road, the last light dimmed to a final softened pitch yet still showed the way, and life felt rich and good as we closed the loop back to our home in the van.

IN DUE TIME the sea lions would be heading from here to California's Big Sur and beyond, the western sandpipers to Alaska's Copper River Delta, and the gray whales clear up to the Bering Sea. Failing to make the steady progress those determined creatures of the ocean and air would enjoy in their peregrinations to where they feed and breed, Ann and I needed to get a head start. So we began to drive north at the end of January.

Spring would advance fifteen miles a day, four hundred fifty miles a month on average, and we would try to keep pace. Counteracting this vernal inevitability, the climate grows cooler by 1.8 degrees Fahrenheit for each degree of latitude north (about sixty-seven miles), all else being equal, which it never is. Any change in elevation, wind direction, precipitation, or microclimate — such as shade on the northern side of a mountain — always bounces the temperature around. In our case, along the Pacific edge, the sea would be a major moderating influence, and in overall effect we expected to enjoy spring-like weather for most of the nine months as we advanced through thirty-nine degrees of latitude. I was reminded of what travel writer Henry T. Finck wrote way back in 1891: "If an excursion agent had planned the climate of the Pacific Coast, he could not have made things more delightfully convenient for tourists. All you have to do is follow spring northwards."

However, at the other end of our journey, on Kodiak Island, it would suddenly, inevitably, be autumn. We knew this. And as certainly as we had to get off the Volcán before dark, we had to beat the autumn storms to the northwestern end of the range, where they rip into Kodiak with a cold vengeance unimagined in Mexico. Though we hated to rush things, Ann and I knew we had to get going.

Following our noses, however, we became hopelessly sidetracked at every turn.

Just northwest of the Volcán we angled into the valley of the Río San Ignacio, shaded by a mass of stately date palms planted by Jesuit missionaries in the 1700s. On the heels of a garbage truck steadily losing contents by attrition to the wind — a plastic bag here, a plastic cup there; six bags here, six cups there — we rolled through town, admired the old mission, and stopped at what looked like an environmental center on the town square.

A gracious young woman with long, black hair, wide, shining eyes, and a finely embroidered dress explained in melodically accented English that they were just starting up.

With my mind flashing on all the problems I had seen, I asked, "Where do you begin?"

She had already thought about this. "With the litter. You might have noticed it's everywhere. In school, the teachers tell children not to throw their garbage on the ground, but then at home they see their fathers do it."

I remembered that in my childhood, back in the innocent dark ages of the 1950s, Americans pitched their trash out car windows. Everybody did it. Do-gooders to whom we are now greatly indebted waged advertising campaigns against this national habit long before the environmental movement of the 1960s and 1970s began. It was one of the first steps Americans took toward an environmental ethic. Not that we don't still have a long way to go.

"You can do it," I said in blindly hopeful encouragement.

She picked up on my enthusiasm and added, "We're also teaching schoolchildren about whales and sea turtles. The turtles are rare now. And the whales! They are wonderful. Have you been to Laguna Ojo de Liebre? Oh, you must see it!"

So we detoured again at the shallow bay often called Scammon's Lagoon, after an American who decimated the whales in an orgy of killing between 1857 and 1859. Two years was all the time Scammon needed to do in an entire population of these magnificent beasts.

We paid fifteen dollars each and a Mexican guide took Ann, me, two French Canadian women from Vancouver Island, and a young couple from San Francisco out in an open motorboat for a tour of Parque Natural de la Ballena Gris — Gray Whale Natural Park.

Rules banned our craft from approaching within a hundred feet of the peaceful cetaceans, but the pilot, in pidgin English, said he couldn't do much about friendly individuals that surfaced closer on their own.

We learned to predict their approach from a smooth slick of water oiling the surface, and we began to regard it with the anticipation — though not the horror — of sighting Moby Dick. Soon the whitish skin of a barnacle-covered mother appeared capriciously out of the depths, slowly coming into focus until softly, smoothly, her back parted the waters and floated above the sea, brine pouring off her roughly ridged spine. With size to match the sea itself, she lay near the surface for half a minute and then silently sank from sight.

In the spring the mothers and babies embark on the longest migration of any mammal — a three-month swim north — passing California in March and April, eventually traveling six thousand miles back to the Bering and Chukchi Seas in the Arctic to feast on amphipods, tiny shrimp-like creatures.

There at the laguna we saw dozens of gray whales, some forty feet long, some with cute little ten-foot-long baby offspring. But the most astonishing experience awaited us after we came back ashore, ate dinner, and went to bed.

Late that night I stepped out of the van alongside the lagoon and noted the water's silvery moonlit sheen. Not a breeze whispered in the grass. The birds slept without a single peep. The night lay hauntingly silent except for one sound: the breathing of whales. Deep, resonant breath — I could hear it — accompanied the hiss of a whale spouting. So many of the big mammals respired that the sound of air was constant, as if the bay itself were breathing.

Hunted nearly to extinction, the gray whales needed a hundred forty years but were back in healthy numbers now, perhaps seventeen thousand. They are the only whale species to have completely recovered from overhunting. We would watch for them during our parallel journey up the coast.

The next day we drove through Guerrero Negro, an industrial town dedicated to one of the world's largest evaporative salt works, which, like the whale reserve, is also located at Laguna Ojo de Liebre. Many miles in extent, it's a hellish place where even the roads are salt and look like ice-covered highways in the dead of Minnesota's winter. The mine means big business, with much of the salt sold in America, and a proposed expansion would encroach on the whales. Even though they'd survived near-extermination, the future of this population was precarious. These charismatic creatures could fall to satisfy Americans' cravings for pretzels and fries. But for now, the expansion plan had been stopped.

NORTH OF TOWN, Ann and I spotted trouble of our own up ahead. At a roadside hut, soldiers in fatigues and army caps held machine guns at the ready.

A young man with a trimmed mustache and crooked teeth gestured palm out, no-nonsense, to stop. In case we didn't, another machine-gun-clutching soldier stood on the roof of the building with a clear shot at our tires or windows. Suddenly our neighboring country felt like a banana republic in full machismo regalia.

Mustering a smile, I offered, "Buenos días, Señor."

"De donde vienes?" Where did you come from?

"De los Estados Unidos." The United States. Of course.

"De donde vienes *en México?*" he asked, impatiently.

"Loreto."

"Donde vas?" Where are you going?

"Back home, Estados Unidos."

"Tienes armas?"

"Perdón, Señor, my español is only *poco*." I gestured with the space between my thumb and forefinger, thinking it wise to avoid the phrase I had earlier sprung on the shop owner in Loreto.

With a thick accent the armed man repeated his question in English, the one intelligible word being *guns*.

"Oh, no, Señor. We have no guns." I shook my head with conviction.

I never thought I'd be lying to a man with a machine gun, but there I was. I always carry a double-barreled twelve-gauge shotgun in the van. It was tucked against the wall, disassembled, at the back of the bed. It was my grandfather's old rabbit-hunting gun — familiar to me ever since I began tramping the brush with him before I could legally hunt. I was planning to take the gun on river trips in the far North, where I would load it with slugs as protection from grizzly bears.

When I entered Mexico I knew guns were not allowed, but I had no place to store the family heirloom and didn't know what the penalty was. The penalty, it turns out, is that they confiscate your vehicle and throw you in a Mexican jail. Probably both of us. Presumably they're concerned about Americans arming the Chiapas Indians who were revolting in southern Mexico, which we clearly weren't doing. But would common sense count at that point in the Mexican bureaucracy, such as it is? I didn't think anyone would ever find the piece unless they had gun-sniffing dogs, but just the same, I hoped the Mexican soldier wouldn't look.

"Drogas?"

As if we would tell him if we had drugs. But we had none. "No, Señor."

"Necesito mirar adentro."

I looked at him, puzzled.

"Inspección." He motioned with his gun at the side door, the gesture so amazingly like what I had seen as a kid in corny old movies.

Much as I hated to arouse suspicion, the side door didn't work. Ever since some unknown driver had backed into it in a supermarket parking lot, slightly denting it, the sliding door had been kaput. Loading its inside running board with our Coleman stove, water jug, and trash basket, we never used the door much anyway. I pantomimed to the soldier that the rollers were blocked. Ann readily opened the passenger door for his use, welcoming him in.

It was weird, having this guy with his tommy gun in our home, in our living room, in our kitchen, in our bedroom.

He pointed to our cooler. "Chiles?"

"No, Señor. Bell peppers, sí, but chilis, no." Do these guys eat chili peppers for lunch? I wondered. But some things you just don't ask.

He scanned the bed, looking for evidence. He was getting warmer, as children say in that game we all played. Then I think he became overwhelmed by our setup—bookshelves, skis racked up against the ceiling, desk and wooden kitchen chair, tiny flower vase tied to the wall. I thought I detected the faint trace of a smile, quickly suppressed, at the corners of his mustache.

Satisfied that we had no guns or drugs, and that no chili peppers were available for lunch, he stepped out.

"Andele." Go ahead.

"Gracias, Señor."

He said, "Qué les vaya bien," or something to that effect. Have a good trip.

Honest to God, I will never again take a gun to Mexico.

THE CHILI pepper laws were strictly enforced at gunpoint, but the littering laws were totally ignored. As we continued northward we saw trash in appalling quantities everywhere. The young woman at the environmental center indeed had her work cut out for her. At pull-outs where we stopped to fire up lunch, whole pickup loads of refuse lay in the mesquite—mattresses, fast food wrappers, bottles, refrigerators with their ozone-depleting chlorofluorocarbons bleeding out, and plenty of cans, especially Tecate beer cans.

On the outsides of sharp bends, trashed cars made up just another category of litter along the roadsides. Always upside-down, two or three of them might lie there completely stripped, some burned out to spooky black hulks invaded by the creeping, snaking arms of sour pitahaya cactus.

Near one of those curves a sign sensibly said, "Highway built for economic development, not high-speed travel." But who's to separate the two? Excess speed was everywhere evident. Once a road is upgraded — in this case realigned and paved — it's used to the limit of safety and beyond. It doesn't matter that signs warn "Curva" and "Peligroso." The drunks who used to crash at twenty miles per hour now crash at sixty-five.

In a testament to widespread death on the road, survivors had planted crosses in the ground here, there, everywhere. And shrines like little doghouses with candles and even statues inside honored the souls of loved ones, violently killed and still missed.

Traveling Baja in the early 1970s, journalist Paul Brooks lamented the imminent completion of the paved road. "Roman gladiators considered the net an even deadlier weapon than the sword," he wrote. "So the highways that enmesh our countryside may ultimately prove more destructive than the gun or the ax." He warned that "soon the heart of Baja will be only a day's drive from the most mobile, gasoline-powered population on the earth."

It had come to pass, and we were among the new travelers. Trudi Angell had told us about the new resorts. Guy Bonnivier had told us about the overkill of fish. We had seen the lineups of campers on the toilet-papered beaches. Now, as we headed back toward the United States at the end of January, we encountered whole caravans of southbound motor homes — thirty, forty, fifty rolling vacation palaces in a pack, TV dishes on the roofs and little yapping dogs inside, all coming to visit this Third World country with its water, its sunshine, and its friendly, good-hearted people.

As we journeyed north, mountains rose from the sea and faded in layers out to the most distant horizon line, showing volcanic cones, flattop mesas, and washboard ridges. Once we reached the horizon, a similar scene telescoped out to the next one, and on and on.

At Cabo San Quintín we gawked in middle-class amazement at the unmistakably feudal commandments of Mexico's economy and quotidian life. The Los Pinos farms stretched to the horizon with fields in tomatoes, broccoli, and beans. On a distant hillside a white mansion, surrounded by palm trees, stood sentinel. Down below, the dusty, potholed dirt streets were crowded with squat buildings of cement block, penurious and windowless, their doors open for air or light, children squirreling about, electric wires drooping limply overhead, mangy dogs on the prowl, men standing on corners talking and curiously eyeballing our van with its two canoes and kayak as we bumped down the divoted streets. Indians from southern Mexico move up here to work for the princely wage of four dollars a day. The farmers pump irrigation water so hard that brackish seawater is infiltrating the once-pure aquifer. Vacant fields at the edge of town had already succumbed to weeds. At a nearby beach, the foam at the high-tide line looked like liquid manure. But beyond town and above it all, seven volcanoes rose up serenely from sea level, the outermost cone a Coast Range island surrounded by the tropical Pacific. All of it, not so long ago, had been a paradise.

Farther north, in a wholly different agricultural style near Santo Tomás, ranches lay on the land where a few cows grazed contentedly. Sycamore trees began to appear along the stream courses, and, Pennsylvania native at heart, I realized how much I had missed trees during the past month. I wanted to go lie under one of them and stare up at those white, leggy branches and just count leaves for a while. To the east, the Sierra San Pedro Mártir rose as the largest belt of wild country in Baja. Back in its midst, in a national park, the peninsula's highest peak, Picacho del Diablo, rose to 10,154 feet.

When I stopped to admire the sycamores, a man came walking by. "Tiene usted algo para comer?" He wanted to know if we had anything to eat.

"Sí, amigo." I gave him a few tortillas.

"Tiene usted dinero?" Do you have any money? I gave him a few pesos.

Before long, a man, woman, and child alongside the road hailed us. The infant was sick, the man explained, faking a cough and pointing to his daughter. Did we have water? We gave them some water in a plastic bottle we said they could keep. Were we going to Maneadero?

While they traveled with us, we tried to converse, with only minor success. When they got out, the man asked for money. "Necesitamos comprar comida para la niña." Ann vaguely understood: We need to buy some food for the child. I gave him twenty pesos, two dollars.

ON OUR LAST night in Baja, we looked determinedly for a camping spot as darkness fell. Ideally I would have driven back out of sight of the road. I had been advised to do this by seasoned Baja travelers as a means of avoiding bandits. But soft, sandy soil made me wary of getting the van stuck, so we just parked in a pull-out.

After dark a pickup with a rusty muffler passed, slowed down, and then stopped. It backed up. "Uh oh," Ann said. "We've got company."

I turned out the van's indoor light and locked the doors. Ann stayed in the back, where she had been reading. The truck pulled in next to us. A man rolled down his window, his fumy pickup still idling. I cracked my window halfway to talk. Unshaven and in work clothes, he seemed to be offering us information of some kind.

"Perdón?" We couldn't understand, and he repeated, louder, as if we'd get it the third or fourth time. Ann finally asked, "Podemos acampar aquí?" May we camp here?

"Sí," he responded. But then he hesitated, searching for words. "Ten cuidado."

We did not know what the man had tried to convey but sensed it was some kind of warning. Ann got out her phrase book. "It says here that *Ten cuidado* means 'Be careful.'" We sat awhile reading, each of us wondering if there was an unusual risk in camping there.

"Hey, Tim," Annie finally said from her spot on the bed.

"Yeah, I think we should move."

We drove back toward town, to where a sign said "RV Is Here," and forked over sixteen dollars to lodge on a cement slab in a weedy lot.

PRESSING ON northward the next day, we searched in vain for Highway 3, which turns east off Baja 1 and climbs the foothills of the Sierra de Juárez before winding north to the town of Tecate, at the

U.S. border. At El Sauzal, a suburb to the humming beachfront metropolis of Ensenada, we gave up and pulled over to ask for directions.

Trying Spanish one last time, I leaned out the window and flagged down a middle-aged woman. "Dónde está el camino a Tecate?" At least that's what I intended to say.

"Tecate?" she repeated after me.

"Sí." I nodded.

She pointed down the road we were on, indicating that we should simply keep going.

"This camino?" I asked, surprised it would be so easy.

"Sí. Tecate." She smiled and wished us well.

We drove on and got lost even deeper in the maze of streets, but there was no shortage of red-and-white Tecate beer signs hanging over local establishments.

Though only a lighthearted misunderstanding, this mixup put me in mind of a far deeper truth about Mexicans and Americans articulated by author Alan Riding. "Probably nowhere else in the world do two neighbors understand each other so little." Our monthlong trip in Baja added to our understanding of Mexico, but more surely, our travels confirmed Riding's view.

Eventually on our way, we watched the countryside grow into a melody of hills and granite outcrops, which put me in a better mood than the roadside culture of Baja had done. Stone walls stood in the foreground, mountains in the distance. Vineyards alternated with pastures now greened in three-foot-high grass. This hilly country enjoys more rain than the desert at lower elevations to the south. Fields lay speckled with homes, some scarcely shanties, some with iron gates and Mediterranean tile roofs. Some, I surmised, were occupied by Americans; more than ten thousand have moved to Baja. When oaks began to appear, with their dark green foliage and gnarled, old limbs, I longed for the savanna hillsides of home.

We braked in low gear down the hill to Tecate, a likable city, well shaded, well lived in, nothing like the hustling, vice-filled border towns of Mexicali and Tijuana. The tree-lined *zócalo*, or central plaza, seemed to cool the whole downtown where we strolled. Though somewhat exhausted by Mexico and troubled by what I had seen, I was still sparked by the lively rhythms of mariachi music in the air. Then we got back in our van and pulled forward to cross the border into the United States.

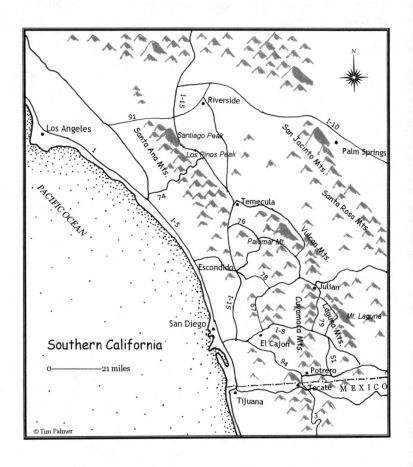

N

Riverside

I-15

91

Los Angeles

Santa Ana Mts.

Santiago Peak

Los Pinos Peak

San Jacinto Mts.

I-10

Palm Springs

PACIFIC OCEAN

1

74

I-5

Temecula

76

Palomar Mt.

Vulcan Mts.

Santa Rosa Mts.

Escondido

78

Julian

I-15

67

Cuyamaca Mts.

Laguna Mts.

Mt. Laguna

79

San Diego

I-8

El Cajon

51

Southern California

0———————21 miles

94

Potrero

Tecate    MEXICO

Tijuana

3

© Tim Palmer

# 3    *Borderlands and Refuges*

DIRECTLY IN front of me lay a four-wheel-drive track of dirt and gravel, unusually straight, considering the hilly country. Just beyond, a barbed wire fence had been strung, east to west. That wasn't enough, not nearly enough, so south of it, and forbidding to my amateur sensibilities, a twenty-foot-wide swath of chaparral had been grubbed out and doused with herbicides up to the edge of a corrugated metal wall. As tall as a man, the wall was shackled in place by four-inch pipe rammed into the rocky ground and topped off with another nine feet of chain-link fence. The fences and dirt road unambiguously marked the United States–Mexico border in spite of an undulant landscape that seamlessly flowed with ravines and swales, ridgelines and summits, and watercourses cutting north or south at will through the wall.

Thankful that I was on the northern side — that I had been *born* on the northern side and had the right to stay — I stood in low evening light on that arrow-straight driveway scraped out for the wheeling of four-by-fours.

My attentive ears picked up the rumble of an approaching vehicle from the ravine to the west. Curious about whoever else was frequenting this border location, but not wanting to deal with complications that might arise if I were found witnessing a "coyote" hauling illegal immigrants north, nor with the suspicion that might result if a U.S. Border Patrol agent looking for contraband were to see me lingering so pointlessly, I stepped off the gravel. I ducked into the brush. I was thankful for the tangle of manzanita providing cover for the birds and me, a good habitat for both of us at that moment. And perhaps it served as cover for others as well; who knows?

Louder now, the vehicle strained against the hill opposing it, and as the sound grew, my apprehension also grew. I was totally innocent, so why get caught by the Border Patrol looking as if I weren't? Yet, a child of the sixties, I knew to avoid dealings with the police.

So, who was coming, a violator of the law or an enforcer of it? It struck me as odd that it would be one or the other, with little likelihood of middle ground. Odder yet, I sensed that the refuge of the mountains had become a battlefield. Or, in my case at the moment, had the battlefield become a refuge? Trying to hide, I didn't know which was true but only that the world, in many ways, was being turned on its head, and the vehicle speeding toward me was an indicator of conflict and trouble and who knew what else.

The driver topped the rise only a few steps from where I crouched, frozen and silent. White with a green stripe—the official rig of the Border Patrol—it hit the crest at a good clip and then speeded up even more, crunching gravel and spewing dust as it passed with a gritty whoosh.

The border is a land of beauty but also of intrigue, chaos, and mayhem, a place where people escape from one political system and enter another. Likewise, the whole collection of mountains running a hundred thirty miles northwest, spanning from Mexico to Los Angeles, serves as a refuge for people who escape more casually from the bustle of cities. And no doubt it's a final stronghold for wildlife that's being pushed and stressed and eliminated on all sides by all these people—Americans, Mexicans, everyone.

I was interested in this geologically and politically ruptured land and in people's responses to it, so my questions took me right to the edge of the barbed wire fence. Here, at the beginning of this search, I looked into Mexico. At the end, I would look down onto Los Angeles, and in between I had no idea what to expect.

Tapping the most bizarre human response to political geography in the entire Coast Range, the borderlands stood as an enigmatic, ironic, fateful strip of mountains, glorious and tragic at once, an expanse of land as integral in a twisted way to hundreds of thousands of immigrants each year as Ellis Island was to arrivals in the past. History now celebrates that tiny isle as the point of excited embarkation, the place where the Americanization of Old World refugees was initiated. In contrast, the mountainous reach of the California-Mexico border is shunned by all but those who are desperate to cross it unseen and those who are hired to stop people from crossing. Remote sections of the border have become best known as drug-trafficking zones. Here is the crux move in a heinous commercial path beginning in the fields of Colombia and ending in every American city.

To the south, beyond the border, and to the north, where I was headed, I saw no difference on the ground; it was all one mountain range. Yet the differences to people are such that thousands risk their lives to make the crossing, to go from *that* mountainside to *this* mountainside.

To consider these differences, try to imagine Mexico City, where many of twenty-three million Mexicans live in conditions of crowding, poverty, and pollution that most Americans can't even imagine.

The Mexican government has recognized the economic and resource apocalypse the country faces because of overpopulation and has attempted to counter the age-old cultural imperatives to produce large numbers of children. Programs since the mid-1970s have encouraged parents to voluntarily have small families. The catchy slogan is "A small family lives better." And it has worked. The birthrate nationwide supposedly has dropped from 7 children per family in 1965 to 2.5 in 1998 by some reports. But keep in mind, that's only the *rate* of growth. The population is still growing fast, up 20 percent in many areas in the 1990s alone, and the absolute numbers to come pose dire consequences for everything from water supply to suitable land on which to live to political strife resulting from poverty and a grossly inequitable sharing of wealth. Faced with these challenges, people by the millions take the drastic step of leaving their homeland behind and immigrating, legally or illegally, to the United States. I would see Mexican immigrants in the coastal mountains as far north as Kodiak, Alaska.

No one knows how many people illegally cross the border each year and stay in America, but the estimates top the hundreds of thousands. Some informed people think it's a million or more, perhaps many more. Just consider a few related numbers. In San Diego County alone, in May 1996 alone, Border Patrol agents arrested 67,282 people trying to enter the United States illegally. When Operation Gatekeeper that year curbed crossing in urban areas by positioning patrol officers at frequent intervals along the border, it pushed activity out to the hinterland, to places like the site where I visited. In a similar remote reach of Arizona, officials caught 60,500 illegals in the month of March. Feeding the flow, a thousand people arrive in Tijuana from interior Mexico and Central America each day, and a quarter of the city's seam-busting population is considered transient, many of them hoping to slip north. An estimated 6 to 12 million illegal aliens already lived in the United States in 2001, the majority of them from Mexico.

The mass migration has continued, and there's no end in sight. Mexico's population of 96 million grows by 2 million a year, and it's not just Mexico City but the whole country that faces widespread crowding, poverty, environmental apocalypse, and oppression. Many other people come from Central American countries plagued by corruption and displacement of subsistence farms by cash-crop plantations that supply the industrialized world with beef, bananas, and coffee, not to mention cocaine. Their reasons for coming are many: to work and earn money through a hard day's labor; to avoid political persecution, and in extreme cases assassination; to have a baby, who will automatically enjoy U.S. citizenship, and thereby make the rest of the family eligible; to join relatives; to sell drugs; to smuggle endangered parrots; to smuggle polluting Freon, now outlawed in American air conditioners; to send money back home for the salvation of parents and siblings; to receive better health care. An estimated 90 percent or more are not fleeing persecution or starvation but are, understandably, seeking greater prosperity.

I wasn't able to talk to illegal immigrants crossing the border. Usually the people I approached smiled, said, "No English," and slipped away as fast as they could. At the counter in a coffee shop, a Mexican man looked away without replying to my opening comment about the weather. Indeed, they would have been fools to answer my questions, even if we had spoken the same language. They would have been fools to trust any promise of confidentiality, and I didn't want to insult them even by asking what they hoped to gain by coming to America. So in other ways I sought perspective on their northern quest by way of these mountains.

Near the border, a Mexican American park ranger who had grown up in Mexico City leveled with me. "People hunger not so much for food as for progress. They're tired of their form of government — abusive, deceitful, corrupted." To illustrate his point, he referred to a recent shootout in Tijuana between federal and state police, each on the take with different drug lords. "The Mexican government doesn't work the way ours does, something you don't realize until things start to go wrong. It's mostly young people who cross — eighteen to thirty-two."

On a nearby ranch, I talked with Donna Tisdale, who had a more troubled perspective. Hearing about my interest, she began by impatiently asking, "How would *you* feel if you'd had two hundred people going through your property last night?"

She didn't wait for my answer. "They break down our fences. They turn on our outdoor water spigots. We hear their voices behind the house in the dark. We can't sleep at night. It's constant. There's no peace of mind here anymore, no sense of security — something you used to have living in the country. We moved out here thirty years ago, but when the government cracked down on illegal immigration in the cities, it pushed the crossings farther out, and now we have to deal with it."

I recalled the tale of a friend. On the outskirts of a peaceable little town close to the border, he sat in the driver's seat of his camper one evening, reading a book. A Spanish-speaking man approached his window, wrestled a hold on him, and tried to drag him out. My friend managed to pull a gun on the intruder, who then ran away.

"We used to see maybe twelve people a year," Tisdale continued in a disgruntled tone of voice. "Now it's two to five hundred a week. The Border Patrol agents say they catch only 5 to 10 percent. Last year they caught about half a million in San Diego and eighty thousand in our local rural area. So multiply that by ten or twenty times to get the number actually crossing." Many of these people go back and forth repeatedly, but many also stay in the United States.

"It's quite a wave of human migration," I said, "and must have effects all over our country."

"Everywhere. It used to be that illegal immigrants came as farm laborers. Most people didn't complain about that. It's different today. Now we see a lot of teenagers, children, old people, and sinister-looking men. My husband has to deal with them all the time and has begun arming himself. He approaches them, and they say they won't use our property, but they're back the next day. They're not afraid of us. And we're afraid of doing more, afraid of retaliation. Here's the problem: a coyote might get $500 for each person he brings or sends across, whether they succeed or not, whether they live or die. At twenty people, that's $10,000 a night. How far would a man go to keep up that kind of business?"

Donna thought there should be more border agents to deter illegal crossing and, more important, a tamperproof identification card so that people could not get jobs illegally. This would be a relatively easy solution to a very difficult problem, provided American authorities had the will and the resources. Illegal immigrants in great numbers are hired as far north as Chicago and Yakima, Washington. Jobs are the major incentive for crossing, and cheap labor is the major incentive of business interests that lobby against reform and even oppose the enforcement of existing laws.

Tisdale continued: "I'm from a farming family and know that immigrant labor has been important, but the cheap-labor lobby in Washington, D.C., goes far beyond the needs of farmers. It forces U.S. citizens out of work, drives wages down, and perpetuates unsafe working conditions." This black market in jobs goes unnoticed or is tacitly supported in communities and among individuals otherwise touting law and order, not the least of them President George W. Bush's first nominee for secretary of labor, who dropped out after the press reported that she had employed an illegal worker in her home.

Seeking the perspective of people who deal firsthand with these problems every day, I went looking for the Border Patrol. Now it was their turn to evade me. At first I encountered agents who advised me to go through the public affairs office in downtown San Diego. But I wanted to talk to patrolmen in the field. The first one I approached coolly put off my questions. "Look," the steely-eyed law enforcement officer told me in a demeaning tone of voice, "You want information, but I can't *give* you any."

I persisted and found two men who didn't mind talking, provided I didn't reveal their names. I'll call them Joe and Sam. They were both supervisors but still spent plenty of time in the field; they were clean-cut, in their thirties, and tired after a long day's work, yet patient.

"What would you like people to know about what you do?" I asked for openers.

They both hesitated at this unexpected question. Joe shrugged and offered, "Well, it's not the easiest job in the world."

No sooner had we started talking in this vein than we were interrupted by another agent reporting with some gusto, "Hey, Minnesota wants the guy."

Earlier in the day, Joe had flagged down a man on the road and ordered him to stop. The man did a U-turn at the Potrero Store, jumped out of his truck, and ran into the brush. Joe pursued, tackled, and handcuffed the man. He was an American citizen wanted for murder in Minnesota. The patrolmen considered this a real score.

"Why do you do this work?" I continued.

"In college," Sam began, "I had the idea that law enforcement was a good thing. I got a degree in criminal justice. After graduation, this just happened to be where I got a job. Turned out I loved it. I was outdoors most of the time. It was a big game of hide-and-seek. Out here, unlike in a city police department, I didn't have to deal with some guy on meth every day or with domestic violence. But then the dopers got into it. And after four or five years, the novelty wore off. Now I've seen it all. A U-Haul once had fifty people crammed into it. I've found bodies in the trunks of cars. My partner once had to shoot a guy who was about to rock me."

"Rock you?"

"Yes, hit me in the head from behind with a rock about *this* size. Still, I like the work. These people are just my clients, that's all. And

I can see their point. If California were as bad as El Salvador or Mexico, I'd take some of the chances they're taking. Most are looking only for work, or public health care, or whatever. But I don't care what they're looking for; my job is to enforce the law. The goal is to prevent illegal crossing of the border."

"So how do you do it?"

"We have road checks on all the highways, including Interstate 8. But most of the work is at the border. Sixty percent of the people we catch are at the border, and 40 percent are at checkpoints. Beyond the checkpoints, let's face it, they're home free."

"Okay, so you're set up at the border. What happens next?"

"Could be anything. If we see footprints, we follow them. I've tracked people for ten miles."

"Do you use dogs?"

"No. We can't use dogs, not even puppy-dog beagles. There's a treaty that forbids it. We have a lot of politically imposed limitations like that."

Quickly changing the tenor, Joe added, "We also watch for lay-up spots, where coyotes pick people up. But it's tricky. The coyotes are well organized and call each other with cell phones when they see us coming or when they find out a checkpoint is down — say, on Interstate 8 after traffic gets heavy — or after the checkpoints close in the rain because of an increased chance of accidents. People cut fences and drive around the checkpoints. They walk around the checkpoints. Some people walk thirty miles to the Laguna Mountains. Fourteen of them died in a snowstorm there a few weeks ago. If we had found those people, we would have saved them; I'll do everything I can to help somebody who's dying of exposure. A lot of them are really screwed by the coyotes. I feel good when I catch a coyote, but catching the drug carriers is the big satisfaction."

"So suddenly this has become a big-money thing."

Joe nodded at this understatement: drugs are a $50 billion a year Mexican underworld industry. "A lot of the crossing is drug related. In one of our areas we get dope every night. Nobody stops more drugs than the Border Patrol. The gangs in Mexico and in the U.S. move the drugs — mostly marijuana, but also heroin and cocaine. And there's a lot of smuggling of other stuff, too, some of it pretty bad, like endangered species of birds, some that can carry tropical diseases into the States—the birds' version of AIDS. The traffic has really picked up in recent years. Now there are a lot of stolen cars in the urban areas. The gangs move the cars, too, but not out here."

"So my van's safe while I go hiking?"

"You don't have much to worry about."

"Are people carrying drugs in backpacks?"

"They carry them any way you can imagine, but the typical dope carrier has a duffel bag. If you see a little brown-skinned dude with a big duffel bag, you know."

Thinking of what the street value of the bag must be, I asked, "Is danger always on your mind?"

"Yes. You might walk into a group of fifty people caught red-handed. They could easily jump you, but it doesn't happen. They respect you, and you both live to play the game again tomorrow. It's like Tom and Jerry. And safety comes first. The number one thing is to go home every night."

Not the least of the questions raised by the illegal immigration issue is, Why bother to limit immigration? With the significant exception of the American Indians, who came here a long time ago, when no other people were around, we are a nation of immigrants.

Long histories of this topic have been written, and news stories break all the time. Scanning the literature, I quickly learned that arguments of the past dealt mainly with the economy and jobs. New immigrants take jobs away from American citizens because the new-comers are willing to work for less money, under illegal conditions, and in unsafe situations, some of them as common as applying pesticides to farmed fields. Job displacement is still a concern and is more so in a tight market.

Some people now worry about the shifting ethnic and racial balance of the American population, a fear that can cross the boundary to racism. Caucasians are now a minority in California, and that scares people who can't imagine being on the other side for a change.

With taxes in mind, many people in the 1990s, including the governor of California, had reservations because the public expense of serving illegal immigrants exceeded any revenue they might bring to the government. And now, population is a big issue, having absolutely nothing to do with race or country of origin but rather just the mathematics and ramifications of growth. To understand what is happening in this regard, it's worth checking out the numbers.

Immigration levels are now higher than ever in American history. Far higher—about six times the amount that was typical until 1970. The rate increased in the 1970s and 1980s and then jumped by another 43 percent between 1990 and 2000 alone. More than 1.2 million legal and illegal immigrants are known to settle in the United States each year. But that's just the beginning of the immigration bubble of growth. Even though family size tends to eventually decline with Americanization, the birthrate among Latinos in the United States is twice that among Anglos.

The U.S. Bureau of the Census projects that most of the population increase in the United States until the year 2050 will be caused by immigration—both the direct numbers of illegal and legal immigrants and the offspring of these new people. This kind of growth alone has accounted for more than two-thirds of America's population increase in recent years, and the rate is going up.

The birthrate among established American citizens is low—about two children per woman. Left to itself, the U.S. population would level off in the middle of the twenty-first century. But because of immigration, the growth rate will increase rapidly, with no end in sight. In a "middle series" projection for growth, the Census Bureau forecast that the American population will more than double by 2100. And given what we see happening today, those projections may be greatly underestimated.

Solidly supported by the research of reputable demographers, a few groups, including the Federation for American Immigration Reform and Negative Population Growth, argue for a voluntarily reduced population and maintain that immigration is *the* population issue in the United States. Until the number of new immigrants can be brought down from the current million-plus per year, the population will grow without limits, and so will the problems of crowding— everything from flooded classrooms to loss of wildlife habitat to traffic gridlock, everything from high taxes to high crime rates, both of which tend to rise when the size of communities rises. An increasing population affects everything from urban sprawl to the cutting of trees, the burning of coal and splitting of atoms, the amount of pesticides applied to crops, and the size of landfills, shopping malls, and prisons.

Interestingly, polls show that a large majority of Americans want less population growth and support much tighter restrictions on immigration.

Supporters of lower immigration levels argue — and this is important — that the significant humanitarian obligations we owe to the rest of the world should not be addressed by allowing new growth that will simply create the same kinds of problems in America that exist in the places where the immigrants are coming from. Rather, we can do much to help people in their countries of origin. We can aid them in working toward population stability, in improving human rights, in educating women. People in the United States can also disassociate themselves from forces such as corporate agriculture that usurp villagers' farmland and drive people away from ancestral homes.

With one-fifth of the world's population (1.2 billion) in deep poverty, poor people, and many others with motivations that go far beyond just eating, want to immigrate to America in virtually unlimited numbers.

Reducing today's unprecedented high rate of immigration is considered by many to be essential if the U.S. population is not to grow wildly out of control until America becomes such a bad place that nobody wants to come anymore. If Americans are ever to cope with growth, reducing legal immigration — averaging more than one million a year in the 1990s — is a big part of the challenge. A simple act of Congress can do this.

But it hasn't happened. Republicans support high immigration because it means cheap labor for businesses, plus more business because of more people. Democrats support it on humanitarian terms. Both strive to capture the growing Latino vote. Meanwhile, the supporters of population stabilization have little voice; even the major environmental groups have abandoned goals they established to stabilize the American population.

If immigration were trimmed to 225,000 a year—the average before 1970—the immigration share of population growth would quickly flatten at replacement level.

Reducing illegal immigration is the other challenge, which brings us back to Joe and Sam, the guys on the front line.

"The more patrolmen we have, the more people we catch," Joe said. "But our post, with two hundred forty officers, covers thirty-two miles of mountainous border, and the fences only keep people from driving through. It's not like in the urban areas, where you can station a patrolman every hundred yards. Out here, people will always be getting through. But if we didn't do what we do, it would be like opening the floodgates."

"There's also not much we can do to deter people from trying again and again," Sam added. "I mean, what they're doing is nothing that calls for punishment. All we can do is take them back to Mexico. Unfortunately, that costs the taxpayers seven hundred dollars for each offense. A big part of the solution to this problem is to crack down on American employers who hire undocumented workers, but there's little manpower in the Immigration Service to do that and little political support for the agency to do its job. And the Border Patrol isn't allowed to operate beyond the border zone."

The issue of illegal crossing raises difficult questions: How do we come to grips with growth? How many people should be allowed to immigrate legally, and for what reasons? Is it unethical to hire illegal immigrants? What can be done to reduce the fundamental push for immigration—the crowding and related problems in the countries of origin?

"Our country is the escape valve for overpopulation to the south," Joe said. "People will continue to try to overflow into the United States until conditions in the other countries are straightened out. That's not going to be anytime soon. And even if it happens, there will still be pressure to come here illegally. So all we can do is our job, the best we can."

ANN AND I camped in Potrero County Park, forty-five miles east of San Diego and only four miles north of Mexico. For a leisurely morning we recovered from our Baja stint, filled our jugs with reliable water at the campground spigot, and then strolled under stately oaks.

*Potrero,* in Spanish, means "pasturing place," and the term is used in southern California to describe meadows or savannas. These beautiful combinations of grass and trees feature broad sweeps of wild lawn interspersed with oaks. The trees stand singly, as in a child's lollipop drawing, or in clusters of shade and shelter.

The reason the oaks grow here is the unusual climate. Now beyond the most relentless domination of the high-pressure system that causes the deserts of Baja, the California coastal region has a hot, dry summer but enjoys a cool, short winter watered by heavy rains. This Mediterranean climate is one of only five in the world, the others being in Chile, South Africa, Australia, and of course the Mediterranean. Covering only 3 to 5 percent of the earth's surface, Mediterranean habitats are among the rarest yet rank exceptionally high in floral variety.

Sitting there with my back against the two-foot-wide trunk of a coast live oak, I reflected on how much I simply love trees. I love their greenery, durability, and persistence, their shelter and food supply for all manner of birds and animals, their embracing arms, their wind-whispering voices. I grew up climbing trees and still do. Not only a tree hugger, though I have done my share of that, I take pleasure in the fact that trees make beautiful furniture, musical instruments, baseball bats, paper for books, beams for houses. In valuing all that, I value the forests that produce the trees.

Comforted there in the shade and shelter of fine oaks, I began to look forward to seeing other trees that would benchmark our Coast Range journey. As we drifted north, the most visible signs of change would be in the forests. Our path would wind through the groves and habitat of one hundred twenty species of trees and large shrubs, each filling its own special niche, performing its own job according to the working drawings of the earth. New arboreal faces would appear as the latitude, temperature, humidity, rainfall, and geology changed. The range of some species would continue for great distances; the ponderosa pine, Douglas-fir, Pacific willow, Scouler willow, red alder, bigleaf maple, Pacific dogwood, Pacific madrone, and Oregon ash extend from southern California to Canada or beyond. The black cottonwood has the longest range, extending from Baja to Kodiak Island, and I wondered if I would see it the whole way.

Looking up at the silhouetted leaves of the old oak's canopy, I now thought of my upcoming months in California as a quercine tour as much as a tour of mountains. Oaks, after all, are to the Golden State what the sugar maple is to Vermont, the royal palm to Florida. Eleven species of the genus *Quercus* would grace the coastal mountains as we traveled north, all of them yielding edible acorns.

The girthy trees at Potrero looked beautiful, but where, I wondered, were the young ones? None to be found. Research shows that a constellation of troubles began back when cows first arrived. Cattle grazed the nutritious native grasses to oblivion, leaving the ground open for invasion by exotic annual grasses and weeds whose seeds were sown via imported hay, cow droppings, and wind. A domino effect followed: The exotic grasses matted the soil and sucked up the springtime moisture. They crowded out oak seedlings. The exotic grasses' prolific seed crops made menu for a plethora of rodents that in turn gnawed on oak seedlings and acorns. Meanwhile, the shooting and poisoning of predators allowed rodents to multiply out of control. Firefighters suppressed wildfires in order to protect ranches and other development, even though the natural cycle of fire was sometimes essential to clear the land for oak germination. Perhaps most important, the cows themselves trampled aspiring oaks, ate the acorns, and bit off the sprouting tops of seedlings. As a result, the most majestic oak species, the valley and blue oaks, scarcely reproduce at all today. The stately trees now gracing California's savanna landscape are not being replaced and will one day die out unless their ecosystem can be fixed. Even more imperiled, the Engelmann oak is endemic to the southern California coastal foothills — it grows on a small range here and in Baja but nowhere else.

An individual oak generally produces up to seven thousand acorns each year, and if only one in a million grows into a tree, the forest can sustain itself. But it's not happening. Plus, suburban development fueled by population growth consumes twenty thousand acres of

California oaklands each year, cutting an ever deeper deficit into the woodlands estate.

The welfare of these keystone species — two hundred vertebrates alone depend on oaks — will be one of the more telling stories of how our society accommodates nature with civilization in the coastal mountains of America. A bellwether for the problems of other life, the oaks are in big trouble.

Distressing as this is, I can't help wanting to be an informed traveler rather than a blissfully ignorant one as I wend my way through this trip and through life. Adventure is a matter of escape. But for me it's also a matter of connecting to the places I travel through. I take satisfaction in knowing how places really work — not just checking out the scenery and shooting the breeze in coffee shops, but understanding what's happening to the land, knowing how people affect it and how it affects them. This is the stuff of which our future is made, and what can be more important — and fascinating — than that? While learning about the unraveling connections of nature can be discouraging, it's also inspiring to know about the intricate workings of the earth, and there's no way such a pursuit today can exclude stories like this one about the oaks.

But for now, here in eastern San Diego County — a region locally hyped as the Mountain Empire — Ann and I reveled in green grass under spreading limbs. It's an easy place to live. Native people would have agreed — I could tell by the cup-like depressions in solid pavements of granite where the Indians for centuries sat and ground their acorns, mortar-and-pestle fashion. They could gather a hundred forty pounds of acorns in a day — well on the way toward the ton each family might eat in a year. They soaked the meaty seeds to leach away acid before grinding them into flour.

Ed Ybarra, the supervising ranger at Potrero, said that people from San Diego and all the way to Arizona visit his park. "If they're from the city, they come because there aren't many people here. If they're from Arizona, they see that our temperature is a hundred and they say, 'Is that all? It's a hundred *ten* back where we live!' People come to these mountains for relief and for clean air. And they've been doing it for a long time. For the Indians, Tecate Mountain was a sacred place."

This nearby peak, called Kuchumaa by native people, is a sacred site where shamans have gone for guidance and young Indians for visions to help them along the path of their lives. Lording over the borderlands one mile from the Mexican line, the 3,885-foot summit now belongs to the U.S. Bureau of Land Management, along with private owners. Indians still come for pilgrimages, though a chain-link fence now guards a corporate communications tower on top.

From Kuchumaa, the California coastal mountains run for seven hundred ninety miles on a northwest–southeast axis (don't be confused by road maps, which tilt the state to make it fit on the maps; San Diego is actually east of Lewiston, Idaho, and far east of Reno, Nevada). The entire mountain complex includes what geologists call the Peninsular, Transverse, and Coast Ranges, as well as the Klamath Mountains in the north. In far southern California, the Peninsular Ranges — named for the Baja Peninsula, with which they merge — link together for a hundred thirty miles.

Watered and rested up, Ann and I set off in the van early the next morning to see what we could of all this.

As the first subrange north of the border, the Laguna Mountains drew us up a windy road and into the zone of the California black oak, a fine tree with acorns favored by the local Kumeyaay Indians.

Even though we were forty-five miles from the sea, we noticed from a high overlook that a belt of ocean fog had fingered inland and flooded the lower contours with moisture. Opaque when seen from above, the fog made it look as if the ocean itself had risen overnight to lap at the mountainside below us.

On Mount Laguna, at six thousand feet above sea level and a mile above surrounding terrain, we hit patches of snow for the first time on our trip. Ponderosa pines grew straight and fat, a long-needled mainstay of dry western forestlands. The mountain-dwelling Steller's jay screeched at us when we stepped out to walk, his wing bars flashing iridescent blue. I took his announcement as an official welcome to higher ground. Like the sacred Kuchumaa, Mount Laguna's summit has been cluttered by an antenna farm, where older radio towers share space with a host of new hardware erected for cell phone users.

Quickly setting off on a trail, I found that oaks and ponderosa pines gave way on hotter, dry slopes to an understory of sagebrush, mountain mahogany, and chamise—a mix of shrubby vegetation known as chaparral. The earliest tips of grasses and forbs pushed up through a rotting litter of old leaves, the green shoots promising a fruitful spring in some of America's most southern high country.

When I reached Garnet Peak, I could see north to the other end of the Peninsular Ranges, a long way but just one leg on the great journey to come. Like a loosely grouped bunch of bananas lying on the ground, the Lagunas link with the Cuyamaca Range to the northwest, then with the Volcan, Palomar, Elsinore, and Santa Ana Mountains. On a similar northbound track but farther east, high country towers above Palm Springs, where the San Jacinto Mountains rise to 10,805 feet, ethereal in my view, with snowy tops seventy miles away.

WE COULD smell the apples as we rolled into Julian, just north of the Laguna Range. With the harvest season long past, it was the cooking of pies that sweetened the air. Here the ponderosas and black oaks had yielded to orchards and then to the architecture of a town not unlike a village in New England. Sugar maples imported from the Northeast shaded two-story Victorian homes. Julian sported hedges and white picket fences, inviting park benches, and a record number of pie shops. New England can boast better apples of more varieties, and Washington can brag about its tractor-trailer apple output, but only Julian combines the orchards, the bakeries, and a town of fifteen hundred souls that one might well regard as American as apple pie. Here at 4,220 feet above sea level the air was crisp as a good bite of a red-blushed McCoun, and an arts-and-crafts industry was spinning in the eddies of the pie trade.

"You know what?" Ann said. "I think we should skip lunch and just eat pie instead." Such dietary abandon is not common for Ann. But she didn't have to twist my arm.

We started at Mom's with a slice of boysenberry-apple, one of a dozen apple combos available. After a shift at the used-book store, we loosened our belts for a second round at the Julian Pie Company.

The sidewalks on that Sunday morning overflowed with three-generation families out for a drive; with middle-aged couples on bed-

and-breakfast getaways, perhaps from the humdrum of mature marriages; and with white-haired husbands and wives who had grown to look alike in their body type, their gait, their wrinkle lines molded by a million joys and sorrows shared together. Even their midriffs bulged in tandem, maybe as a result of repeated excursions to Julian. I wanted to talk to people, but irrespective of the touristy flair of the cute little place, most folks had a big-city aversion to eye contact.

Not so with the Walter Matthau lookalike who was giving away samples at the Apple Alley Bakery. "Umm, good," I proclaimed.

"Have another for the road," he generously offered, which was all the encouragement I needed.

"So, tell me, why is Julian the pie capital of California?"

"Hey, we're the pie capital of the *world*." He even sounded like the veteran movie star.

"Okay, the world. Why?"

"It's the apples. All around you are orchards."

"Yes, I noticed on the way in."

"It's not just apples. Pears and cherries, too. Come in the fall and it's like driving through a fruit stand. Since 1905 people here have been making pies. It was a good change of pace."

"What were they making before that?"

"Trouble. They were shooting each other and claim-jumping at the gold mines. Living in an orchard is better. Here, have another sample."


THE FRUIT TREES were fine and the pie was tasty, but ever longing for the native forest, Ann and I drove into the Cuyamaca Mountains (pronounced *Quee*-a mack-a), our second subrange in southern California. Along Cold Stream Trail we found our reward — coast live oaks growing three feet in diameter and one double trunk six feet across, giants in a region where I had expected little but brushy chaparral on hot hillsides.

The mountains there offered a fine refuge from the urban lowlands to the west and the parched ranges to the east, including the Anza-Borrego Desert, but they lacked real wildness. Cuyamaca Rancho State Park had its asphalt lot, with required fees. Private ranches fragmented the forests. Even on public land, cattle fences gave the cows free-roaming privileges on miles of mountainside while keeping all us people in a skinny, weedy paddock at the shoulder of the road. Corrals for loading beef alternated with new vacation cabins, no doubt cherished by urbanites who came for the greenery but who nonetheless pushed back the wild edge as they bulldozed their driveways and built there.

Leaving that weakened wildness behind for the time being, we ramped onto Interstate 8 westbound toward El Cajon and San Diego. Quickly I had to work at getting my speed up to par — it was the first time I had driven faster than fifty miles per hour in a month. Traffic hummed like one big techno-organism pulsing down the freeway, tens of thousands of people commuting home after a weekend fling in the mountains or desert. This brand of traffic is a California phenomenon as regular as the tides: urbanites roll up the mountain slopes at the beginning of the weekend and back down on Sunday night.

Dropping on a ten-mile, 6 percent grade late in the day, we bathed in the golden light that translates so stereotypically into a West Coast ambience of the good life, sweet and casual: the guy and girl in the convertible, his smile handsome and kind, her hair streaming back from her sunglasses. You know what I mean. Even we — a married couple in an overloaded van, with books crowded onto shelves and boats lashed on top — even we felt light and airy simply because the light and the air were so potent in their seductive powers. It all just really felt good.

The low-angled sun radiated onto granite boulders and set them aglow. As we dropped farther, the air of Pacific influence softened the rays once more into an atmosphere of hazy comfort and warmth, and it was almost too much. Behind us, the mountains rose like cutouts of yellow-green, each one fading into a lighter tone than the one before it.

Even on the interstate there was something oddly exciting about this plunge toward city and sea. It all spoke to something so very Californian — the sun, the speed, the air, the fault scarps behind, the surf ahead. At moments like that a person can forget about some onerous realities and believe that California is still the mythical island where dreams will indeed come true.

El Capitan Reservoir flooded the San Diego River behind a dam and reminded me of the essential connection between mountains and people throughout the Coast Range: high country rakes the clouds and provides the water needed for life down below. It's the mountains, in fact, that make human life and cities all over the West possible. Without mountains, the urban throb of places such as San Diego would be more like a dusty blow on an alkali plain in Baja.

Tapped to the max, the rivers flowing from the Coast Range of far southern California are all dammed except for the Santa Margarita, north of San Diego. With fine riverfront habitat, that stream is irreplaceable to the wildlife it supports. And — talk about connections — it also provides essential silt that rebuilds Pacific beaches that would otherwise erode under the constant force of surf. In contrast, beaches at the mouths of the dammed-up rivers are disappearing for lack of sand flowing down from the mountains. This struck me as no minor problem for the local scene, because what could be more southern Californian than beaches?

Not going that far west, we exited beneath the impressive rise of Rattlesnake Mountain and turned onto lesser streets half a dozen times until we arrived at the home of Jack and Hazel Lynch. Finding a warm welcome, we sat down in the living room, which was brightened by Hazel's paintings on the walls, a pot of steaming tea, and a stack of cookies.

Of magnificent, gentle spirit, Jack Lynch was a man I had wanted to meet ever since his daughter, Christy, told me about him some thirteen years before. White haired, with bushy brows and a snowstorm of a mustache, he had eyes that still gleamed even though his health was failing. He had a respiratory illness that defied diagnosis. "I'm not sure what's going to happen to me," Jack admitted with a shake of his head, and immediately I could feel the value of every moment — the value of every moment in his life and in mine.

I knew Jack loved the mountains, so I asked him to reflect on their importance to his family.

He began with a type of story I never tire of because it's always

laden with chance and consequence, always brimming with optimism and hope. It's the story of arrival — of how we each came into
our chosen place on earth.

"The servicemen who got to see California during World War II
were never quite the same afterward," Jack began. "It happened to a
lot of us. After serving in the Coast Guard out here, I married Hazel
and we moved to southern California. We lived in Escondido. I taught
high school there. We had an old 1936 Chevy and loved to go for
rides. One day we drove past Rattlesnake Mountain, and I thought,
How beautiful, how serene. This was really the backwoods back
then. Ten years later we bought this house with the same view of
Rattlesnake. We felt we belonged here. The mountain quickly became a part of us." Jack paused to let the idea sink in.

"That feeling of belonging must grow through a lifetime of wonderful experiences," Ann commented, giving Jack a chance to catch
his breath.

"Yes, you're right, Ann. Up there," Jack pointed, "up to the very
top, at twelve hundred feet, I took my three girls when the youngest
was just *this* high." He flattened his hand down below waist level.
"On our first trip they put their names in a can and we buried it on
the summit. It's our backyard mountain, you see, and for years we felt
that it was our own. There were no other houses around then. Only
an orchard of orange trees lay behind us. We could ride horses the
whole way up into the Cuyamacas and cross only two roads."

It occurred to me that what Jack described, quite simply, was the
elusive but universally sought condition we call quality of life.

"Now you can't even walk up there. It's all posted as private property. More people moved in. Developers even proposed a thirty-story
apartment building on top of Rattlesnake Mountain. For a while the
entire fortune of that place was riding on a few people who lived
down below and thought the view was important." Jack took a deep
breath.

"The fortunes of mountains everywhere are tied to the people who
live near them and care about them," I offered.

He nodded. "Isn't it a paradox that something as durable as that
mountain would depend on the frail actions of a few people who

adopted this place as their own? And it's a tragic paradox because the forces we fight against can be so powerful."

"But the mountain is still there, still beautiful," Ann said.

"Yes, it is. People stopped the development. To build the apartments would have required a zoning change, and we blocked it."

Jack reflected further on a life well spent, on the joys of raising a family with an appreciation for nature, on a timeless search for accomplishment and a sense of belonging in a world troubled by increasing stress and difficulty.

"I guess we each do what we can. I taught school and raised my girls. During summers I worked as a ranger for the Park Service, showing visitors the wonders of Kings Canyon National Park. After we bought this place, I let half my yard go natural. The native grasses and wildflowers grow where they want. With all the other changes around us, we no longer see bluebirds or horny toads. They're gone. But my wild backyard's still my little Shangri-La. It's just a hundred feet wide, but I let it be." We all paused for a sip of tea.

It's hard to be both informed and hopeful, so when I talk with older people who have lived through great changes, I'm curious about their wisdom of acceptance, especially if they know enough to avoid denial of the problems yet also evade a sense of total resignation. I had to admit, hearing Jack talk about the changes around his place made me feel depressed. Yet somehow he managed to find joy in his miniature mountain refuge. He had found some satisfaction with a bigger picture he seemed vaguely to envision. How could he remain hopeful? I had to inquire. Yet I had to be ready for an honest answer. "What will happen here?" I asked. "And what hope do you have for a better future?"

Jack shook his head. "There'll be no end to the changes. There will be another Los Angeles here, I'm sure. The traffic is already horrendous, and where there used to be eight horses behind a fence there are now eight hundred people.

"California changes, but it happens gradually, and people get used to it. We're like the frog that never jumped out of the pond because the temperature increased so slowly he didn't realize he was in trouble. Then it was too late; he was too weak to jump. The new millennium will bring a world we can't imagine. But for here, for now, we're fortunate. Nestled up against our mountain, there's some feeling of security. While I have that mountain in sight, somehow I still believe we can make it, that we can do what we need to do. Looking at a mountain inspires hope in people."

In retirement, Jack did what so many dream of doing: he pursued what he was truly passionate about. For him, this meant writing poetry about his place and his life.

With his mind still on the difficult and perhaps unanswerable question of hope, Jack said, "May I read a poem to you?"

"Oh, please. What's it called?"

"It's called 'Flight of the Condor.' The condors, you know, are our largest birds, and they used to fly over these mountains. Maybe they will again someday."

> *His was a life of short flights*
> *though he dreamed of condors*
> *and of heights unscalable*
> *where the purity of driven snow*
> *unmarked and glittering in the sun*
> *promised a timeless freedom.*
>
> *Stark and pure as before the fall,*
> *simplicity such as this he sought*
> *though not on so grand a scale,*
> *for being born to a frenetic world,*
> *the sublimity of his soul*
> *was weathered by noisy vicissitudes.*
>
> *And so he turned containment*
> *into the art of the minuscule,*
> *banked the furnace of his muse*
> *with common fuel, and having closed*
> *the damper down waited in hopes to pour*
> *from that crucible the golden ore.*

After another cup of tea, Ann and I said good night. Jack died the next year.

DRIVING NORTHWARD toward the next set of mountains, Ann and I curved up through orange groves and then onto the steep grade ascending Mount Palomar. That evening we found a mountainside pull-out level enough for sleeping, and as dusk faded toward darkness, southern California lay spread out below.

It looked far better than I had expected. From three thousand feet above sea level, the view showed mountains and hills rolling and folding away in a hundred creases and pale-lit valleys. The sun's dimming light colored the slopes of pines, oaks, and orange groves in purple, hazed by moisture from the ocean.

With no city upwind of us at that point, the air wafted straight from the sea, and it had the most delectable freshness to it, damp in a rich and full-bodied way yet not a bit clammy or muggy. Stirred into this was a delicious twist of aridity as the breeze brushed across the water-hungry landscape.

Warm with the moderation a big ocean provides yet cool with the falling temperature of elevation and of the night, Pacific air settled sweetly into my lungs, like the taste of a really good Julian apple, both sweet and tart at the same time. Again and again I noticed this in unpolluted areas along the coast, and I could tell I was developing a true passion for Pacific atmosphere.

I had regarded southern California between Los Angeles and San Diego as one monolith of subdivisions and strip malls. But it's not. Just east of the coastal edge and into the mountains, I couldn't help but be impressed at open country with scarcely a light to be seen at night. Valleys lay beyond valleys where whole new cities could be built, and probably will if adequate water can be found.

In the morning we wound up to the Palomar Observatory. With an art deco dome gleaming in white concrete, it's the most famous astronomical observatory in the world and gives this mountain, among all Coast Range summits, the greatest name recognition. In one fell swoop, Palomar's sixteen-foot-diameter telescope doubled the size of what an interpretive display called the "known" universe, though it struck me as hubris that anyone would say they know something simply by seeing a speck of light.

Palomar had replaced the Mount Wilson Observatory in the San Gabriel Mountains east of Los Angeles when the air there became too polluted and lit up at night, but the same fate awaited Palomar with the growth of San Diego and Escondido. Today, the telescope has been eclipsed by electronic devices that can "see" two hundred times as far. Palomar, on this natural landmark of the Coast Range, has become for the most part a historic landmark to science.

Just down the road from the dome, and with no art deco pretensions, Palomar also hosted a prickly antenna farm—a high-tech display of discs on metal poles, Erector set towers on three legs, spear-pointed receptors with multiple blades probing the sky, spheres the size of tennis balls bolted up in rows, and endless other assorted hardware designed to reap man-made waves and electronic impulses from the sky. I was reminded of a Wisconsin study revealing that a thousand-foot TV tower, between the years of 1957 and 1994, had killed 121,560 birds of 123 species. One tower! In 1998 the Federal Communications Commission reported that there were seventy-five thousand communications towers of all sizes in the United States, and with cell phones dependent on these high-tech mountaintop junkyards, another thousand towers were expected to be built in 1999 alone. In the Telecommunications Act of 1996, lawmakers even ordered the National Park Service to turn over public summits to the telecommunications industry. Worse yet, Republican congressmen —so fond of habitually saying they favor local over federal control— used their federal muscle to ban state and local governments from regulating the towers. Beyond the uglification of our finest mountaintops, concern has been voiced about the health effects of electromagnetic radiation emitted by some towers and even by cell phones themselves. The cellular industry people make no estimate about the number of new towers that will foreseeably be needed.

Up there on Palomar, where antennas had replaced trees, I couldn't help but think of the irony. To call home and do business by cell phone from bustling airports and clogged freeways means that one's missives must travel by way of these remote mountaintops.

Palomar sits as an isolated uplifted mass, and to reach our next link in the northward-angling ranges—that scattered assortment of bananas on the map mentioned earlier — we needed once again to go down. The dirt road we took ranked as one of the more dizzying road plunges drivable. The sharpness of the switchbacks barely accommodated the turning radius of the van's power steering, and the gradient dropped in a low-gear, brake-stinking, ear-popping pitch toward a dotted quilt of orange groves.

Except in the small Indian reservations — thirteen of them checkered onto the Coast Range foothills of San Diego County — "For Sale" signs littered the landscape most of the way to Temecula, a small-lettered name on the map but on the ground a sprawl of newly plastered neighborhoods, Mediterranean Levittowns sporting identical pantiled roofs overhanging pink walls. An isolated Engelmann oak preserve was saved, but elsewhere behemoth earthmovers molded this frontier suburbia into cul-de-sacs awaiting demand from those fleeing the cities and older suburbs as those older communities are filled with immigrants. So goes the fate of southern California: less and less nature, more and more development.

The size of the peninsular mountains increased with the Santa Ana Mountains, boldly rising to the north. After advancing along the eastern side, we turned off Highway 74 to drive up to the high ridges, visible only through a pall of deteriorating air. Official signs threatened hour-long delays for road construction, and sure enough, we joined a long lineup including not many cars but plenty of light trucks, sport utility vehicles, and pickups pulling powerboats. Such vehicles account for half the auto sales in California these days. Ticked off that they couldn't just go, some men honked their horns in anger. Sentiment was turning ugly by the time the flag-woman flapped us on for the breathtaking climb. Low gear then tugged us up pavement notched into the eastern face of a fault scarp. From our acrophobic view, civilization seemed to recede as if we were on a slowly launching rocket, never to return.

Topping out after the hot pull, we left the maddening traffic behind and wheeled north onto a quiet mountain byway. The road wound farther up, a skyline drive where fantastic views opened to the hazy gray of the Los Angeles urban area below. Canyons swooped down like the gliding flights of condors to chaparral cloaking this northernmost of the Peninsular Ranges. It all smelled spicy with resinous greenery. The now-expected antenna farms for cell phones scarred the summits, but little else scratched up our view, and we settled into a pull-out where, with decades of experience, I judged we could sleep unbothered for the night.

After dark we strolled to a clearing where the airy vista dropped to valley lights, pinpoints signifying a world apart from our refuge. I reveled in the fact that there, so close to multi-millions of people, we could enjoy a setting so mountainous, so apparently remote. The land up there on that quiet evening did not appear to be under lock and key but seemed simply to exist, much as I, too, simply existed, touching down for the moment on a new section of the earth where I felt at peace. With such feelings I looked forward to a quiet sleep.

Just before dawn, in that pleasant retreat within the sky glow of Los Angeles, our slumber rudely ended with a "Blatt!" from a car horn, way too quickly followed by "Bam bam bam" on our door.

I rallied fast to defend my territory, wondering what would be required. Fueled by a suite of cave-guardian hormones coursing quickly into my bloodstream, I parted the curtains, and through starkly shadowed light beaming from a pickup truck's bright beams, I saw a man in a USDA Forest Service uniform. This wasn't good, but it could have been worse.

"You have to leave," the man yelled while I pulled on my shorts as rapidly as a fireman called in the night. "You can only camp in a campground." He shined a lunker of a five-cell flashlight in the window, blinding me for an instant.

"Okay, I'll leave."

I jumped into my jeans and shirt and emerged to talk, curious about the need for policing the road so vigorously. What goes? But the ranger was already officiously copying down my license plate number—an intimidating transfer of data that triggered the sinking feeling that someone else was in charge.

"No fires, either. If you're found cooking a meal even in your vehicle, you can be cited. Fire hazard's high. I'm just giving you a warning, but if you're caught again, you'll be cited." The fit man of fifty or so with red hair and rosy face was not the macho young cop-impersonator I had expected but now seemed more a forest ranger of true dedication, and I had the feeling I'd like the guy in some other context. Any other context. But, too bad, he was anxious to speed off and nab another boondocker before dawn.

"I see you have Wyoming plates," he said as a softening afterthought. "Well, you can't just park and camp around here. There are far too many people for that." With what I perceived to be a tone of apology and allusion to social trends over which neither he nor anyone else had any control, he added, "This is a whole different ball of wax down here."

Boy, no kidding. The pull-out had seemed like a remote enough spot to me. What could I be hurting? The attitude seemed to be that people were a problem and they needed to be corralled.

In fact, the rangers here in the national forests rimming Los Angeles have good reasons for this policy — car theft, rape, murder, and gang activity among them. Rumors have it that Angeles National Forest, east of the city but a lot like our interrupted site in the Santa Ana Mountains, is a major dumping ground for dead bodies and stolen vehicles. Yet the problems were not evident in my travels, except for some gang graffiti like what you see almost everywhere in West Coast cities. A sheriff's department investigator later admitted to me that the dumping grounds part of what I had heard was true but that criminals rarely *committed* their crimes in the mountains. They just dumped the victims there.

I kept an eye peeled for the unsavory at the fringe of LA, but typically I ran into athletic young men wearing Lycra and puffing their way uphill on mountain bikes after a day in the computer industry, women in sweatpants on chatty walks with their girlfriends, families camping for the weekend and trying to reign little boys in from treetops and the brinks of waterfalls, and bird-watchers with binoculars half strangling their necks. Rather than indicators of violence, I saw couples in love and showing it off as a Californian's sacred birthright to be affectionate in public.

Only once did I see a weirdo who provoked me to glance backward over my shoulder. Some say I was lucky, but perhaps the truth lies in between my good fortune and the paranoia that can overcome people who watch the news all the time.

After recovering from our early morning wake-up, Ann went to work on her book while I hiked up Los Pinos Peak, 4,500 feet high, and enjoyed the sight of mountain beyond mountain. The range's twin summit, Santiago Peak, locally called Saddleback, rose to 5,680 feet nearby. Canyons zigzagged down from the backbone of the Santa Ana, but they terminated all too soon at the open jaws of a hungry civilization, reminding me of a funhouse sliding board that expels you without pause into the mouth of a dragon. Looking north, I could see toward the lowlands where the Santa Anas fade into the Chino and Puente Hills. Then the flatter pavement and the city take over through a twelve-mile topographic gap skipping to the southernmost rise of the Santa Monica Mountains.

All day I kept my eyes peeled for lion tracks on the trail. Biologist Paul Beier in the late 1980s fitted radio collars on thirty-two mountain lions living in the Santa Ana Mountains. Within a few years cars and trucks had creamed seven of them. And traffic is just one of the diffi-cult hazards that crop up where civilization abuts the wild. Indicative of another, and with the tables turned, a child was attacked and seri-ously injured in 1986 by a mountain lion just downhill from my Los Pinos hike. In this policy-setting case for park managers, a judge rep-rimanded the state and county governments for not warning people about the dangers they might face in the outdoors. The public was forced to ante up $2 million. Seeking to avoid further liability charges involving the cats, which show a disturbing preference for children, Orange County flatly prohibited anyone under eighteen from enter-ing Ronald W. Caspers Wilderness Park. I tried to imagine myself again as a seventeen-year-old, itching for adventure and pumping testosterone that I had no idea what to do with, and being banned from this wild public place. Would I have stayed out of the park? Of course not.

Unlike the protocol for dealing with aggressive grizzly bears — you're supposed to play dead if you've got the courage — the thing to do if a lion attacks is yell, throw rocks, fight back. In the mountains I normally walk with ski poles as a way of turning hiking into a full-body sport. And there in lion country I took some comfort in thinking I could wave my poles at a snarling cat and maybe even give it a poke in the ribs, if it didn't snap my spinal cord before I so much as laid eyes on it. The main advice to hikers is to keep children close and never let them bring up the rear of the line.

With all this in mind, I didn't really have much to worry about. The felines are so shy that in my entire life, much of it spent outdoors, I've only ever seen the faintest glimpse of one lion, a thrilling moment on the flank of Junipero Serra Peak, a coastal mountain farther north.

From the Los Pinos summit, in hazed light, the San Bernardino Mountains rose behind a soup of petrochemical air to the northeast. Though girded by suburbs that lay down there in the smog, the Santa Ana mountaintops surrounding me remained a refuge, a world of nature up against some of the least natural detritus of civilization one could imagine. Like so much of California, the scene in front of me was one of stark contrasts. But for now, in early February, the monkey flowers bloomed on the moist, sunny slopes and the afternoon air caressed my winter hide. At moments like that I thought of my bird's-eye view from mountaintop to megalopolis as the God view down to the mortal world.

The roughly thirty- by fifteen-mile expanse of the Santa Ana Mountains isn't a lot smaller than the famed Teton Range of Wyoming, and I couldn't help but think that for all the urbanization in southern California, the large swaths of public open space in the bordering mountains are extraordinary. Though Los Angeles has the dubious distinction of protecting less open space as a percentage of incorporated area than any other major city in America, few others can boast such large expanses of *surrounding* open space. The mountains here offer a model of what needs to be.

But is it enough? More and more people need more and more recreational space. The valiant efforts of park planners and managers are not keeping up with the growth; they're not even coming close. California's population increase of three million people in 1990 alone caused an increase in recreational demand equivalent to the use of thirty Yosemite National Parks. Five thousand acres of developed parks and 25,000 acres of natural resource parks should have been added to the public estate just to keep pace, according to recreation expert Pete Dangermond.

Furthermore, wildlife biologists all agree that to sustain an ecosystem of truly functional proportions, connection of corridors between the mountains of southern California and throughout the Coast Range is imperative. Just consider the bighorn sheep. Once in plentiful numbers throughout the Peninsular Ranges, they've been reduced to only about two hundred eighty individuals scattered in nine herds through hundreds of square miles between the San Jacinto Mountains and Mexico. This is down from twelve hundred sheep as recently as 1978. Any population of wild animals either needs a large area to support enough members for an adequate gene pool—thus avoiding the degenerative problems of inbreeding—or needs corridors to connect one territory with another so that occasional mavericks can infuse local groups with new DNA.

As top predators, mountain lions also need large areas simply to hunt. One study found that the habitat of a single lion contained 210 to 350 deer, and it takes a lot of land to support that many animals. Young males need even more room to roam and find new territory.

Though they seem large, the existing reserves within the coastal mountains are in fact not adequate. Furthermore, California's booming human population is steadily encroaching on lion land. Even at the protected tracts, fat-tire bikers and hiking families increasingly visit the mountains, peopling the lands the lions have long claimed. According to biologist Beier, the Santa Ana lion group will probably be extinct in twenty years if we don't protect additional habitat and reduce the conflicts.

Biologists think it's still possible to link the Santa Ana Mountains with wild areas to the south by way of an Interstate 15 underpass and a golf course. It seems odd to think of a young lion tunneling under traffic or passing the ninth hole on his journey to find a mate, but we're down to those kinds of corridors, and even they will be ineffective if action isn't taken soon.

From that summit in the Santa Anas, I tried to spot our own corridor for traveling north, and I didn't see even a golf course. For our own Coast Range journey, I could tell that some serious challenges lay ahead.

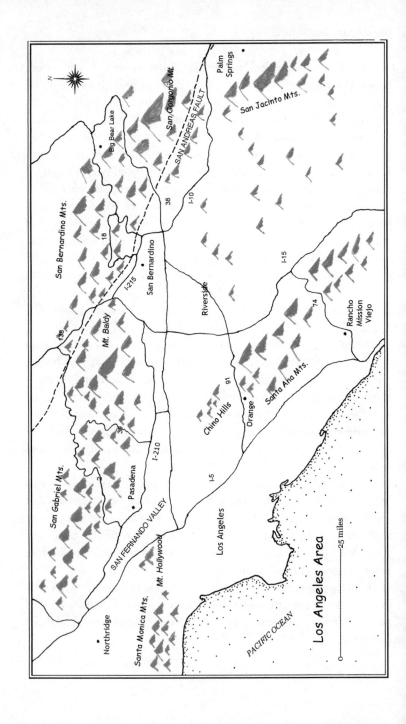

# Los Angeles Area

San Gorgonio Mt.

SAN ANDREAS FAULT

Palm Springs

San Jacinto Mts.

Big Bear Lake

San Bernardino Mts.

I-10

38

18

I-15

San Bernardino

I-215

138

Mt. Baldy

Riverside

74

Rancho Mission Viejo

San Gabriel Mts.

38

91

Chino Hills

Santa Ana Mts.

Orange

2

I-210

Pasadena

I-5

Los Angeles

I-210

Northridge

SAN FERNANDO VALLEY

Mt. Hollywood

Santa Monica Mts.

PACIFIC OCEAN

0 — 25 miles

# 4 | *Rising Above Los Angeles*

WITH AN impressive sea of civilization ahead, Ann and I rolled down the west face of the Santa Ana Mountains by following the canyon of San Juan Creek. Mottled-bark sycamores cantilevered over riffles and waterfalls, and red-tailed hawks screamed overhead, all of it thus far within the public-land refuge of Cleveland National Forest. At lower elevations, a blanket of native bunchgrasses survived among invading prickly pear cacti, a mosaic of chamise chaparral, and a splendor of stiff-armed oaks, gnarly and ancient and holding their own for now in a hostile world.

But soon enough, like the leonine cats seeking new territory by sprinting across freeways and sleuthing around subdivisions, we were out of our element. Mankind's frontier bucking up against mountain country proved not to be a pioneering edge of bushwhackers or some forgotten remnant of rural hardscrabble at the fringe of society. Rather, the interface of humanity and the wild in the western Santa Ana Mountains was the thoroughly posh Rancho Mission Viejo. To serve tile-roofed Mediterranean homes — palatial spreads often housing only two people — the streets lay in curvilinear precision. Chemlawns shone spotlessly green, palms lined the thoroughfares, and watered beds of flowers were tiered as orderly and colorfully as bouquets at an open-casket viewing. Indeed, something had died, and the showy flowers represented an effort to accommodate the loss.

I feared that this next set of Coast Range mountains would be the most difficult for us, the least friendly to the way Ann and I live, and the most disruptive to the interactions with nature that we sought.

"How are we going to get through this?" Ann asked as we sat pondering our fate, each of us with one eye on the map's amoeba-like splotch of red urbanity and one on the smog and suburbanization already swamping us.

"We'll just have to make the best of it," I said in what must have been a tiresomely optimistic tone. Underneath a layer of denial I harbored my own sense of dread, and I deeply appreciated Ann's willingness to accompany me through thick and thin, even into what now awaited—the maw, the epicenter, the popcultural Mecca—I wasn't sure what to call the urban area other than LA.

"It could all be quite interesting," my wife rallied, reminding me that it was another Rancho Viejo where we had visited and eaten freshly slaughtered goat in Baja only one month before. "Talk about contrast; this place is about as different as can be from there."

While putting a temporary hold on some of my other exploratory ambitions, such as climbing peaks, canoeing rivers, and biking back roads, I adopted the goal of understanding the inevitable interface of urban and wild. With that mission, I was drawn with a compelling new sense of curiosity to the places where sprawling city met forbidding edge of mountain slope.

Okay, I questioned, what do the mountains really mean to this city? The high-country view of Los Angeles is not the typical perspective one gets at the beach, or in Hollywood, or at Disneyland. But what difference do the mountains make to this place? Whether or not people are aware of it, how much of life do the mountains shape around here?

First I was faced with the designer aspect of the streets and home-sites at Rancho Mission Viejo. They reminded me of my days studying landscape architecture and of my decision as a young man to avoid taking a job in a firm that produced stereotypical clusters of condos, golf course communities, and private residences. Not all landscape architects do that kind of work, but a lot of them do, and at the entry level I would have had few options to choose the kind of work I wanted.

Instead, I entered the profession of planning. In it I had hoped to influence the larger shape of communities toward solutions that worked well for both people and the land. Over the course of eight years I accomplished some modest things and failed in other ambitious goals. But aside from all that, I learned a lot about the process and the problems of development, about sprawl and floodplains, about steep slopes and mudslides, and on and on, and now, twenty years later, I had a new opportunity to put all that exposure to work as I struggled to comprehend no less than Los Angeles where it intersects with its mountains.

For miles the single-family homes of Rancho Mission·Viejo dittoed onward, outward, interspersed with horse trails and riding stables, golf courses and commercial nodes shining with showy cars. At the development's headquarters—plush, cool, ultra-Californian with oaks and eucalyptus—a grainy wooden building had been architecturally jointed with fine taste. I stopped there because, as I rolled down off the mountaintop and into the hilly suburbs of the LA fringe, I had wondered just how far the new development would ultimately go. Would anything but the publicly owned lands of the national forest be left open? I thought I knew the answer, but when you're writing a book, you want to be sure. So I asked the woman behind the desk if they had any information about the design of the property, about future plans. Maybe I could even see some drawings. My old landscape architecture expertise was welling up inside of me.

"I beg your pardon," she said, successfully deflating me in four short words because I knew she had heard me.

"Well, for example, can you tell me how many more houses will be built?" Surely any investor in a home there would want to know the same thing: Will this place continue to look like it *does,* or will it look like where I just *came* from?

"Oh, we don't give that kind of information *out.* This is a private company, in the same hands for a hundred years." A public relations specialist, essential for dealing with my ilk, wouldn't be available for two days. I wasn't about to wait at this glorified subdivision that long, so I left clutching a few brochures. Reading them, I learned that the current owner's history indeed began with Mexican land grants and cattle ranching. But since then the company had gone way beyond beef. It developed ten thousand acres in the 1960s and sold them to Philip Morris Companies Inc., hardly a Spanish land grantee. Fifty-two thousand acres remained slated to become new neighborhoods that "50,000 persons may be calling 'home.'" There, right in the brochure, I found what I had been looking for. Fifty thousand more people on this runout of mountain slope, and they'd spawn just as many cars, with a high pet-per-person ratio of cats and dogs prowling and decimating the local birds and wildlife. That was what massive suburbanization in wild foothills meant to me, but obviously I wasn't the typical reader of this slick promotional piece. Thinking about all those roaming house pets, I wondered, Would there be anything left even of the national forest?

With unanswered questions everywhere, Ann and I drove on, now finding whole hillsides labeled with signs saying "Homes, $300,000 and Up" and "Will Build to Suit." In the Santa Ana foothill city of El Toro, brand-new high-end subdivisions lay everywhere. Gated against criminals, outsiders, and, let's face it, everybody, those compounds, I'm sure, served as refuges to their owners just as whole mountain ranges stood as refuges to me. I'm sure the homeowners see the fortifications as necessary to guard their accumulated wealth, as essential for comfort and security, and as the only way to cope with what has happened to the world. But, look: this radical level of privatization represents no less than a revolution in the way we regard living space — private and public — in America.

To resort to a private compound for security now struck me as a case of abject poverty. Or a lot like living in a prison. From the looks of those barred-up places, it was not clear if the criminals were locked out or the residents locked in. To be satisfied with such a tiny habitat seemed like a resignation perhaps appropriate during wartime siege, perhaps in medieval times, but not as a way of life today, and especially not an affluent way of life. All those neighborhoods seemed to be rich in building materials but agonizingly poor in living space.

Behind those gates, maybe it would be soothing to regard the rest of society as someone else's problem. Since Proposition 13 was passed in 1978, Californians have faced systematic tax cuts and a retreat from provision of public services, education, and amenities such as libraries, parks, and recreation. It has all led to an era when improving the larger society is not considered much of an option anymore. On top of those funding limits, picture the rate of population growth: enough more people in California each year to fill a city the size of San Francisco plus a few suburbs and then some. The state is left with a chronically decreasing supply of public infrastructure per capita.

Wholesale abandonment of the social contract and the embrace of unlimited growth through history's highest rates of immigration leaves white flight and reinforcement of the heavily mortgaged bunker as the main response to some deep underlying problems of our age. In triply locked gates, "Keep Out" signs, iron bars on windows, electronic surveillance, alarms at driveways, and private security forces, which outnumbered police in California by four to one, the response to population growth and social ills was clearly evident all around the Los Angeles foothills of the Coast Range.

Meanwhile, at a collective level, shopping malls—architectural paragons of the consumer culture—have replaced public spaces in the minds of many people. Ann and I were shocked to learn that Girl Scouts in southern California go "camping" in shopping malls overnight. They call these window-shopping slumber parties camping! Old people walk in the malls for exercise, not because the weather's bad outside but because the neighborhoods are no longer considered fit to walk in, and community open space no longer exists.

Looking for space of our own, we tried to stay on the flanks of the Santa Ana Mountains while winding north toward the city of Orange, and we saw precisely where the rolling swell of foothills encountered the ocean of stucco and tile. Because it was Sunday, one developer's fleet of bulldozers, payloaders, road graders, behemoth backhoes, and spike-wheeled dirt packers rested in formation like a division of tanks, like a private warlord's army of yellow equipment two machines wide and a quarter mile long occupying the front lines. At this leading edge of civilization's war on wildness, the earth had been reduced to bare dirt. Clawed-up soil stretched behind the fat-treaded Caterpillar fleet and down the hill, abruptly ending in a brand-new city of tile roofs. It was coming, coming, as surely as the population of the Los Angeles urban area had expanded from a World War I cow town to the $500 billion urban engine roaring uphill at the turn of the twenty-first century.

In a classic history of the region, Carey McWilliams called southern California "a gigantic improvisation. . . . a product of forced growth and rapid change." To show the phenomenal rate and extent of development, he inserted into his book a table reporting on the 1940 census, when 3.5 million people lived here. With convincing eloquence McWilliams lamented the changes growth had already wrought. Well, the current population is six times that great. And the figures in another sixty years will probably make today's southern California look as quaint as McWilliams' nightmare looks to us today. But even more telling than the increase in population is the acreage consumed. While the numbers of people grew by 45 percent between 1970 and 1990, the suburbanized area increased by 300 percent, a ratio that might well define the word *sprawl*.

What I saw served as evidence of California's known statewide population increase on the order of three-quarters of a million people every year (many additional arrivals escape census counts). What I saw also described "California One," so named in a plan drafted by the nonprofit organization California Tomorrow. In 1972 that group identified the Golden State's dour fate — if effective growth management measures were not taken — as a "tortured place" where cities were spread out and slurbed together, where people relied on their cars and created gridlock, and where more freeways continued to tear up the land and the neighborhoods while only adding more traffic, more pollution, more cost, more stress. "California Two," on the other hand, promised a thriving and beautiful place if Californians embraced reasonable planning approaches to the problems posed by runaway growth.

In spite of fair warning, California One is clearly the legacy we find today. In fairness to the organization that described these scenarios, they didn't have a chance at California Two, given the rates of immigration.

Nowhere is it more clear: our rules of social and environmental conduct were designed for a small population on a large landmass, but today we have a huge population on a relatively small landmass. Ann and I now sat in traffic through mile after mile of commercial strips en route to the next range of mountains.

BORDERING THE Los Angeles urban area to the north, the fifty-mile-long face of the San Gabriel Mountains rose up so steep and tall in our windshield that it looked like a phony Hollywood backdrop through the urban haze.

It's naive even to think about mountains, or land development, or anything at all there in front of that escarpment, without also thinking about the San Andreas Fault. Eight hundred miles long, it begins its geologic knife-cut east of the Laguna Mountains near the Salton Sea. From there it runs northwesterly through the consequential fold where we had now arrived, between the San Bernardino and San Gabriel Mountains east of Los Angeles. As one of the largest and most exposed seismic fractures anywhere on the earth's crust, the San Andreas and nearby related faults mark the boundary between the Pacific and North American Plates.

Geologists have discovered that these plates are discrete sections of the earth's crust that float and slip on top of the hotter, semi-solid rock underneath. They move at different speeds and in different directions, and over time they have covered great distances. Two hundred million years ago, for example, North and South America adhered to Africa — a heritage that's imaginable when one looks at a world map and meshes together the outlines of the continents. They fit like the two pieces of leather stitched together on a baseball.

The Pacific Plate includes the land west of the San Andreas Fault plus most of the Pacific Ocean floor and is moving northwestward at an average of two inches per year. Los Angeles will slip north of San Francisco in about twenty-five million years, though by no means intact.

Most of the Coast Range south of San Francisco is on the Pacific

Plate. Already I found myself wondering: Which side of the fault am I on? Am I on the Pacific Plate or the North American Plate? And it's hard to wonder about which plate you're on without wondering about the consequences of being caught in an earthquake.

"Which side are we on now?" Ann asked as I tried to locate the fault on a geologic map I had filed away for this phase of the trip.

"Half and half."

"Well, then, let's get out of here."

We always hear about earthquakes as disasters, and no doubt, movements on this and dozens of related faults cause extreme damage to anything built in harm's way. Northwest of Los Angeles, for example, the Northridge earthquake in 1994 moved the San Fernando Valley eight inches and cost more than any other natural disaster in U.S. history, $42 billion. This one sector of the Los Angeles urban area consumed nearly half the federal disaster assistance funds for all the United States over a six-year period.

A city simply cannot exist in the Los Angeles basin without exposure to earthquakes. Certainly a safety margin of green space near the fault lines could be reserved from development to avoid some of the most inevitable damage, and regulations in fact now ban building directly on known fault lines, something that seems as basic as banning picnickers from a rifle range. But no matter where you go, the tremors and their effects will be felt.

Without earthquakes, however, North America would still be attached to Africa and Europe. One look at these mountains shows that earthquakes are true forces of creation, the original shapers of the land. Without them, there would be no Coast Range, nor the related rainfall, snowmelt, water supply, and forests that serve people's needs.

Perhaps owing to a continental rift across Nevada that is now pushing that megablock of land to the west, the San Andreas Fault at the San Gabriel Mountains takes what geologists call the Big Bend. This is a kink in the fault's dominant northwest–southeast alignment. For a short but significant distance it bends decidedly west. Reflecting that shift, and visible to Ann and me, was the bold and extended east–west axis of the San Gabriels, one of the five Transverse Ranges.

These are big mountain masses lying at an oblique but intersecting angle to the north–south Peninsular Ranges. The fault later resumes its northwesterly direction to San Francisco and beyond, but right here, the kink of seismic contortion forms one of the more complex mountain masses in America.

Remember that the Pacific Plate — west of the fault line — represents the inexorable northward march of the entire coastal mountain mass, all the way from the tropical tip of Baja and beyond. Throughout this length the two plates slip alongside each other, an extended seismic happening but nothing compared with the extravaganza awaiting at the kink. There, just east of Los Angeles, the northbound Pacific Plate bulldozes into the east–west axis of the San Gabriels, a broadside collision pushing mountains up quite fast in geologic time. Riddled by faults and rattled by earthquakes, the slopes of this two-mile-high geologic behemoth are breathtakingly steep. Thoroughly shattered by seismic thrusts, the steep terrain looks as if it has been fed into a big food processor and piled up for tossing as soon as a little dressing can be added. Just walking around at the fault near Interstate 15, I could see that the ground was more like mineralized mulch than bedrock.

All these factors lead to a rapid disintegration of the San Gabriel Mountains even as their ridgeline is pushed up ever higher, ever more erodibly into the sky. The frail roots of plants are all that nominally hold the slopes together. But those plants burn on a regular basis. Indeed, fires rage frequently across the chaparral- or brush-covered slopes, and after rainstorms soak and lubricate the friable soil, it's primed for rill erosion, mass wasting, landslides, mudflows, and debris avalanches of awesome weight and crushing ability. With such forces of destabilization in place, it's a simple matter for gravity to level what seismicity so boldly but precariously pushed up.

As I thought about what all this meant for LA, I realized that the mountain material that erodes off these ranges is in fact what has created the Los Angeles basin — both the flat plain near sea level and, more obviously, the long, gentle, steady slope that characterizes the urban areas within a few miles of the mountains. Some of the alluvial deposits — just another name for dirt originating on the mountains and washed down to a lower spot — are fourteen thousand feet deep! The slides, mudflows, and floods emanating out of each canyon have, with the homogenization of time, spread the eroding material across wide fans known as *bajadas*. Los Angeles has been called many things, but most simply it is a floodplain surrounded by mountains.

The average acre of mountainside in the San Gabriels loses seven tons of rock and dirt per year, most of it in cataclysmic mudslide events following intense storms that have delivered as much as twenty-six inches of rain in twenty-four hours. The slides deposit their cement-like aggregate in depths that swim houses and then completely inter them or else shatter them to smithereens indecipherable from the dirt itself. Single slides running at five hundred feet a minute deliver mud, rock, and soil that spew across the lower slopes in grave-covering layers of two-, four-, ten-, twenty-foot depth. Anything in the way of these multi-kiloton forces of disintegrating mountain may as well have been in front of Pompeii's lava. Residents discover this again and again when homes, cars, garages, roads, and bridges are plucked from their moorings and crushed to wet, brown pulp by the encroachment of boulders as big as buses, all of it backed up by the weight of a descending mountainside. Though biblical in proportion, these slides are no rare event; exceptional floods of debris occur somewhere in the Los Angeles basin about once each decade.

To live on those eroding slopes — which means virtually every steep mountain slope in the region — is to live on an avalanche path. Even worse, to live at the mouth of a canyon is to look up the proverbial barrel of a gun. A very large gun.

Rather than question the wisdom of living there, and rather than restrict development by telling any group of bankers, real estate agents, and builders no — rather than do any of that — the city spends over $60 million a year maintaining debris basins, dry reservoirs dug out in the canyons in an attempt to arrest the natural process of mountain erosion and *bajada* buildup. The basins are intended to catch the rock and mud before it engulfs houses. Over the years, more than twenty million tons of such rock and soil have been trapped, deposits that are then reexcavated and trucked away to prepare for the next slide.

The long-term futility of this exercise is enough to inspire a downhill spin on the myth of Sisyphus. The cost is borne not by those relatively few people who choose to live in the mudslide zones, nor by the developers who fail to inform buyers of impending doom, but by the taxpayers at large. And even with all that effort and expense, there are frequent overflows of the catchment basins and wet avalanches in drainages lacking debris dams.

The mudslides are only one of a medley of natural hazards that excel in southern California. Floods and wildfires also claim the lives of residents, destroy billions of dollars' worth of property, and sap the taxpayers of billions more in disaster relief, fire fighting, and levee building. But unlike the ubiquitous earthquake hazards, these other disasters could largely be avoided if people would just respect their mountains.

Look at it this way. The Los Angeles urban area is essentially an oval of city, a hundred miles by forty miles in extent, with tentacles reaching into adjacent flatlands, up gentle slopes, and into canyons. Lucking out with a clear day, Ann and I could see one whole arc of this oval when we reached a pull-out high on the flanks of the San Gabriels. Around the edges of this vast area a veneer of development climbs the lower slopes of the mountains. The hillside zone can easily be seen on maps because there the straight-line grid of streets turns to a curly fringe of winding roads. Now think of this edge of development along the mountain front as the skin of an orange—it's that thin in relation to the rest of the city. Yet virtually all the hazards of mudslide, debris avalanche, and wildfire occur in that thin strip.

The mud has always slid—otherwise there would be no Los Angeles basin of relatively flat land down below, composed of earth that once did the sliding. Likewise, the brushfires have always burned. As I would see later, chaparral was *made* to burn. And floods have overflowed the riverbanks ever since rain began to fall on the earth. The problems exist not because nature is nature but because people have built homes in the way. The problems exist because development of mountain land is neither voluntarily avoided by people nor restricted by government regulations. The main strategies that government has assumed are to try to change the rules of nature and to pay people for the damage that is bound to occur.

I'm reminded here of something that California's great conservationist Gary Patton once told me. As a society, we regard the laws of nature as optional when in fact they are absolute. Meanwhile, we regard our own customs and laws as immutable when in fact we can change them whenever we collectively decide to do so. In our minds we have perfectly reversed the way nature and culture actually function.

Here in the mountains around Los Angeles, we think we can stop mudslides, though we can't, and we don't think we can prevent people from building in the way of mudslides, though we can.

As a result, the refuge of the mountains has become a battleground of people versus natural process. Some call this "people versus acts of God," which is very close to simply saying "people versus God." And, as the ravages attest whenever a debris slide flushes out a wall of mud and puréed houses, the battle is futile.

If people simply recognized the hazards and costs involved in the development of this steep veneer of the city, a lot of problems would be on the mend. In fact, in a visionary plan for Los Angeles in 1930, the eminent landscape architect Frederick Law Olmsted Jr. proposed hazard zoning to ban building and rebuilding in the most disaster-prone areas. But real estate interests of the day killed the idea. Meanwhile, taxpayers at the local, state, and federal levels have been socked with endless bills for the damage, and again and again they've subsidized redevelopment on the same disaster-prone slopes.

HERE AT THE ultimate North American limit, where westering pilgrims and real estate tycoons alike butt up against both sliding mountainsides and the deep water of the Pacific, Californians have collided with other limits as well. This was all too evident to Ann and me on a ridgetop walk we took near the retired Mount Wilson Observatory in the San Gabriel Mountains: the city had all but disappeared by midafternoon. The pall of smog posed a definite limit on our vision and on the quality of air to breathe.

This is a phenomenon of only the last half of the twentieth century. In 1946 historian McWilliams wrote, "The charm of Southern California is largely to be found in the air and the light." He raved about a profound sweetness in the air, a softness in the light. Ann and I saw it ourselves from the flank of Mount Palomar and other spots that survive unpolluted by virtue of their location. We shared McWilliams' enthusiasm. He wrote that "the skies have a lazy and radiant warmth" and that these ephemeral qualities had "no counterpart in the world."

Then, in 1951, the term *photochemical smog* was coined for the growing, darkening haze. This noxious brew of hydrocarbons and oxides of nitrogen reacts with sunlight to form ozone, a chemical substance that's essential at high levels in the atmosphere, where it protects us from ultraviolet light, but is poisonous to life in its low-elevation form. The principal source of the damaging chemicals was and still is automobiles; here, their belching tailpipes create one of the smoggiest places on earth.

Like mudslides, air pollution is also a story of the mountains, and like so many aspects of the Coast Range, it speaks to the interface of mountains and sea.

The high country bordering the Los Angeles basin acts as a big leeward wall blocking the free escape of air and causing a stagnating effect, enough to figuratively gag the basin below. That's troublesome enough, but greatly accentuating the problem, the fresh air drifting in from the chilled Pacific is cool. This accounts for the pleasant oceanside breeze in places such as Santa Monica. But the cool ocean air is heavier than the sun-cooked atmosphere lying inland, especially in summer. Thus, the cool air clings to the ground and fails to rise or blow away, a phenomenon called an inversion. Trapped in the LA basin, the cooler air holds hostage the region's pollution. With what might be regarded as an ironic sense of justice, the mountains require that the people who produce the foul air also live with it.

The thickness of the smog has given rise to the strictest air pollution requirements in America, including bans on the open burning of trash since the 1950s, and to requirements for smog reduction devices on cars today. Tighter restrictions and big investments in clean air have paid off to the extent that the per capita rate of pollution is well below what it was in 1980. The burning eyes, sore throats, headaches, and chest pain are not as bad as they once were. Where a whole forest of ponderosa pines in the San Bernardino Mountains died of ozone and smog poisoning, young trees have begun to sprout back. But that means only that the air is better compared with the gas chamber of the past.

Southern California's air still exceeds federal health standards for one pollutant or another on half the days in a year. Improvements aside, it's not the kind of air informed people would really like to suck into their bodies by breathing six to ten million times annually. According to the South Coast Air Quality Management District, fifteen to twenty thousand people in the LA area die each year from respiratory conditions directly related to poor air quality. If the purely human implications for health seem unalarming, consider this: by solely meeting federal standards, which don't promise good air but are only the minimum requirement for some statistically derived definition of health, the Los Angeles area alone would save $9 billion a year in health-related expenses. This affects not only the victims but everybody who pays high bills for health insurance. And the figures don't address all the ways people would feel better, live better, and see better with cleaner air.

Even the incomplete gains of two decades of hard-fought regulatory success are tenuous because right-wing politicians argue the corporate line for deregulation. Mostly unsuccessful at trying to legalize bad air, they resort to hamstringing regulatory agencies by cutting funds for monitoring and enforcement. And even though the pollution per mile driven has been reduced, there are many more cars today. Besides that, people drive far more miles than they used to; since 1980, car use has increased at twice the rate of population growth. Worst of all, and most avoidable in this long litany of worsening, avoidable facts, the current fleet of sport utility vehicles—so popular even among people who have little exposure to either sports or utility—are pigs at the gasoline trough. For no reason other than political influence they've been exempt from important air quality rules. Hundreds of thousands of drivers use them on routine commutes when a regular car would do just fine.

THE MOUNTAINS not only contain the air in the bowl of the Los Angeles basin but for years contained the sprawl as well. Any location within the basin was fair game to suburbanization, but people were unwilling to make the painstaking commute over high passes to distant locations beyond. It's somewhat of a myth that southern California has spread without shape or discipline. Rather, it has sprawled until it hit the mountains. Ann and I could see this by looking out from the San Gabriel Mountains to the nighttime glitter surrounded by the darkness of mountain barriers.

But today, a mania of commuter leapfrogging runs rampant. From the mountaintops you can look eastward to new cities splotched on the desert and to a surveyed grid of subdivision after cookie-cutter subdivision checkering arid land beyond Palmdale. Mini-markets occupy dusty intersections in the Mojave Desert, the trashy roadsides tormented by billboards for personal damage lawyers and bikini bars. Looking down at the desert's failing condition from a high vantage point, I was reminded of an early-twentieth-century photo of the San Fernando Valley clad in pasture and orange groves where Hollywood now sits beneath a perpetual smoke signal of smog. And predating those old photos, the same valley had once been a *potrero* and savanna. Spanish explorer Gaspar de Portolá called San Fernando "el Valle de los Encinos"—the Valley of the Oaks. Now, as other observers have noted from airplanes, it looks like El Valle de las Piscinas—the valley of backyard swimming pools.

Population growth, cars, and cheap gasoline are the causes of both sprawl and pollution. Adjusted for inflation, fuel prices are now lower than ever in the history of the automobile, and as a result people commute a couple of hours one-way to affordable housing on the far side of the mountains. But in this devil's bargain, the marathon commutes of desert residents not only pollute the air but also erode the quality of family life; parents spend their time in their cars instead of with their kids.

Looking out at all this sprawl and smog, and considering the hazard of mudslides and the diminishment of nature, it's easy to be discouraged. But being as optimistic as I could about people and life, I looked on this troubling scene from my perch above Los Angeles and wondered what could be done. Now, at the passing of what might be regarded as the century of sprawl, this problem has become recognized as one of the most important community and environmental issues of our time. Leading a Sierra Club campaign against sprawl, area resident Tim Frank said: "Rather than being against development, we are for community. We're for development—or redevelopment—of compact, vibrant, livable communities." Though it astoundingly avoids the unavoidable issue of population growth and thus immigration, the Sierra Club campaign seeks to promote urban growth boundaries, revitalize established towns and cities, protect open land outside the boundaries, and cut subsidies for sprawl. Such subsidies include federal mortgaging policies and public spending for sprawl-inducing investments such as water lines and freeways. The Urban Land Institute reported that public facilities for suburban sprawl cost 40 to 400 percent more than equivalent facilities for compact housing. Other subsidies include the sacrifice of public land and offshore areas for oil drilling—which means that commuters' gasoline is heavily subsidized—and cleanup following oil-related disasters such as the wreck of the *Exxon Valdez*.

If efforts to control sprawl fail, where will it all end? Eighty percent of California's 33 million people in 1998 lived within thirty miles of the coast. Projections now call for 58 million people in the state by the year 2040, the equivalent to five more cities the size of Los Angeles. Where will they go? How this increase of 25 million can be accommodated, even in the best of scenarios, must challenge anyone's imagination. But if the new growth comes as sprawl, the costs in land and taxpayer expense will be especially extreme.

At the mountain interface with Los Angeles I had seen firsthand the limits of steepness where mountains begin to slide, the limits of pollution where the view disappears, and the limits of space itself as sprawl encounters the undeniable edge of the ocean on one side and the increasingly permeable barrier of mountains on the other. This all struck me as the ultimate extension of the principle I had seen in effect at San Javier in Baja. There, a village could support no more families because the farmland and water were used up. Here, a large urban area encounters limits of its own, requiring new approaches in community design, technology, and lifestyle.

EVEN IN THE month of February, heavy weekend traffic clogged the mountain roads as Ann and I wound back down the dogleg bends of Highway 2. Recreational hinterlands for the urban area, the Angeles and San Bernardino National Forests see more use than any other national forest in the country. After all, 20 million people live within a three-hour drive. More than 5 million visitors a year go to Big Bear Valley in the San Bernardinos alone — more than visit the famed Yosemite National Park.

But even with its urban edge, even with its recreational mob, the mountains rimming Los Angeles continue to overpower and amaze.

Whitened by snowfall, San Gorgonio Mountain in the San Bernardinos rises to 11,502 feet, the highest in the entire Coast Range south of British Columbia. In the San Gabriels, San Antonio Peak, nicknamed Old Baldy, reaches 10,064. These heights tower over a lowly base of 1,500 feet, resulting in some of the greatest vertical uplift in America. Mount Whitney is the country's tallest peak outside Alaska but rises from a 4,000-foot valley floor, so the relief here is comparable. Landmarks of the Rocky Mountains such as the Grand Teton climb significantly less because they veer up from valleys already 7,000 feet above sea level.

The mountains edging the greater Los Angeles area are said to constitute the longest urban–wildland interface of any nontropical city — some six hundred eighty miles and growing as urban development usurps farmland that historically buffered the city from the mountains.

For all its artifice, for all its sprawl and foul air, for all its crowds of commuters, this metropolis remains a city of nature as well. Both an amenity and a bitter pill to swallow, the mountains expose Los Angelenos to the workings of the natural world and offer rugged refuges literally at the edge of town.

I DROPPED ANN off to visit an old college friend and drove alone on the winding climb of Los Angeles' best-known hillside. Giant letters spelling *Hollywood* had long ago been blocked across the slope. That name has come to mean so much in American culture, but its origin can be attributed only to mistaken identity. Because of its red berries, people thought that the toyon—a common small tree of the chaparral—was holly. Somehow I just can't see *Toyonwood* having the glitzy appeal that its misnomer has given to the movie industry.

Up on the hill I parked the van and locked it. When leaving my home and vehicle in big cities, I usually snap curtains up inside the windows so that predatory cruisers cannot see how much fenceable stuff I have inside. But this time I would be gone for only a few minutes to take a picture.

I walked a short distance and noticed that a lone man in an old gray Camaro had pulled in right next to the van. I set my camera on the tripod for a good shot, but each time I glanced back, the man in the car was looking either at me or at the van.

Cautious, I returned and drove farther up Mount Hollywood, took a left turn and then a right, and eventually emerged at another overlook with a higher view of the city. The same car pulled in directly behind, almost parking me in.

I grabbed my bear spray—a Mace-like aerosol—and stuck it within reach under my seat. Creeped out by this stalker and his persistence, I drove back down to a lower overlook. But when I stopped again, the same car appeared in my rearview mirror. Disgusted with the feeling that I needed to arm myself in order to step out of the van and shoot some film on Mount Hollywood, I returned to the Griffith Observatory. There, among a crowd of people, I was paradoxically alone again in the center of America's second-largest urban area.

The winter day was otherwise glorious, spring-like with life's eagerness for the growing season. Hardy flowers popped into bloom, and opalescent grass pushed up new blades by tapping the moisture of winter rain. Birds sang in the toyon, and schoolkids visiting the observatory seemed to bubble with vernal enthusiasm.

Looking west now—the coast of California here runs not north–south but east–west with the contrarian alignment of the Transverse Ranges—I could see the rise of the Santa Monica Mountains ramping up, each earthy mass higher than the one before it. Ridgelines faded away one after another to the end of sight. Unlike the California mountains Ann and I had visited so far, these rose directly from the sea, or fell straight into it, depending on whether you're coming or going.

My exploratory zeal had been deflated by the problems of the mountains around Los Angeles, but now I was ready for the freshness that a new land promised, for the abrupt edge of rock and water that had been missing since we left the rugged terrain of Baja. From my vantage point above Hollywood, the hazy mountains lured me toward their wave-resistant shores and hidden valleys ripe with springtime.

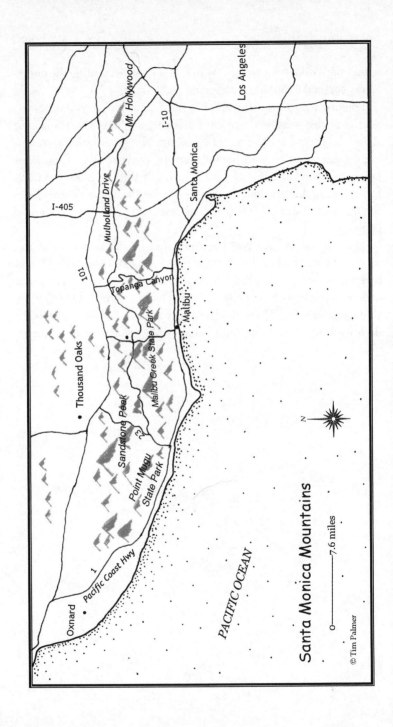

# Santa Monica Mountains

Los Angeles

Mt. Hollywood

I-10

Santa Monica

Mulholland Drive

I-405

101

Topanga Canyon

Malibu

Malibu Creek State Park

Thousand Oaks

Sandstone Peak

23

Point Mugu State Park

1

Pacific Coast Hwy

Oxnard

PACIFIC OCEAN

N

0 — 7.6 miles

© Tim Palmer

# 5    *Mountains and Fire*

T HE SKY was clear, the breeze from offshore, the world's widest ocean silver-blue. From where I stood, the Santa Monica Mountains showed off a rhythm of rock and topography, artful patterns repeated here and accented there, all seeming to beat with a pulse of life on the whitened granite ridgeline and then down through the chaparral thickets for twenty-five hundred feet to the sea, the slope so steep that just looking at it made me tend to tip over. The glass-and-steel architectural summits of Los Angeles stood in a pall to the southeast, but the wind came from the oceanic west, whistling sweet, moist, and clean across our next range in the coastal mountains.

Scented with the new growth of grasses and wildflowers, dry in the crisp interlude between late-winter rainstorms, the air came from a special recipe, not just sustenance to the lungs and bloodstream but deliciously more than that, dulcified with earth and ocean both. The whole package — rock, grass, sun, air, sea — had a tingling effect that I could almost feel coming up into my core by way of my feet, thus far anchored on good earth. But the mountain feeling was so light, so carefree, so high that I almost felt like taking flight.

Walking farther up on the two-track remains of a dirt road, which had been shut down for erosion control when this mountaintop became public parkland, I approached a woman. She sat perched on a flat rock just above the trail. Perhaps in her fifties, trim, tan, with long, graying hair, wearing a dark blue athletic bra and running shorts, her shoes kicked off to the side, she faced the setting sun, her eyes apparently closed, a heavenly hint of smile on her mouth. Her upturned hands reached toward the source of her light and her warmth.

I hated to intrude. But I had little choice because the trail passed so near to her. She detected my approach on the gravelly path and awakened without alarm to my presence. We made eye contact, and she veritably glowed from within, a joyous, peaceful person, no doubt. In her presence I couldn't help smiling.

"Hi."

"Hello." She smiled as well, her eyes squinting and wrinkling in the character lines that helped me guess her age. "I'm thanking God for the last rays of the day."

It struck me suddenly that here, in this woman's eyes and heart, was the proverbial California sun worship at its finest, without vanity but rather with reverence and vitality that goes to the essence of life itself.

"You don't need to explain," I said. "I understand."

"Could it be more beautiful?"

"If there's a way, I don't know how."

I wanted to talk to her more but didn't want to be a pest at that special sunset moment, so I continued on.

After a few more bends in the trail I encountered a young couple rock climbing. They had set up their belaying line through a bolt at the top of a slab of granite that offered just enough knobs and divots, just enough cracks and jams, to be interesting and athletically doable. The man stood with a length of rope threaded through the stainless steel brake and slung to his harness, pulling in the slack while his girlfriend stepped up. They talked back and forth: "Yes, what a smooth move," and, "Oh, no, I don't think I can stay on this hold for long!" I wanted to watch but felt like a voyeur. This public rock had become their own private place for the intimate dance of the climb. He held her body within a quick tug of safety while she reached, stepped, twisted, hugged the granite, and turned herself into the inverse shape of the rock itself. She had quite literally become one with the mountain. As I distanced myself, their voices became simply tones, his deeper and quick, hers higher and melodic, the two of them nicely paired. I imagined them living their lives that way.

Finally, at a meadow near the summit, I passed a group of men and women, eight or ten of them standing in a circle in a clearing behind a low ridge of rocks. They couldn't see me. They were singing, or something. Like stringed instruments, they hummed along with an occasional deep-diaphragm "Bahhhh" and a falsetto "Ahhhh," altogether a full-bodied tone that definitely perked up my ears and made me stop and spy further. My first eavesdropping impression — that it was weird — soon yielded to fascination because the voices sounded so harmonious. Their collective chorus then descended in tone to a resonant "Om" that vibrated among the surrounding guardians of rocks. Then came the words.

"I am the channel of healing."

"I am the channel of peace."

"I am the channel of life."

I took these three claims as my cue to move on, but just then a flute picked up a spacey but captivating tune. To my ears it all still seemed pretty strange, though I couldn't help thinking that the flute sounded like a distant coyote song. This prompted me to scan the horizon, where mountain ridges in the ephemeral light matched the highly improvisational sound track.

And then, with the high-pitched notes fading on the gust of an ocean breeze, someone began to beat a drum. Adding bass and belly, a deeper drum sounded. After a few steady bars someone began striking triplet and off-beat accents on a high-pitched drum, and at that point I could hardly stop myself from joining them. What can I say: I'm a drummer. I always have been. I mean a real drummer. I've played snare drum, a trap set in a jazz band in the sixties, rock and roll in the classic era of the seventies, bongos, congas, wooden boxes that sound like hollowed-out logs, and timpani to tunes by Sibelius in an orchestra. Drums reach deep into the visceral and the unconscious, yet they broadcast sheer joy and make your body move with carefree abandon. A good drumbeat draws on the deepest past, yet it's as vitally present as each and every beat of the heart.

Now, with the ocean crashing far below and the springtime air alone a hormonal stimulant, drums hammered out the rhythm of life on that sunset mountaintop while the last rays of the day beamed down on us. It all seemed so alive, so good, so right.

EVERY MOUNTAIN range is different, but to me the Santa Monicas now seemed completely different, occupying a special place in my personal pantheon of up- and down-country. Being southwest of the San Andreas Fault, they're on the Pacific Plate, so they're inching north toward Alaska along with Baja, the Peninsular Ranges, and the streets of LA. Originating somewhere in Mexico, these mountains retain a core of whitish granite, to which I'm partial. But much of the mass of the forty-six-mile-long, seven-mile-wide range is sedimentary or volcanic in origin, darker and more crumbly, with exceedingly erodible soil when disturbed.

I found thriving in this dirt a blend of the shrubby low growth called chaparral, pocket groves of conifers on north-facing slopes, lush woods along stream bottoms, and bald, rocky outposts where one could almost get blown away on the stiff winds of spring. The Coulter pine grows here, with its fourteen-inch, bear-claw cones — the heaviest pine cone anywhere. A third again as large as a pineapple and heavier, they drop off the trees like resinous bombs; I definitely would not want to be standing, or even parked in my van, underneath when one falls.

No doubt the Santa Monicas seem special in my mind because they face the Pacific so well. Maybe it's different if you grow up at the seashore, but I grew up in the interior, so whenever I approach an ocean, I'm unrestrainedly delighted. I seldom take for granted that here, the familiar element of land ends. The mystery of deep water begins.

As a member of a terrestrial species, I find it easy to forget that only 29 percent of the surface of the earth is land. But here, with that wet horizon running from my far left to my far right, with six thousand miles between the base of the Santa Monicas and the island of Japan, I could believe that there's a lot of water on the planet.

Behind me, America rose and fell for three thousand eastbound miles of dependably solid topography, but at my front, the final slide of the mountains ended in the western sea. Somehow just seeing this change infused me with the *power* of change. Change — whether the end of land and the start of the sea or the end of one era and the beginning of another — requires us to think, to act, to respond to the world. To do all that — to make the changes or even to simply roll with them — can be empowering in many ways. Here in the Santa Monicas, simply seeing the change in front of me touched on all those chords.

Then, too, from my high perch looking out to the Pacific, the idea of limits was real because the land of America comes to an undeniable end here. There isn't any more. Yet the ocean is not limited but infinite in both its appearance and its fundamental nature — of water forever flowing in via rivers at the same time an equivalent amount evaporates into thin air — and so my gut feeling there at the edge is always one of unlimited possibilities. I can stand at that Pacific shore with twenty million southern Californians at my back but a primeval wilderness out ahead, and I feel good, hopeful, even joyous. Almost satisfied.

Certainly a large part of my attachment to the Santa Monicas involves no metaphysical stretch and in fact differs little from anyone else's attraction to the beach or to expensive real estate. Simply put, I like a view of the ocean.

At a secret campsite I can sit in my van, work at my table, and look out across the Malibu Coast Fault to the sea. In a region where the land has systematically been put under lock and key — you pay to take a stroll in a state park; you pay for a parking spot at the beach; you pay even more to walk on private land; you pay an enormous amount of money if you want to own land yourself — this secret site is one place I've found where I can stay awhile, quiet and alone.

In most places there are rules against doing this, and for good reasons. Number one, there are too many slobs. But I am careful about my impact. I pick up the trash left by other visitors. I do not drive onto vegetation or soft soil where I would leave muddy tracks rutting the earth. I avoid nesting birds and do not hassle wildlife with my camera. I seek a private spot far from the road when nature calls, avoiding watercourses and wet areas and digging an adequate hole with an ice ax to bury my waste. Almost everywhere I camp I eradicate exotic, invasive, noxious weeds that displace native vegetation.

It's a fabulous thing, I believe, to still be able to stop and live on the land, unfettered and free, the way trapper Jedediah Smith did when he first came through California in 1827, the way writer J. Smeaton Chase did when he toured through here on horseback in 1911. But opportunities to live this way up and down the California coast today are almost nil.

Sitting at my campsite overlooking the ocean, I remembered that I had caught one of my first glimpses of the Coast Range near here. Back in 1967 I hitchhiked south from Yosemite to visit my uncle and his family in Los Angeles. From the freeway on that balmy evening, I could see the Santa Monica Mountains tapering down from high green chaparral. I was impressed at how mountainous the fringe of the third-largest city in America was. The truck I traveled in rolled down into the honking maw and those steep slopes faded in darkness as the sun set. They faded in my mind as well after that flicker of twilight romance, when I wondered what was up on top of those summits and behind those purple ridges of rock that seemed to be guarding the city, or, perhaps more accurately, to be guarding what lay beyond from the city itself. Now, thirty years later, I was finally there, ready to see for myself.

Though Ann and I hated parting company, our trip to the Santa Monicas presented a rare opportunity for her to visit her aunt and spend a few days with her aging grandmother, who suffered from Alzheimer's disease. When Ann was a little girl, her grandmother took her traveling each summer. Those trips no doubt stirred Ann's sense of curiosity and wonder about the world — traits that now make our nomadic life together not only possible but abundantly rich in intimacy and shared experience. So her grandmother has been important to both of us in this way. The coming week would be a sad time for Ann, but one she wouldn't miss.

After joining her for the first part of the visit, I set out alone with a simple agenda. I had no great peaks to climb or rivers to run; here in the Santa Monicas I sought just to enjoy the land and learn about it.

I must admit that there's a certain excitement, intensity, and zest that accompanies solitude. Now I was completely free to go where I chose, to stop when my foot happened to find the brake, to linger and pursue a story or a slowly ripening sunset with my camera. Of course, I can do all that with Ann; she's patient and understanding of my needs, as I am of hers. But when we're together I cannot pull up stakes unexpectedly or lollygag inexcusably without some concern that she will be inconvenienced. Surely everyone who has a partner knows what I'm talking about. And, let's face it, independence is fun. Setting off alone for even a few days now strummed on some resonant strings that lurked back in my memory of single life. Before I met Ann, I lived alone in my van for years, writing about what interested me and traveling wherever I wanted, whenever I wanted to go.

Failing to suppress a slight smile at all these thoughts, I looked at the mountain range on my topographic map. I saw that the Santa Monicas lay like a great east–west loaf of French bread, slightly curved. The cartographer had colored most of the loaf green, as open space. But in its eastern reaches blocks of gray, indicating pavement and homes, roughened the edges. And like patchy clouds on the evening weather map, a low-pressure front of urbanity crowded in on the easternmost green space and then completely enclouded the mountain at the Highway 101 corridor, leaving Griffith Park and Mount Hollywood as an island of green torn from the loaf and left out to dry.

I'd already been to Mount Hollywood, so I started my Santa Monica tour at the promising head of Temescal Canyon. After puffing rapidly uphill for an hour, I stared out across the city of Santa Monica and beyond to Los Angeles International Airport — the fourth-busiest airport in the world. I confirmed from my mountain lookout that planes indeed land on average every twenty-five seconds.

In no place was the contrast of mountain land rising from an enormous city more clear. My nearest foreground resembled a wilderness, but the white and gray of the city awaited immediately at the bottom of the slope with the same absolute certainty that a football field lies at the bottom of the stadium steps. "The mountains are so close to the city but so far away from it," a man named Levi later explained, capturing the essence of the Santa Monicas from his own hiding spot — a Jewish retreat camp farther up the road.

In Topanga Canyon I struggled against speedy if not reckless traffic on the sinuous two-lane. J. Smeaton Chase passed through here during his horseback trip to Oregon in 1911. In his classic *California Coast Trails* he wrote: "I was impressed by the ruggedness of the mountain slopes, which rose in striking mass and contour, and in places pushed the road into a mere defile, overhung by precipices of fine height and verticality. At the northern end of the cañon are many neat little hillside farms, mainly of Mexicans, and the dust of the road was plentifully marked by the scamperings of children's naked feet."

No naked feet on that road today. Nor overhanging precipices. They had been blasted away to accommodate the cars.

Turning away from the parade of impatient commuters insanely squeezing every mile per hour they could out of the blind-ended bends, I parked and hiked to the bald overlook of Eagle Rock, where canyons dropped away in twisted, chaparral-tangled pathways to the sea.

I decided to hit Malibu for an early dinner and soak in the beachtown scene. Of course, a lot of ordinary people live there, but the archetypal Californian tended to catch my eye.

Ready to take advantage of what the place uniquely had to offer — ocean waves — a young man stepped out of a rusty Volvo with a short yellow surfboard racked on top.

"How's the surfing today?" I asked, only to be rebuffed with a cooler-than-thou stare through sunglasses.

"Not bad, dude," he deigned to say. He could tell I was not a surfer, though in fact I have stood up on a board for a few seconds now and then.

At Coogie's Beach Café I got a table beneath a big curve of window facing the mountains. While taking in the beautiful view, I couldn't help overhearing the conversation of the couple next to me, an exploratory dialogue between a nerdish man and a strikingly trim woman in black tights, her hair as blonde as straw and as straight as if it had been ironed. She was in the movies, yes, but so far only Grade B horror flicks. "Oh well," she said, "you have to start somewhere."

Outside, a man wearing a starched white shirt and superfluous suspenders and a woman in a black dress that lacked any pretense of a neckline kissed lengthily at the edge of the parking lot butting up against the freeway, a scene that would have tickled filmmaker Woody Allen and piqued his penchant for the absurd, especially when it occurs on the West Coast.

Traffic was surging in both directions on the Pacific Coast Highway — PCH, as they say — and I recalled the quaint history of access to this once and always extraordinary place. Her husband long dead, May Knight Rindge owned the entire Malibu coast and ranched here, posting the whole area against trespassers. Troubled by travelers who did not douse their campfires, she even closed the roads through her ranch, leaving the beach below high tide as the only legal passage along this part of the Pacific coast. Defending her property with gun at hip, she eventually lost an access case in court, and in 1928 the county built the Roosevelt Highway along the route of today's PCH. Reduced to poverty through her lifelong battle to keep Malibu as Malibu, she ultimately auctioned off her estate to avoid a sheriff's sale. I couldn't help but think it was a broken heart that killed May Knight Rindge two months later. In those last weeks, would her life have felt like a failure because of the development of Malibu?

When J. Smeaton Chase passed this way, he apparently ignored Mrs. Rindge's "No Trespassing" signs. He saw only one or two people on the entire route.

Among the thousands I saw, I struck up a conversation with fellow travelers Bobbi Poolan and her college-age daughter, Tess, from Bucksport, Maine. As we eyeballed the surf at a public access spot, Bobbi explained, "We're on a journey, I guess you could say." They had driven across the country to Oregon and then down to here.

"You're an adventurous pair," I offered.

"Oh, we're just out to see the world, that's all."

White haired, petite, and not averse to chatting with a stranger, Bobbi continued: "We knew there was this huge city down here and that the air was awful, and so we wondered, Why would anybody want to live there? But now we know. It's the weather! Can you believe it? This is February!"

"It's not Maine," I agreed. I warned her that air pollution would get worse as they ventured down the coast. But she knew.

"I wondered why they don't *do* something about it," she commented. "They all say, 'Oh, you should have seen how bad it *used* to be.' But I thought, Imagine if this were Maine! People would be out there with signs protesting and getting authorities to clean it up. And then I remembered: Maine has 1.6 million people. How would you ever accomplish *anything* in a place with as many people as Los Angeles?"

"It would be like expecting the air to be clean in New York City."

"Oh, well, nobody would ever expect *that!*" Bobbi, from Maine, and I, most recently from Wyoming, which boasts a population of 0.4 million people, both agreed that bigness has its drawbacks.

"Well, shall we boogie?" Tess eventually cut in.

Bobbi signed off with "We'd better get going."

"Where do you go next?"

"Tess, honey, what's the name of that place we're going to next?"

"Guatemala."

GOING IN the other direction, I entered Malibu Creek State Park. In this wild enclave of stream valley cutting past steep-sided peaks, the trails wind all over. Many people have seen this state park without even knowing it. The opening scene of each TV episode of *M\*A\*S\*H* was filmed there, transforming the Santa Monicas into wartime Korea. The park has also been billed as France, Africa, Arizona, the South Pacific — almost anyplace Hollywood needed it to be. In fact, the film industry owned the place until 1974, when the state bought it from Twentieth Century Fox and also acquired nearby ranches owned by Ronald Reagan and Bob Hope. Reagan bought another ranch farther north, in the Santa Ynez Mountains, where there were fewer people.

Along this Hollywood theme, I really wanted to see the forest where Tarzan had his treehouse and grapevines. A childhood hero of mine, Olympic swimmer Johnny Weissmuller, was filmed here in his exploits as Tarzan of the Jungle, which I watched religiously as Saturday morning reruns of corny old flicks made during my parents' youth. Weissmuller inspired me to rig my own backyard woods with ropes and treehouses, to which I attribute a personal transformation from ninety-eight-pound weakling to scrappy little wildboy.

Now I saw that the cameramen had been challenged in making a few sycamores, within an arid valley wholly lacking precipitation nine months of the year, into a tropical rainforest suited to the bare-chested ape-man, the bare-legged Jane, and the banana-wielding chimp called Cheeta. Finally seeing the artifice involved after all those years, I felt more satisfied about my own childhood digs, where I had struggled to imagine that a maple and cherry grove in Pennsylvania was really a jungle. In fact, my Tarzan setup was a far better facsimile for the Edgar Rice Burroughs fiction than the one Johnny had to put up with here, near Hollywood.

Though it's difficult to swing from one to the other, valley oaks, *Quercus lobata,* were more in line with my current interests. Scattered in grasslands, they grow larger than any other western oak, and the southern limit of their range lies near Malibu Creek. Once covering Edenic panoramas of California's central and coastal valleys, the girthy trees are now limited to isolated stands and lonely individuals. But where they can be found, the real-life forest is like a fantasy without any Twentieth Century Fox intervention, props, or cropping. Up to five feet in diameter, valley oaks speak of long-gone times, each canopy an umbrella to the sun. Root mass to treetop, they stand as great monuments to nature.

I went looking for the Mendenhall Oak, reported to be seven hundred years old, aged even when the Spanish arrived. A tree of that stature deserves a pilgrimage, and I thought of it as a shrine. So I was aggrieved to learn that the giant had burned and fallen down in 1982. Standing at the site of its decomposition, I longed even more to see a grove of the ancient oaks, to cool my brain in their shade, to rest my back against their great, living bulk. But I would have to wait.

Having scratched the surface of Malibu Creek State Park, I set off to see more of the Santa Monicas, simply looking for whatever was there. This hit-and-miss approach appealed to my hunting instincts, which go way back, not only to my rabbit-hunting days as a kid but perhaps to the genes of my earliest ancestors, who no doubt hunted for a living.

To find the essence of a place requires hunting, which involves an element of skill, an element of persistence, and a big element of chance. I'm rewarded in my search by what psychologists call intermittent reinforcement. I never know when I'll score, or where, so I unfailingly try again, and again, and again, like a pigeon in an old-time behavioral lab pecking at the switch that would someday release a bite to eat.

Up in the hills I stopped at the Malibu Country Club, which obviously had a relationship with these mountains, since they ran smack through the links, right past the clubhouse, and next to the greens. "Are the mountains important to you here?" I asked the local golf pro.

"No, I wouldn't say so. This just happened to be the place to have the golf course. The money is the thing. We get the best people here."

"Yeah, well, okay."

Next I came to the driveway of a structure that from the distance looked like an Olympic-scale hilltop gymnasium, all stainless steel and glass, something that might have appeared in *Goldfinger* had that cultic flick been filmed in the 1990s. Somebody had sited this building — more like science fiction than architecture — on a lightning-rod promontory of the mountains. So, I reasoned, wouldn't it be interesting to see what the owner *thinks* of the mountains?

Waiting at the heavily barred, electronically monitored gate complete with audio hookup, camera monitor, and unambiguous "No Trespassing" signs, a young woman leaned against her car.

What luck.

I stopped. While I was awkwardly mulling over what I'd say, she offered me an unexpected greeting.

"Are you the guy checking out the house for the film shoot?" This question, of course, would be asked only in the mountains around Los Angeles. And all I had to do was say yes. But what would my movie be about? Okay, there's this billionaire recluse who believes that global warming is going to cause flooding up to the five-hundred-foot elevation, pushing everybody in Los Angeles into the mountains, where only a tiny fraction of the population can actually survive. Next, she's going to want to know who my actors are. This was all beginning to seem doable — my own little Hollywood fantasy. But bullshitting is not my strong suit.

"No, I was just wondering what sort of building that is up there."

"It's a private residence." She nodded her head and looked at her shoes.

"Is the owner around?"

"No. No." No matter what I said next, she would probably think I was a nut, so I figured it was best to leave.

Next I came to a sign that said "Camp 13." This had potential. But what really caught my eye were women in blue-shirt uniforms grubbing out brush along the road. I braked sharply without a logical thought in my brain and turned in while the women swung their heads and looked up at my van, with its two canoes and kayak on top in that dry, riverless terrain.

In a parking area in front of a cluster of institutionally white buildings, twenty more women were doing a morning workout, the count-out-loud, jumping-jack style rather than the sexy steps of Jane Fonda. Some African American, most white, none Latina, these women all wore blue work shirts. Several green fire trucks with donut-shaped coils of hose were parked at the ready. Many of the women eyed me suspiciously as I walked to the office of this cooperative endeavor between the Los Angeles County Fire Department and the California Department of Corrections.

With little delay I found Tom Duda, a fire crew supervisor. On hearing of my interest, which of course included fire in these mountains, he set me up for a conversation with Becky Collins and pulled her out of the ranks of sweating women. The two of us sat down at a nearby picnic table.

"I'm a swamper," she said, beginning with no prompting or lack of personal identity. She didn't say I *do* swamping. She said I *am* a swamper.

"I run the back line. See, the foreman's up front with the saws — two saws, and two women each with Pulaskis and McClouds. Those are the hand tools you fight fire with. I'm making sure the line gets set right. I have the universal tool — the shovel. The foreman says, 'I want four feet of line to the sky.' That means clearing away all the vegetation to a width of four feet with no overhead brush. This line serves as a firebreak. Or at least it's supposed to. The idea is that you stop the fire by eliminating its fuel, even for a short distance. It's a challenge for us girls. It's men's work. We bust our asses. It's hard. We hiked in three miles to a fire once."

Sitting there in the shade, Becky had painted nails with no scratches on them and wore a fair amount of eye makeup. She had pulled her hair back tightly, giving her face a severe look that it otherwise might not have had, but keeping her hair out of fire's way. There was nothing frail about her. She was fit and tough and no-nonsense, I could tell all that right away. And her thirty-two years had put some age on her, as you might expect of someone who ends up in the state prison system. But now she smiled and leaned forward. "Let me tell you about my first fire."

"Sure, go ahead."

"They trucked us in and then we walked. When we got there we couldn't believe it. Flames thirty feet high. We were the only women. Men were falling out and we were replacing them."

"Falling out?"

"Yes. Exhausted, dehydrated, black-faced, weak-legged, spent."

"Okay, I get the picture."

"In all that smoke you couldn't see. We had to stick together. The winds were like blasts out of a furnace, erratic. We started working on a line off to the side of the fire. The foreman went out ahead to see where to run the line. But he didn't come back. And he didn't come back. In a minute he radioed us. He was in trouble, in the flames. He couldn't see. As the number two person on the crew, I jumped in, ran ahead. We all tried to keep in voice contact as we spread out our line. You see, from one voice to another we hoped to find our way back out.

Then I met him as he was struggling back down the path. He coughed a lot, bent over to the ground. We gave him a hand. We had to go back. There was no way anyone could hold a line."

"Not the kind of place you're anxious to return to."

"No. The foreman said, 'It's going to burn the whole way to the coast.' And you know what? It did. These are tremendous mountains, and they burn with tremendous fires. You gotta respect that. We put a line in front of fifteen or twenty houses and saved them. That's all anybody could do. You gotta know when to let it burn. It's definitely a lot bigger than *you* are." Becky paused.

I said, "Little boys grow up wanting to be firemen, but little girls don't, do they?"

"Of course not. Let me tell you, I never imagined I'd be doing this. None of us did. These girls come here and say, 'I can't do it, I can't do it.' But they can. We train hard, and in a fire nobody has to tell us what to do."

"So how do you train?"

"First we get in shape. I came here and said, 'Oh, my God, these people are trying to kill me.' But they said, 'Why are you psyching yourself out? Just get up there on that trail and climb that mountain.' In a month I saw that I could do it. And we learn about fire. Every day we learn something new. Then we do drills, cut line. Tom, up ahead of us, he falls out on us — he's playing dead. I call him up on the radio. He has a broken leg and the fire's coming in. We have to get him out before the flames reach him. See, that's how we train."

"And then I suppose the Santa Ana winds start moaning, and it's fire season."

"You know it. In the fall those hot, dry winds start to blow from the desert and pretty soon the alarm blows and we run. The women are jayed up. 'Yahoo, we got a fire!' We jump into the truck. We all go in there as a crew. You might have had a spat with a woman — you know how it is — but we go in there and work together. It's a thirteen-to-one crew: thirteen women and one helluva reputation. Over at the Cascade fire we put in seven, eight hours hot-lining with the air crew — the hotshot guys who get dropped in by helicopter. Their leader said: 'You know what? You women put in a better line than my boys do.'"

Becky paused. Now the fire was over in her mind.

I waited.

"I'll have been here two years before I leave. This is the biggest thing I've ever done in my life, more than what I ever wanted to do or thought I could do. You cry. You laugh. You hurt. It's tough. But there's nothing you can't conquer."

She looked down for a few seconds, and I thought a tear might come to her eye. But then she laughed and added, "There's nothing you can't beat. Except maybe the fire itself when it blows up in the chaparral with a thirty-mile-an-hour wind fanning the mountain." She paused again. She looked up at me and smiled slightly, and a bit of tear *was* in her eye.

"Do you mind, Becky, if I ask why you got put in prison?"

"Sells."

"Cells?"

"Yeah, sells. Selling drugs. I was stupid. I thought money was everything. I got twelve years. I'd already been busted but kept selling. I'll be out this summer. I'll have given four and a half years of my life."

"Has anything changed in that time?"

"Listen. *Everything* changed. I think this fire fighting is the best thing they have in prison. The thing is, these guys trust you. The foreman says, 'I need this, I need that.' So you do what's expected of you. People like Tom Duda are great. Those guys are like big brothers. They're there for you. And the guy's not a counselor or social worker or anything like that. He's a fireman. They've taught us so much."

Becky continued, "Look, let's say you come in here, you never had goals in your life. You learn what you need to know. You do your job, pay proper respect, and stay home. You get a résumé together. You send it out. Then one day an employer calls these guys up and they say, 'Yes, she can do that.' You see, I couldn't have asked for a better place to come. I had a choice of going to drug rehab or here, but I don't have a problem with drugs. I just sold them. Coming here has made all the difference."

"So what's next?"

"I have three boys. My mom's taking care of them back in Modesto. I see them every three months. I'll get back to my boys. I'm going to be okay now. Now I know I can get a job. I can run a computer. But what I'd like to do is work on a hotshot crew. A lot of women have stayed with this and got jobs on the hotshot crews in places like Redding."

"And what do you think of the mountains?"

"Well, without the mountains there wouldn't *be* any of this."

Becky's eyes went far away and then came back again. "You know what it's like when you went to camp as a kid? Well, it's neat up here. Every morning you get up and the air is fresh. It's always pretty here. You notice things you never notice on the streets—the different types of trees, and the way the wind's blowing, and the best way up the mountain. We climb that mountain, right there, a few times every week. If we can climb that mountain, then we're in good enough shape to do our job. If I can climb that mountain, I know I'm going to be okay."

FIRES IN THE mountains of the Coast Range offer career changes and virtual prison escapes for some people but pose frightening hazards for those who have built homes in harm's way. Major fires of a thousand acres or more strike every two and a half years on average in the Santa Monicas and other mountains surrounding Los Angeles. In 1980, for example, fires in the San Bernardino Mountains destroyed three hundred homes, caused $42 million in property damage, and charred eighty-four thousand acres. Santa Ana winds—a result of autumn low-pressure zones over the coast and high-pressure domes over Nevada—blow with nearly zero humidity and speeds of twenty to ninety miles per hour over the mountains of southern California. Those winds fan blazes that leap ahead in hundred-foot jets of flame. The whole effect can cause a fire to rage completely out of control until the weather changes or the fire tries to burn seawater.

Wildfires in the chaparral of southern California's coastal mountains burn faster and more intensely than any other wildfires in America. With torch-like volatility, these blazes bear little resemblance to forest fires I've helped fight in Idaho and Oregon or even to notorious burns such as the Yellowstone fires in 1989. East of Los Angeles, sixteen miles of the mountain front once burned to the ridgeline in a single day. In 1993, 250,000 acres burned in southern California. Firebreaks — swaths cleared of all brush and burnable material — can be cleared a quarter of a mile wide, but the big infernos can throw embers like Roman candles for a mile and a half, leapfrogging ahead of any containment efforts. Two hundred fire engines might be called out at a time, and about all they can do is park near houses and spray water on roofs, letting the flames burn around them, as if the houses were rocks sticking up in the middle of a whitewater rapid of flames. Even these limited efforts are made at great risk; these wildfires are nothing like the usual house fire in town. Any sense of predictability is lost when the chaparral becomes so hot that aerial ignition occurs: radiant heat explodes out ahead of the fire line, a firefighter's worst nightmare.

Chaparral, the dominant brushy form of plant life on these and many of the coastal mountains and covering about 12 percent of California, is quite literally made to burn. It's what ecologists call a disturbance ecosystem: to be healthy, it needs to be disturbed. Left unburned, the thick tangles of vegetation — chamise, ceanothus, toyon, manzanita, yerba santa, poison oak, and others — become old and woody, clogged with dry branches and leaves, which don't rot in the dry climate. Up to twenty-five thousand tons accumulate per square mile, enough to make quite a conflagration. The chaparral needs fire to break dead material down into ash and nutrients that can be reabsorbed by the soil to nourish new life.

If that's not enough evidence that these plants were born to be eaten by flames, consider this: to retain water during the dry months, the leaves of many chaparral shrubs are covered with waxy materials. These chemicals double as pyrophoric resins, which make the leaves exceptionally quick to ignite and hot when burning, like the wax on the cover of a cardboard milk carton.

Many of the shrubs are capable of resprouting from still-living root masses, so new growth can begin at once after a fire. Equipped with two-tiered root systems, these hardy plants put out shallow tendrils to catch winter rain as soon as it falls and deep roots to probe for underlying water during summer drought.

New shoots green up following the first showers of winter, and wildflowers pop up with rainbow sprays of color as soon as spring arrives. Known as ephemerals or fire followers, these sprout from seeds that may have been lying in the soil for fifty or even a hundred years, patiently waiting for the fire to come. Deer and smaller wildlife thrive on the succulent, vigorous new growth. After one fire, the deer numbers increased threefold.

The plants compete for space, water, and light, maturing in twenty-five years as a thick mass of shrubbery that sends the hardiest hikers scrambling for evasive routes. As the stand ages further, dead leaves, twigs, stems, and trunks accumulate, eventually forming a large portion of the plant mass, until the chaparral tinderbox burns again. Under natural conditions, this happened about once every thirty years.

But in the urbanizing world, fire suppression has increased the amount of mature chaparral. And the ever accumulating dead material only promises to burn hotter when the flame inevitably finds the fuel. Fifty-year-old chaparral burns with fifty times the intensity of twenty-year-old growth.

By burning mature chaparral in controlled situations between November and March, land managers can restore the natural condition of this flora somewhat, and with restoration comes protection from the intensely hot fires that plague mountain neighborhoods. The Forest Service and California Department of Parks and Recreation intentionally burn when they can, but the backlog of overmature chaparral covers large spreads of map, and liability in areas where houses have encroached has become a sticky issue. Once in a while a controlled burn somewhere in the West unfortunately blows out of control and ignites houses, prompting landowners to blame the government and sue. As a result, the legal system has pushed land managers to allow enormous conflagrations to occur as "acts of God" rather than stage controlled burns that in some unusual circumstance might accidentally destroy a house that was built in an area prone to wildfire.

And the liability issue gets even worse. In Topanga Canyon, a homeowner sued the county fire department, claiming that a controlled burn would make it impossible for him to sell his house, not because it would be burned but simply because the chaparral around it would be blackened when his real estate happened to go on the market.

As a result of these lawsuits, hotter, costlier, riskier fires are now inevitable across the populated mountainsides, and when they do burn, firefighters such as Becky Collins and Tom Duda labor at far greater personal risk. Picture this: the 1996 Corral Canyon fire in the Santa Monica Mountains leapt a thousand feet in seven seconds—a hundred miles per hour! It caught a squad of firefighters engaged in defending canyonside houses. One dedicated fireman was severely burned while hosing water on flames so that his fellow workers could escape.

Beyond the unnatural accumulation of dead fuel in unburned chaparral, firefighters in suburbanizing mountains face troublesome hazards because they are now hamstrung in techniques such as back-burning. In this classic strategy, firefighters deliberately ignite a border of brush at the periphery of the ongoing burn. They do this at night, when it's cooler and the flames are controllable. In the absence of strong daytime winds, the main wildfire sucks the back-burn into its center because the heat of the main fire rises and creates in-draft. It's an ingenious, time-tested defense, critical in the strategic arsenal of every fire boss. But owing to heightened liability concerns, if a deliberately set backfire happens to singe even one house, the firefighters are often forbidden to back-burn.

The fires cause infernos of damage, but commanding just as much respect, they prime the mountainsides for Part II of the southern California disaster revue: the mudslides and debris avalanches we saw in the last chapter.

It's easy to understand that the litter, roots, and duff of organic matter normally weaving together loose particles of soil disappear after a fire. When water hits this unlaced dirt, far more washes off than when the ground is covered with vegetation. This alone is bad enough, but the phenomenon of post-fire erosion in chaparral is far more extreme than just that.

The same resins and waxes that hold valuable moisture inside the leaves of chaparral shrubs and that volatilize like waxy milk cartons have yet another characteristic of great consequence. In the years of organic accumulation — when unburned leaves pile up in the soil underneath the plants — the resins accumulate as well. Eventually the fires burn them, vaporizing the waxy aliphatic hydrocarbons into gas. Much of this vapor rises in the pungent smoke of chaparral fires. But — and here's the important part — the vapor wafts downward as well, penetrating directly into the soil. Though the temperature on the soil surface might be eighteen hundred degrees, the fine soil of the region is such a good insulator that it remains cool just a few inches underground. There, when the chaparral's resinous vapor hits the cooler soil, it recondenses. The same chemicals that once waxed the chaparral's leaves, and thereby kept the water inside, now coat the underlying soil with a similar effect: the dirt there is water-proofed and becomes hydrophobic, or unwettable. It's something like cocoa, which in large globs initially repels water, especially cold water.

When winter rains come, they cannot soak in beyond this layer of waterproofed soil, so the entire upper layer of burned dirt quickly becomes saturated, like slurry, and sloughs off en masse, producing southern California's notorious flash floods, mudslides, and debris avalanches. The mountains, the chaparral, the fire, the soil, the rain-storms, and the mudslides all connect inextricably in the ecology of this tumultuous place.

Like the mudslides and debris avalanches they trigger, wildfires are avoidable. In the same way we know that slides are likely on steep slopes, and debris avalanches are likely at canyon mouths, we know that wildfires will rip across these mountains again and again. As one Los Angeles County fireman told me, "We can tell pretty much where a fire is going to go. You look at burns in the thirties, forties, six-ties, nineties — they're often in the same patterns. Each time, the Santa Ana winds blow over the top and down the canyons in shapes that sway back and forth; you can see the lines in the vegetation." Historical maps of the fire routes bear this out.

A big game of Russian roulette, fires have burned the entire moun-tain front in the Malibu region three times since 1900. At least once every ten years a firestorm of awesome intensity rages somewhere in southern California's mountains, destroying hundreds of homes. Yet there are no restrictions that ban house construction in frequent fire paths. Anybody who wants to take the risk can do it.

The fire department points out that houses at the head of a canyon — where it tops out at the ridgeline — sit in an exceptionally dangerous position, graphically called a chimney. The fires climb the canyons and hit the ridges with inferno force. Locations within canyons are likewise prone to extreme and unavoidable damage.

In chimneys, in canyons, on ridgelines, and on steep slopes I saw many ruins from the devastating fires of 1993 and 1996. Pads of concrete lay like abandoned basketball courts, with shards of walls and unburned rubble crumbling in the sun, everything else bonfired to vapors or black crisp. Swimming pools collected mosquito-breeding water. Windblown trash had settled in burned-over lots — eyesores in millionaire neighborhoods.

This is not like poor people occupying floodplains because they can't afford to live anywhere else. In the fire and mudslide zones, coveted for their ocean views, it's expensive homes that are being carpentered up by crews specializing in preferred real estate.

ANN'S AUNT, Birute Vileisis, owns a beautiful, elegantly modest home two thousand feet above sea level on a Santa Monica mountainside. I asked her about living there when I returned to pick up Ann.

"I had looked at properties in Topanga Canyon but didn't like it down there," Birute told me. "It was dark, with a lot of tires on the roofs and old cars abandoned in front yards. But up here, near the top of the hill, you can see the ocean. We're above the fog belt. I thought, 'Gosh, I could *live* here!' The view overwhelmed me. I was working down in Santa Monica, and I wanted to move to the country."

"You must have been lucky to find a house like this for sale," I said.

"It was on the market for over a year because of the landslides, which had closed the main road to the PCH. You could still drive another, longer way, but I got a bargain." Birute pointed to the house in front of her, its roofline at eye level. "*That* house wasn't there yet, and the ocean view was even better."

"More people everywhere," I acknowledged.

"I'm from the East," Birute continued, "and so had no idea of the winds, the fires, the mud. I was drawn to this place for the view, the pure air, and the chance to live in the country. I wanted enough land to garden. Everybody warned me about mudslides, but I know I'm on bedrock—a geologist's report was required for the sale."

Where we sat, on a brick patio surrounded by a colorful garden of native flowers and shrubs, the ocean breeze whispered like a zephyr and the sun softened us through the moisture of mild Pacific air. It was heavenly. I could understand that being there was worth some personal risks.

"I wanted to do the landscaping correctly," Birute said, "so I started by taking a course at UCLA. I wanted to be in tune with what was around me. I tore out the lawn and put in a garden of these beautiful drought-resistant plants. In one truly joyous moment, I turned around and there was a huge bobcat, with spots on its legs, tufts on its ears. We stared at each other for ten minutes. Owls sit on my roof and hoot."

Encountering the unexpected exigencies of country life, Birute has discovered the occasional rattlesnake in her garden. "The first time, I called a neighbor and he came and chopped the snake to pieces. I felt awful. This mountain had been the snake's home. After that I called another man and he came and caught the snake and relocated it to another canyon. Now I catch them myself. It took some adjusting, driving these roads with a rattlesnake in the trunk, but it's not really any problem."

"Good for you," I said. "It must be wonderful living here, but isn't the commute awful?"

"It takes forty-five minutes, but when I come home, my spirit's restored. A lot of people don't want to live in the hills behind Malibu, with the fires and other problems, and I can see why. But for me, it's worth it."

As we sat, I gazed around at the green of chaparral, tall and thick uphill from the house, freshly burned and regreened on the hillside below. "It looks like you had a fire right here."

"Oh, yes. The fire came right to *there*." She pointed to the edge of her patio. "It was a momentous year, 1993."

"You seem to have managed okay."

"Yes, but I didn't know it while the fire was raging. That morning the Santa Ana winds arrived at full force. As usual, I drove down to work. Then the fire began. At one o'clock a neighbor called me at the office and said that the flames had topped the ridge to the east. The smoke made a black mushroom cloud, and the blaze was curving down like a tornado right toward my house. I jumped into my car and flew up the PCH. From the bottom of the hill I could see flames as high as could be. A fireman stopped me, and when I asked about getting to my house he said, 'Lady, do you want to get *killed?*' All I knew then was that the fire was burning the whole way from Calabasas and over the top of the Santa Monicas and down the canyon in front of my house."

"It must have been difficult to just stand and watch."

"A lot of us were watching. By four o'clock the fire was at the ocean. I cried out my emotion. My house! My cats! Everything I had! Up in smoke! Grit and cinders blew and everybody's face turned black, and then I looked up at the sun, an apocalyptic orange cherry in the midst of black clouds. Flames still shot up like skyscrapers in the canyon. Helicopters hovered all around, and loudspeakers kept announcing that people should leave. Then I drove to one of the bends in Las Flores Canyon. From there I saw the roof of my neighbor's new house, just below mine. It was still there."

Lucky Birute. The fire outran two residents who were racing the flames in their Jeep. They burned to death. Fanned by seventy-mile-per-hour winds, the blaze drew thousands of firefighters from as far away as Oklahoma. Seventy pumper trucks were stationed at one upper-end neighborhood. Queueing up on roads leading to the area, fire engines, water trucks, and bulldozers ran eleven miles bumper to bumper. Even so, two hundred fifty homes burned.

"Two days later they let me return," Birute continued. "My front door had been knocked in. I later found out that firefighters forced their way in to breathe — to get air. An eerie moonscape lay all around, and soot covered everything in the house. Three fire trucks had pulled into the driveway that serves these five houses, and they kept spraying water. Other houses along the main road burned because the fire trucks couldn't park there without blocking traffic on the road —it had to be kept open for emergency vehicles and for people still escaping from their homes. But they could park on our cul-de-sac, and that's what saved us.

"Houses around mine had been destroyed, but I resolved to stay. The grass grew back after the first rain, and I appreciated the rebirth out of ashes. Having been close to nature in its most terrible moment, I appreciated it more. But then came more mudslides along the PCH. Three months later the Northridge earthquake hit, at four thirty-one A.M. I thought a train was coming through the house. I couldn't believe the sound. Everything shook. Out toward the ocean I saw green explosions all over the place. They were transformers blowing up. When I came here I knew there were hazards, but this was ungodly! Even so, my house withstood a fire and an earthquake. I took it all as a good sign."

NOT SO GOOD are the signs of more and more development in the Santa Monicas. New construction by millionaires and billionaires has become epidemic. From an airplane, the growing network of roads, snaking around the ridges and canyons and slicing traverses across the mountainsides, looks like a diagram of how to butcher a cow.

People want to move up to higher slopes, believing that the fires and slides won't come again, won't hit *them*. And the houses are getting bigger all the time. Given the many options for disposing of discretionary wealth in both self-serving and philanthropic ways, it's curious that so many people choose to build larger houses, escalating from what might be a perfectly adequate two thousand square feet for two people to three thousand, four thousand, and on up to the utterly ridiculous—ten, fifteen, twenty thousand.

Before leaving, Ann and I hiked to the top of nearby Calabasas Peak. From there, the skyscrapers of downtown Los Angeles showed through a thickening smog to the east. Dozens of homes lay scattered on hillsides above Santa Monica, and uncounted others clung to mountainsides or to scraped-off spots on the ridges. Some sat on slopes so steep that the front door entered at ground level but the back deck soared on I beams forty feet off the ground. Driveways veered up at angles demanding a low gear ratio on slopes you would never see developed in places where it snows. I could make a very good living around here doing nothing but building retaining walls; they shore up crumbling hillsides everyplace where people have sought to accommodate their need for flatness with the reality of the Santa Monica Mountains.

While all this development was going on, few costs of government escaped the budget-cutter's ax in the era following the tax freezes of the 1980s and the federal devolution of the 1990s. But the endless expense of fire fighting for all these hillside homes goes scarcely noticed and rarely questioned. It took $100 million to mobilize fifteen thousand firefighters in 1993, and no one seemed to deliberate over who should pay or how much should be spent. No one seems to question that we've dug ourselves into a trap of doing this again and again, with no end of ever greater disasters in sight.

Worsening a bad situation, government disaster relief provides tax breaks, low-interest loans, and outright grants for rebuilding in the same hazard zones. So in these high-risk, high-end neighborhoods, all those tax dollars go to rebuilding multi-million-dollar homes. Analysis has shown that each fire is followed by reconstruction of larger and more expensive homes. Rather than regulations being tightened to reduce future disasters, rules have at times been relaxed to accommodate fire victims. Instead of learning from these repeat performances and launching efforts to prevent disasters through thoughtful land-use policies, the director of the Federal Emergency Management Agency in 1993 promised southern Californians "all the aid they need to rebuild homes and lives" after the fires.

In 1930, forward-looking landscape architect and planner Frederick Law Olmsted Jr. recommended hazard zoning as the best way for Los Angeles County to curb the costs of mudslides, floods, wildfires, and earthquakes. He envisioned attractive and functional greenbelts at the most damage-prone lands in the Santa Monicas. He proposed that ten thousand acres between Topanga Canyon and Point Dune — the section of the Malibu coast that burns repeatedly — be acquired as public open space. Olmsted's plan was truly visionary. If it had been adopted, there would be few worries when fires visit the mountains each fall. People could just sit back and watch nature be nature. But too much money was being made by selling lots, which now go for a few hundred thousand dollars at rock bottom and up into the millions when amenities such as a sliver of ocean view are added.

It's not that there hasn't been any interest in limiting or directing some of the growth. Malibu originally incorporated as a city in order to kill a plan to build a major sewage treatment plant there, a scheme that would have allowed the population to grow to 405,000 in an area severely constrained by environmental limits—ocean, fire, mudslide, flood, earthquake. Instead, voters elected slow-growth candidates by a wide margin. But out across the mountains, zoning is administered by the ever boosterish county, and according to local ecologist Paul Edelman, "almost all the development proposals get approved after some haggling. With each lot, the roads get pushed out farther, the chaparral cleared away a little more." Fire hazards mount and the dream homes become charcoal briquettes to the blazes of newspaper headlines.

While land-use regulation does little to keep hazard zones unhazardous, neither do the risks themselves repel prospective owners. Malibu real estate agent Steve Duboff told me: "Even with the big fires that destroy dozens of houses, we don't see a blip in the market. People forget very quickly. Most rebuild. They're here for the lifestyle, the privacy, the clean air, the good weather. The chance of another fire? Sure, it could happen, but they'll take that chance."

The final result here in the Santa Monica Mountains is what fire historian Stephen J. Pyne called a "lethal mixture of homeowners and brush."

Without effective zoning to control construction on hazardous land, public acquisition is the only helpful option. The impressive open spaces, parklands, and trails I enjoyed in the Santa Monicas owe their existence to a heroic history—however incomplete—of land preservation. At Topanga State Park, for example, nine thousand acres have been called the country's largest wildland within the boundaries of a city.

To protect what remained became a cause of southern California conservationists who saw this as one of few places within America's second-largest metropolis where a sizable sample of nature could be saved. In 1963 landowners banded together as the Friends of the Santa Monica Mountains to fight freeway and sewer extensions that would have opened up the hills even more than the scribbled network of existing roads already had. Pushing for federal protection as the only option to get a grip on development, the group persuaded the U.S. Department of the Interior to study the Santa Monicas for their park potential. Then, in 1974, California senator John Tunney recommended a national urban park with funds to buy 100,000 of the 191,500 mountain acres not yet committed to development at that time. In this once-only opportunity, land could have been bought for $2,000 an acre. The $200 million price tag was only twice the taxpayers' cost of the 1993 fire alone. In one of those regrettable moments in America's environmental history, the bill died, a victim of real estate interests.

Arising out of those ashes, and piggybacking onto a federal initiative to establish parks where the people are, the United States Congress passed legislation to create the Santa Monica Mountains National Recreation Area in 1978, the prototype for a new concept called green line parks. Rather than have the federal government buy up solid blocks of land, the strategy was to mix softer approaches: to encourage local governments to zone, to acquire easements that leave land in private ownership but prevent development, and to buy critical tracts opportunistically. But federal money for land purchase was not forthcoming until the state and local governments adopted ordinances to complement conservation plans. So while the planners planned and awaited local government approval, the developers developed and delayed the approvals. With each passing day and year, real estate prices skyrocketed, limiting what public agencies could ultimately buy.

What has happened in the Santa Monicas is a classic case of fragmentation. Where large parcels could have been bought inexpensively before the building boom, the mountains have now been subdivided into hundreds of homesites and additional thousands of split-off parcels not yet built upon. The first superintendent of the

national recreation area aimed to put 70,000 acres in federal ownership for public use. Facing opposition from developers and from
private-rights zealots who condemned the federal government for
everything and anything, and also facing soaring real estate inflation
and a tightening federal budget, the national recreation area had
picked up only 22,000 acres as of the late 1990s. Fortunately, the nonprofit Santa Monica Mountains Conservancy had also continued to
buy land and acquire easements from owners who agree not to
develop. An unusual piece of the nation's open-space estate, the
national recreation area remains a scattering of parcels within a
boundary that encircles 100,000 of the Santa Monica Mountains'
total 250,000 acres.

The shortage of funding for public open space, recreation areas,
and wildlife habitat stands in stark contrast to the money spent in the
private sector to develop these mountains into hundreds of multi-
million-dollar estates, to the hundreds of millions of taxpayer dollars
spent fighting fires to prevent the new houses from burning down,
and to the disaster relief provided to those whose homes get burned
or crushed by mudslides. In pushing to increase funding for open
space nationwide, the Sierra Club in 1999 identified the Santa Monicas as a national priority, arguing for a $59 million appropriation.

With effective regulation of new building unlikely, the fate of these
mountains rests with the Santa Monica Mountains Conservancy and
the National Park Service in their efforts to buy what's left of the
undeveloped land.

FROM THE 3,111-foot top of the highest Santa Monica peak, called
Sandstone, the view could have been to the Coast Range wilds
before the boom, before the smog, before the PCH. Ann and I had
sweated while climbing to the summit, and from there, in a chill
breeze, Los Angeles seemed far, far away. I would never have guessed
that in the Santa Clara Valley—the next river basin to the north—a
twenty-one-thousand-unit development promised another San
Fernando Valley in the making. From Sandstone, just mountains and
mountains folded down out of sight.

They all rekindled my drive to go deeper into the canyons, to go higher up the peaks, to lose myself out there in country that was wilder than where I had lately been spending my time. Yes, well, soon I would be able to do that, and as my California friends sometimes say, you should be careful about what you wish for.

In a canyon below, I found one of California's finer groves of sycamores. From fat and barrelish trunks, leggy limbs kicked far out into space, the bark white and mottled in olive and tan, the leaves rustling in the Pacific air. Some of the branches were so big I walked out on them—gangplanks ten feet off the ground.

From that valley in Point Mugu State Park I hiked to another high summit on a trail that runs the length of the Santa Monicas. From there I could see northwest to the cities of Oxnard and Ventura and on to the Coast Range's distant northward repetition of peaks and peninsulas. Santa Cruz Island rose out of the Pacific like an apparition, misty air skirting its base at sea level and giving the impression that most of the mountain lay underwater.

I looked west to that island, now protected in northern Channel Islands National Park; north to the Santa Clara Valley; and east toward the built-up flats of Thousand Oaks and the San Fernando Valley. With all that around me, the Santa Monica Mountains themselves were clearly an island amid a world of urban change, separated and isolated, but not separated and isolated enough.

In the Santa Monicas I had found something animated and joyous about mountains, with people appreciating the nature of the place. I also found something sad and melancholy about it all. What was it? The loss of wildness? The nearness of LA's smog? The opulent wealth displayed carelessly on site after fire-prone site? Without the fear of fire, without the innocence of isolation, without the stability of ecological balance—without all this, what future exists for this special place on earth?

With ocean waves on one side and urban sprawl on the other, I could see how small this range is—an outpost, a remnant, a struggling survivor—but it is still a place with possibilities for nature as fate unfolds. Where will the next fire blaze through, the next earthquake strike? Will the relentless push for development break the backbone of this fragile, fragmented mountain world? Will the efforts of the Santa Monica Mountains Conservancy save what's left before it's too late?

Hopeful about those efforts but not entirely successful in fighting off a troubling sense of despair, I gave up for now and lay down on a granite boulder at the top of the ridge, the surf swooshing in distant foam, birds whistling back and forth above me. The pull of gravity seemed to draw me into the rock. I felt weighted, barely floating, as if I were just keeping my head above the waterline, like the tops of the Channel Islands out in the Pacific.

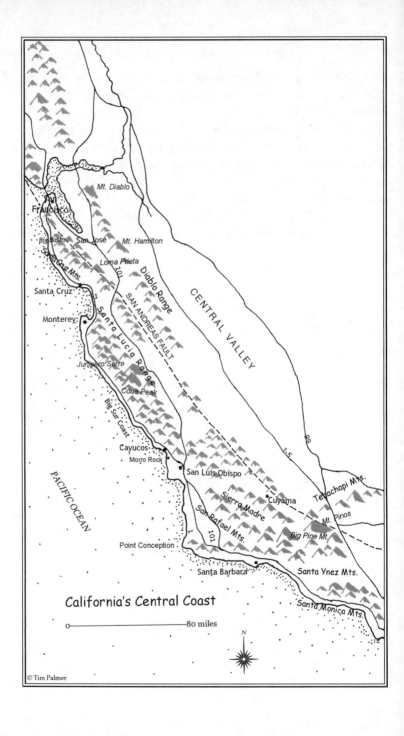

California's Central Coast

0 ——————— 80 miles

© Tim Palmer

# 6 | *A Dream of Condors*

T HE SNOW in our path lay two, three, and four feet deep. Dressed for the coastal mountains of central California in balmy March, I wore only shorts and a tee shirt. We had paid more attention to the hazards of sunburn than of frostbite. But now I began to wonder. The bottoms of my feet felt numb. The sun had already set, deep in the trees to the west. And still the tires of our heavily loaded mountain bikes sank into the rutted, snowy path as we tugged on them with brute force, the bikes acting as if they had no wheels at all. One step at a time, we approached the high mountain pass, which seemed to recede with each step we took. Yet we *had* to get through. We had to make it over to the other side before dark.

Puffing for air, I turned to watch Greg pull his bicycle through the six-inch-deep rut I had broken, his wiry body angled forward. With one hand gripping the handlebars and one affixed to the seat, he muscled his bike along, though it fought him in every way, sinking and skidding, the wheels clogging with slush, the pedals rasping at his shins if he stepped too close. Not only that, his bike was coupled to a one-wheeled trailer tightly packed with gear. The trailer hung low, and its tire sometimes failed to hold it up out of the snow, leaving its whole width to resist forward motion.

"If we did this very often," I yelled back to Greg and Mary, "we could develop a bad attitude about snow." I said this in jest; in most circumstances, I love snow.

Greg has an insatiable, deep, thorough curiosity about the world and an easygoing sense for good conversation, but when times get tough, he doesn't say much. He was just doing what he needed to do, hauling his gear, some of Mary's, and some of mine.

Behind him, Mary struggled as well, pulling her bike along in the same track. She had packed her equipment into panniers — saddlebags straddling the rear tire. This husband-and-wife team now joined me on a diminutive island of melted-out pine needles. Looking at the brighter side is a family trait for Mary, which I know because I'm her cousin, and I've seen it in both my mother and her father, not to mention myself. "Oh, well," she said in great family style, "at least the storm isn't going to hit us."

Through the tiniest of gaps between tall sugar pines we could see the soft light of an evening sky, the sun capped by clouds but no longer threatened by them. I had forgotten all about the weather report, but Mary was right to be thankful. Rain would have forced us to turn around and thwarted the entire trip, not because this unexpected snow could get any worse — it couldn't — but because the roads and trails below snow line would become quagmires of clay and mud, our bikes nothing but greased pigs in one of those county-fair free-for-alls. If there could be any sense of relief at the height of this crisis, Mary had put her finger on it. None of us wanted to deal with mud after we were done with the snow. And whatever the hazards confronting us, we definitely did not want to turn back after peddling hard for two days already.

As a subrange of the coastal mountains in central California, the Sierra Madre rise monumentally out of the drylands of the interior and align themselves along the greater range's northwest–southeast axis. To their immediate west, the San Rafael Mountains run parallel, and the two ranges merge at their southern ends. There, at the high point of connection, Big Pine Mountain loomed as the crux of our trip, the lofty target of winter storms that shower rain on most of the coastal mountains. But here they dump snow, a lot of it. By March, this had consolidated into the crusty mush that so confounded us. Even though the heavy accumulation had been melting in the warm afternoons for weeks, it refroze every night and endured far beyond its season.

In a complicated geologic junction box south of Big Pine, the Sierra Madre and San Rafael both mold into the flanks of the Santa Ynez Mountains, which are the westernmost of the Transverse Ranges — the expansive east–west block of topography north of Los Angeles. Directly over the Santa Ynez lies the ocean at Santa Barbara.

This accumulation of three subranges lends a fat and formidable bulge to the coastal mountains here, which is exactly what had attracted me. Mary, Greg, and I planned to complete a crossing from the central California drylands to the ocean, a hundred-mile route we called "Cuyama-to-the-sea."

The maze of ridge after sparsely watered ridge continued with resounding wildness, considering that the roar of multiple freeways in America's most infamous megalopolis was only a few hours' drive away. At the core of our trip, a sixty- by twenty-mile block of wildland was occasionally scratched by a foot trail or rutted double track, but that was about it.

Springtime snow notwithstanding, the best way to explore this formidable washboard of seismic uplift is with the knobby-treaded, low-geared mountain bike, and Ann and I had talked about doing the crossing together. If it had been a river trip, there was no way she would not have gone. But Ann can resist the spine-rattling mountain bike. More to the point, a week was required for the four-day journey, counting preparation and recovery, and Ann could not take that much time off, given the approaching deadline for her book. So, lacking my soulmate and usual traveling partner, I broached the idea with Mary and Greg Bettencourt, who find biking as irresistible as Ann finds whitewater boating. They jumped at the excuse to get away, and they proved to be the perfect traveling companions, considerate, knowledgeable, supremely capable.

In March, travel here is risky because the winter rains can still drench you with smothering force, and the weather prediction had kept us all guessing. The forecast called for a light storm. But we could make the trip only on that one weekend, so we hoped for the best, knowing we might be thwarted midway.

Just east of where we began, across the weed-infested, overgrazed Cuyama valley and then across the low rise of the bone-dry Caliente Range, the San Andreas Fault slices through the Carrizo Plain with some of the most visible and traumatized fault lines anywhere, the epicenter of continental drift. Additional related fault lines fenced our route to the west. The aftermath of all the combined slipping, sliding, and folding lay everywhere evident in upthrust rocks, ruler-straight stream courses suddenly shunted into right-angle turns, and berms of soil where the earth had slumped like an unappetizing glob of oatmeal. In short, a scrambled-egg amalgam of rock, dirt, and grit loosely configuring the steep slopes riddled our route to the sea.

Except for a compact tool kit, my load of gear, crammed into rear-tire panniers and strapped on top of them, did not exceed what I would take if I were backpacking, though it seemed as if it did. With the weight riding high and rear-heavy, my bike bounced left or right at the slightest provocation. Within minutes of my starting the trip, a minefield of rocks in the erosion-clawed two-track ascending Aliso Canyon challenged me at every crank of the pedals.

No matter how hard I tried to avoid the most irksome rocks by keeping a watchful eye on them, I hit too many. My progress would be nip-and-tuck, but then in a split second I would crunch into a kingpin cobble and skid to an abrupt halt, sometimes forcing myself to make a painful dismount. As I struggled along on that hot afternoon, drenched in sweat but gamely believing I could survive by iron will, Mary said in her calming way, "Let me tell you, I was intimidated when I started out mountain biking. I never had any talent for playing stick-and-ball sports with my brothers. But this is different. Here, you balance and move your weight around, choose which way to go, miss the big obstacles, and roll over the little ones. I'll only ever bother you with one tip. Are you ready?"

"Yes. Anything."

"Here it is: Never look at what you want to avoid. *Always* look where you want to go. Remember, where you *look* is where you *go.*"

Pondering the broader implications of this truth that might well be universal, I ratcheted my way up the mountain and hit fewer rocks.

Once the grueling remnants of the jeep road ended, the hard part began. A narrow path switchbacked up the eastern front of the Sierra Madre in hairpin turns I couldn't begin to ride. In between the impossible bends, the trail angled up slopes of pulverized shale like stomped-on graham crackers while dagger-pointed yuccas bristled from both sides and threatened to puncture my tires if they so much as touched the thin rubber sidewalls. A master biker, Greg somehow kept going, even towing the "Bob," as the little trailer is called. Mary and I walked our heavy bikes a couple of miles to a dirt road on the ridgetop, where we found Greg sitting on the ground, welcoming us as he bit into a Clif Bar and reflected with satisfaction on all that surrounded him.

Here, west of the San Andreas Fault, the ranges buckled up like a carpet might do in the middle if you pushed on one end. In a geologically uncertain world, earthquakes had sliced and torn and made the land into what it temporarily was, and then even small amounts of water had gone to work, digging in the dirt and breaking it all down by sculpting the canyons and valleys the three of us were now determined to cross.

From that main backbone of the Sierra Madre I spotted a glimmer of snow in the Sierra Nevada, a hundred twenty miles east. To the west, the ocean lay beyond the Casmalia Hills, south of San Luis Obispo. To the southeast, Mount Pinos rose to a blunt 8,831 feet, the tallest mountain in the Tehachapi Mountains — one of the five Transverse Ranges. Below us, scattered with ranches, the Cuyama valley looked like a miniature Central Valley of California and resembled what that industrial breadbasket might have been at the turn of the twentieth century, before the pumps and pipes, the farms and freeways, the cities and endless suburbs now bursting with California's population explosion. A few fields of irrigated alfalfa and geometrically dotted pistachio and apple orchards greened the keel of the Cuyama valley, otherwise a desolate lowland baking in the rain shadow of these peaks, which rake off the ocean's water and leave little for the warming, descending air on the eastern side.

Just downslope in the other direction — to the west — lay the San Rafael Wilderness, which in 1968 was the first area set aside for protection in the National Wilderness Preservation System. This designation, affecting only federal land, bans logging, roads, motor vehicles, and mountain bikes. In the canyon separating the northwest–southeast massifs of the Sierra Madre and San Rafael, the wild Sisquoc River cuts northwestward. This and Sespe Creek, to the south, are southern California's only rivers designated as Wild and Scenic — federal status that bans new dams once proposed by real estate and agricultural developers.

Befitting those efforts to rescue nature, three condors soared into view on the thermals out beyond the ridgeline. I rushed for my binoculars, which were tucked away in a pocket of the panniers. Larger than vultures, with wings that held a straight and stiff look, the condors looked like remote-controlled toy airplanes over the bulky mass of the Sierra Madre. *Large* toy airplanes. The great blue heron, for comparison, boasts a wingspan of seventy inches. The bald eagle has a wingspan of eighty inches, the trumpeter swan an eye-arresting ninety-five. But the condor's wingspan can top one hundred twenty inches. *Ten feet!* Not so large, the adolescents in front of us had recently been released from captivity.

Once common along our route the whole way from Baja to British Columbia, this largest North American bird had dwindled in number to an extinction-bound fifteen in 1984, owing to loss of wild habitat, electrocution on power lines, and pointless shooting by vandals. Condors were also poisoned by the lead in buckshot and bullets used by hunters who killed game but didn't take it home to eat (federal regulations finally phased out lead shot in 1991). Perhaps most ravaging, ranchers applied poisons, including a nerve toxin, Compound 1080, throughout the condor's range to exterminate ground squirrels, which were thought to be chewing up forage that cows might otherwise eat. A hundred fifty thousand pounds of poisoned grain were once air-dropped on 653,000 acres of ranchland, a Rhode Island–sized blanket of death that staggers my mental grasp of how twisted our relationship to land can become. Wreaking havoc everywhere, the fatal toxin polluted water supplies and worked its way up the food chain when predators or scavengers such as the condors ate the poisoned rodents and, in turn, convulsed and died.

After six of the remaining birds disappeared in the winter of 1985, the U.S. Fish and Wildlife Service captured the rest of the condors and bred them in captivity. Not a single one remained in the wild. By 1992 the captive population had increased enough that some adolescents could be released. But now a whole generation of these homely creatures hatched in zoos had never even *seen* the wild, never lived under its demanding rules. Not surprisingly, the young condors showed little fear of people. They swooped into buildings; eight of the black-feathered beasts surprised one man in Pine Mountain by strutting into his bedroom. They approached hikers, and while having a finch eat out of your hand, as the little birds did for Saint Francis of Assisi, is one thing, having a bald-headed, carrion-reeking bird with a wingspan wider than a dump truck step up to their roost was unnerving to people. Biologists moved the recovery sites farther into the wilderness and, by frightening the young condors, tried to condition them to avoid humans. By the year 2000 twenty-nine of the endangered birds had been set free in the mountains of southern California, and their trainers hoped a new population would take hold in the wild.

I remembered Jack Lynch saying that someday the condors might be back. Now, as I stood in the brisk wind watching the soaring survivors in their return to the mountains of home, the place seemed to ring with a new wildness, a new life, that I'm sure would have pleased Jack. The old California dream of easy living beneath the palms, of beach bumming, of making it big in Hollywood, of slick convertibles —that dream now seemed so obsolete. My California dream, there on a Sierra Madre ridgetop, was a dream of condors.

At that moment, the pleasure of traveling in the mountains struck me so vividly: springtime freshness in the air, radiant shine of the sun, resounding quiet. It was just us and the birds on that mountaintop, and for a while the rest of the troubled world ceased to exist. Perhaps we can bring the condors back from the brink of extinction, and if there's hope for them, maybe there's hope for the rest of life.

The first night, we camped at the head of Lion Canyon, a boulder-strewn amphitheater of bulbous sandstone near the summit of the Sierra Madre. Staring down on us from a ledge, Painted Cave and its ochre-toned rock art proved that the campsite had been used for some time. People have long taken advantage of the nearby spring and the coolness that elevation affords in a viciously hot summer. Greg and Mary knew the site because they had been there before. As we set up camp and talked about this range and that range, this canyon and that, it seemed that my cousin and her husband had biked everywhere during the past ten years.

While I took my turn cooking dinner that first night, I inquired about the Bettencourts' arrival at the central coast of California. Greg's path owes quite simply to his family history: he was born there. More revealing is the story of his return.

He had grown up in the beach town of Cayucos, north of San Luis Obispo, wedged between mountains and sea on the alluvial plain of the Santa Lucia Range. Greg spent summers working in his father's scuba diving shop but was denied the redeeming pleasure of this childhood fate. Plagued by seasickness, he never enjoyed going out on the water, which one must do in order to go diving under it. So he tended the store and filled air tanks for the divers.

Misplaced there at ocean's edge by a cruel twist of inner-ear physiology, Greg was a terrestrial boy, made for the mountains, which bordered Cayucos even more evidently than did the ocean. After all, you have to go to the beach or an overlook to lay eyes on the flat Pacific, but you can see the mountains all the time because they climb straight up from town. Yet people generally don't look that way. They look toward the sea.

And so did Greg, even though he couldn't go there, and as a teenager he declared there was nothing to do in Cayucos, a town so small that the pouring of a new cement footing made news. After high school he departed for college, with no intention of looking back. Now, with the clarity that fifty years of trial and error lends to one's vision, he said: "I was struck at the time with adolescent stupidity. It took me some years to develop a brain."

Part of this process, in college in San Diego, was meeting my cousin, Mary Gremer, who grew up in Bellflower, next to the industrial engine room of Los Angeles called Long Beach. Mary's parents had moved there from Pennsylvania following World War II because their first son suffered from asthma, and the good, dry air of Los

Angeles was considered therapeutic for people with lung ailments. Today, this enormous stretch of the imagination shows just how fast and how far things can deteriorate. But at any rate, Mary and Greg married, went to Tucson, Arizona, for graduate school, and with a baby, Jeremy, two years later moved back to the Los Angeles suburb of Orange, where Greg had scored his first job.

"There we were," Mary recalled, "living in this huge urban area. We weren't in any riots or mudslides or anything like that, but there was always this *thing* out there. It was symbolized by the little boy next door. His mom was on drugs. He lied. He stole. He walked right into our house. He gave me the creeps. I hadn't gotten my nursing degree yet, and I mostly stayed home with Jeremy."

Meanwhile, Greg taught high school at a time when many of the problems now afflicting teenagers and schools in epidemic proportions were just beginning to pass over the slippery hillside of irrevocable change.

"I could see the way it was going," Greg recalled. "The money was getting tighter, the schools worse, the kids more disaffected. After an especially bad day I drove home, discouraged. I sat down to dinner with Mary and Jeremy. I didn't know how to put it, so I finally just blurted it out. 'Mary, you can't raise kids here.' From that moment on, I couldn't wait to go home to Cayucos."

Remembering that fateful moment, Mary said, "I was a city girl but had always wanted to live in a beach town. So I said, 'Okay. Let's go.'"

Even though he had grown up at the foot of the Coast Range's slope, Greg never really knew the mountains bordering his town very well, but that was about to change. A significant technological breakthrough had occurred while he was gone: the mountain bike was invented. After returning to Cayucos and taking the new fat-tired two-wheelers for a spin, Mary and Greg were hooked. They simply loved mountain biking.

They sought out virtually every dirt road and trail within fifty miles. Their exploits included forty-mile days, aching climbs up thirty-degree slopes, spins into unknown box canyons swathed in poison oak, and spine-mushing descents on bedrocked trails that clung to skinny ridgelines or nominally adhered to the side slopes of canyon walls. They worked to maintain their trails, digging waterbars to prevent erosion and caring for their new mountain places.

"Mountain biking is fun," Mary said of their joint passion. "It keeps us fit, and we love the technical challenge of negotiating rough ground. But the main thing we like is *being* here. We like seeing the country. Experiencing these places firsthand broadens our view and awareness. Now we can look up at a mountain and know what it's like. That might not seem important to people who have never known mountains. It didn't used to be important to me. But once you know them, it's like recognizing an old friend on the street, compared with running into some total stranger."

All their biking for years had been done as day trips. But when I suggested a four-day journey to cross the formidable lineup of Coast Range topography, Cuyama-to-the-sea, Mary and Greg both sparked to the idea, and so there we were.

On our second day we peddled a symphony of airy ridgelines, the canyons tumbling away from us left and right, the views immense out to peak beyond peak from our roughcut path on the skyline. Of course, you can't cross three mountain ranges by joyriding like that, and we knew our route would get harder. But just how hard surprised us all.

We followed the Sierra Madre ridge until it began to merge with the San Rafael on the formidable slopes of Big Pine Mountain, which rises to 6,828 feet. Encountering a prelude to trouble, we hit mud in a melt zone near some snowdrifts. Then we hit snow itself—old, crusty, deep snow that forced us onto our feet and into slogging, backbreaking postures as we pulled the weighty bikes through the drifts. Topping a rise near the head of Madulce Canyon, we dropped again onto dry ground, fostering a cruel optimism that the northern face of Big Pine might not be too bad.

But it was. Far above the chaparral of our earlier ridgelines, we hit snow in a forest where Coulter pines and bristlecone firs yielded to the water-loving, cold-tolerant incense cedars and sugar pines—the largest of all the world's pines. From repeated freezing and melting over the past months, the snow had firmed up enough that we didn't break completely through, but it remained soft enough that the bike tires gouged deep, and our shoes sank enough to leak icy, wet crush over their tops.

Since I didn't have the additional drag of the trailer, on which Greg had carried even some of my gear ever since I underwent torture climbing out of Aliso Canyon, I broke trail, one step at a time. Fallen logs forced us into teamwork as we lifted the bikes over each one. Flowing water had hollowed out small stream crossings. I broke through one of these up to my waist in snow, yelling back, "See you guys later." As I climbed out I wondered what would have happened if the cavity had been deeper or the stream had been flowing harder.

At any given time a hundred feet was all we could go without stopping to breathe and rest. Then another hundred, and another, and another. Bend after bend lay shaded by the trees, with no end in sight, and we struggled on and up, on and up. In three hours we put on three miles, not much better than a crawl. To check for frostbite on the numb soles of my feet, I pulled off a running shoe and a sock full of sopping ice water. Mary and Greg, in thin biker's shoes, had it even worse but didn't complain a bit. None of us complained, yet I think we were all beginning to wonder what would happen if our situation worsened—if darkness caught us, if anyone got hurt and we had to camp in the wet and the cold. We were not prepared for a bivy in the snow.

Finally, with the sun long set, we began the eagerly awaited descent, and after turning a critical bend southward we began rolling again, the slush flying loose from our spokes and brakes. Cold mud splattered our legs. We dismounted to walk through another drift or two, but then we were whizzing downhill unimpeded.

Really unimpeded. In no time we graduated from a welcome downhill grade to an elevator shaft of free fall, and with some distress I found that no matter how hard I squeezed on my brakes, I failed to get enough bite. At one point I had to dodge the sudden wreckage of a landslide and nearly crashed. Blaming the problem on the melted-out wetness of my rims, I shouted ahead that I needed to stop. Greg quickly recognized that my front brake cable had slipped loose, and it's the front brake that counts most on downhill pitches because body weight is shifted to the front wheel. As darkness crept up on us and an unstoppable chill fingered its way down our necks and up our shorts, Greg tackled the repair job with skill derived from hundreds of such adjustments.

Next we searched in vain for a campsite while dusk faded toward darkness. Bone weary and dehydrated, we came to a trail intersection, where Greg stopped to look for Bluff Camp, nowhere evident. Our primary need was water. "Let's just head for the stream," I said. "I can hear it."

Bumping down a lane toward the swish of a riffle, we happened on a Forest Service cabin. Greg recognized the site from a description in his guidebook back home.

Cold, wet, and beginning to shiver in the growing darkness, we leaned the bikes against a picnic table. "After we filter some water, I think we should just put up the tents and get in our sleeping bags," I suggested. "We can eat tomorrow's cold lunch for dinner and call it good. We have to get warm soon."

"Okay," my friends agreed, all of us shooting for bare-bones survival at that point and willing to pass on Mary's home-dried stew, even though we knew it would hit the spot.

On a whim, I tried the cabin door.

It opened.

We stepped inside. The day's last light faintly revealed hunting-camp decor. A kitchen table, woodstove, woodpile, Coleman lantern, and separate room full of bunk beds greeted us. Warmth and comfort were suddenly ours for the taking.

While Greg and I filtered water from the nearby stream, Mary prepared dinner at the kitchen table. Then I fired up the woodstove, which looked a lot like an antique iron six-burner I had lived with for a decade during an earlier lifetime, three thousand miles away in the 1970s. Soon we were sipping steamy drinks and spooning hot stew, later gripping mugs of hot chocolate and leaning our butts against the warmth of the stove. With dry feet and a popping fire, we couldn't believe our good fortune. I later learned that the Forest Service cabin is normally locked.

Though Big Pine was clearly the height of land, day number three brought rigorous up-and-down biking followed by a spectacular hour-long descent of thousands of feet into valleys that looked like a clay model of the earth as seen from an airplane window. My hands ached from gripping the brakes, but I didn't dare let go, even when a bug flew into my eye. Hairpin turns wrapped around rocky shoulders and then plunged farther down, lower, lower to the valley of Indian Creek. After we crossed another divide, a final thigh-spasm climb brought us into the Santa Ynez River valley and the relief of camp number three.

On the fourth morning we kicked our bikes into high gear and breezed down the dirt road, ready for the final episode of the trip. We planned to surmount the Santa Ynez Range in a profoundly simple way: up one side, down the other. The mountain's opposite slope lorded over Santa Barbara, with its rustling palms above a gracious beach, its wave-moistened light, its sensuous Pacific air absorbing the aroma of flowers that bloom in every corner of open space, private and public. Spring and summer, fall and winter, it's all so easy there. In fact, the climate on the mid-California coast is the most uniform in America. Because of the moderating ocean, which cools the land in summer and warms it in winter, the annual temperature variation is only ten degrees. The tantalizing beach at Santa Barbara was our goal for the day, and we looked forward to the sweet-scented end of a long, sweaty trip.

Low-gearing directly up the Santa Ynez, I gazed back east toward the mountains' rumpled merging with the Tehachapi Mountains and marveled at the Coast Range's continuous nature. To the west, the Santa Ynez slanted toward its terminus at Point Conception, which juts into the Pacific forty miles beyond Santa Barbara. A landmark of geography, the Point is the apex of the coastline's consequential bend from west to northwest. It marks a narrowing of the continental shelf, the beginning of colder waters more exposed to northern ocean currents. North of there the continental shelf narrows, the winds increase, the surf swells. Northern plant species begin to appear. Point Conception introduces the first taste of northern California, even though it's less than a third of the way up the length of the state.

At a resting spot partway up the Santa Ynez we could see back to the punishing terrain where we had journeyed for four days. A panorama of hills led up to ridges that hid canyons and then rose to higher ridges before summiting on the far distant skyline—the same one we had crossed, unbelievably, only yesterday.

Panting my way uphill again, I imagined the final, glorious scene of our hard-sought goal: the Pacific. But as we gained elevation, we could see a flood of ocean fog puffing through gaps in the skyline. Then, when we finally reached the Santa Ynez summit, we stood lost in a gray soup of cloud, the final, climactic drop of three thousand feet to sea level completely blotted from sight. Greg summed it all up: "Delayed gratification."

Through the high fog we descended toward the towns of Montecito and Santa Barbara via the Romero Trail. Greg's earlier description of this as "a jeep road that has reverted to a single track" completely failed to do justice to what I now faced. For this finale of the trip I had imagined a coaster of a drop with a brilliant ocean view. But what I found was a painfully narrow ditch of a trail composed wholly of rocks, angular and sharp, with slashes of bedrock crossing like curbs thrown in my way, with frequent drop-offs where a single failing—say, a couple of fingers slipping off the brake—could result in an error of great consequence. Mary and Greg thrive on these challenges. I struggled with my poor ability to steer and the constant shock of hitting one rock after another, banging down from one ledge to the next. Lacking shock absorbers except for the fluid in my spinal discs, I beat my backbone and my equipment to bits. I tried to ease down the endless escarpment slowly, but in doing so I sacrificed the momentum that mountain bikers rely upon to carry them over small and medium-sized cobbles. Suffering badly, I began to step off the bike and ease it over the most difficult spots.

By gradual degrees the trail improved. Soon I picked up rolling speed, and then we spun down, down, down, the Pacific coming slowly into focus as we dropped by increments beneath and beyond the gray layer of fog. Then the ocean was finally unrobed in all its glory, still two thousand feet below. Wind in hair, sun in face, I followed my friends as they banked their bikes around curve after curve, each turn opening up a new and thrilling frame on the world below.

We hit the pavement and breezed onto chic residential streets of

Montecito, where estates of West Coast grandeur hid behind walls, gates, and hedges bursting into white and pink blooms. Mary led the way through heavy traffic and onto a bike trail that curved out to the seashore, colonnaded by palms. The ocean on our left, we rolled into Santa Barbara and dropped the bikes on the grass. Wasting not a minute, I pitched my helmet, shoes, and socks in a pile and waded into the Pacific, Cuyama-to-the-sea now complete.

"Pizza in San Luis" was the mantra after our four-day workout. Smaller than the big urban hubs along the Pacific, San Luis Obispo is to me the Queen City of the Coast Range, a place of architectural charm, pleasant neighborhoods, and downtown vitality. It's still a manageable size, though growing fast. With less sprawl than the usual California model, it sits in the middle of Los Osos Valley, named for grizzly bears. In 1837 alone one man shot forty-five of the long-clawed beasts in this temperate Eden. Some say there were more grizzlies here than anywhere. Sharing this idyllic valley, a chain of volcanic plugs called the Seven Sisters cones up in a picturesque row, one after another from urban edge to ocean.

During a few days of recovery back at Mary and Greg's place, I jogged with Ann on the Cayucos beach. But soon Bishop Peak, the closest of the Seven Sisters to San Luis Obispo, lured us toward its bouldered profile. A skinny path led first through plush grasslands and into the shade of coast live oaks and then to unyielding rocks, where we twisted and squeezed through strategic slots and finally spider-gripped at their faces until we stood on a wind-whipped summit.

The town lay like a toy Plasticville below. To the northeast rose the formidable Santa Lucia Range. One of the longest subranges in California's entire coastal block, it runs a hundred twenty miles all the way to Monterey. To the southwest the green of the Irish Hills did justice to their name, though power lines crackling with electrons from the Diablo Canyon nuclear power plant scarred the velvety skin of grassland.

Diablo Canyon had been the alternative site to Bodega Bay, north of San Francisco, where the Pacific Gas and Electric Company (PG&E) originally planned to site its flagship nuclear reactor, four hundred yards from the San Andreas Fault. Though it has earthquake problems of its own, Diablo Canyon was at first preferred by the Sierra Club as a better option. Thanks to the work of David Brower, the group later repealed its approval in what many people regard as a turning point for the Club and, for that matter, the entire conservation movement, which became more assertive and attentive to issues of broad environmental consequence. Amid massive civil disobedience, in spite of an earthquake scoring 7.5 on the Richter scale a scant two and a half miles offshore, and after correction of errors when blueprints were "mixed up," Diablo Canyon was built in the early 1980s.

Though hidden by hills from Bishop Peak, the reactor's science-fiction domes and blockish buildings of thick, white concrete stand at the edge of green mountains and blue sea. It reminded me, once again, of the connections between the Coast Range and its cultures. Though remote, the antenna farms, the mountain reservoirs, and now the power plant are just a flick of the switch away from the demands of everyplace.

From our view facing northwest, the captivating chain of the Seven Sisters ended with the monolithic Morro Rock. Its mass bites up out of the sea like a giant tooth, a Rock of Gibraltar if ever there was one in America.

On that magical evening, the more vulnerable summits stood beautifully fringed in fog. But the scene was far from unmarred. In a view otherwise as fine as in any national park, three behemoth smokestacks pointed skyward from the base of Morro Rock, where PG&E operates a gas-fired power plant. And a large chunk of the rock had been blasted away to build a jetty.

In my mind's eye, from that high view, I now undressed the land of its freeways, its encroaching sprawl, and its power plants, and the scene that remained showed a deftly formed beauty, hardrock cones above oak savanna. It all tiered down to the Pacific, which beat at the base of Morro as though that rock were a guardian of the whole continent, taking a courageous stand out there to break the force of the ocean for everything else.

As darkness deepened on our springtime evening, the fog filtered farther in from sea. It misted the neighborhoods of San Luis Obispo, scattering auriferous light. Its swirls animated the scene the same way waves enliven the seashore, and it reminded me again that an exquisite blending of earth, air, and water lies at the essence of these mountains wherever I go.

Windblown waves of green grass washed up against the mountain slope below us. They made a pasture for cattle, but here, in springtime, it didn't have the grazed-over, weed-infested look of most other ranchland I had seen. It seemed to convey some wisp of hope for harmony in the productive land below the peaks.

Bob Blanchard's father, with unlikely preparation as a career accountant, bought a dairy farm near Cayucos to make his escape from Los Angeles at the early date of 1949. But dairies have their own challenges, and the herd of Holsteins became an albatross.

"Swearing to never again own anything with hooves, my father switched to oranges and avocados," Bob explained to me nearly fifty years later. Not so hoof-averse, and loving the open lay of the land he had been born with, Bob sought out a ranching career without family pasture to build upon. This meant he had to lease land from someone else.

Where the Irish Hills west of San Luis Obispo slant down toward the sea, they taper onto a terrace as green in springtime as the pastures where farmers bred the first Hereford cows in England. North America ends there with a twenty-foot cliff above salty breakers. This fine four-mile-long spread is part of PG&E's compound, fenced off as a buffer zone for the Diablo Canyon nuclear power plant. Bob had been leasing the land for his cattle, and he continued after PG&E bought the ranch.

"PG&E paid thirteen and a half million for this spread," Bob explained. "The investors, of course, charged the company as much as they could for the loaned money. So PG&E charged as much as *it* could to lease the grassland for cows. This didn't even put a dent in what the company owed, but it forced us to run as many cows as we possibly could." The cows, of course, ate as much as *they* possibly could.

As in every place we humans touch shortsightedly, it was here, where root meets soil, that the system of life support broke down. The process is one of the world's more common forms of exploitation, called overgrazing.

Sparing me the details of the inevitable root rot, soil erosion, and weed infestation, Bob jumped ahead and said, "PG&E had to form a land stewardship committee to look at how they were managing this property. I knew we could do a better job, and I was willing to change the way we were doing things."

A capable-looking man, Blanchard wore a corduroy shirt, jeans, and cowboy boots, though not the pointy-toed kind. With blue eyes and a subtle smile, he had the classic rancher look, though he wore a ball cap instead of a cowboy hat. "Out here on the coast it's too windy for a cowboy hat," he explained.

As he drove his pickup past a lawn-like pasture, Bob said that once on the path of range improvement, he put up fences so he could control the wanderings of his cows. Now they graze in one of twenty-five different paddocks at a time. They get rotated while the ungrazed grasses rest and recover. "The fences are expensive, but they're worth it," Bob said. In each rotation he lets the stock eat grass but not so much that they repeatedly bite off new growth, damage roots, or disturb the soil enough to invite a takeover of exotic and useless weeds — otherwise a pandemic across California and the West today.

"They call this a high-density, short duration strategy. It's managed grazing rather than continuous grazing, which is where you just turn the cows loose and let them go where they want. After switching to the new system, I realized one day I had recovering ryegrasses out here. I hadn't even seen them before. Without the cows biting them off all the time, they had a chance to compete with the weeds, and now they're winning. The ryegrasses, bur clover, and filaree aren't native, but they're usable and good for the cows. With better management, the poverty grasses like foxtail and needlegrass begin to decline. If grazing is well managed, the more noxious weeds don't get a foothold." I encouraged Bob to tell me more. The grasses certainly looked good there in the spring of the year.

"I got into this environmental stuff because it's fascinating. When you realize that this diverse system is what everybody wants, and then you look at good grazing, you see that we can have both in this climate. I now have more birds on the land than when I took over the lease. Some shrubs grow here, and the mix of plants doesn't hurt; I don't have a problem if it's improving the habitat of a wild animal. If the grass started getting crowded out altogether, then I'd say it's bad. But it doesn't."

Bob uses eight acres to raise each cow and calf. That compares poorly with the one or two acres needed in the East, but it compares well with fifty or as high as two hundred acres in arid regions of the West. "This is good range," he said, "so I can cut my production costs. That's the only way you can make a living at ranching today. With managed grazing, I'll have a lot of nutritious brown grass in the summer and fall, and I won't have to haul in hay. If I had to do that, I might as well not even think about making money off a cow. My costs have dropped from eighteen dollars per month per cow to fourteen. As I harmonize with nature instead of butt heads with nature, the economics improve."

Looking beyond his own tract of improving ground, Bob said, "The big problem is that most people can't make a living off ranching. A lot of guys are going broke. They see that they can sell their land for development and make a killing. So they do. I hate to see it, but you can understand how it happens."

The rancher continued on this theme. "Beef is still one of the biggest agricultural commodities in San Luis Obispo County, but I'm afraid it's not as important economically as it is aesthetically. Fewer and fewer ranchers are committed to the cattle business. The old spreads get divided into hobby plots, ranchettes, and subdivisions. If we don't do some land-use planning that preserves large grazing areas, cattle ranching will be lost. But throwing rules and regulations at a guy won't work. If the public wants this open space, and I think it does, then we need to pay a rancher for his development potential, or allow for a transfer of development rights, or something like that. If we don't do that, we just won't have the quality of life we're accustomed to here on the central coast. And without that, what have we got?"

WITH SO MUCH coastal ranchland up for development, the Trust for Public Land and other conservancies in California have been scrambling to preserve the open space that makes the quality of life here so fine. In 1998 they protected 1 percent of the state's shore from subdivision, the most mileage saved in many years. One of their successes is a four-mile reach of oceanfront grassland north of Cayucos that otherwise would have been sliced up for lots and condos.

Sites such as this, together with parks, wilderness areas, and other kinds of refuges, make up 16 percent of California that's protected as natural areas—places for nature to do the important work it does. That's a good start, but it excludes many critical hot spots and corridors of habitat essential for the survival of native animals and plant life. More than half the state's coastline remains in private hands. Much of this is still open space, unchanged in years, which gives the illusion that it will stay that way. But even in remote areas, coastal land is highly vulnerable. Governments and conservation groups hope to buy or secure easements on another five million acres statewide by the year 2010, but to do that will require $12 billion. The Planning and Conservation League and other sponsors hope to pass a major bond issue to raise some of this money.

NORTH OF Cayucos and San Simeon, feeling as if we were stepping into the Land of Oz, Ann and I entered the realm of Big Sur. Eulogized in the poetry of Robinson Jeffers, who called this "the greatest meeting of land and water in the world," the ninety-mile length of coast is where the Santa Lucia Range drops like a sliding board into the sea.

Because the topography is so extreme, most of Big Sur lacks beaches and instead confronts the Pacific with rocky cliffs. Mountainsides and bluffs are covered with plants of the increasingly rare coastal sage community. Redwoods shade tight canyons, and up higher the Santa Lucia Range climbs to massive slopes entangled with chaparral and finally to conifers that triumph on north-facing slopes. Where beaches do occur—charmed quarter-moon crescents at the mouths of streams—they lie isolated and intimate in their thrifty brokering for existence between big mountain and big ocean.

We stopped at Salmon Creek, which approximates the southern end of the historical range of salmon. These large, silvery fish spawn in streams but migrate to the ocean to live. Or at least they try. But none are left here. If only in name, Salmon Creek signified our progress north in a journey toward the salmon's ultimate habitat, which by default of the dammed and developed rivers in the lower forty-eight now exists primarily in Alaska. Ann and I scrambled along the creek's edge, peering into pools and searching with unjustified hope for the charismatic fish.

But who knows? Struggling populations survive in many of the coastal streams north of here, and if their numbers and habitat can be improved, maybe someday a stray will return and reestablish a local population in Salmon Creek. As recently as the 1980s, steelhead —fish with a similar life cycle—spawned in Cayucos Creek. At one time steelhead spawned in Malibu Creek, and they've recently been found in a stream near San Diego.

For now, Ann and I were rewarded by alder leaves unfurling in springtime greenery and buttercups brightening the ground. The scent of pungent bay leaves filled the air like a vernal tonic. From the woodland trail we could hear the distant music of both surf and waterfall, all this sensory detail painting a picture in my mind of the mountains in a dream—another California dream in which the swoop of condors is further enlivened by finning schools of salmon returning to their ancient homeland and once again providing food for the rest of life, including us.

Just a short way up the road, we offered respects near the southern end of a four-hundred-fifty-mile belt of redwoods in a fog-dripping hollow aptly called Redwood Gulch. The trees grew tall and straight, their foliage soaking up the light and letting only thin cathedral-window shafts reach the ground. Having come through the Coast Range's cactus phase in Baja and into its oak zone beginning near the border, we now celebrated our entry into the range of the redwood. In northern California these tallest of all plants would reach their skyscraping pinnacle.

To really experience the mountain flavor of Big Sur rather than just the side-hill feel that tends to dominate when you drive on Highway

1, we once again met Mary and Greg, along with their mountain-biking buddy Ron Dexter, and set out for the top of Cone Peak. To get there we turned east from the coast and negotiated the spectacular switchbacks of the Nacimiento-Fergusson Road. Grass and chaparral yielded to redwoods and Douglas-fir as we chugged uphill and entered cool and woodsy enclaves.

Where the road topped the Santa Lucia crest, the energizing winds of a Pacific high-pressure system delivered crystal-clear air on a stout blow from the northwest. We parked, unloaded the bikes, and began to ride on a dirt lane that took off to the north. For six miles we peddled through the forest of bay, oak, madrone, and bristlecone fir, also called Santa Lucia fir. These striking trees have long needles with sharp points. Bracts like drooping hair curl out of the cones. The famous botanist David Douglas first described this rarest of firs here in 1831. It was also on this mountain that another great botanist, Thomas Coulter, first documented the Coulter pine, with its bombshell cones. Adding further botanical interest, local ponderosa and sugar pines here are disjunct — reproductively isolated — from other stands of those great trees that grow plentifully in the Sierra Nevada.

Greg and Ron, real mountain-bike animals, tended to outdo each other and sprinted ahead, leaving the rest of us in the dust. Ann and I took time to dodge rocks. We stopped to identify birds — finches and siskins as disjunct here as the trees they live on. Though fully capable of a faster pace, Mary hung back with us.

I had singled out Cone Peak because in the United States outside Alaska it's the highest point so close to the ocean, 5,155 feet high and only 3.4 miles from the water. This was easy to believe after we ditched our bicycles and hiked the final 1,400 vertical feet to the top. I hoofed vigorously with Ron, who along with Greg obsessively kicked stones off the path, a habit extending from years of maintenance work on their favorite mountain bike trails.

The view from the summit would have been worth twice the effort. Far to the south, and pleasing me for the final time, I spotted three of the Seven Sisters in the San Luis Obispo area. Northward, and eleven miles in from the ocean, Junipero Serra Peak rose to 5,862 feet, the highest peak in the Santa Lucia Range. Ron and Greg pointed out additional summits, their banter focusing on which peak was which, where the trails ran between them, and when they had once traveled that way or someday would.

Scanning it all, Greg said: "I can't think of a ride here in the Coast Range that doesn't involve a steep climb. We've gone to the Rockies to ride, and at first we were concerned about bigger country. But it's no steeper, no more mountainous. The only thing harder is the extra altitude — the lack of oxygen. There, you start from seven thousand feet and go up to ten, eleven. Here, we start at zero and go up to five."

Having spent years of my adult life in Idaho and Wyoming, I was fascinated by this two-tiered vision of western geography. Most of the Coast Range summits south of Canada lie at a lower elevation than the valleys in the Rocky Mountains. Just imagine if there were no intervening miles between the two ranges; it would look like two giant steps of five thousand feet each. From now on, when I return to the Rockies, I will picture the Coast Range as an entire mountain complex lying underground from what I see.

After a spread of peanut butter and jelly sandwiches, we hiked and biked back down, reboarded our vans, and crossed eastward to the interior valleys of the Santa Lucia with a special, long-awaited goal in mind. The coast live oaks on the western slopes had impressed me ever since camping in Potrero County Park, near the Mexican border, but I dearly wanted to walk through a savanna of valley oaks — the really big ones — and Greg knew exactly where to go.

At the southern side of Junipero Serra, we stepped into the most splendid grove anywhere. Bursting with spring growth, scattered amid grasslands, these kings of the oaken world stood with trunks five feet or more in diameter. I walked up to the first giant and put my hands on the roughly plated, deeply furrowed bark. Far more impressive close up, everything about these trees was magnificent — girthy trunks, single limbs three feet across, hundred-foot spreads of canopy. We stepped quietly through their midst at sunset, a soothing, godly time of day, and to be anything but reverent in that place would have felt wrong.

Then, with nighttime coming on, we exchanged goodbyes. Mary, Greg, and Ron returned to Cayucos, and Ann and I stayed to camp among the enchanted oaks. The next day we backtracked to the coast and regained some northerly momentum.

But not much. Puttering along Highway 1 again, we reveled in scenic views from pull-outs high above the Pacific. The terraces there seemed to have bolted up off the ocean floor all of a sudden, as if the earth really had been created in only seven days. Canyons cut deeply into the slopes and allowed the sea now and then to finger its way into the escarpment. Seeing this endlessly irregular outline of the continent made it believable that California's 790-mile length of coastline increases to at least 1,400 miles if you actually follow the ins and outs of the zero-elevation contour.

Just looking at that chaotic edge, I had a hard time imagining that a road was possible at all. Riddled with west-cutting canyons of repulsing steepness and depth, the slanted Pacific face of the Santa Lucia posed a formidable barrier to any north–south travel. Until 1937 only fragments of trails and roads could be found. The historic route since the time of the Gaspar de Portolá expedition in 1769 had bent inland, using the amenable north–south valleys of the interior.

Early residents of Big Sur fought construction of the road because it cut into their property, required extensive earthmoving, and promised an influx of outsiders to a place where the locals had a fair emulation of paradise going on, a bit like May Knight Rindge's situation before the Pacific Coast Highway chopped up Malibu. The Big Sur segment of Highway 1 might never have been built at all if not for California's 1915 Convict Labor Law, which set prisoners to work on road construction. After an initial estimate and state bond issue of $1.5 million, and even with chain gangs doing the dirty work, the completed road cost $8 million.

That 500 percent overrun, however, was only the tip of the Highway 1 iceberg. Fighting with extreme topography in a mountain range that's only two million years old and obsessed with reshaping itself is an endless job. While construction alone had been a herculean task, the upkeep now requires a comparable effort over and over again.

Not only are the Big Sur slopes some of the steepest on the Pacific front of America, but also the soil covering them turns to slurry when lubricated by rainfall, all of it resting precariously atop fractured and rotted bedrock, if any bedrock at all. Squads of bulldozers, backhoes, and dump trucks work for weeks, months, years at a time just to fix single slides.

Sometimes fixing means peeling off the slope for a thousand feet of rise — open-earth surgery with the bluntest of scalpels here at poet Robinson Jeffers' greatest meeting of land and water in the world. The J. P. Burns slide made California history as the single largest earthmoving project ever undertaken by the California Department of Transportation, which has shoved around a lot of dirt in its day.

In 1983, when two hundred inches of rain pummeled the summits of Big Sur until frogs could have drowned, a slide cut loose and shut down the road for a year. Greg Bettencourt's young cousin Stuart Negranti worked there as an apprentice bulldozer operator. His colleague and teacher, Skinner Pierce, doubled as a deep-sea diver, abalone hunter, and notorious gambler. Blading through the oozing rubble of the landslide, the men came to an especially dicey spot. Pierce commandeered the bulldozer, insisting that Negranti stand aside because he had kids to be fed at home. Two days later they found the bulldozer at the bottom of the ocean, with no sign of Skinner Pierce. Today, driving Highway 1 is a classic honeymoon thing to do, but maintaining the road is no frivolous pursuit for work-ers on the ground or for taxpayers footing the bill, which in one recent year topped $16 million.

Despite the endless difficulties, and with hubris that can only astonish, business boosters and the fast-car people, including the state's highway engineers, floated proposals to make this seaward-sliding road a freeway, four lanes and all. Fortunately, the state took action in 1976 to limit Highway 1 here to two lanes.

Development, of course, comes in the wake of access. Under the existing county land-use plan, four hundred homes on the Big Sur coast can increase by another thousand, a change that's bound to make parts of Big Sur look more and more like the fragmented Santa Monica Mountains.

To get away from the asphalt, Ann and I walked down to the beach at the mouth of Willow Creek, a breathtaking spot. We strolled for a while and then sat before the breaking surf, joyous that we would be visiting the ocean—"Pacificking," we called it—for some months to come.

We had the kind of day you want at Big Sur—clear, with the famed Pacific High system of northwesterly winds piling up big, diaphanous waves. We sat in the sand, a bit hypnotized by the steady onslaught—eight thousand waves a day chewing at the Coast Range even as it continues to rise.

A couple of virtuoso surfers balanced on the landward slope of aqua blue swells, which were translucent at their peaking crests when afternoon light beamed through from behind. Gulls squawked where Willow Creek fed water back to the ocean, the whole hydrologic cycle so neatly completed before our eyes.

While we sat there, a young man walked by, a sad and lonely boy if I ever saw one. So I struck up a conversation. His name was Josh. Looking wistfully out at the water, he soon confessed that he used to be a surfer. Now he was a Christian.

Baffled by his sense of conflict, I raised what is surely the obvious question. "Why can't you be both?"

He looked at the ground and explained, "You can't have two gods at once."

Tickled that surfing would be so elevated in his mind, appalled that he would limit himself in such a way, I could think of nothing to say. Together we watched the surfers, at one with their waves. I suspected they were the envy of all three of us.

Josh moved on in his waveless misery and left us alone with our ocean.

"Maybe we should take up surfing," Ann suggested.

"As a religion?"

"I don't think we could ever be that good. It would just be another way to go Pacificking. You know—then we'd be *in* it."

"Where would we put the boards?"

"On the roof rack—just push the canoes over to the side."

"But that would be like having two gods at once."

"I think we have room up there for both of them."

We sat close to each other, so happy for the beach, the mountains, the quiet time together. We weren't surfing at all, but I must say that something about the scene felt quite reverent; there was something eternal and redemptive about a piece of earth and sea so unspoiled.

Nothing much happened, if you can call the onslaught of those blue-green, foam-capped waves nothing. But then we were blessed with one of those special moments that often seems to come as a reward for sitting still in the outdoors. Though a bit early for the usual migration, a whale spouted out in the blue, the first we had seen since Baja. The world's largest mammals were headed north, bound for Alaska, just like us.

AT THE MOUTH of the Salinas River—what was left of it after total agricultural diversion—the oceanfront ridge of the Coast Range was broken. The Santa Lucia had tapered down from the south; the Santa Cruz Mountains ramped up to the north. Then, just beyond the intriguing town of Santa Cruz, we turned inland and wound up a coastal valley between tall, rolling slopes, eventually arriving at the Swanton Pacific Ranch with an appointment to see Wally Mack.

A professor at California Polytechnic State University in San Luis Obispo, Wally managed a school-owned estate of woodland, cropland, pasture, and chaparral where students came to live, work, and learn about better ways of managing resources. A husky, handsome man obviously suited to the outdoors, though he'd taught forestry in a classroom for years, Wally, along with the students, researched better ways of caring for the land—what they called "best practices."

"Eighty percent of our agricultural students are now from urban backgrounds," Wally began. "When they come here for eleven weeks, it's a lot different from anything they've ever done. They harvest their own food, plan the menus, cook for each other, live together, and work hard. It's all part of the education, and most students love it."

On the three-thousand-acre spread rising from sea level to the windy tops of mountains, Wally and his staff and students raise vegetables, graze cattle and goats, and cut timber. In some respects, the ranch is a microcosm of California, where 55 percent of the land is used for grazing or logging. That being the case, the grazing and logging may as well be done with some foresight, which is the motivating goal behind the Cal Poly program.

Wally drove me up to a spacious green pasture on a ridge overlooking the ocean, where goats enjoyed a knockout view. Students had strung a temporary electric fence around the pasture, and inside, among the fifty goats, a tall, serene, creamy-fleeced llama chewed its cud with crooked bites. Wanting a better angle for a picture — goats in front, ocean behind — I put a leg over the fence.

"Don't go in there!" Wally clapped me quickly on the shoulder. "The llama will send you running. She thinks those goats are hers. She'll protect them at any cost. It's the most effective protection you can get. You don't have to kill coyotes or mountain lions if you have a llama."

"Okay, no problem." I took the picture from outside the fence, the llama keeping a cool, downcast eye on me.

We walked up a timbered valley for a mile, to a logging site where scattered large redwoods had been plucked out, and Wally explained the Cal Poly timber program. "This was all clearcut after the 1906 San Francisco earthquake, so the next generation of trees were all the same age. That might be okay if you're just going to mow them down as soon as you can, and if you don't care about anything but logs, but an uneven-aged forest is far better for wildlife, for other plant species, and for the watershed. What we're doing now is converting this woods from even- to uneven-aged. With trees of all ages, including dead and decaying ones and seedlings in small, sunny openings, the forest offers more diversity of habitat. The worst thing you can do is cut the cavity trees — the really old ones with nesting holes in them. We need those for predators such as woodpeckers, which keep the insect pests in check."

"This isn't your usual commercial logging job, is it?"

"No. But it is successful commercially. In spite of what some people in the industry would have you believe, you don't have to clearcut redwoods to have economic forestry. We're proving that here. There are actually a lot of foresters who don't like what commercial timber harvests have done to forests for the last fifty years. No doubt you'll see what I'm talking about as you head into northern California. Traditional foresters have seen no way out. But here in the Santa Cruz Mountains, we're showing that there are alternatives."

ANN AND I returned to Santa Cruz and then drove up Highway 9 along the diminutive San Lorenzo River, leaving the seashore behind with mixed feelings because these recent weeks near the ocean had been so good, so fine. Light rain peppered us; the ground was spongy, the air damp, the fog hanging low in valleys. The evergreen canopy soaked up the light like dark draperies, and we looked forward to what lay on the other side.

The small towns of Felton, Ben Lomond, and Boulder Creek had a woodsy air about them. Scattered log cabins looked as if they'd once offered secluded retreats for San Francisco urbanites. Now the towns were lived in year-round by working folks who had set up businesses here or who commuted to Silicon Valley. So close to, yet worlds away from, the microchip paradigm, wood smoke curled from chimneys on that cool day in March.

To see some of the best of the Santa Cruz Mountains, Ann and I drove to Big Basin Redwoods State Park, set aside as California's first state park in 1902, when tree huggers of the day convinced the legislature to purchase the land. The tall conifers reach for the sky and thicken the ground with their duff and deadfall, all of it interspersed with the flashy green broadleaf madrone, the adaptable Douglas-fir, and the persistent tan oak. Ann said, "It feels like northern California now, doesn't it?"

"The fog, the water, the trees — I think you're right." At Big Basin we tasted the splendid array of life we would enjoy as we moved farther north. But first, the hills of San Francisco awaited.

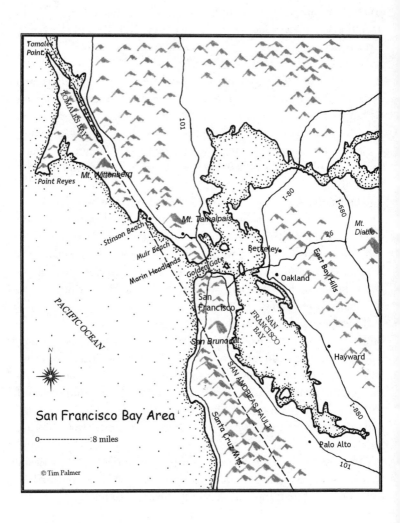

Tomales
Point

TOMALES BAY

101

Point Reyes

Mt. Wittenberg

Stinson Beach

Muir Beach

Mt. Tamalpais

Marin Headlands

Golden Gate

San
Francisco

I-80

Berkeley

Oakland

26

I-680

Mt.
Diablo

East Bay Hills

SAN
FRANCISCO
BAY

PACIFIC OCEAN

San Bruno Mt.

Hayward

I-880

SAN ANDREAS FAULT

N

San Francisco Bay Area

0 --------------- : 8 miles

Santa Cruz Mts.

Palo Alto

101

© Tim Palmer

# 7 | The People's Mountains

At RUSH HOUR Ann and I barreled down Highway 17 from the shady Santa Cruz Mountains toward sunny San Jose. Traffic in our two lanes streamed along lightly, but an outbound onslaught of cars and sport utility vehicles hemorrhaged from Silicon Valley at day's end. In strange terrain, and looking forward to a short stop on our way to San Francisco, we watched for the sign to Los Gatos, and when it appeared, a miraculous break in the traffic occurred, as if the waters had parted just for us. I hastily wheeled left and crossed the two oncoming lanes.

But it wasn't the road we were searching for. In fact, it was nothing but a cracked-asphalt frontage lane that dead-ended at The Cats tavern. We soon realized we had made a big mistake. Cars in a collective din of internal combustion flew by at sixty, seventy miles an hour, both southbound lanes as full as hydroelectric penstocks except that the water in this pipeline flowed uphill. We couldn't turn left, couldn't even turn right. In ten minutes we saw more cars than we had seen throughout Baja in an entire month.

Welcome to rush hour, I thought, a trauma to us but a quotidian event on virtually every road leading to and from America's fourth-largest metropolitan area, where seven and a half million people live clustered around San Francisco Bay and its fringe of filled-in marshes, lowlands, hills, and mountain slopes.

Ann finally said, "Why don't we just fix our dinner here and wait for the traffic to thin out?" Defeated by the exodus of everyone who had driven into the urban area that morning, we turned our back to the traffic. We boiled spaghetti in our van right there at the urban border, acutely aware how the edges of coastal mountains mark boundaries not just of topography, habitat, and climate but also of culture.

Avoiding rush hour was the first lesson we learned in this part of our journey, and I knew there would be others as we delved into the urban landscape. In Los Angeles I had considered the ways the mountains affect the city and its development — the broad brush of earthquakes, mudslides, and fire: in sum, the natural, though violated, laws of geography. Here in the San Francisco Bay Area I wanted to climb the hills and also learn how people responded to the coastal mountains. What did they think about them? In the south, I had seen friction and conflict at the interface of city and slope. In San Francisco I was hoping to see something else.

Like many people, I was jazzed by the city and its buzz of civilization so elegantly situated near water's edge. I had spent some months there in years past, but now, for the first time, I realized that the hills regarded as so distinctly San Franciscan belong to the Coast Range. Telegraph Hill, Russian Hill, Pacific Heights, Mount Diablo, Mount Tamalpais — all belong to the Coast Range complex. While the mountains around Los Angeles serve vividly as a topographic barrier to the endless sprawl, the mountains and hills of the Bay Area impressed me as gems of scenery and opportunities for outlook woven into the urban culture and around which the fabric of life is tailored. In Los Angeles, the mountains contain the city; here, they enhance it. Along with the ocean and its bay, they make San Francisco into what many people call the most beautiful city in America.

After finally arriving in San Francisco, Ann and I were counting on a special night out — an urban date as a change of pace. Eschewing innumerable other fine restaurants, we delighted in Café Pomodoro, with great Italian food we could afford and a cozy, friendly atmosphere. In part, we were splurging as preparation for some abstinence. Ann had to fly to a conference in Baltimore the next day to give a talk about the history of wetlands—a preview of her book. She would take some time to visit her family in Connecticut as well, so I would have to fend for myself in the city.

After dinner we held hands at our little candlelit table, waiting for the creamy *panna cotta* with strawberries on top. Ann made me promise to be careful. I made her promise to tell her wetland story with the enthusiasm she really felt for it. The next morning she flew east, and I went right to work.

Work? By bicycle I tackled the hills of San Francisco, walking the sharpest climbs and enjoying the neighborhoods in between. Lots of them. But I saved the best until last. In low evening light I pumped up steepening streets to a central landmark. A monstrous communications tower rose up there—a steel-girder Erector set hundreds of feet high, the multi-legged mother of all antennas among all the antenna-polluted Coast Range summits, the ranking eyesore in the entire Bay Area. But just in front of that tower, Twin Peaks overlooks San Francisco. What better place to check out the view?

Racing the sunset, I banked into the hilltop parking lot and immediately dodged two idling tour buses disgorging crowds of suited Japanese. Without delay they busied themselves taking one another's pictures in front of the view. In the low light, their camera flashes flicked again and again, the total effect a slow-motion stroboscopic study of unshadowed Japanese faces pasted onto twilight America.

Though the mountains there wore a deceptive urban mask, the commanding vista from that summit showed with utter clarity that indeed I had biked up to the backbone of the Coast Range. Chilly with evaporating sweat, and so windblown I could hardly open my map, I scrambled to identify the landmarks before the light faded away.

To the south lay San Bruno Mountain, an isolated mound thirteen hundred feet high. After a heated land-use battle in the 1970s, Bay Area conservationists had saved 1,950 of the 3,600 acres of San Bruno —the largest contiguous open space on the San Francisco Peninsula and one of the more sizable wild mountains within urban America.

Public action spared most of the slopes from the bulldozer and cement truck. But on its north face, ranch houses as blockish and white as bedsheets hung out to dry zigzagged up streets that had been bladed into the hill as if slashed by Zorro's sword. New developments still chewed at unprotected eastern flanks, rich in the rare vegetation botanists call Franciscan habitat.

Southwest of San Bruno, the San Andreas Fault zippered through Daly City. Then, for the first time, it headed out to sea like a torpedo aimed northwest, destined for a few more glancing yet bruising blows at the coast of California. Unlike Los Angeles, San Francisco resides on the North American Plate, immediately east of the fault.

Thirty-three miles to my east-northeast, the famed Mount Diablo reached to 3,849 feet. In my view at sunset, only the upper half of this interior Coast Range landmark treaded water above the East Bay smog. The core of an old volcano, Diablo is what geologists call a piercement structure and represents what's left after molten earth from Franciscan rocks was squeezed like toothpaste up through cracked and leaky layers of sediment. Today's still-significant peak remains after 20,000 vertical feet eroded off the fiery old giant. On a clear day, it is said, you can see more from Diablo's double-top summit than from any other mountain in the world except Africa's Kilimanjaro. The reason owes not so much to height as to relativity; Diablo stands alone, with few other big mountains nearby to block the view. Beneath it lie the deracinated hills of the East Bay area, with four-garage homes and designer malls where the blue oak savanna sadly fades from memory.

Closer to my outlook from San Francisco's Twin Peaks lay the Oakland and Berkeley Hills, quilted in grass and chaparral at the edge of highly flammable neighborhoods. As in southern California, this landscape is just so much kindling subject to the inevitable forces of nature. In 1991 the notorious Oakland Hills fire charred 3,354 homes, the ultimate suburban chaparral firestorm and third-worst urban fire disaster in U.S. history, after the San Francisco earthquake of 1906 and the Chicago fire of 1871. One house was torched every five seconds for an hour. Twenty-five people died. If not for a shift in wind, the famed Claremont Hotel and University of

California campus would very likely have burned. The next time it may be worse. With federal disaster relief checks in hand, owners replaced virtually all the homes with new ones 20 percent larger than their fire-feeding predecessors.

The next disaster, however, may be an earthquake. The Hayward Fault, cracking along the base of the hills the whole way through the East Bay area, is now considered more dangerous than the San Andreas. The U.S. Geological Survey estimated a 30 percent chance of a tremor scoring at least 7 on the Richter scale in the next thirty years. With its epicenter here, ground shaking from a magnitude 7 event would be twelve times worse than that of the 1989 Loma Prieta earthquake, which caused quite a stir in its own right. The Hayward Fault may be the most populated in the world, far more built upon than the San Andreas.

In the neighborhoods directly below Twin Peaks, tiny streets penciled out like contour lines and a tightly textured mosaic of roofs checkered all the spaces in between. Farther below and ruler straight, Market Street arrowed purposefully toward the Bay. The Mission — plaster-white and lacking the trees that greened other districts — slanted busily off to the south, and to its north rose the Financial District's shadowlands of steel and concrete. From my view, the skyscrapers seemed cobbled together like a sculpture of oversized blocks and Tinkertoys.

In all directions, the hills of the city mounded up as if the earth underneath had swollen and arisen with streets and houses intact, and now all that infrastructure was slotted and tilted and wedged onto slopes to which buildings clung by friction holds and cement-footing fingernails. As sunlight faded further, the view began to sparkle with the lights of night.

A busy place, Twin Peaks hummed not only with Japanese and other tourist groups chattering in a smorgasbord of languages but also with runners, lovers, and little old people who sat in their cars and stared at the view or deliberated over the *Chronicle*'s crossword puzzle while soaking up the last light of one more precious day — one more twilight before retiring to endure the night.

I biked back down in the darkening hour, trying to keep my

promise to Ann by avoiding traffic as best I could. At a good clip I cut through Golden Gate Park—slightly larger than New York's Central Park. Then I panted up a steep hill to Pacific Heights. Really steep. From that high-end neighborhood my brakes screeched enough to attract annoyed looks from pedestrians the whole way down the northern side. If I had been dragging a paraglider, I surely would have taken off. With this thriller of a drop behind me, I rejoined the van at the Marina Green, a sweet recreational green space hugging the Bay.

The next day I walked the streets and absorbed the San Francisco vibe. Even in the era of AIDS, crack cocaine, and gang activity, a soulful sense of excitement clicks in when one looks out over a thousand rooftops to water dotted with sailboats, to the inverted rainbow arches of the Golden Gate Bridge, to the misty headlands of Marin County slanting down to sea. Nature and city seem to coexist.

Perhaps not coincidentally, people in San Francisco seemed happy and energetic. There was something in the air; I couldn't help feeling it myself. A simple deep breath always made me smile. Plus, I naturally become more outgoing when Ann's not around. I see this as an indication of how satisfied and fulfilled I am in her company. Together we are happy to the point of turning inward, isolating ourselves somewhat. But when alone, I'm more aware of others around me, more interested in striking up conversations and helping other people if I can.

A large gay population lives in San Francisco, so when I spoke to men, I sensed that they were either hopeful or fearful that I was gay. You can't quite speak to people if you don't first catch their eye, so, confounded in my friendliness to men, I tried to make eye contact with women along the waterfront trail to the Golden Gate. This proved to be quite a challenge. After a long string of downcast eyes from women who seemed to regard me as a rapist cleverly disguised as a tourist with a smile, my first connection was a grin from a little African American girl. She zipped by on a bicycle with sheer joy in her heart. The second was with a spunky San Francisco native who had walked her dogs nearly every day for most of her eighty-five years. A young, pretty woman did once smile at me. She was accompanied by her pit bull.

Taking none of this personally, I regarded the lack of eye contact from men and women alike as half protection from issues of sex and half the fact that — of course — this is a city. Quite simply, there are too many people to be friendly with.

So I drove across to the East Bay, where, I thought, Berkeley might be a better place to hang out. The pier there offers a good outlook to the wide surrounding swells of water and to the hills; perhaps it would be a good place to chat with folks about the lay of the land.

First I tried to talk to the black fishermen. After a few nominal answers to the old question, "How's the fishing?" they turned their faces out to sea to let me know we had nothing in common. Nothing. The other groups there — Asian men and older couples — didn't come forth with much English. They acknowledged my niceties with nods and the cautious smiles of those who still feel like visitors in a strange land. Missing Ann more now, I began to feel the deep creep of urban isolation setting in.

In the parking lot there I talked to an out-of-uniform cop, and though he was a friendly, unofficious kind of guy, his perspective didn't help matters. If you want to feel good about the world, never talk to a police officer, not even a nice one. They know too much. Working in plain clothes, this man rode the buses in Oakland for a living. He caught people selling drugs and stealing books of transfer tickets, which they hawked at half price.

"I would expect that seeing the seamy side day after day eventually colors your view of the world," I commented, thinking of the current trend in my own demeanor.

"It saddens me to see it all," he bemoaned of our society. "There are such huge problems with youth and crime. It goes back to the parents; so many don't care."

"And even when they do, there are so many other influences in our culture," I said.

He puffed some air out of his cheeks. "The big gangs, like in LA, aren't so bad here, but we have no end of neighborhood syndicates and small groups. They fight each other and compete for crime. It's all over the Bay Area." The young cop shifted his weight and tipped his ball cap back to expose a prematurely furrowed forehead. "I just arrested a drug dealer on the corner. Another takes his place. One of the kingpins got killed off last week, 'the man.' Now there will be a bloody power struggle to see who takes over. The stakes are high, and everybody has guns. I'll tell you, from murders to petty theft, 85 percent of crime is drug related."

"What about up in the hills?" I asked, ever curious about my mountains. "What happens there?"

"Bodies are dumped in the hills. That's where the gangs and the drug traffickers take dead people to ditch them. Cars get broken into up there. East Bay parks have problems. If I were you, I'd be careful. You can get broken into anywhere. It's not just red or black cars with CD players. Vans get broken into as well. Maybe people think they're full of stolen goods or something." He glanced over at my rig — boats on top, water jugs on the back — and, I think, concurred that the notion was absurd in my particular case.

With a surprising willingness to talk, the officer continued: "I got into this work to make a difference. Now I'm just trying to keep my head above water."

He had a lot to do, and his last comment didn't leave me much to say. "Yeah, well, good luck," I wished him, thankful I didn't have to do the work he does.

"I just hope to someday win the lottery."

My own luck prevailed, and in spite of the officer's grim prognosis, I had no trouble with anybody.

Later I returned to San Francisco, where I befriended some homeless guys who collected impressive numbers of aluminum cans and redeemed them for a shopping-cart living. "Hey, you guys are saving the salmon," I congratulated them. "You know, it's aluminum smelters that use the electricity from dams on the Columbia River, and it's those dams that are driving the salmon to extinction."

"Stupid sons o' bitches," one of the men said. "We need fish more than we need these fucking cans."

I fixed him up with an extra ball cap, as the springtime sun was burning his receding hairline to a crisp and making him look even angrier than he really was. I gave another an old wool blanket that Ann didn't care much for anyway, just extra bedding to us but quite useful to him, he assured me, in the shivering, damp nights to come after San Francisco's summer fog sets in.

The fouler tempered of these two men smashed another can with a stomp of his foot and pitched the pancaked remains into his shopping cart, telling me he had been to Vietnam twenty-seven years ago. Perhaps he had been nuts before he ever got drafted. But it's certainly plausible that the war ruined him, and I may have been spared his fate only by the luck of the draw: lottery number 236. I will never forget. My draft-age colleagues up through 194 packed their bags for boot camp or Canada. Some never came back. I stayed home and protested the war they didn't want to fight in, and I enlisted in what to me was a more sensible war: the fight for a healthy environment.

The second homeless man seemed gentle of spirit, living on the streets for reasons unknown. But even though he explained nothing, I could understand his not fitting into the patterns of society.

Leaving them to sleep beneath overpasses and inside cardboard boxes, I drove the van back into the pricey Marina neighborhood where I parked each night at eleven, to retire in style. I found it harder to park there at night now than it was twenty years ago. I could tell there were now more cars per capita but no more parking spaces.

One night I had no choice but to park in front of the same house I had slept in front of the night before, and the police came knocking in the wee hours.

"Hey, buddy, the guy in the house here called up and yelled at the chief, and you're going to have to get out of here. They've got an ordinance against sleeping in your car."

"What's it hurt?" I asked the men in blue. But every single one of them hates to explain the laws they enforce, and most avoid any attempts to do so.

"Look, man, you gotta go."

Not really fearful of being busted, I drove farther west, to a quiet street nearer the Golden Gate, and settled in again for a second take on the night.

The yellow light of the city glowed above nearby buildings. Traffic inexplicably running at two A.M. produced distant white noise. A muffled foghorn hooted on the Bay. Now and then a car door thumped shut, and the steps of a walker once clicked by on the sidewalk while the chain of his dog jingled. But all in all it was quiet, remarkably quiet and peaceful for such a large city.

The loud noise in this neighborhood came during the last earthquake. Located entirely on unstable fill, including a great ooze of mud dredged from the Bay plus unconsolidated demolition debris such as boards and junked furniture from the 1906 earthquake disaster, this posh neighborhood suffered heavy damage in 1989 from a relatively minor and distant tremor. The district may well be leveled to smithereens when the Big One occurs. In what could be a truly nightmarish sequence of events, the fill beneath the streets and footings is expected to liquefy with brine; earthquakes mix artificial earthen fill and salt water as if they're dirt and water shaken together in a jar. Floating on top, but unrecognizable at that point in its history, will be the once-chic Marina District.

Yes, well, someday. I shrugged off the hazard myself with as much hope and denial as anyone. For the moment, urban living in the Marina District remains so exquisite that even well-informed people don't seem to care about the risks. They just hope their hefty investment survives intact for their lifetime, and that their lifetime isn't prematurely ended by their hefty investment crashing down on their heads.

Eventually I gave up on socializing with strangers and started calling old friends. First I met up with Mark Dubois, who had come to town for a meeting with international activists working to stop World Bank dam-building schemes that flood out whole tribes of people for a little bit of hydropower. Early in the morning we walked to the low hilltop at Fort Mason, each step opening a new view of the city and its landforms.

Years before, I had met this charismatic giant of a man, six feet, seven inches tall, when he helped lead the unsuccessful effort to save the spectacular Stanislaus River from damming. Then, branching out beyond the Sierra Nevada, he started International Rivers Network, the first organization for river protection worldwide. Now fighting for the whole globe but steeped in a lifetime of connections to California that were bound to surface in everything he saw, Mark pointed across the Bay to Angel Island, a summit of coastal mountain that peeked up beyond Alcatraz. "Some years ago I camped out there," Mark recalled. "It was back when we were working on the Stanislaus. In the morning I rolled up my sleeping bag and left the island before dawn in order to kayak over here for a meeting. I was keeping my eye peeled for freighters and tankers in the fog when all of a sudden, out of the darkness, I heard this 'Whoosh!' A V formation of cormorants was flying six feet off the water. Then another formation, and another, hundreds in all. I later learned that they roost in the East Bay for the night and then go out to sea to fish by day." Mark paused, leading me to think he was recalling more than the daily cycle of bird flight, and then added: "Right there by this huge city they reminded me of the peaceful magic of the earth, the rhythm of life that few people ever see. It still goes on, even here."

"And the mountains come right through the city as well," I said. "Tell me, Mark, as a kid, did you think of the hills here as part of the Coast Range that runs from Mexico to Oregon?"

"Growing up, I never did. The Sierra Nevada or the Klamaths were the mountains. These were just hills. I didn't even know what to call them. But then on a trip from Sacramento to here, my friend Alexander once said, 'Hey, we've got a few hours. Let's climb that mountain.' It was just off Interstate 80 where you pass through the Coast Range. So we jumped a cattle fence and jogged up the slope, finally looking out across a whole world down below, the Bay Area on one side, more hills and then the Central Valley on the other. There was an amazing continuity; you really could see how the hills linked southward to Diablo and also ran north. Down below me the city had totally changed the lower land, but the hills were still there, a lot like they were when my great-grandfather arrived during the gold rush."

PART OF THE reason the rugged Bay Area perimeter looks somewhat the way it did when Mark's ancestors arrived is the work of Larry Orman. He has as much knowledge of these hills as anyone, and he set aside some time to talk with me. His wife was off on a business appointment, so Larry bundled up their baby in a stroller and we walked through his Berkeley neighborhood.

As a teenager in San Diego, bodysurfing at the Pacific Ocean's edge, Larry had watched that pleasant city "destroy itself" with sprawl. He recalled Mission Valley as "a kid's paradise with a river and dairy farms that became shopping malls overnight." But while in Germany for a year during his undergraduate days, Larry saw that sprawl wasn't inevitable. "Over there, it's like this," he said, gesturing at the compact little houses surrounding us. "But you take one step and you're out of the city, into the country. One step. They enjoy an effective version of what we call urban growth boundaries. As a result, they have the qualities of both city and country. They have farmland so they can feed themselves; they're not totally dependent on faraway food sources that could be cut off by war. They minimize the suburban zone of asphalt, traffic, and commercial strips in favor of cities that work and countrysides that are truly rural."

"Great. But how do you make that model relevant to American culture?"

"I wondered about that, too," Larry admitted. "So I enrolled in the University of California's graduate program in urban planning. There I became involved in a Bay Area citizen group called People for Open Space."

Back during my own career as a county planner, I had heard of this nonprofit group, and I knew it had written one of the first good anti-sprawl proposals in the country. Folding in a host of citizen activists for neighborhoods, parks, farmland, trails, and land-use reform, the incipient movement sought to ensure the health of the Bay Area's towns and cities by safeguarding open space. When Larry graduated, he became director of the organization, which he later guided through its transition to a group now called the Greenbelt Alliance. "Of all the open-space approaches we could take," he said, "creating a greenbelt around the Bay Area offered the best return for our effort."

Larry had become a dean of the environmental community in the Bay Area. Gray haired, he was intensely engaged at every moment yet smiled easily at frequent ironies and mishaps in the stories he told, interrupting himself to make casual observations about the occasional skateboarder or dog walker. I could have guessed that Larry is a fine photographer — which he is — because he seemed alert to all that was around him, whether it be the repugnant architectural style of snout houses, which face the street with nothing but garage doors, or the broken limbs of eucalyptus brought down by recent winds, a sign that the winter storms were still going on.

"So what do the coastal mountains have to do with all this?"

"The mountains," Larry responded, "have to do with *everything*." As if he had been awaiting my question for years, Larry began to rattle off the connections. "This was once a tremendous agricultural area because of all the fertile soil that had eroded off the volcanic slopes. With its varied topography, the Bay Area has more different microclimates than most places in the world, and as a result, we have all kinds of agricultural niches. For example, Petaluma is great for dairies because the fog cools it in summer, and cows love cool weather. In the Central Valley they have to give the cows drugs to keep them from being heat-stressed. In the Bay Area our volcanic soils are well drained, especially on the more gently rolling hills. Because of that, the Napa Valley is one of the best wine-producing regions anywhere."

Taking another tack, he explained, "Here the San Andreas and related faults shape the land and create major hazards to development. And related to those faults, big peaks provide landmarks for community and neighborhood identity all around us. Just look at Mount Tamalpais, Mount Diablo, and Mount Saint Helena, north of Napa. Mountains are very close to people all the time. We look up and see them constantly. And from up on those ridges, you can see down and be aware of your place in the world. In the Bay Area, millions of people can go to great mountain country on the city bus, and they do."

"There's nothing else like it, is there?"

"It's vastly different from Los Angeles. When I was a kid visiting there, back when the air wasn't so bad, you could often see the mountains above that city, and with that, you had a sense of your limits. The ridges around the place made an edge. They still do, but now you hardly ever see it because of smog. Here, the mountain edges are still a real thing. People here aren't any more virtuous than in southern

California, but our open space is closer to us. And the local governments are smaller and therefore more accessible, so it's easier for
people to convince their leaders to make sounder decisions. I sometimes think we have fewer problems of all kinds overwhelming our
society here, and that leads to more people caring about the place
where they live." Finally, Larry explained that the San Francisco area
has a world-class reputation for natural beauty, and it's the hills that
make it so.

I had never thought of it in quite so stark terms, but Larry had an
interesting point. In flat terrain, you can't see the land very much,
and anything you build, no matter how squat or banal, obstructs the
view. At that point the land is out of sight, out of mind. But with hills
and mountains nearby, you can always see some land. And only by
*seeing* something do we care about it. It's often said that we protect
only what we love, but perhaps just as true, and even more basic, we
protect only what we see.

Larry ran further with this idea: "People in the Midwest are not as
engrossed in saving open space, and one reason is the fact that they
have no hills to look at from where they live. Here, people care pas-
sionately about open space because the ridges and mountains always
rise in the background. Look at all the pictures of the Bay Area on
postcards and calendars. Almost every shot has hills in it. Mountains
are the motivating force for protecting open space here. Just think
about the rich history of people's movements to safeguard the
Berkeley Hills and the Marin Headlands."

"So what does the Greenbelt Alliance try to do?"

"It tries to set boundaries for urban expansion. Beyond those lines,
you protect the land through zoning and some acquisition. A lot of
this has been done; there are good plans to protect farmland, and
public agencies have bought land where they could. But a lot of it has
not been done."

Back at home, after tucking the baby in for a nap, Larry ushered
me into his office. "Let me show you something," he said. He unrolled
a map titled "At Risk: The Bay Area Greenbelt," a collage of land use,
color-coded from a dense gray urban core through widening red

fringes threatened by sprawl and into a soothing green of farmland and mountains.

He walked me through the map and itemized the threats to his geography of home. Out of 4.5 million acres in the Bay Area, 950,000 are publicly owned. Another 750,000 are already urbanized. "What happens to the remaining 2.8 million acres will determine much about the quality of our future. During the next thirty years we may double the acreage in urban use. It's now going at the rate of ten to twenty thousand acres a year. While that's happening, we have to save what's most important."

"We need to buy more public open space to keep up with the sprawl," I suggested.

"Yes, but we'll never be able to buy enough. So the Greenbelt Alliance works mainly on getting good zoning on the ground—local regulations that limit how much development can be done on steep slopes, on ridgelines, and near parks. Mainly it seeks to limit sprawl-type growth."

Reflecting on my own experience as a planner, I asked, "Can't good zoning be undone?"

"It's a question of political will and constant vigilance. In Napa County we had a citizen initiative that locked in the zoning for thirty years. Good zoning in Marin County has held for the past three decades, with strong support to keep it. And the zoning is getting better. In the 1970s, what people called an 'agricultural' zone allowed one house per couple of acres. That's the worst thing you can do—it eliminates farmland and open space and accelerates sprawl with low-density development. The Greenbelt Alliance has succeeded in increasing agricultural lot sizes to 100 and 160 acres in some ranching areas. We need that kind of protective zoning if we want farms and ranches here in the future."

Larry convinced me that if a regulatory approach to land use can work anywhere, the Bay Area is it. The birthplace of dozens of environmental groups, including the Sierra Club, and a crucible of progressive planning going back to the 1970s, this area has legislators averaging 86 percent on environmental voting records. In contrast, southern California politicians rated 42 percent, and officials from interior California scored a retrograde 23 percent.

Larry had left the Greenbelt Alliance in 1995 and founded another nonprofit to help citizen groups use computer-generated maps. The Alliance's campaigns have continued to have remarkable success, securing urban growth boundaries by popular vote in over a dozen communities and counties and working to direct new building to sites inside cities.

Another dream of local open-space activists is the Bay Area Ridge Trail, encircling the region for four hundred thirty miles and linking together its mountain land. One-third of the ridgeline belt is now public land. To protect the rest and link it by trails is a long-term project that will take decades. But as Larry Orman said, "When you invest in a vision and stay with it for years and years, you finally get results."

ONE OF THE more significant results is the seventy-four-thousand-acre Golden Gate National Recreation Area, a bastion of public open space designated by the United States Congress in 1972, running northward for twenty miles along the Pacific coast from the southern end of San Francisco to Point Reyes National Seashore. It embraces a handful of city and state parks, historic sites, and federal land, and additional private tracts were acquired for the public estate.

The coastline, more than the mountains, was the motivation for protecting what may be the greatest urban park complex in America, but the mountains are clearly central. Because of the variable topography, habitats include seven distinct natural communities in the short jaunt from Marin County's Mill Valley, east of the oceanfront hills, to the sea. Here are salt marshes, broadleaf evergreens such as California bay, and coniferous forests including redwoods, grasslands, chaparral, coastal scrub, and ocean beaches — more varied than just about any other cross section of three and a half miles in America.

To get a feel for this area, I set out with my backpack from San Francisco and headed north on a five-day hike to Stinson Beach. I planned to take my time and sleep out, following Henry David Thoreau's advice and letting the night overtake me "everywhere at home." I carried a tent, warm clothes, my camera with three lenses, food, and four quarts of water, which is enough to see me through a whole day.

Impressed and a bit intimidated by a twelve-hour storm that had just broken up, I packed my sturdiest rain gear — a yellow slicker with overalls like the commercial fishermen wear. But the sun shone bright for now.

On Saturday afternoon at the Marina Green I joined an eyeful of runners and joggers, roller-bladers, kite fliers, power walkers, dog walkers, people in the slow flow of tai chi and the fast clip of rope-jumping, nappers in the grass, and sightseers from many nations.

I had arranged to meet my friend Tom Hicks under the southern end of the Golden Gate Bridge, and there he was, appraising the surf with kayaking in mind. He often launched his whitewater river boat there and rode the waves, occasionally getting trashed by six-foot breakers. I had met Tom through Ann when they both led wilderness river trips for Outward Bound in Utah. Inspired to help people understand the need for river conservation, he founded the Headwaters Institute, which trains commercial river guides so they can impart a conservation message to their clients. Tom and I babbled on about our lives since we'd last seen each other, a couple of years earlier, the woman he was crazy about, the frustrations of running a river education program and convincing people to help pay for it, and so forth.

Crossing the bridge was dizzying because of its height and its awesome drop to an angry tidal bore. No wonder it's the favorite leap for local bungee-jumpers and suicides. Tom and I suspended our conversation, which was drowned by the roar of traffic, a mad-commuter intensity in multiple lanes just an arm's length from our precious sidewalk.

On the northern side we wound down a path and crossed under the bridge among the girders and beefy towers of cement and steel, the Golden Gate's sixty-year-old underbelly looking like the construction site of a new skyscraper. Then we climbed above the northern abutment for a gull's-eye view. I looked down to the sudsing waters of the Bay and back south across that most memorable of all American bridges, and once again I could see the Coast Range as a continuous block, dipping here below sea level for the mile-and-a-quarter crossing to the cliffs of Fort Point in the city, to the shaded bluffs of a old army base called the Presidio of San Francisco, and to neighborhoods leading back up to Twin Peaks.

"Can you believe it?" asked Tom, a Connecticut native. "You can walk out of that city with a sleeping bag on your back and be on a trail in an hour. What a place!"

The Golden Gate's gap in the mountains is such a narrow, strategic fold in topography that impressive batteries of cannons were anchored there during World War II to defend the nation from Japanese attack. I stood on one bunker trying to imagine an armed invasion of America.

Tom and I opted for a crumbly trail that took us over rounded summits of a hard sedimentary rock called chert with views back to the city, a gleaming civilization of chalky buildings armoring multiple hills above the water. We hustled out to Point Bonita, the extremity of land on the northern side of the Gate, and stared straight down to the spumy surf, the waves unimpeded since their departure off the shores of Asia. Farther north, at Fort Cronkhite, a hundred people frolicked on the spit of sand separating sea from lagoon, and waves swept in forcefully, tackling one little boy trying to run from them. Here Tom said goodbye, returning to his San Francisco commitments. I kept going, alone now, but only for a few moments.

On the grade approaching Wolf Ridge I met Ann Marie, who, unlike younger women in the city, didn't seem to fear me. She worked for a nonprofit group that helped place senior citizens as mentors to young people. Gray haired, fit and trim, in jeans and a visor cap, she stepped right along as we chatted.

"It's nice here, isn't it?" I understated as we paused together to survey the wraparound of ocean, headlands, city.

"I've moved away three times," Ann Marie confessed, with the obvious implication that you can't move away again unless you've first returned. "First I went to New York, following a guy. Next, with my husband, to Eureka. Last, to where my daughter is living, in Eugene."

"That's a good place to live," I offered.

"It is, but I didn't like it. Too many people had a ghastly narrow-mindedness, concerned about the most petty things. When I came back to the Bay Area for the third time, I decided to stay. I'll be doing this hike for a long time."

We each waved goodbye and offered warm wishes. Ann Marie curved east toward Highway 101 while I tromped ever northward. Steep climbing took me to my first-day target, Wolf Ridge. It was late now, and with the sun dipping below the ocean's horizon, I found a swatch of grass where I could bed down unseen. I quickly heated dinner on my tiny gas stove. Then I sat and looked.

Like so many of my Coast Range views, this one linked country I now knew with other country yet to come. I saw south to the familiar Santa Cruz Mountains. Mount Tamalpais rose on a long, inviting incline to my north. Farther up the coast, Point Reyes jutted out into the ocean like a tugboat towing the continent west, and I felt like heading out there to the prow just to see where we were all going.

On day two I descended to Tennessee Valley, where thousands of people wander down a dirt road to a beguiling cove that's boxed in by cliffs, with surf crashing about and wind lofting the wings of gulls, pelicans, and cormorants. After relaxing for a while, I climbed north to airy views and then dropped to Muir Beach, where I sat and lunched until Andre rolled in.

The first person to have shown me these hills and mountains, Andre Pessis lived in a tumbledown shack along Redwood Creek twenty years ago, not far above the line of storm surges at Muir Beach. He tuned car engines by day and played music by night, ambitiously writing songs and sending them off to publishers and performers with the stereotypical California dream of making it big. Now he has. In the intervening years he has sold more than eighty songs to artists such as Bonnie Raitt and Huey Lewis, whose hit "Walking on a Thin Line" is about the difficulties of a Vietnam War veteran Andre knew. The pace of success has changed Andre's life, but he took time off to meet me there and compare notes on our recent pasts. I was delighted that Kimberly, his partner of fifteen years, came along, and after I ditched my pack in their car, we all strolled across the beach and up the steep trail to an overlook above the sea.

Stories of arrival in California are often, like my own, tales of seek-

ing a new and creative career, of reinvesting in the vigor of life after a
failed marriage, of grasping for something golden in youth or in
midlife years, when you realize that you have to stretch or you'll never
really live. People come here to open pathways to a life considered
impossible elsewhere, if indeed such alternatives are considered
elsewhere at all.

When we all sat down on the ground at the overlook, I sprang my
favorite question. "Kimberly, how did you happen to arrive here?"

"In California? Oh, by a long, roundabout road. Do you really want
to know?"

"Sure I do," I assured her. "I collect arrival stories like some people
collect pretty stones on the beach."

Kimberly leaned against Andre, and her eyes rolled up at the
clouds as she thought about where to begin.

"Okay. My mother and father were from Pennsylvania and Ohio.
They were having problems and decided to get a fresh start by going
to California. I guess it was a common belief that you could *do* that
back then—that some new *place* could help you. And maybe it was
true. After all, those were the golden days of this state. So with four
kids and a dog in the car we all set out for Stockton, in the Central
Valley, where my father knew someone. But in Texas we ran out of
money, and Dad had to take a job in a slaughterhouse for three weeks.
When he came back to where we were camping we about gagged, he
stunk so badly of dead animals. I don't know how he did it.

"After the first payday we moved on, staying in motels with bed-
bugs. When we crossed the desert, the car started steaming, and Dad
peed in a bottle because the radiator leaked and we had no water to
add to it. Finally, we broke down for good in Provo, Utah, and stayed
four years. Dad took jobs anywhere he could find work. I loved it
there, living among the Mormons. They were nice to us, but Dad
didn't like them because they were always trying to convert him.
Eventually we got a new car and made it to Stockton. Five hard years
after we left Pennsylvania, everyone faced the truth and admitted
that, for all we'd gone through, the place was awful. So we moved to
San Jose after Dad got a job at Lockheed. He and Mom stayed there.
But as soon as I turned eighteen, I moved to San Francisco to live

with my sister. It was 1961. I had to go to work, full-time, right away. I've been working ever since, for the last hundred years, it seems."

Cloud cover was beginning to thicken overhead, nothing threatening but enough to give me the slightest bit of a chill. "You all earned a little California sunshine, since getting here took five years," I said.

"Three days for me," Andre chimed in with his sly little repressed smile.

His story, though less wholesome by degrees of magnitude, was no less wrought with fate, consequence, and hope.

"In New York City it was dirty and violent," he began. "Everybody I knew was on drugs. I was on drugs, too, and didn't see any way to fit into the bigger system. It was all so perverted. I went to work for my dad, but that was a disaster. I got a job with UPS loading packages but then got drafted just after Vietnam had heated up. I already knew guys who had gone to the war, and I wanted nothing to do with it. That war just wasn't right, and I didn't want to be a part of the killing. As stupid as I was back then, that's one thing I did know." The three of us sat there on the ground and laughed at the strange ways knowledge comes to us.

"When my army physical was scheduled and I saw I really had to go, I got an appointment with a psychologist. I acted severely withdrawn. He wrote a letter saying I was mentally ill. When I went into the physical, buck naked in line with all those other guys, I chewed and slobbered all over my papers. I acted pretty weird, which didn't take a whole lot of practice. I sweated this out quite a bit. Then, when I got the letter saying I was rejected, I said, 'Yeah! I'm *free!*'"

As Andre paused, I asked, "So what did you do back then if you were really free?"

"Simple. You went to California."

"But it couldn't be that easy, arriving here," I replied, holding my hands open to the Pacific Ocean below while the moist wind slipped up the hillside and ruffled my hair.

"No. In fact, it got quite bizarre at that point. With this girl I had just met, I got a drive-away car—somebody needed to have it driven to San Francisco. They allowed five days, so I bombed out in three, at a hundred five miles per hour. It's a wonder we lived, but, you see, that gave me two days to look around with the car. I stopped at a gas station and asked the first person I saw — a black guy — where he'd live if he could live anywhere at all. He said Muir Beach. Julide and I came out for a look, and I couldn't believe how beautiful it was. But there was no place to live out here, not for cheap, anyway. Then everything got way bad. Julide was Turkish, incredibly exotic looking. But as with other exotic things, after a while you realize that what you *thought* you had was not what you *really* had at all. She was cheating on me whenever I was gone. Then she took acid and totally flipped out. I felt horrible because I was the one who gave her the drugs. So I decided to do the right thing and take care of her until she got better. It took a long time, but what I eventually learned was that she had always been flipped out. Her name was beautiful — it's pronounced 'Julie-day'— but in Turkish it means 'chaos.' She couldn't have been better named."

"A relationship can bend your life in strange ways," I offered.

Andre raised and lowered his eyebrows in agreement. "No kidding. But after six months, Julide left me, and for the second time in a year I said, 'Yeah! I'm *free!*' Suddenly everything came up roses. I scored a job in a band with these guys who fortunately had very bad taste and hired me as a singer. We started getting jobs. We opened for Van Morrison. The next thing I did was move out to Muir Beach."

"Andre, do you mind if I repeat this story?"

"No. Hey, everybody's entitled to a wild and crazy youth, and I had mine, that's for sure."

The three of us looked down into the valley where Andre's shack used to be, where I had visited and camped in my van along the creek when I first came to live in California, in 1980.

I'm one of those people who took to the road when their first marriage failed, though in my unusual case, I had already intended to do this. I just ended up doing it alone, and for a much longer time than I had planned. Instead of launching short trips to collect writing material, followed by months of work at home, I ended up on one grand journey that has continued for twenty years so far.

Like Kimberly and Andre in their own arrival stories, I had some bad luck that turned into good. At the time of my breakup, I had just received a contract from the University of California Press to write a book about Mark Dubois' dam fight on the Stanislaus River. Much like my friends, I came to California unrooted, and even at that late date—long after the California-dreaming days that drew others so powerfully—I liked what I found. But unlike Andre and Kimberly, who settled down, I have come and gone, owing to my writing choices, my geographic curiosity, and my efforts to find the right relationship with a woman. This final goal was like searching for a needle in a haystack, at which I finally succeeded when Ann miraculously appeared six years ago.

My continuing itinerancy does not leave me feeling homeless. On the contrary, I feel at home in many places, and one of them used to be just below where the three of us now sat. I had parked there at Andre's place, working at the wooden desk in my van, sharing meals and heartbreak stories of my personal life with my car-mechanic, songwriting, rock-and-roll buddy. Like me, Andre had recently been through a breakup with his woman partner of ten years.

Though our pasts were incomparably different—our lives on entirely divergent paths, our professions and avocations in fully separate circles—Andre and I became good friends. Not the slightest bit judgmental and with an anchor of common sense that his own checkered past might seem to belie, Andre became a fine sounding board, supportive in the best kind of way, which includes room for disagreement. He would tell me if he thought I was off-base. Plus it was fun for a serious guy like me to be around someone with his sense of humor.

I'd scarcely seen Andre in the past fifteen years, but today it felt good to be sitting together again, perched on that mountain with him and Kimberly. Each of us had traveled far and adventurously in order to be where we finally were.

Like Andre's old life and mine, the Muir Beach cabin site was now completely grown over. A strangling jungle of young alder trees blanketed the place like vines on a Mayan ruin.

"There's no sign of the cabin," I said, pointing that way, a bit of wistfulness in my voice.

"It's gone," Andre confirmed, "except for some wild squashes growing out of our old compost heap."

"And a lot of memories."

"That's just the way it ought to be," Andre said, turning away from the direction of reverie where I was headed. "In fifteen years down there, we were flooded five times. That place was *made* for alder trees. After all those floods, the sound of hard rainfall still drives me nuts. I have to use earplugs during heavy storms. I'm glad we live on a hill now. We don't have the ocean out the front door, but we can walk right onto the mountain whenever we want. We do it every few days. Trails connect directly into our street from Mount Tamalpais."

We walked back to the car. I fooled with my pack a bit, keeping the conversation going for a while. Then there was no denying that it was time to go.

"Hey, have you heard the weather report?" Andre asked with a wrinkled brow and a sideways glance. "It's supposed to rain for five days. Hard at times. You know what that means. I might have my earplugs in, but give me a call if you need somebody to come blot you up out of the mud."

The afternoon had flown by. To bivouac for the night, I retraced my steps southward and back up the hill to a remote little bench and pitched the tent, a bit of emptiness in my heart. Having been warmed by my old friendship, I felt lonely now. But looking around, I took some satisfaction in the fact that just across the valley lay Muir Woods, a redwood grove named for John Muir, whose ghost — just figuratively speaking, of course — accompanies me many places I go.

Coming here one century before me, he was America's first great land preservationist, an eloquent disciple of wilderness, an itinerant traveler, and an enthusiastic commentator on the land of his time. He might have once sat right there where I camped, also alone and looking down at the redwoods later to be named for him.

I would cross paths with this predecessor of mine repeatedly in my travels from here north, and I can't help but contrast Muir's sensuous passion for nature with the response of his contemporary J. Smeaton Chase. While Chase's *California Coast Trails* is interesting and revealing of trail routes and daily life, Muir's work explodes with vitality and the love of raw elements. Chase took shelter in pubs and stables; Muir climbed the tallest tree so he could sway like a bobolink on a reed in the midst of a mountain storm. It is Muir, of course, who kindles my spirit, who lived a life of learning about nature and embracing it wholeheartedly. "Climb the mountains and get their good tidings," he advised. "Nature's peace will flow into you as the sunshine into the trees. The winds will blow their freshness into you, and the storms their energy, while cares will drop off like autumn leaves."

Marin gentleman William Kent bought the redwoods across the valley specifically to save them from logging, only to have the local water company then try to condemn his land for a dam and reservoir. Ingeniously thwarting this plan, Kent gave his three hundred acres to the federal government and persuaded President Theodore Roosevelt to declare them a national monument in 1908. Though Kent had not met Muir, he admired the man's work and so had the park named in his honor. With a message just as relevant today as it was then, Muir wrote to Kent thanking him for saving the redwood Eden: "How it shines amid the mean commercialism and apathy so destructively prevalent these days." Perhaps this is silly, but with Muir's woods across the valley, I no longer felt alone.

In the opposite direction the sun set, so picturesque, so California-like in beauty, though behind a thickening screen of moisture. The wind had picked up, noticeably damp and southerly as it pressed against my face and left me feeling clean and refreshed but not entirely dry or secure.

No doubt, the weather was changing. That's the way it is at this season, early spring. A southerly wind often announces the approach of a low-pressure system that brings rain, in a fascinating interplay of weather I'd been trying to understand ever since I left Baja. As much as the geologic formation of the Coast Range itself, the imperatives of climate affected everything I would see and do for as long as I was in these mountains, so the weather was worth understanding.

THE BIG PICTURE all begins with the Pacific High weather system, a high-pressure zone that dominates the West Coast of the United

States south of Oregon. It's the northern end of the same high-pressure zone we experienced in Baja, and it results after the warm, moist air of the Tropics has risen with its impressive heat, rained on the equatorial latitudes of the earth, and then cooled off at a higher elevation, become heavy, and descended back to the earth, hitting most effectively through the 25- to 40-degree latitude range. The northern end of this — the 40-degree line — is at Chemise Mountain, one hundred seventy miles north of San Francisco, though the High in early summer can expand to fill most of the Gulf of Alaska.

As this high-pressure mass of heavy, cool, dry air descends to the earth, it warms up, further diminishing the possibility of rain because the descending and therefore warming air retains water vapor better. It also spreads out as it comes down, and it expands. This creates the Pacific High pressure zone, centered in the northeastern Pacific, which pushes away other air, including storms to the north and south.

In the Northern Hemisphere, outward-flowing air such as this is deflected to the right, or clockwise. This is because of the Coriolis effect: a motion independent of the earth's surface, such as wind, will not appear to follow a straight line because the spherical earth is turning all the time underneath while the wind blows.

Owing to the Pacific High's center out in the ocean and to the clockwise spinning of the high-pressure air mass, the descending winds consistently approach California from the northwest in the warm months from April to November.

In contrast, the storms that hit the Coast Range are often bred in the Aleutian Low — a low-pressure zone residing north of the Pacific High. The low-pressure trough advances southward when the otherwise repelling high-pressure dome moves toward the equator in winter. Exactly the opposite of high-pressure zones, low-pressure areas are made of rising air, which cools as it climbs and is therefore unable to hold its water vapor. This promptly condenses as rain or snow. Because this air is flowing in toward the low-pressure vortex, the storm centers spin in a counterclockwise motion, and as they advance from west to east, the leading edge of this spin is often felt as wind from the south.

As a result of all this, California has its Mediterranean climate of dry summers owing to the Pacific High and wet winters owing to the southward-dipping storm track bred in the Aleutian Low. In January and February, when the Pacific High recedes to its seasonal weakest, the storm track advances southward.

The farther north you go, the less effective is the high-pressure system and the wetter and longer the winter. For example, the rainy season in southern California occurs in December through February, a short siege. Even at that, the storms are often few and weak. But on the northern coast of California the rainy season runs from November through April and includes predictably big storms of long duration. In British Columbia, plentiful rains often begin in August, with September and October the wettest months. In southern Alaska — beyond the normal reach of the Pacific High — it's often rainy year-round except for May, June, and July, and even then storms can come at any time and cloud cover can dominate.

By now, in March, the storm track had usually retreated up to northern California, but it could still slip down whenever it found a weakness in the repelling winds of the Pacific High, which is exactly what I was seeing in play from my campsite perched between Muir Woods and the big, wet Pacific.

To understand the weather here, you also have to know about the enmeshed relationship between sky and ocean. Prevailing winds of the Pacific High push the water at the surface of the sea enough to create the California Current, which runs southeastward along the West Coast. This moderates the summertime temperature of the land by cooling it with water brought down from the north. Because the Coriolis effect turns the southbound ocean currents to the right, the surface currents angle away from the coastline. To replace the blown-away surface water, cold water from deep oceanic canyons wells up and stirs undersea nutrients responsible for marine life and the once-rich commercial fishery of the West Coast.

When this cold water from the upwelling comes in contact with the relatively warm and moist atmosphere above it, the air next to the sea is rapidly cooled, bringing it down to its dew point, which causes the water vapor to condense. This explains the frequent summer fog along the coast of northern California and Oregon. If the high-pressure system weakens, the winds subside, the upwelling decreases, the surface-water temperature increases, and the fog is minimized.

But the fog hangs just offshore much of the time, and the only question is how far inland it will come. Because it's generally clear and cloudless above the fog layer in summer, the sun tends to burn the fog off soon after it reaches land, if not before. But strong winds can carry the fog miles inland. For example, when central California heats up in the summer, that hot inland air—growing lighter the hotter it gets—rises rapidly above the Central Valley and blasts like a furnace blower up the slopes of the Sierra Nevada. To take its place, prevailing eastbound winds suck in the damp ocean air through topographic gaps such as the Golden Gate or the Klamath and Eel River canyons. The inland fog that results is responsible for the dairy belt Larry Orman talked about as well as the redwood belt of northern California. Those trees need the summer moisture provided by the fog.

In winter, the encroachment of the Aleutian Low causes the wind to shift. Instead of coming from the northwest, it often comes from the southwest. Following its lead, a northbound ocean flow called the Davidson Current is created along the West Coast and brings warm water in from the south, further moderating the temperature in what was already a very moderate system.

While the maritime influence evens out the temperature throughout the year all along the Coast Range's Pacific front, it also causes microclimates that offer variety unimagined in other regions of the country. San Francisco can be shrouded in summertime fog while the East Bay bakes in sun. A couple of city blocks can make all the difference. The mountains play into this mosaic of microclimate, blocking the fog or clouds here, whisking them along there. The gap through the Golden Gate, for example, gives winter storms unfettered access far inland; the effect can be seen two hundred miles away in the Sierra Nevada, where huge dumps of snow are delivered downwind from the Coast Range's most notable gap.

Now for one more complication people have heard a lot about since its broad implications first became known in 1983: El Niño is a condition of warm ocean water that affects Pacific currents, storms, fog, fisheries — the whole works. This important weather-making phenomenon begins way down in the tropical Pacific. There, near the equator, where the water heats up intensely, prevailing winds are governed by low-latitude temperatures and the spinning of the earth. These winds do not blow to the east, as they do at temperate latitudes farther from the equator, but rather to the west. This powerful force literally piles up water on the west side of the ocean. The accumulation of tropical waters skimmed off the top of the sea — the warmest of the warm — can be two feet higher in the Philippines than at the eastern side of the ocean bordering the Americas. But — and here's what counts for us — the west-blowing winds periodically subside for reasons unknown, and sometimes they even reverse, allowing the heavily heated water, on top of colder ocean layers, to level out by sloshing back across the Pacific. This redistributes the warm water to the eastern, or American, side, raising sea level and boosting ocean temperatures by ten degrees or more.

With warmer El Niño water lapping here on the eastern side of the Pacific, the air above it is warmed as well and therefore holds more vapor, so storms become more common in the Tropics. These effects cause the jet stream of upper-elevation air currents to shift, often resulting in wet winters in the southwestern United States and dry ones in the Pacific Northwest. In California, the effects are often split, though some notoriously wet winters in the Bay Area have accompanied El Niño.

The warm ocean water of the El Niño cycle also reduces upwelling and so results in less fog and markedly poorer ocean conditions for fish. In the 1980s and 1990s, the effects of El Niño were far more pronounced than ever before, leading some climatologists to suspect global warming as a cause.

There at my high and exposed campsite in the shoulder season of spring, the Pacific High had faltered, allowing rainfall to approach the coast. Further biting into my comfort zone, the clouds were pushed up over the mountains, causing the air to cool, which would force it to drop even more water. Mountaintops of the Coast Range often receive three times the rainfall of nearby land at sea level. The precipitation can increase by an inch annually for each fifty feet of rise — an interesting prospect, since I planned to hike to the top of Mount Tamalpais the next day.

A gust of tepid southerly air rustled the tent in the early morning hours and then ripped at it just before dawn. I knew what was coming, so I scurried out at the first grayness of dawn, yanked the stakes, gathered the poles, and stuffed all my gear in my pack for safekeeping.

I headed down the trail in the faintest morning light, and even with a heavy breath of jeopardy in the air, I didn't feel threatened. Rather, my spirit surged with joy at the freedom of backpacking — of facing the world with whatever I could carry and being free to go wherever my legs wanted to take me. The sense of being capable pleased me deeply, though something else was also at play.

Creature comforts had been left behind. Andre's offer notwithstanding, technological backup — such as catching a ride if I didn't want to walk — was not an option. Now even the sunshine had been taken away from me. Yet I still had what I needed, and those essentials seemed all the more satisfying because of scarcity. The more that's taken away, the more precious is what remains.

The threat of the storm strangely intensified this scarcity-based euphoria. I could hike in my rain suit; I could survive the storm by pitching my tent wherever I needed to. At least I hoped so.

On a picnic table at Muir Beach I broke out my breakfast cereal when the first spit of rain caught me on the cheek. A National Park Service maintenance man was cleaning up the weekend's trash, and I commiserated with him about the piggish nature of our fellow citizens. "Weatherman's calling for heavy rain and high winds," he warned, eyeing my pack.

Hustling on with visions of a wooded grove sheltering me from the storm's direct onslaught, I made my way up the highway north of Muir Beach and reconnected with the Pacific Coast Trail where it angled off the road toward Mount Tamalpais. As I aimed toward my destination, layers of cloud descended from the summit like cream poured over the top. The sky's darkening gray kept pace with the sun's hidden rise and lent an increasingly ominous feel to the morning. Four mountain bikers rattled down the studded trail so fast they looked as if they were engaged in deliberate full-body vibration as some new brand of California therapy. The last one stopped long enough to tell me, with dripping eyebrows, that the air was thick up above.

At my first opportunity I abandoned the trail and crested eastward over the ridge to gain some wind shelter on a well-drained slope. Near the umbrella of a fir grove but not quite in it because poison oak grew thickly there, I pitched the tent. No sooner had I crawled in than the first big drops, like chilling pellets, stung the fly, pinging off its tightly guyed surface and then pattering as wetness softened the fabric. There I stayed, prone or propped in my Crazy Creek chair, the wind beating on nylon threads, the rain pouring by the bucketload. With just cloth between me and the storm, I registered nuances in wind, in drop size, in rainfall intensity that I never notice when indoors. Just a few miles from San Francisco, battened down in my tent for nineteen hours, it occurred to me that you don't need to go to Tasmania or Kodiak Island to find some really foul weather.

I read a book, napped, wrote notes, and peed in a Ziploc bag, which I then reached out into the downpour to dump. The alternative—going outside—would have drenched me in one second flat. After dark, at eight o'clock, the wind eased but the deluge did not. Finally, at three in the morning, the rain quit.

Well rested after this hibernation, I stepped out of the tent at daybreak. As soon as I hit the trail, a bombardment of hail punctuated the end of the storm and announced the arrival of a colder wedge of air blowing up under the warmer rain clouds. This had rapidly cooled the clouds and produced the stinging grand finale of the storm, potentially a good sign for the weather ahead. With luck, it would not rain for five days as Andre had warned.

Mount Tamalpais is a backyard, a recreational escape, a physical fitness course, a social medium, a spiritual quest, a natural history lab, a meeting place for trysts, a red-tailed hawk's home, a tourist destination, an afternoon shadow on trendy towns to the east, a landmark to sailors at sea, and a dazzling backdrop to views all over the Bay Area. Selecting from a maze of trails, I strode briskly through shining green meadows and glades where rainwater still clung like jewels to grass and spiced the smells of willow, Douglas-fir, and chamise. The Coulter pine gave way to chaparral on south-facing slopes. I traversed toward the summit, weaving in and out of bay-scented canyons and climbing, always climbing, the weather brightening as I went.

At the top I found a small and immiscible collection of local residents and tourists, who, like birds, had appeared as soon as the storm passed. Kids played hide-and-go-seek among the rocks, and mountain bikers walked the final pedestrian pitch to the 2,571-foot summit, which tops out a scant three miles from the Pacific. To the west I could see the ocean fading out beyond the curve of our globe, a sight that never fails to thrill me, though I'm sure that if I had been at sea for months or weeks or maybe even just a few hours, the sight of Mount Tam rising as dry land would thrill me even more.

As the most seaworthy evidence of the Coast Range, twenty-two miles offshore the Farallon Islands jutted up out of the Pacific, almost mystical in their partially seen nature. During a fifty-year period beginning with the gold rush, twelve million bird's eggs had been plucked off that jagged hundred eleven granitic acres for the sourdoughs' breakfasts. A national wildlife refuge now protects the Farallons as one of the largest seabird colonies in the contiguous states.

To my south, the Marin Headlands, which I had just spent three days crossing, folded down like a topographic model, and beyond the span of the Golden Gate Bridge the city shone like a fictitious Mediterranean capital.

Clouds rose from valleys all around me while the ample moisture of the rainstorm reevaporated, in places spiraling upward as if Olympic-sized vats of water were being boiled for corn-on-the-cob down below. Mount Diablo rose darkly in the southeast, so cone-like that I could imagine it smoking in volcanic revenge at the suburbia clawing at its base. The real roar of Highway 101 lofted the whole way up to the top of Mount Tam, even though the road was so distant and shielded that I could scarcely see it. To the east, the neighborhoods of Sausalito and Marin City flattened out into the Bay on fill dumped decades ago to make more land out of precious wetlands once considered worthless.

Finally, to the north, I saw hills and hills, mountains and mountains, lime-colored *potreros* and snag-top tufts of conifers. Redwoods greened the gulches where the fog clung tight even at midday, and clouds grayed the background of distant new lands where I was headed.

When I climbed up one side of a rock and down the other, I found myself next to a little girl with her lunch spread out. "This is my home," she announced without reserve. "What are *you* doing here?"

A bit intimidated by this possessive little thing, I said, "Me? I'm taking pictures and looking for a place to eat my own lunch."

"It's pretty here, but I wish that God had a camera in heaven and could take pictures there for us."

"Maybe they'd look just like this."

"I'll bet they would look ten times prettier than this."

"Emily!" I heard her mother yell from another rock nearby.

As I left, Emily said, "I hope that you have a *job* taking pictures, and that you get money for them."

Chewing on the little girl's overly hopeful expectations for the hereafter as well as my own career, I ate lunch in a rocky enclave at the summit. Then I reloaded my pack and began the long declination toward Stinson Beach.

Some distance off the trail, on a skinny bench of land edging a steep meadow, I camped one more time, buttoning up every stitch of clothes to stay warm in the biting north wind. As I finished dinner to a star-collecting sky, the nighttime city shone once more in the distance, craftily framed left, right, and above by the silhouetted limbs of oaks. Beyond them, fir trees serrated the hills, which were alive with the hoot of a great horned owl and the yip of a coyote. The Bay's Golden Gate outlet lay roughened in white moonlight as if fish had left a million little tracks on it. I squirmed deep into my sleeping bag, the lights of San Francisco sparkling out my front door, so near but so far.

The last day's descent toward Stinson Beach took me to gloriously undulant grasslands with oaks standing magisterially at meadow's edge, deer on the lookout with perked ears, and the ocean beating in surf far, far down. The waves advanced unstoppably in parallel lines

—from that elevation I could see hundreds of them at once—evidence of the wind and the weather, which governs everything along this mountainous seashore. To the northwest, Point Reyes rose sharply as the leading edge of land.

I RETURNED once again to San Francisco, Ann returned from her trip east, and together we headed directly to the Point Reyes National Seashore for a happy reunion at one of the seismic hot spots of our trip.

After its long severing of California's southern interior and central coast, the San Andreas Fault first launches out to sea just south of San Francisco; then it briefly returns inland at Stinson Beach for the twelve miles necessary to lop off the Point Reyes Peninsula, almost making it an island. Leaving Highway 1 there, Ann and I crossed again to the Pacific Plate, where for several days we would content ourselves with drifting north at the tectonic pace, headed for Alaska in millions of years rather than our van rate, which would pop us up there by July if all went well.

We skirted the western side of Tomales Bay, more descriptively called Earthquake Bay because it overlays the fault. Capping the ridge above us, the granitic rocks of Point Reyes had journeyed from the Tehachapi Mountains region of the Transverse Ranges north of Los Angeles, delivered by the ongoing slip of the Pacific Plate. It's difficult for the untrained eye to see fault scarps because eroding soils soften the lines and plants grow over them, plus some faults lie deep underground, but along the Rift Zone Trail we could see in a straightforward display how the 1906 earthquake had realigned a fence. While the North American Plate portion stayed put, the Pacific Plate side leapt northwest sixteen feet—by any measure a lot for inanimate rock. The tremor registered 8.25 on the Richter scale, or 7.7 on a scale called the moment magnitude scale, which geologists are now using.

Standing on a grassy hillside studded with oaks and imagining such raw power of the earth is one thing; imagining it in the cities straddling the fault lines is another. The San Francisco earthquake and the fires it triggered destroyed 490 city blocks and 28,000 buildings.

The response was to cover up the losses and loosen building restrictions in order to expedite reconstruction. How our governments would deal with such a disaster today is beyond anybody's grasp.

But offering some clue about this, the Loma Prieta earthquake, giving a little shoulder-shake to the Bay Area in 1989, damaged 21,000 homes and commercial buildings and caused $8 billion in losses during a few tremorous moments. One section collapsed on the upper deck of the San Francisco–Oakland Bay Bridge, a span on which four thousand people are crossing at almost any given time. Loma Prieta, it turns out, released only one-thirty-fifth the energy of the 1906 quake, and its epicenter was seventy miles away from San Francisco and twelve miles underground. For this relatively minor event, analysts reported that all emergency response systems were stretched to the max.

The real hazards are not from the moving earth but from falling cement and shattering glass, from ruptured gas lines that explode and incinerate, from collapsing overpasses that crush cars like pennies flattened on railroad tracks so that you can't even make out Abe Lincoln anymore. When the Big One comes — and a large quake is due in the Los Angeles area or the Bay Area soon — I'd rather be in this grassy field at Point Reyes, where a shower of acorns will most likely be the main hazard.

Standing in that field, face to sky, foot to dirt, one could almost say, "Go ahead, God, bring it on." The only sizable earthquakes I've felt have been in wild areas, once in the southern Sierra Nevada, when the earth roared, rocks tumbled from cliffs, and branches quivered as if ten-ton gophers were tugging on the roots of pine trees. I happened to be sitting on the ground at the time, eating cereal. It was a wondrous experience, reminding me of John Muir's response when a rock-splitting tremor shook his own Yosemite Valley. "A noble earthquake!" he exclaimed in one of his quaintest quotes.

Parklands such as Point Reyes pose few earthquake hazards compared with urban death traps on the fault line, but this could have changed at several junctures in recent history. With what must have been a sense of corporate exemption from natural law, the Pacific Gas and Electric Company planned a nuclear reactor at the fault line along Bodega Bay, just north of Tomales Bay where the San Andreas again slices across a small neck of peninsula. Before that, in 1961, the state proposed expanding Highway 1 to six lanes here, which would have made Point Reyes as accessible to San Francisco as Malibu is to Los Angeles. Then, in 1967, the Bolinas Harbor Plan proposed the dredging of a lagoon for a sixteen-hundred-boat marina, and in 1971 a subdivision plat was drawn for a new city of fifty thousand people huddled along the fault east of Tomales Bay. All these ventures were stopped, but not without strong citizen campaigns.

In one of those, conservationists persuaded Congress to designate the area as Point Reyes National Seashore. Dairy farmers' opposition was muted when they were given life tenancy and long-term agreements to continue farming. A 1965 master plan called for a plethora of new roads and park development, but the National Park Service bowed to the public outcry and left the Point mostly the way it was.

For the big overview of this flagship of America's national seashore system, Ann and I hiked to the top of Mount Wittenberg, at 1,470 feet the highest summit on the peninsula. Girthy Douglas-firs shaded the ravines. Bishop pines cooled the hillsides. Bay trees, which I often think of as small, grew to oakish dimensions. The morning fog slowly burned off above Drake's Estero and from the rocky barrier of Point Reyes itself. Home to seals and sea lions, signpost to whales that navigate offshore, this six-hundred-foot cliff lay bared to the wind and waves. Salty mist swirled as the surf pummeled the land out there, a place with some of the windiest weather ever clocked. It once blew fifty miles per hour for nine days—winds strong enough to knock down chimneys and uproot trees. For twenty-four hours it once blew eighty miles per hour, with gusts up to a house-crushing hundred twenty.

Much as Point Conception marked a geographic boundary in southern California, Point Reyes is a turning point at this latitude. Thirty-four species of plants reach their northern limits here in Marin County, so we would not see them again on our trip. But ninety-seven reach their southern limits, and for them we would keep our eyes peeled as we traveled north.

On another day we hiked to the far northern end of the peninsula, where tule elk have been reintroduced, replacing cows after a century-long reign of the bovine. There at Tomales Point, on the northern extremity of Point Reyes, the San Andreas Fault strikes back out to sea.

Though a ceiling of fog blocked the sun from dawn to dusk, the bottom hundred feet of atmosphere remained clear, and as we advanced down a long slope to the final spur of land separating the bay and the full-blown Pacific, our view opened up to breakers and waves terrorizing the rocks. Nonchalant about it all, orange-billed oystercatchers pecked at limpets in the splash zone as if it were just another lunch counter.

We stepped out to the very point where the cutting edge of land meets the erosive blade of surf, and I wondered how another sixteen-foot northward lunge would feel there, on the prow of the Pacific Plate.

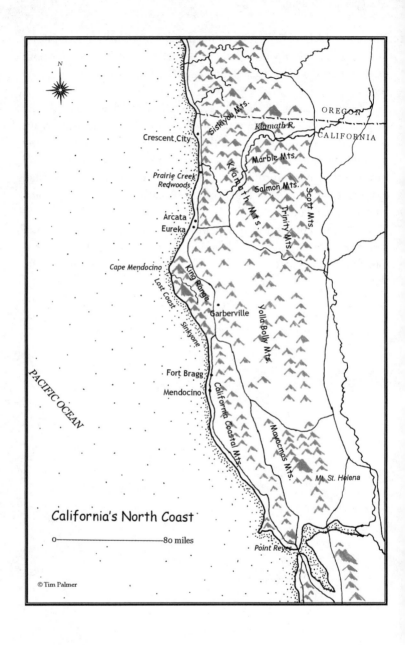

# California's North Coast

0 ——————————— 80 miles

© Tim Palmer

# 8 The North Coast

U NTIL YOU'RE lost somewhere east of Mendocino, you don't have any idea what kind of mountain range is up here," said Ronnie James. Like a lot of other people, she had moved from urban California to the North Coast, meaning the Pacific front north of San Francisco. A slight woman, she had hair that bounced in dark curls, a face that expressed a full range of emotions, and a presence that reflected a no-nonsense grip on the world.

"People think everything you own up here mildews. That's definitely true. They think that housing is substandard, that wages are low and services poor. That's all generally true. They think that the population is a bit strange, and there may be some truth to that. They think that if they step off the road they'll get shot by a pot grower. That's not true, though I suppose it is possible."

"But you've survived," I said.

"Yes. I stay on the trails when I go walking in the parks, and I don't go hiking on private land at all."

"Except when gathering mushrooms?" I asked, aware that the skeins of tan, ochre, and purple yarn lying around her house had been colored with wild mushroom dye.

"Well, yes, I do wander around in the woods then. And it can be pretty creepy at the height of the season."

Ronnie grew up in the San Francisco Bay Area, lived for seventeen years in the Central Valley city of Modesto, and then moved to the university town of Davis, where she stayed for ten years. "It was fine at first," she said of this half-step north, "but then I started getting sick all the time. Bronchitis, the flu, an aching back, insomnia. You name it, I suffered it in the Central Valley. It's horrible for allergies and exposure to pesticides, and the place has an epidemiologic history all its own. My great escape was to drive up the coast, which I had been doing for a long time. I camped in the Mendocino Woodlands as a Girl Scout when I was nine years old. I think the place got into my blood that way. Whenever I came up here, I felt *great.* So the minute both boys graduated from high school, I was on the way."

A steady rainfall of two days' duration drummed on the roof of Ronnie's wood-frame home south of Mendocino, a late-season storm but nothing unusual where the "free water" days of rainfall can number well over a hundred per year. "After desert-like Davis, the climate must have required an adjustment," I suggested.

"Only in the positive sense. I *love* the rain. When the winter storms start in November, I'm thrilled. Yes, it rained ninety days in a row one winter. That was a bit much. But the green outside suits me. And the green under your carpet — you learn to deal with that. When the real estate agent brought me down this driveway and I saw the redwood trees, and the rain was pounding on the ground, I knew this was the place. It wouldn't be what it is without the rain."

"No rain, no redwoods, no mushrooms," Ann threw in.

"Oh, yes," Ronnie acknowledged, "back to the mushroom season. You wouldn't believe the competition. Some people carry guns. They stake out territories, informally, of course, because they're either on public land or on private property, where they trespass. At a minimum they're armed with a knife, because you cut the mushrooms with a knife. So there I am, a lone woman in the woods with a bunch of guys carrying knives and guns. I tell them I'm looking for dye mushrooms. Those are different species from the edibles. But mainly I avoid other gatherers, especially the scuzzballs who collect commercially by raking the ground, which of course destroys the fungi. It's the mushroom equivalent of strip mining for the sake of gourmet restaurants and big sales to Japan. There's virtually no regulation. You're supposed to get a permit for gathering on state land, but the agencies don't have funding for enforcement."

Settling into her chair and propping her slippered feet on a coffee table, Ronnie reflected further to Ann and me about the idiosyncrasies of her adopted homeland. "Employment in the North Coast tradition of logging actually peaked in 1954. Except in mill towns such as Fort Bragg, few people now work in timbering." In my own reading about the area, I had learned that once the big trees were cut, many of the logging companies moved on, just as they had done a century ago when they left the East to come to California. This time they went back to the Southeast, where politics are easy to manipulate and where their pulp crop regrows quickly. Or they moved on to Indonesia and Siberia, where there are no regulations. "Cut and run" still seems to be the operative phrase.

As loggers and their families abandoned the North Coast for work elsewhere, hippies in great numbers moved in during the 1970s, buying rural properties where they could live closer to the land, plant a garden for subsistence, and perhaps cultivate a modest commercial plot of marijuana. North Coast author Ray Raphael described this movement as "a reaction against the materialistic excesses and spiritual complacency of mainstream America." He wrote that "the new pioneers wanted to recreate a new society on the outer edge of the old." With the unexpected infusion of low-key wealth, local businesses, including many with otherwise extreme intolerance to the counterculture, were reinvigorated in a curious two-way assimilation. But then big money led to industrial-scale drug operations and a nasty web of competition and violence during the 1980s.

"Now," Ronnie resumed in her own short course on local history, "the tourist business is big and all kinds of people have moved in. Most of the servers waiting on tables have college degrees. They're here because they want to be, or because they're escaping something somewhere else. Myself among them. For one reason or another they just can't live out there over the hill. A lot of them simply won't tolerate the frenetic pace of the mainstream culture. We also have our share of misfits, including modern hate groups. You know who I mean: anti-Jew, anti-gay, anti-government, anti-black, -brown, -red, -yellow, -green. One out of fifteen people might fall into that category."

"It's not your typical retirement countryside."

"No. Retired people generally like sunshine and communities where you can get medical care within fifteen minutes. It's definitely a different breed here. You need your friends to get by up here, to weather the loneliness, the cloudiness, the long, gray winters. Stores and restaurants even close down in the bleak months. Most of the young people are out of here after high school; they want to see the world."

Ronnie smiled, tilting her head at the rain on the roof. This all sounded a bit grim and gray—a nice place to visit but not a place where most people would stay. I think my expression tipped Ronnie off, and she changed her tune. "The upside is that we're all in this together. While friendships are often disposable in the city, here you have only *these* people. You have to bury the hatchet and get along. When the power goes out, friends call to see how I'm doing. You read about those cases where a woman screams in a parking lot in Los Angeles and nobody comes to help her. Well, that would never happen here. People would come running from all over, and whoever the perpetrator was would be in big trouble. We're all constantly on the edge of disaster here, quite literally, with the San Andreas Fault just offshore."

Ronnie no doubt is part of a subtle support system among friends and even mere acquaintances, but she also jumped into the community headfirst as president of the Mendocino Woodlands Outdoor Center—the camp she had attended as a child. Secluded in the redwoods along Big River, folded deep into the Coast Range, the facility was part of President Franklin D. Roosevelt's New Deal, one of forty-six similar camps built through an employment program during the Great Depression. "The idea," Ronnie explained, "was to make camping available to the middle class. And it worked. We have families that have been coming here for sixty years. The presidential retreat, Camp David, was one of these camps, though it has changed over time while the Woodlands has remained intact." To keep it that way, Ronnie has spent several years battling logging plans for the state's adjacent demonstration forest. "The demonstration," Ronnie said, smirking, "is to use various methods to cut the forest down and then see what happens." All the giant trees had once been logged off, and now three-quarters of the maturing second growth along the Little North Fork of the Big River had been cut as well. But the Woodlands group managed to save a buffer around their camp and to convince the state to buy more recovering forest in the Big River watershed.

Ronnie described herself as "an oldest child who has a need to take care of others," and now that her two sons were out working in the world, she volunteered at the local senior center and cared for injured wild animals at her home. Current residents included eight owls and hawks, a spotted fawn, and a squalling bear cub. The California Department of Fish and Game delivered handicapped fauna to Ronnie and directed others to do the same.

The bear cub, for example, had been collared by a local logger, who claimed that the mother had abandoned her baby. This never happens. It makes more sense that the sow was shot or killed when the tree that she and her cub had taken refuge in was felled. At any rate, state officials found out about the illegally caged cub and ordered the man to deliver it to Ronnie. It now cried in a plaintive, heartrending voice that, no kidding, sounded like a high-pitched "Maaaa-ma." Ronnie responded by feeding it a baby bottle of special-formula milk. She would nurse the little animal until a rearing facility in Washington State could take it. The bear would be returned to the wild when it was old enough.

"These animals are not pets," Ronnie warned. "They don't live by our rules. When you see Oscar, my great horned owl, you'll want to touch him. But listen, *don't* do it. He doesn't like it. I'm privileged to be so close to wild creatures, but to have a relationship with a wild animal, you have to know it on its own terms. And when you do that, you get a whole different slant on life. They live very much in the present. That fact brings everything into perspective. It raises the question, What's really important? And a big difference between humans and wild animals is that we have choices in how we behave.

They don't. Here's what it boils down to: they do everything the way nature has directed them. As people, we don't even know what that is anymore."

Ronnie was right. So often we don't even know what nature directs us to do. I mulled this over after we left, and Ann and I talked about it as we did with other thought-provoking tidbits we unearthed along the way.

"It's a matter of instinct," I offered, thinking of the way animals respond without training.

"For the animals, yes," Ann said. "But for us, it's also a matter of learning to live in accord with the earth. Look at the clues we found in the burned-up hills of the Santa Monicas and in the mudslide paths of the San Gabriels."

With new resolve I regarded my trip northward as an opportunity to find direction. Just what *is* nature telling us to do?

INTO THIS region where wildness was both lingering and disappearing, Ann and I drove north beyond the mill town of Fort Bragg, whose ripsaw edge had softened with tourist business, and then through the comfortably unremodeled village of Westport and on up the coast to the Usal Road. Highway 1 turns inland there to a junction with the busier Highway 101. By prearrangement, near the Usal turnoff, we met Greg Bettencourt's niece, Casey, and her boyfriend, Michael, who lived in Arcata and would drive our van north while Ann and I walked through seventy miles of wild country.

This was Sinkyone Wilderness State Park and the Lost Coast, the longest stretch of California's Pacific edge without a road near the shore. Our first twenty-eight miles lay mostly in Sinkyone. One of the earliest targets of Earth First! activists who staged sit-down protests to delay logging at the magnificent Sally Bell Grove, the Sinkyone was reprieved by lawsuits that eventually led timber giant Georgia-Pacific Corporation to sell 7,200 acres to the Trust for Public Land and the California State Coastal Conservancy in 1986. Those groups added 3,300 acres to the existing state park and passed the rest on to the InterTribal Sinkyone Wilderness Council, a consortium of ten

California Indian tribes that began to close logging roads and reforest clearcut slopes.

"Come with me," I had encouraged Ann when I planned this expedition. She was down to the final readings of her manuscript, down to polishing a word here, a sentence there. It was the exact opposite of where I was—step one—collecting raw material in gross and undiscriminating piles that might or might not appear in my book at all. I could hardly imagine what lay ahead for me, but Ann could see the end of her book in sight and so opted to see Sinkyone and the Lost Coast as an eight-day vacation.

"I have the feeling this is going to be a very special place, so I don't want to miss it," she said. "And I can use a break from my work. I think a week away will give me the fresh perspective I need to finish."

At Usal Creek we slung our packs onto our backs, waved goodbye to Casey and Michael, and began to climb, the first steps of our trek taking us to a different world. A canopy of Douglas-firs, redwoods, and tan oaks blocked out the day's diffuse light until we emerged at the top of a thousand-foot pitch amid meadowlands and scrub on steep slopes eroding into the ocean, which is where these rocks of a long-forgotten terrane originally came from. This pattern of geography would enchant us for days to come: mountainous headland, deep forest, remote beach. It was like an escape to a large temperate isle.

But it's not for everyone. Winter brings boot-sloshing rains, and with the Pacific High weather system having less effect as we go north, the days-long storms can last until summer. Allowing little relief, the fog sets in about the time the rains let up, moistening everything. The skies soak in gray, and the emotional spin-off plagues people susceptible to the clinically recognized seasonal affective disorder, its acronym, SAD, being more than letter-language.

Much to our distaste there at the height of springtime, ticks played out guerrilla warfare on our skin. We plucked them off our pantlegs hourly, before they could sneak inside to our legs, and we comprehensively searched our bodies for unwanted guests at bedtime. Beyond being creeped out by the little bloodsuckers, which can't be brushed off with the usual sweep of the hand, we were concerned by the fact that these pinhead vampires can carry the dreaded Lyme disease. Difficult to see, let alone extract, some ticks appeared to be nothing but pore-sized specks of blood, which could result from any routine brush with blackberry bushes. Examination with our hand lens—essential equipment for the whole California coast in springtime—would reveal the wiry legs of a tick that had quietly bored its head through our epidermis to tap our warm hemoglobin. Whenever that happened, we diligently freed ourselves with tweezers. Ann and I have a fair tolerance for nonhuman forms of life, but we unapologetically hate ticks. All by themselves, these germy, skin-penetrating parasites may keep Sinkyone a wild and uncrowded place, at least in the spring.

Our trail skirted the knob of a mountain whose top, in very slow motion, was literally sloughing into the sea. It made me wonder if we just might go with it, swept to surf in one grand finale of erosion. Once a dense forest, the knob's trees reflected the downward movement of a veneer of jellified soil. Instead of pointing straight up, the conifers looked like quills of a porcupine radiating across the rodent's curved back; they protruded at graduated angles toward the ocean, the lower trees nearly horizontal and primed for the crash. The total effect was of a great landslide frozen for examination in process.

This Franciscan mélange of rock, typical throughout northern coastal California, is the legacy of exotic terranes—small, drifting offshore plates related to the great Pacific Plate but separate from it. Eons ago these terranes collided with the North American Plate, and while most of their mass was subducted under the continent, a lot was also smeared up against the North American edge, resulting in a jumbled, fractured rock mass. The Franciscan complex readily erodes with water or gravity or both, especially at the seashore and riverbanks. As a result, the Eel River, not far north of us, was said to carry the largest dose of silt per unit of water in America. Plentiful serpentine lends a greenish tint to many Franciscan rocks.

Climbing beyond the eroding mountainside, Ann and I entered a cloud forest of grandfather conifers, matte-finished in gray. Moisture wisped through the thick biomass, condensed on the needles, and then rained onto the ground. Called fog drip, this accounts for up to

30 percent of the moisture in northwestern forests and as much as thirty inches of precipitation a year. The old-growth forest thus moderates the climate to the benefit of all life. A summer surrogate for rain, fog drip keeps the trees growing year-round.

Shedding our packs so we could rest at an overlook above Dark Gulch, we met Lonnie and Chuck, bright eyed as they took in the view, each with hair to the shoulders. She wore a Guatemalan skirt and a lip ring as well as multiple earrings; he sported dreadlocks, a beard, and piercing blue eyes. "It's *so* beautiful," Lonnie said. "Can you believe places like this still exist?" They had hitchhiked up from Santa Cruz.

Suspecting that hitching was more difficult now than in the halcyon days of vagabonding, when I did a lot of it, thirty years ago, I asked how it had gone. "It was totally easy," Lonnie said with a toothy smile. "The nicest people picked us up." Chuck added, "A fifth-generation local man brought us the last leg and told us how the area has changed since the loggers took all the trees away."

"How far are you going?" Lonnie asked us.

"To the mouth of the Mattole," Ann replied.

"Nice," Chuck commented, drawing out the word.

"How about you?" Ann asked.

"Oh, three or four days," Lonnie answered. "We don't have a car to worry about, so we can hike to most anywhere and then connect to the road and hitch home. We just see how it goes and take it as it comes."

Take it as it comes. Yes. Be open to what is here. One could do worse.

That night we camped on the beach, where I stoked our tiny campfire. Ann performed her usual alchemy with dried food and a few pinches of spice, and while we spooned chili with gusto after a hard day's hike, another feeding frenzy ensued nearby. Just offshore, at the mouth of Little Jackass Creek, fifty brown pelicans gathered along with svelte western grebes, common murres, Brandt's cormorants, and half a dozen seals, all diving or stabbing frequently for anchovies or sardines at the surf line. A seal surfaced and peaceably bobbed two feet from a pelican, the whole interspecies group a vivid reminder of the abundance once so common along the entire coast. After dark, the squawks, chirps, barks, and grunts of the diverse cast continued.

Another window to the organic abundance of this region opened two days later at Duffy's Gulch, where a redwood grove a thousand years old darkened the deep ravine. On the trail, two hundred feet above the valley floor, we could look straight out to the boles of trees rooted along the stream far below. Behemoth dead conifers had fallen and created whole landscapes of mounds like glacial eskers where trunks lay in rot. These actually contained more living mass — now in the form of lichens, invertebrates, insects, and microbes — than an upright, living tree trunk. Craters appeared in this pit-and-mound topography where root balls had been unearthed when the giants crashed down, creating varied habitat for plants and animals. Salal and evergreen huckleberry adorned the fallen redwoods and firs and would produce wonderfully edible berries later in the year. Floral displays of ferns grew tall enough to hide a whole tribe of forest people.

As with mountain creation and erosion, and rainfall and runoff, I was reminded here of cycles — the conceptual wheels of life. This time, the carbon cycle expressed itself in the buildup of plants from nothing but soil, sunlight, water, and air. Climaxing in the growth of a three-hundred-foot-tall tree, the cycle continues with death as a critical element. Through decay, carbon and nutrients are returned to the soil, atmosphere, and water, allowing new growth to race ahead in life's unbroken chain.

Standing there in the ancient grove of recycling trees, or at the mouth of a stream returning its life-supporting water to the ocean, or on a fault line where one side rises up while the other sinks undersea, I felt in my gut that I was a part of these other cycles. I, too, would live and die, edematize and evaporate, transmogrify to a redwood or a rodent when my elements finally rot up. My life was in a cycle like all these others. Except for my metal belt buckle and tooth fillings, I wasn't much different from the rest of the natural world.

Now, seeing the great beauty in that natural creation around me, I felt good about the humbling fact that I was destined someday to contribute to the beauty. For that matter, it's not so humble to think that my ashes or bones could someday become a redwood.

But what I really felt was satisfaction in life and perhaps even in my own inevitable death. Because this is not a feeling or even a thought that comes to me when I'm in developed places, and especially not in ugly ones, the importance of this natural landscape now seemed profound. After all, can one aspire to a more important emotion than the ultimate satisfaction with life?

Hungry for lunch — anxious to keep our own life cycle going here — we ate on rocks above the surf at Bear Harbor. A curved, isolated sickle of beach lay below, but otherwise steep slopes veering up mountains monopolized the seashore for miles to the north and south. Walking up the gulch, beyond bleached stacks of driftwood, we passed through gardens of ferns and alders, every part of nature thriving in exquisite detail, each a perfect sample of what it was, of its station in life, each scene elegant in ways completely different from the scene before and after it.

So it went up the Sinkyone coast — in and out of forests, up and down mountain faces more rugged than any others on the perimeter of the forty-eight states. Sinkyone is like Big Sur minus the road, plus the big trees. And, of course, the rain, the fog, the ticks.

Strolling toward the Needle Rock Visitor Center on a dirt lane, we met Gary Slattery, a seasonal ranger who had stopped to weed his garden. His garden was the whole park, and its infestation with weeds was severe. By *weeds* I mean not wild plants but exotic vegetation introduced here from other parts of the globe. To get his take on the current invasion of America did not require much prompting.

"French broom — the shrub that's spreading all over this hill — it's crowding out the natives. It's fire resistant, and the seeds stay viable for forty years. We used to control it somewhat with herbicides, but State Parks doesn't use them anymore. Now we're trying to pull it out, but it's impossible to keep up. And even if we got rid of the French broom, there are other exotics. Early Californians imported eucalyptus trees from Australia, and now they displace the oaks and cottonwoods." Big trees, the eucalyptus are beloved by people who regard them as naturalized members of the plant community, but their damage touches native lives in devastating ways. Some songbirds, for example, are killed when they try to extract nectar from the eucalyptus flowers and instead get black gum stuck on their faces. The birds are literally tarred to death. Native plants pose no similar hazard. Often planted around houses, eucalyptus also have a high content of resin, so they're far more flammable than oaks in the fire ecology of the Coast Range. "And exotic thistles are spreading like crazy," Gary added.

Ann commented, "The park is great, but if the native plants and animals die out because of exotic weeds, it's no less a loss than if it had been logged or developed."

Gary shook his head in frustration. "I wish more people understood that. We do what we can, which isn't much. We just hope someday there will be acceptable biological solutions so we can really get rid of these noxious invaders."

I resolved to pull identifiable weeds wherever I went, continuing in a public way a personal heritage of weeding that goes back to a childhood garden of beans, corn, and tomatoes.

Before we resumed our walk north, Gary said, "Let me warn you, around the next bend we just saw a mountain lion. It had killed an elk. We dragged the carcass off the road, but the lion will hang out nearby for some time. Be careful."

We would like to have seen a lion under some other circumstance. But facing the possibility here, we wondered, Just how do we be careful about a cougar guarding her food supply in the middle of our path? We concluded that we'd make noise, move quickly, and not bend over to tie our shoes. The lion, we hoped, would stick to the tastier ungulates. A good food source for the cats, Roosevelt elk have populated these mountains plentifully since their reintroduction some years ago.

Beyond Needle Rock, where a corrugated dirt lane ventures a long way down from Highway 101 to the wilderness park visitor center, we pressed on north, ever astonished at the Sinkyone school of beauty: stunning details and clean-cut edges between flower garden and shrubbery mass, forest glade and forest depth, driftwood pile and sandy beach. The designer nature of it all caused me to reflect on my landscape architecture days and to realize again how limited any effort to re-create natural beauty really is.

Ponds lay pocketed between narrow and pointed ridgelines thrown up as if by afterthought on the seaward side of the main mountain range. These features indeed looked as if another half mountain had been smeared onto the continent during the docking of an offshore terrane, which is exactly what the geologists say happened. The San Andreas Fault lies just offshore, almost within spitting distance.

Douglas irises bloomed with gorgeous furls of purple, and on March 18 I photographed Ann in front of one as a thirtieth-birthday portrait, her beauty and that of the irises a perfect complement on that green hillside above the sea. My birthday came two days later—the near-equinox of March 20. I often say that I was born two days after Ann, slyly omitting that an interval of nineteen years just happened to occur between my first day in this world and hers.

As a joint celebration—a rebaptism, if you will—we decided to jump into the ocean. For all our travel near the sea, we hadn't done this since Baja. The water everywhere had been too cold and rough. It was still cold and rough, but now jumping in seemed like an enlivening, exhilarating, youthful thing to do—a birthday thing—and perhaps a fitting plunge into whatever lay ahead during our next year or next decade of life.

The day had warmed to a sunny nugget of springtime, and now, late in the afternoon, the light lay low but still warm enough to make the dip thinkable. The Sinkyone water no doubt was frigid, but then it always is, gyrating off the California Current from Alaska and herded by upwelling winds of the Pacific High. The water temperature does not change dramatically from winter to summer. In fact, water temperatures off southern Oregon and northern California are actually higher in winter because the direction of the ocean current is reversed. In any event, come summer we would be up north, coping with glacial runoff clogged by icebergs. So right here, right now—this was the warmest ocean water we were going to see all year.

"Let's do it," Ann said, a twinkle in her eye.

Descending to Whale Gulch, where a rain-fed stream of charming repose gurgled onto the beach, where the radically uplifted face of Chemise Mountain soared away to the north, where the cliff shores reigned supreme and the waves of the Pacific acted as though nothing had impeded their progress since the island of Attu, we dropped our packs on a driftwood log. We unlaced our hot and sweaty boots, peeled down to our birthday suits with the joy of the birthday kids we really were, and waded in knee-deep.

The surf pounded ashore with surges up to our thighs and to critical thermal zones beyond, and the uneven line of the water's edge as it scalloped up on the beach told us to beware of a steep underwater incline with rips that could conceivably pull us out — not the kind of birthday celebration we had in mind. But none of it looked terribly bad, and after testing the shallows and allowing a big set of waves to play out, we waded deeper and then plunged into the ragged, foamy surface of the water.

The Alaskan chill shocked our systems and awakened us from a state that we certainly hadn't considered somnolent, yet now there was suddenly *more* to life, something fresh and even alarming about life and all the world around us.

The turbulence sandblasted our legs, and small stones, sucked out by waves, plunked against our ankles when we regained tentative footing in troughs between the foam. Wet from head to toe, we felt we had done it — enough already — and we scurried back to shore with the joy of returning sailors, even though we had been at sea for only about fifteen seconds.

"Somebody's coming," Ann said.

We had seen so few people that we'd begun to feel as if the Pacific coast were all our own. But sure enough, a man was walking straight toward us.

"Let's put our clothes on."

Ann was already scurrying for her underwear with an unmistakable sense of apprehension, and I rushed for my shorts as well, a flush of warmth and tone coming into my chest and arms, the protector hormone still doing its thing after all those years since Neolithic times.

A fit man with windswept hair, a trimmed gray beard, and an aquiline nose approached, carrying a walking stick long ago smoothed by the friction of his palm. Somehow, that alone told me he was okay. Frank Letton greeted us by harmlessly, confessing, "I walk down here four times a week but have never seen anyone swimming in the ocean."

"Well, it's now or never," I said, without explanation of the glacial waters to come in our summer, and Frank seemed to accept my response at face value.

He was an immediately likable guy, and we fell into a conversation no doubt enhanced by social deficit; there were so few people around that it was fun, even in our somewhat exposed state, to chat.

He had grown up along much more swimmable waters, in Florida, and his story of arrival here was unique in detail but similar in gist to the stories of other hand-hewn home builders on the coastal mountainsides of northern California. With an unpausing certainty as to when and where to begin, he said, "I was studying physics at Syracuse, and in those days if a physics graduate wanted a job, he went to work for the Defense Department. You worked on war. But I went to Berkeley instead, for grad school, in 1969."

"The year of People's Park!" I butted in, referring to the occupation of an urban green space by hippies who loafed and threw Frisbees and smoked dope and gardened there. They ultimately prevented the authorities from leveling the park for paved tennis courts.

"It sure was. And People's Park was just the tip of a social revolution going on. Life was getting pretty crazy. And when it does, you wonder what you're doing there. On top of a lot of cultural flux, a man I knew was shot that summer in Berkeley, and I remember thinking, 'To avoid working for the Defense Department is not enough. It's about time to leave altogether.' When I was sitting around in a coffee shop one day and reading an alternative newspaper, a buddy piped up, 'Hey, Frank, look at this. We can get some land real cheap in northern California.' 'Okay,' I said, 'Let's go look at it.'"

"And here you are," I commented, speeding up the story a trifle so that Ann and I could put some more clothes on.

"I bought the land," Frank continued, "right up Whale Gulch from here, but I couldn't build a house yet. I had to work and make some money first. So in Fort Bragg I bought my own fishing boat and trolled for salmon from San Francisco to Washington. That's back when there were still fish. You could make a living then; that wasn't the problem with fishing. The problem was that you couldn't have a good relationship with a woman. At least I couldn't. My partner now says, 'I'm glad you got rid of that old boat before we ever met.'"

"Excuse us while we grab some more clothes," I interrupted.

With his physics background, Frank had become fascinated with alternative energy sources, which served him well because his home and those of all his neighbors lie off the grid. He now helps people who live without conventional power to use alternative energy. He advises them in setting up systems for solar heating, and he builds hydropower generators running off minimal water from a two-inch pipe that doesn't hurt the fish in the streams.

"And what do other people around here do for money?" I asked, not wanting to put Frank on the spot, yet wanting to know how common the marijuana livelihood was.

"Some work in the school we started up. Some grow dope. Everybody knows that. I don't grow any. I don't like the prospects of going to jail. There's too much else to live for. What do *you* do?" Frank asked, with what appeared to be genuine interest rather than simply a desire to change the subject. His curiosity reminded me that our occupations were anything but evident, whether we were on the beach with backpacks or in a van decked out with boats on top. Ann and I just *looked* as if we were having fun all the time.

Hearing about my book, Frank offered, "You'd be interested in the Mattole River restoration effort. The local people have been working hard for some years now. The loggers tore the place up pretty badly, but through grassroots efforts we've fixed a lot of the damaged stream banks and are bringing the salmon back. It can be done — at least we hope so."

Ann and I, still in lightweight attire when a heavy sweater was called for, began to shiver a bit as the sun set behind an opaque bank of clouds. The wind simultaneously picked up — a moist blow with some unsettling determination in it. Looking out to sea for the weather, we all gazed up the coast at one of the more impressive edges of North America, a cliff front that after some incomparable miles of gorgeous heavenward slant tapers back down to sea at a low flattop peninsula.

Pointing along the line of our sight, Frank said, "As near as I know, no one has ever walked the coast from here to Shelter Cove. A few years ago a local girl tried it. She was forced to climb up the cliffs when the tide came in. She had her clothes in a bundle but dropped them. Then it got dark. Her father went looking and found her in the middle of the night, dressed about like you guys were a little while ago." It was Frank's first even subtle acknowledgment of our under-dressed state.

The young girl had had quite an adventure, and after Ann and I bundled up for the evening, I gave some thought to what adventure really is. Certainly it involves a change from the routine—doing something different. It also involves being in a spot where something could go very wrong or very right, and you're never sure which it will be. Sometimes all that's required is to be vulnerable—to be available and open for something to happen rather than guarded against the world.

The girl's adventure was based in real earth, real places, real elements of water, rock, waves. Many of my own adventures, over the years, had been rooted way back in childhood visions of Indians and fur trappers and New World explorers. My fantasies were rooted in dreams of unknown territory across wide oceans or down whitewater rivers in search of new homes, new lives, new knowledge, and new meaning in its many surprising forms. Like the girl who set off for Shelter Cove, I had engaged with real places, real people, real challenges that I could, at least conceivably, go out there and find. How different this seemed from the fantasy worlds of children I know today—off in cul-de-sacs of spaceships or robots, of monolithic power, of computer games. They live by remote control, with no roots in the earth at our feet. If that is the basis of childhood adventure today, and if the critical skill is knowing where all the buttons are, what would be the basis of adventure and happiness for these kids later in life? In not being able to answer this question, I wondered if I was just being old-fashioned. But can you be open or vulnerable to *buttons* in a meaningful way? The great environmental, cultural, and spiritual visionary Thomas Berry once wrote, "For children to live only in contact with concrete and steel and wires and wheels and machines and computers and plastics, to seldom experience any primordial reality or even to see the stars at night, is a soul deprivation that diminishes the deepest of their human experiences." Rather than facing a world of deprived souls, why not get kids out in nature? I have real admiration for people who work in environmental education and for parents who take their kids on trips in the outdoors.

Like the girl who had been caught by darkness, Ann and I didn't really have a plan for the night. Now, given the lack of light, we decided to simply stay where we were. While our safety could conceivably be an issue on that micro-beach, we were clearly above high tide by three vertical feet. We knew because the tide, coming up about fifty minutes later each day, had peaked while we were talking to Frank. So in a pocket of sand up against the mountain, we pitched the tent off to the side of a spot where small rocks had tumbled down and piled up as if in the bottom half of an hourglass. Contented there at the very edge of land, and excited by the horizon reach of prospect our little site so freely offered, we cooked dinner and ate, with a view unsurpassed.

Yet the moist wind continued, and before going to bed we couldn't see any stars. We turned in, perhaps less concerned than we should have been about the prospect of being overtaken by a rogue wave — an odd roller that can top all others by several feet. A year later, in fact, one of those waves swept two people to their death on this coast. But ignorantly untroubled, we drifted off to sleep, secure in each other's arms.

At two o'clock I thought I saw explosions of light. Was it just the illusion of a flash that I sometimes see when I blink in near-sleep? I kept my eyes wide open, and sure enough, it was the real thing, lightning. But distant. Just a freakish flash, I thought, no doubt touching down on one of the high mountains some miles away.

But the lightning brightened to the southeast, zapping a glow on the yellow tent for a split second, followed by the timpanic sound track of thunder. Surely the storm would be minor down where we lay. It's the mountains, I reasoned, that push the damp air up and cause the hardest rain. And it's the summits, closest to electric charges in the clouds, that get struck by lightning, which in any event is not common along this coast because the normally required after-noon buildup of temperature doesn't happen often.

Louder, brighter, louder, brighter, the incipient storm awoke Ann, usually a sound sleeper. I decided to go out and pee before showers might pin me under shelter.

What I saw outside the tent was quite alarming. Lightning flashed not only across the southeastern sky but also to the north, on the abrupt rise of Chemise Mountain. Not just distant strikes strobing the horizon, these bolts pierced the ridges like arrows, and the jagged white lines fractured the sky like geology-book diagrams of seismic faults — here the Santa Ynez, there the Malibu Coast; here the Hay-ward, there the big daddy San Andreas.

Wet bullets splattered against my skin and, caught naked there for the second time, I went running for cover. Inside the tent again, I briefed Ann on our deteriorating conditions.

The thunder grew to rifle-crack intensity and followed the light-ning flashes by only a few seconds. Then by one second, which meant the strike had occurred just a thousand feet away. Then the thunder didn't seem to follow the lightning at all. It was simultaneous and earthshaking in its abrupt and explosive booms. I could almost feel the vacuum, a contraction that seemed to override the beating of my heart. What would an electric shock feel like?

The tent lit up like a fireball, leaving my vision bright red until my eyes readjusted to the dark, at which time the light exploded again, keeping me blinking in wonderment.

The first danger, Ann and I reasoned from the thin security of our sleeping bags, was that the vibrations of thunder would shake loose a large rock, avalanche-style, from the mud slope directly above. I was glad I had pitched the tent off to the side of the known hourglass-rockfall, but who knows where a whole boulder might plunge when tumbling off a muddy mountain?

Hearing a downpour like a dozen garden hoses on the tent's roof, I now worried that the whole mountainside, with an obvious procliv-ity to slide, would become greased and movable and bury us in its lubricious ooze like a couple of future fossils. I'd watched other unstable slopes become saturated in two hours' time and send mudflows down their flanks, and I didn't want to be tented at the business end of any such earth science demonstration. I decided that if it rained for two hours — or maybe less, depending on how things looked — we should evacuate.

But where would we go? What barely passed for a trail descended the very slope that was most likely to give way. Instead of climbing up its gooey face, we could seek refuge on a small terrace on the other side of the creek. But it seemed too isolated, and if it rained that hard, the creek would flood, not only preventing us from fording but also conceivably washing us off the site where we were now tented. If the rock avalanche or mudslide didn't get us first.

In the dark of the night the mind works overtime, pondering the inscrutable and the silly. Would a flooding creek raise sea level right here, where it dumps into the ocean? Of course not. But now I strained to listen for waves as well as mudslides over the drum of rain on our sagging roof.

Suddenly this black, downpouring night, illuminated only by micro-seconds of electrified white light from God's own flashbulbs, seemed to be a composite of California coastal hazards: tidal surge, mudslide, flood. An earthquake was just as likely or unlikely as at any time, but the slope, being wet, was far more prone to collapse. And though I didn't know it then, our camp was a bull's-eye, virtually on top of the San Andreas Fault. What a birthday site this was turning out to be! Would Frank return on his stroll tomorrow and find us not swimming naked but clinging to a wet hillside like the girl who so adventurously had tried to walk to Shelter Cove?

Scared now, I pulled on my rain gear to go for another look — to see if the slope had grown muddy, to see if the stream had inched up, and to begin evacuation if necessary. But outside the tent, the rain now didn't sound so loud, didn't seem so threatening. When illuminated by lightning, the hillside looked unchanged, unscathed. The stream lay as placid as a stagnant pond. Nonetheless, I planted a twig at the waterline to monitor the rise.

I rejoined Ann in the warmth of the tent and realized that maybe I was getting carried away. Yet suppose something awful did happen. Suppose Ann got buried in mud and I couldn't find her. If I survived,

I'd have to say that I had known better, that I had been aware of the danger but failed to act. Paranoid or not, I decided that my two-hour evacuation plan was still the prudent approach.

Returning to bed, I checked my watch and hoped with every moment that the rain would let up and save us the onerous escape in sticky, wet sand, in mud, in chilling wind, and of course in rain.

Finally, it did ease up, but about the time my eyes relaxed a bit and shut, the downpour reintensified. On again, off again, on and off. But with each cycle, the heavy rains came a little lighter, the pauses lasted a little longer. The thunderclaps now followed a suspenseful pause after the lightning strikes, indicating that the vortex of the storm had drifted away.

Ann unzipped the tent door and we looked out. Yellow bursts of lightning flashed over the sea, and though it made no sense to me that the storm had retreated in that direction, it had. Finally, the air grew quiet, and peaceful moments passed, and I slept again with the deep appreciation of a survivor.

ON A DAMP and freshened morning we left that beachhead, reinvigorated by the night's display of power and surrounded by a wet beauty polishing everything that was green. That meant almost everything. We hoofed up a trail of eye-stopping scenery, across the watery rush of Whale Gulch, through woody forests clinging to temporary cliffsides, and into glades of native wildflowers.

The view back southward showed miles of shoreline in foreshortened, alternating coves and headlands etching off into the distance, ridge after ridge piggybacked on top of one another. Finally summiting the bony spine of Chemise Mountain, Ann and I lunched at 2,598 feet but only one mile from the ocean. Along with several peaks in the King Range farther north, also located along the San Andreas Fault, this was one of the steepest drops to sea from a major mountaintop in the Coast Range south of Canada, the gradient, though not the height, outdoing Cone Peak at Big Sur. Again clouds rolled in, blocking our view beyond the manzanita, chamise, and tan oak that entangled us.

After lunch and a quick downhill jaunt, we emerged at a road and had to walk three miles on pavement down to Shelter Cove, the site of a recreational subdivision, which is also bisected by the San Andreas Fault in its brief foray ashore. For all we knew, the big schism could have been just another survey line between lots for sale; it was that close.

Partway down the hill, at a building pad scraped level by earth-movers, we stopped at a store, enjoyed a Ben & Jerry's ice cream treat, and read the local bulletin board. Notices advertised a new Veterans of Foreign Wars post, information about veterans' services, a lost dog, meetings of Alcoholics Anonymous, a potluck dinner, and many houses and empty lots offered by owners and real estate agents. Explaining this, the woman behind the counter said that many of people buy lots or homes, discover how remote they are, and then change their minds. "Or," she said, "they listen to their own heart murmur one day and decide they want better access to medical care." Or they inherit a half-acre lot, and with no inclination for their parents' dream, they sell.

We licked our ice cream on a bench while a woman with two children waited for a ride, a motorcyclist with a deformed face talked to himself while browsing the free box of donated clothing, and a older man in cowboy boots and double-knit pants stared at the bulletin board. Two mangy dogs rounded out the sad scene there at the gateway to Shelter Cove, which would have been quite a spectacular highlight to the California coast if it had only been left alone instead of converted into the cookie-cutter lots of a subdivision struggling for sales, to pavement buckled by earthquakes, and to a sewage treatment plant that — according to a public notice posted in front of us — now required an expensive upgrade. The subdivision had been started before the California Coastal Commission regulated major building along the shoreline.

Moving on, we tried to hitch a ride down the switchbacked road, but the drivers were older people who never even think about picking up strangers, or hustling workmen in plumbing vans, or mothers with children and, no doubt, the usual sense of guardianship that babies add to a young woman's fears. As if the cards weren't stacked against us enough, the entire group hit each switchback at a squealing rate of speed. Our goal soon became not to flag down a ride but simply to avoid being run over. Redeeming our unfortunate fate, black raspberries — my favorite of all — had ripened along the road. Picking our share as we walked, we hoped they hadn't been sprayed with roadside weed killer.

Encountering traffic and second homes in the middle of a wilderness trip heightened our desire for the wild beaches yet to come, and fortunately the Lost Coast section of our hike lay just ahead. When we reached the shore we found continuous sand backed by springtime slopes of grass and chaparral with pockets of conifers that climbed the relentless incline of the King Range. As extraordinary as the wooded mountainsides and artful details of Sinkyone, this part of the walk thrilled us with surf-breaking beauty, broad sweeps of sand, driftwood tangles, quiet coves, hidden canyons, and grassy fields. Rising from salt water, Kings Peak is the highest in the region, topping out at 4,087 feet within 2.8 miles of the ocean. Most of the area is protected as the sixty-thousand-acre King Range National Conservation Area, where the U.S. Bureau of Land Management tries to lessen the decades-long impact of cows and motorized vehicles.

I had looked forward to this wilderness at tide's edge. After all, what could beat the joy of beach walking for days on end? But soft sand absorbing our momentum alternated with plentiful rocks requiring us to step from stone to stone, after a while a shock to the joints. Worst of all, the beach sloped into the sea, as beaches by definition do, and so we constantly walked on a side slope tilted west. With every step my left foot landed lower than my right. Where possible, we sought level micro-topography, such as at the top of a wave-cut terrace, but there at the ultimate edge, the tilt of North America dipping into the Pacific was one of those difficult features to mitigate. My lower back began to ache.

Each night found us on a beach well above the tide line but paradisiacally situated with a view of the ocean as well as the deteriorating rocky buttresses rising from it. Piled up in knotted balls, ribbons of giant kelp had washed ashore. Some stretched out longer than an old bullwhip, though they were just scraps, really. The longest plant in the world, living kelp can grow in strands up to fifteen hundred feet long. Clouds and fog came and went, but for more than our share of time on this soggy front of America we enjoyed sunshine, brilliant on the flowery slopes and blue sea.

Not alone during those clement days, we saw three teenagers backpacking their surfboards out from Big Flat, a man and two daughters struggling to have a speakably good time as they hiked, a troop of Boy Scouts yelping it up in the surf, a party of six women and two men lounging in cutoff lawn chairs and sipping wine, and more couples like Chuck and Lonnie—longhaired backpackers from Berkeley and Arcata who beamed with joy at the beauty around them.

In some sections high tide can prevent safe travel. Here the waves batter the rocks and allow no way around. Partly by luck and partly by planning, we managed to skirt several of these points of land when the tide was still coming in but not yet peaking. North of Shipman Creek we watched an intimidating set of waves drench the rubble of rocks at the toe of cliffs, the troughs between waves revealing an adequate running track if only the next wave, after its traverse of the Pacific, would just wait a few extra seconds.

We, of course, were the ones who did the waiting, letting a big set pass and then planning our escape when smaller waves staged up offshore. We hoped that when we cleared the rock wall impeding both our progress and our view, there wouldn't be another rock wall sentencing us to a sudsing drench at sea level. Sprinting across the watery sand while one wave retreated, we ran flat-out where the ocean had lapped just seconds before. We cleared the monuments of rock that had blocked our route and dashed up the beach on the other side, relieved that dry sand lay within reach.

The next morning, at the mouth of Kinsey Creek, Ann and I lounged in a warm sunrise, me taking pictures, she painting the purple details of mussel shells and the crumbly escarpment of cliffs. In no rush to leave such beauty, we embarked at noon, about the time the northerly winds picked up enough force to sandblast our legs and drown our conversation.

At Spanish Flat, full-length logs of driftwood had been flung ashore, even into the meadow far above high tide, evidence of a multi-megaton tsunami. Approaching land as fast as five hundred miles per hour, these tidal waves result from earthquakes or related landslides under the ocean. To model the effect, just push your palm quickly against water in a bathtub. The dry-docked logs most likely came from the 1964 tsunami that swallowed the North Coast after an earthquake in Alaska. An eighteen-foot wave near the Oregon border took out thirty blocks of Crescent City as if it were a toy town. Tsunamis can reach a hundred feet in height, with enough force to wipe out portions of many towns. Seismologists say to evacuate if a tremor lasts twenty seconds or more. The waves could come ten minutes after the quake.

A rabbit quickly darted from the base of an old, waterworn trunk; after floating at sea, the driftwood now created its own ecosystem of cover and shelter. Insects chewed on the punky rot of woody refuse delivered by the tsunami, serving as one more reminder that changes in nature are slow and scarcely detectable to the human eye, but that change arriving at a few hundred miles an hour is also a part of the mix. Evolution and revolution both play strong roles in the ongoing saga of the Coast Range.

For our last night backpacking we camped south of Punta Gorda, where a stiff northerly blew in a nonnegotiable mood. In the lee of a boulder, our campfire danced like a dervish to swirling eddy-winds. After dinner we zipped up our jackets and went tidepooling, sliding clumsily on the slick surfaces of rockweed, sea cabbage, and surf grass while we checked out the anemones, starfish, mussels, snails, limpets, and chitons. Late light cast warm rays on a grassy mountainside that arose directly from the tide line. Pelicans and cormorants winged by, and porpoises gulped air in their dance step of leap-and-plunge. The scene reminded me of Baja, but there the mountains had been brown. Here they were green.

Our final day took us to Windy Point, where, sure enough, a northwesterly howled. As if controlled by puppet strings, we leaned far forward but didn't fall over, our jackets ballooning, our hair plastered back as if in a convertible going sixty. Finally, we reached the Mattole

River, a wide stream slicing across a sandy spit before surrendering to the ocean. Seals fished in the mixing zone at the mouth of the river while cottonballs of clouds sailed on the stiff winds of a Pacific High.

THE MATTOLE tops anyplace else in California for rainfall. On the gauge at Honeydew, 100 to 150 inches is not unusual, and Wilder Ridge, between there and Kings Peak, might see half again as much. Annual rainfall here can exceed the 200 inches regularly measured in the Coast Range east of Lincoln City, Oregon, and sometimes rivals that on Washington's Mount Olympus, which ranks as the wettest place in forty-eight states.

The Mattole River begins inauspiciously near Whitethorn, a back-woods community of weather-battered middle-aged houses, trailers suffering under steady fog drip, and mossy cabins surrounded by more junk than in West Virginia. With mud puddles, peeling paint, and loitering residents, this little grid of dirt streets has a bit of a Third World feel to it, like some old-time elephant-tusk trading town at the edge of African wilds. More than anyplace, it has the reputation of being a dope growers' haven and an outpost of cultural conflict.

People here are familiar with the acronym CAMP. While the heinous crack, crank, and heroin ran rampant, a Ronald Reagan–era anti-drug program targeted marijuana with a deployment called the Campaign Against Marijuana Planting. Federal officials escalated earlier cat-and-mouse games to paramilitary maneuvers. Anti-government wackos in places such as Montana fabricate laughable tales of black helicopters from the United Nations monitoring their every boring move, but the helicopter part of their paranoia — here on the North Coast — is real. Outdoor marijuana plots are spotted from the air and destroyed by tough uniformed SWAT teams.

The crackdown pushed surviving dope growers to be more clever. Now people grow their crops on somebody *else's* property or on public land such as the national forests. Some small growers hang marijuana plants in pots concealed in trees or grow their plants indoors. Facing intensified risk, many of the easygoing hippies and casual growers who long characterized this cottage industry abandoned the still-booming business to a hard-core lowlife element that has little to lose and is willing to risk mandatory jail sentences.

One friend described Whitethorn's population as "hippie-thugs"— people with long hair, beards, and guns. Another called the town the armpit of Humboldt County, noted not only for the culturally embedded marijuana but also for harder drugs, including the scourge of rural America, methamphetamines, which make men sleepless and violent.

Not proving any of the appraisals I had heard, we picked up two hitchhikers on our way to Whitethorn. The first, a sixteen-year-old boy with a horrible complexion, was incensed about the industrial logging nearby. He called it "an invasion by a bunch of timber beasts who don't care anything about our home." After a few miles I came to the second hitcher, and as I braked to let him in, the boy muttered, "This guy's an asshole." The two didn't speak to each other, but both were polite and appreciative to me.

While Whitethorn functions as a community center, so to speak, the thick woods of the Mattole River basin are scattered with people living quiet, private lives on the land. Their houses are hidden by trees and evident only in faint glints of midday light on tin roofs or driveways making thin scratch lines in the emerald forest. A fair percentage of these rural residents have banded together and for twenty years worked to restore salmon in their river—the effort Frank Letton had told me about. Mattole fish have never been adulterated by hatchery stocks, which can weaken the native gene pool of wild fish. An especially critical population, the Mattole stock is one of the southernmost wild salmon runs on the West Coast. This valuable food source dwindled from 10,000 spawners in the 1960s to only 200 in the 1990s.

Logging and overgrazing had caused erosion, higher flood runoff, and correspondingly lower dry-season flows. The fishes' spawning beds were alternately smothered by silt and dried up. In the modern era, when nine-tenths of the forest was cut down, it was no coincidence that the northern California and Oregon coho salmon population plummeted by 97 percent. Residents of the Mattole basin saw firsthand the connections between forests and water, soil and fish, and they worked to save residual pockets of undamaged watershed, such as the two-hundred-acre Sanctuary Forest.

Other tracts of ancient forest would have been completely chopped but for protestors who formed human chains around the beloved trees. Faced by loggers who yelled, among less civil phrases, "Go home," the Mattole protectors replied, "We *are* home. *You* go home." At Sulphur Creek the loggers chased, beat, and tied up protestors who stood in their way. But the feisty Mattole guardians persisted, and courts eventually took their side, ruling that the California Department of Forestry and Fire Protection had failed to consider the objections of other state and federal agencies when it approved the clearcutting. With the help of the State Coastal Conservancy, the Sanctuary group went on to acquire thirty-four hundred acres, and a new fabric of recovering ecosystem is being stitched together. Though the ultimate backwoods basin, this unlikely enclave may be a model for California's future because here local people have taken responsibility for their place.

Well downstream from Whitethorn, the country store at Honeydew might be the smallest general store anywhere that offers tofu and ginseng tea on its shelves. The local bulletin board advertised not Veterans of Foreign Wars and Alcoholics Anonymous news but rather African drumming and aikido classes way out there in the woods.

Below Honeydew the river meandered and brought life to small ranches that occupied cleared meadows, the plots tended in a mountain-farm idyll that pulled my nostalgia strings to the breaking point. My Appalachian heritage was to blame. In my youth, such scenes of tranquil beauty had been imprinted on me as the ideal landscape, and as my tastes matured and I learned more about the forces of change on the earth, the flavor of those places to which I had bonded did not fade. Rather, it grew with the promise of living lightly on the land, of growing food yet still honoring nature every step of the way. Driven partly by fact, partly by memory, and partly by wishful thinking, I still longed for the mountain farm of leafy Appalachian slopes and riffling rivers. And here at the Mattole was the closest thing I'd ever seen to a West Coast counterpart. With rare balance and charm, homesteads not remodeled by aluminum siding lay tucked into hillsides at the end of curved driveways, all of it edged by field and forest, the sweet waters of this little river murmuring timeless messages to all who would listen.

It takes an hour or more just to drive from this rainy, dripping valley out to Highway 101, at which point you're still nowhere, figuratively speaking, two hundred forty miles north of San Francisco and fifty miles south of Eureka. Nearby Garberville hardly counts. Once a logging boomtown, the place looks burned out now that the big timber is gone. A cruise on local streets showed a high incidence of overweight smokers and dour-faced inhabitants whose collective health looked depleted, as if by some sinister agent in the drinking water. Or perhaps by the local drug supply. Or perhaps by a head-splitting hangover that followed the terminal binge of logging. However, a new element, which liked the place for what nature offered, was settling into woodsy cabins around the fringe of town and slowly changing the social profile. As one resident told me, "The town is schizophrenic with loggers, pot growers, and environmentalists, all in strong numbers."

Back on our coastal route north, just beyond the mouth of the Mattole, the highly significant Cape Mendocino appeared with an impressive rock called Sugarloaf Island a quarter mile or less offshore, depending on the tide. A charter member in anyone's geologic hall of fame, this is the site of the Mendocino Triple Junction, the most truly awesome of all seismic convergences south of Alaska. Here the Pacific Plate, Gorda Plate, and North American Plate all come together in an earthquake extravaganza of uplift and seismic bumper cars, signified by the vertical profile of this rocky monolith. The National Earthquake Information Center's map of seismicity in California shows the Triple Junction as the second-densest cluster of tremors, outdone only by Mammoth Mountain, on the eastern side of the Sierra Nevada, which is hardly a fair comparison because Mammoth is an active volcano geologically ready to pop, and its plentiful earthquakes are mostly small. Here near the coastal cape, residents of nearby Petrolia feel an earthquake about once a month.

At this point the San Andreas Fault finally veers west, splinters apart, and disappears for good undersea.

Unlike the Pacific Plate's slippage northwestward and mostly alongside the North American Plate—a lateral dynamic that characterized the San Andreas system from Baja to here—the offshore plates north of the Triple Junction collide more nearly head-on with North America. The oceanic plates are directly subducted—overrun and mostly buried—in the Cascadia Subduction Zone. Here we left the San Andreas behind but seismically jumped out of the frying pan and into the fire; head-on subduction has the potential to produce the largest earthquakes of all.

The whole crash-car derby is something like an eighteen wheeler headed west and rolling right over a little Datsun puttering eastward. The smaller vehicle is obliterated under the grinding wheels of the larger while the equivalent of the car's roof gets caught in the oncoming bumper and slathers up in front of the unstoppable truck, on which we Americans are all riding. It's that accretion that accumulates at the continent's edge and creates the coastal mountains we now see, many of them composed of sedimentary rocks, which are lighter than the sinkable undersea basalt.

The Cascadia Subduction Zone extends for seven hundred fifty miles to the northern end of Vancouver Island. North of there, an even more dramatic collision awaits as the whole tectonic bonanza works up toward its mind-boggling climax in Alaska, just where Ann and I and the springtime and the whales were all headed.

But there, stark and clean, bristling with sharpness, Sugarloaf Island fisted up out of the sea as though the earth had just punched a hole through the ocean, not unlike Morro Rock near San Luis Obispo, though without the smokestacks, power plant, and jetty. As I sat there by the road looking at Sugarloaf, it was evident that revolutionary change had taken place over the ages, and I couldn't help but feel that further rapid changes could occur at any moment. Staring at the scene harder and longer and without interruption, and letting my eyes float in and out of focus in a slightly spacey way, I got the feeling I was watching the earthquakes happen right then, that I was a spectator to the formation of a new edge of continent on that very day. Indeed, the mountains here rise at a record rate of three inches per year.

At this point, and only from here to the Olympic Peninsula, the coastline turns from its northwesterly slant to a truer north–south orientation, which is how most people seem to regard the entire West Coast.

A road of extraordinary sights and blessedly little traffic, the Petrolia–Ferndale byway offers one of the finest paved bicycle routes in the coastal mountains, swinging past the sunset shadow of Sugarloaf and then climbing high over the Bear River Range. This roaded ramp taxes even the iron legs of century riders and then free-falls to the picturesque town of Ferndale. There, the delightful view from the local hillside cemetery showcases blocks of Victorian houses bounded by dairy farms at the pastoral delta of the Eel River. Every few years this artery possessively reclaims its broad lowlands, flooding the fringe of town.

Twenty more miles north, Ann and I entered buzzing Eureka, the urban capital of the North Coast, headquarters of the once-dynastic logging industry. The town had backslid from its economic overshoot, for some years a victim of compounded decrements in resource abuse. But now it was gentrifying with metropolitan refugees. Craftspeople and artisans had been drawn to Eureka long enough that a major magazine recently named this former sawdust center the best small city in America for the arts.

Across Humboldt Bay lay Arcata, the green capital of America. Though itself a logging town within the memories of many, Arcata may now rank as the ultimate holdout of the 1960s counterculture, outdoing even Santa Cruz and Berkeley. The town has achieved fame for its tolerant disposition, natural foods co-op, used-book stores, and fine university. Longhairs are common and skinheads rare. Humboldt State University does well in natural resource studies and draws students who prefer mountains and woods to the shopping malls of the other California. The city has a model recycling program, its own sustainably managed forest, and a sewage system that waters wetlands and nourishes whole flocks of waterfowl.

The proud owner of an old Volkswagen bus near the co-op had wallpapered his vehicle in bumper stickers typically found in Arcata though rarely displayed all at once: "Support Organic Farmers" / "Pro-child, Pro-family, Pro-choice" / "Peace Is Possible" / "Love Animals, Don't Eat Them" / "Rescue the Rainforests" / "Test Peace, Not Nuclear Weapons" / "Nuclear Weapons, May They Rust in Peace" / "Good Planets Are Hard to Find" / "Love Your Mother" / "Go Organic" / "Smart Bombs or Smart Kids" / "My Child Was Born at Home" / "Why Be Normal?" / "If You Think Education Is Expensive, Try Ignorance."

While Ann and I ate dinner at Nancy Reichard's house with a group of her friends one foggy evening, a loud rap sounded at the door. It was the police, generally unwanted guests at dinnertime. "I just thought you'd like to know that somebody out front left their car lights on," the officer notified us with a smile.

Ann and I liked Arcata, and so did Nancy. For some years she had directed a nonprofit program to restore streams damaged by logging. She now split her time between helping small cottage businesses get started and mediating environmental disputes. Happy to take some time off, she walked with us the next day along the Mad River, which emptied into the ocean nearby.

Nancy spoke fondly of her twenty-five years living on the North Coast, which began when she enrolled at Humboldt State. Like many students, she bonded to the place, tolerated the rain and fog, and stayed. She witnessed great change in that time. The age of forest destruction wound down and the age of recovery began. "Through watershed restoration efforts started in the 1970s we could soon see improvement in stream banks and the forests alongside them. It felt good to be patching things up. But whether or not the salmon and steelhead will come back, we don't yet know."

"Is that a Sitka spruce?" I blurted out, not wanting to interrupt but irrepressibly excited.

"Yes, it certainly is," Nancy said. "We're near the southern end of its range." This full-bodied evergreen grows along the coastal edge and from then on would grace our travels wherever we approached the ocean. More than other trees, it needs magnesium, which is abundant in salt spray. Though it was another seventy-five miles to Oregon as the crow flies, this magnificent tree's dark presence made me feel as though the Pacific Northwest had begun.

"So where did the stream work take you?" I asked, wanting to hear more of Nancy's story.

"It led me to be more interested in who was doing what, and to whom, and why. A lot of psychology goes into land restoration, and over the years I've seen people change in the way they think about this place. In terms of public awareness, it's a whole new world up here. Fifteen years ago, if you talked about a watershed, meaning all the land that drains into a particular river, no one knew what you meant. Now they do. And now they know that nearly everything touches on that concept. The endangered status of the salmon really got people's attention. They'd like to bring those fish back. They know that healthy streams are needed to do it, and that to have healthy streams we need healthy forests as the source and protector of the water. A few decades ago, people nearly got murdered in the battles to establish and expand Redwood National Park. There are still some intense conflicts, but now we are using new and different means to resolve them."

Nudging the new era along, Nancy made her living by helping people work together. As gentle and congenial a creature as I could imagine, she directed meetings of opposing parties and skillfully aided them in understanding each other's point of view. Committed to her home, tolerant of its people, she was helping lead the way to what this place would become.

Looking at the plethora of grassroots efforts on the North Coast, from the restored salmon redds of the Mattole to the cooperative grocery store selling organic, pesticide-free produce in Arcata, I thought of Nancy and others like her as the bearers of the new California dream. It's one of living peaceably on the land in ways that don't ruin it, of accommodating one another's reasonable needs without ruining anyone else's future, of living a truly fulfilling life in communities that work well and on land that's allowed to do its most fundamental job — that of supporting life.

After staying a couple of days at Nancy's place, we couldn't help but feel a bit recharged about all this. In leaving, Ann and I bid a fond "Good luck" to Nancy. We wished we could have taken her with us and somehow dropped off clones at innumerable stops where people need her along our route north.

BEYOND THE surf-booming headlands of Patrick's Point State Park, beyond the exhilarating wide beach at Dry Lagoon, we pulled off at Prairie Creek Redwoods State Park, really hyped up with anticipation. We had seen redwood trees here and there since Big Sur, but now we were about to enter the heart of the big-tree belt.

Redwood country is the Holy Land of tree lovers, and we relished the fluttery thoughts of simply standing in a great redwood grove.

Quickly we were rewarded. Just a few feet from where I parked the van, the great boles and branches disappeared into the fog above while the roots disappeared into the spongy soil below. The trees stood as living monuments to whole millennia since their births. Together, our outstretched arms reached a small fraction of the way around the largest trees, one of them sixty-two feet in circumference.

The groves of shaggy-barked giants rose cathedral-like, with fluted columns soaring in search of light. Light, after all, means life, and light's scarcity on the rainy, foggy North Coast makes the competition intense. Thus, the world's tallest trees have evolved and triumphed as the masters of finding light, and they do this by reaching for the top of the canopy. The loftiest tree is about 365 feet tall. Growing only in the narrow strip along the western front of mountains, where winter rain and summer fog keep the forested mountainsides wet, these dinosaur-age organisms are accompanied by an understory of ferns, salal, evergreen huckleberry, rhododendron, and a delicate shrub called ocean spray. The tree's range corresponds with the strongest zone of offshore cold-water upwelling, which produces the fog. The redwoods need a steady supply of water and cannot survive at drier locations because they lack root hairs to efficiently tap soil moisture.

As I looked across the stream bottoms or mountainsides, the aggregation of trunks appeared like a solid mass, the big trees overwhelming everything, including whatever chatter might have been going on in my head. Their fine and lacy foliage blotted out the sky.

Withstanding the test of time, the redwoods resist fire with their thick, resinless bark. The trees thrive in the deep soil of lowlands and cope with the inevitable floods by putting out a new network of shallow roots whenever a layer of fresh silt is deposited around their trunks.

Though they can reproduce from seeds, 98 percent of the redwoods emanate from shoots, thanks to an unusual and ingenious quirk of physiology. The trees produce a burl of tough tissue around their trunks. Within this, embedded buds spring to life if the burl is damaged or irritated — if the tree is blown over by wind, for example.

On the select group of redwoods that arise from seed, the swollen burl tissue encircling the incipient trunk begins to form from day one. Strange as it may seem, after four or five years the weight of the burl can become too much, and the seedling collapses, momentarily defeated by itself. But from the fallen burl the little redwood immediately sprouts a new, more vigorous root system. The struggling seedling is now reincarnated as a supertree of phenomenal power, and it resumes its growth, this time not stopping for anything, pushing up to the sky for twenty-two hundred years.

The one thing that kills off redwood trees is logging. Because the wood is highly resistant to rot and weather damage, it has been a favorite for house siding, outdoor decks, and hot tubs. New generations of redwoods can grow at a rapid rate after logging — in a limited, tree-farming sense — but the productive, life-affirming mix of ancient trees, including dead and dying ones, with all their associated habitat takes upward of two hundred years to develop. The industry-owned second growth is recut before it reaches anything close to that age.

The giant trees once grew in many great groves running along the Coast Range's Pacific front, from Big Sur to southern Oregon. Only 4 percent of that original redwood forest remains uncut. With this statistic in mind, I stood trying to imagine the tree in front of me — the most charismatic of all flora — being severed at its base and crashing to the ground for an afterlife as decking underfoot in California suburbs or as paneling in Japanese living rooms. Parks protect over half of the old growth that remains, much of it in small groves but here running with impressive continuity through whole valleys, almost out to the ocean, and north–south along a fifty-mile length of the mountains.

As the most significant privately held grove, the Headwaters Forest, east of the Mattole, became the site of America's most intense battle ever to rescue a virgin forest from the rip of chainsaws. After years of political squabbling, court fights, civil disobedience in the trees, and demonstrations by thousands of people against a Texas tycoon who had taken over the once-local Pacific Lumber Company, the federal and state governments bought seventy-five hundred acres for nearly half a billion dollars. But significant sections of the Headwaters tract remained contested, important habitat for the marbled murrelet, a bird that feeds at sea but nests amid the ancient trees. Now endangered, the murrelet dropped in number in California from 60,000 to 6,500 because of lost nesting sites. Hundreds of other species also depend on ancient forests such as Headwaters.

Midway through the north–south alignment of Redwood National Park, the Klamath River flows gloriously out to sea. In its two-hundred-mile path through the coastal mountains — the longest river route through the Coast Range south of Canada — it ties together diverse aspects of California and the Pacific Northwest. This is one of only seven rivers south of Canada that carve the whole way through the coastal mountains. Among the other five, the Chehalis of Washington, the Columbia, and the Sacramento cross where the mountains are low and the valleys wide. But the Klamath, along with the Umpqua, Rogue, and Siuslaw of Oregon, cut with unmistakably bold incisions through the backbone of the range.

Collectively known as the Klamath Mountains in northern California, this is one of the widest unbroken masses of mountains in America and includes the Trinity, Salmon, and Marble Ranges. The Siskiyou is the northernmost subset, sometimes considered separate from the Klamaths as it extends into Oregon as far as Port Orford on the coast and Roseburg inland. The Klamaths mark America's largest relatively wild section of the Coast Range south of British Columbia. Linked in the geologic past to the Sierra Nevada and now to Pacific-hugging ridges, the Klamath Mountains host plants from both these ranges as well as from the ancient past; the region went unglaciated in the ice ages and thus represents a rare forty million years' worth of uninterrupted evolution. All this, coupled with sharp climatic gradients and varied rock types, results in the world's most diverse conifer forest, supporting thirty different species of cone-bearing trees.

Along with the Olympic Peninsula, which is much smaller, this region offers the best opportunity along the coast between Mexico and Canada to restore a whole ecosystem of mountain land. Wild corridors can still be linked across a 170- by 80-mile sweep of topography. A significant step in this direction was the 1990 defeat of the Gasquet–Orleans Road, which would have bisected the wildest terrain. Another was a policy of President Bill Clinton's administration that set many remaining old-growth stands off limits to logging because of the northern spotted owl, marbled murrelet, and other imperiled wildlife that needs the ancient forests.

Regretting that we didn't have time to visit the tumble of peaks and canyons in California's northern interior, Ann and I clung to the Pacific front in order to meet our schedule of summertime exploration in Alaska. But there at the Klamath River bridge, fold upon fold of terrain lay to our east, telling us there was so much more to see. Knowing this hardened our resolve to make the most of each single day.

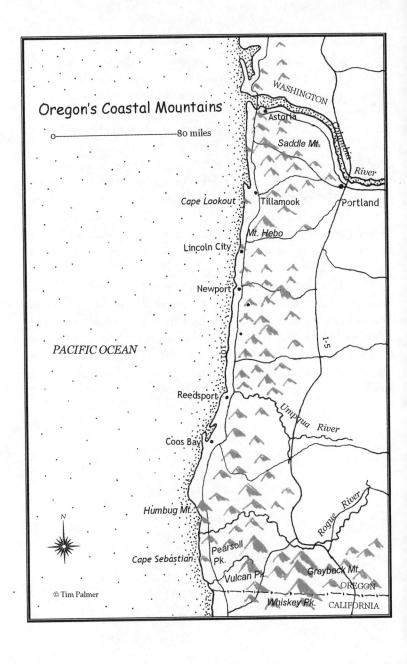

Oregon's Coastal Mountains

0 ————————— 80 miles

WASHINGTON

Astoria

Saddle Mt.

Columbia

River

Portland

Cape Lookout

Tillamook

Mt. Hebo

Lincoln City

Newport

PACIFIC OCEAN

101

I-5

Reedsport

Umpqua River

Coos Bay

Humbug Mt.

Rogue River

N

Pearsoll Pk.

Cape Sebastian

Vulcan Pk.

Grayback Mt.

OREGON

© Tim Palmer

Whiskey Pk.

CALIFORNIA

# 9 Kalmiopsis to the Columbia

THE PLEASURES of an eternal spring now seemed like a normal part of our lives. The birds really know what they're doing, and like them, we had been migrating with the new season's advance of low-angled sunniness, its scent of birth and germination, its juicy green salad of fresh fields with wildflowers popping out all over.

Springtime joys had been replaying themselves ever since Ann and I launched our trip in Baja three months ago. But as we vanned our way up the languid lower Chetco in southern Oregon — the river shining back at us in teal green, its gravel bars cobbled in nimbus gray — the season infused us anew. The alders burst with yellowy green leaves, and freshwater springs dripped like honey from primitive boudoirs of ferns while songbirds and waterfowl winged determinedly north toward the great show and feeding frenzy of summertime at the upper latitudes. March 31 delivered such spirited balminess. But at that time of year you never know, and on April 1, when we entered the Siskiyou Mountains, we encountered our wintriest conditions thus far.

Climbing rapidly in elevation, we left the greening alder leaves and unfurling skunk cabbages behind, and soon the road whitened with spots of slush from a storm that had blown through in the night.

Then, more serious, fresh snow covered the road, a crystalline blanket marred only by the melted-out tracks of a truck that had come before us. Soon those burly mud-tire prints failed to melt the snow but rather packed it beneath them, and finally the tracks disappeared altogether where the driver had pulled over and given up.

Missing my cue, I wondered, What's the problem? But I soon learned that the narrow road increased in pitch the way a jet does soon after leaving the runway. Fighting gravity with a distinct disadvantage, the van's wheels began to spin. My momentum now gone like yesterday's whiff of springtime, I heard only the whirl of wet rubber on ice. Painstakingly I backed down the hill, sliding for heart-thumping seconds before my speed neared zero, at which point I released the brake to correct my steering, only to slide and palpitate again.

Happily without incident, we parked near the truck, dug our sweaters out from under other clothes, and bundled up in our winter's best. We zipped our jackets to the chill but shaded our eyes against the first direct rays of sun and began our hike up Vulcan Peak, at 4,655 feet one of the higher mountains on Oregon's Pacific front.

Another Vulcan! As we set off in deep snow we couldn't help but recall our ordeal on the Volcán las Tres Vírgenes, the Baja monolith so elaborately armored by cacti. But here, with the snow effectively repelled by gaiters and mittens and such, we felt more at home. In fact, Ann and I usually spend the cold months living in the snow, shoveling it and sliding on it daily for at least an hour or two on our telemark skis. But not this year, and so the cushioning white flakes underfoot felt good as we stepped down and squeezed the air out of them. We enjoy water in the solid form, even without our skis, and the unifying brightness of snow always strikes me as beautiful beyond any grasp of logic. The nip of frosty air in the lungs felt refreshing.

Soon the sun shone boldly over the Siskiyou crest, and its golden glare made us squint even with our shades on. The sky became polarized blue, and the forest was skirted with manzanita and stunted pygmy pines whose earthy green had been heaped with airy white.

Here in the Kalmiopsis Wilderness, a family of infertile soils called peridotite weathers from serpentinite—a greenish rock that floated up from the core of the earth to the ancient seafloor and later become exposed when offshore terranes slathered themselves into above-water existence against the North American Plate. The depauperate peridotite lacks plant-world staples of calcium, nitrogen, sodium, and potassium, and so it prevents most trees from entering life's great competition. Furthermore, the local soil excels in the heavy metals of nickel, chromium, and cobalt, debilitating to most vegetation but creating a niche for obscure specialty plants that have adapted. The trees that do grow — Jeffrey pine and incense cedar, for example — describe homuncular versions of their great cousins on fertile dirt. The forbs, shrubs, and dwarf trees on peridotite are so unusual that botanists from all over come here to examine them with hand lenses and taxonomic keys.

The serpentinite-based soils intermingled with others supporting larger trees, and as the morning sun warmed the burdened boughs, meltwater lubricated the snow, which sloughed to the ground, allowing the branches to spring back up. With scaly evergreen foliage flattened by evolution's rolling pin, the Port Orford cedar's elegant two-dimensional splays were especially adept at this melt-off, pop-up survival mechanism. Having become rare throughout its southern Oregon and northern California range, this cedar displays fluted, furry bark and magnificent reddish wood that's just the ticket for finely crafted furniture and the hulls of sailboats. A single bole can bring ten thousand dollars or more in the Japanese decorative market — more than the long-cherished redwood. Oregon's increasingly rare cedar is heavily consumed as a substitute for Japan's esteemed hinoki cypress, which is nearly extinct.

It's no coincidence that my first sighting of this emblematic tree of the region happened along a trail far above the highest reaches of the local road system. Cedars once excelled on lower terrain along streams and lakes, but a vicious attrition now means they are seen mainly beyond the reach of roads.

The reason for this is an exotic fungus originating with ornamental plants introduced from Asia. The dreaded *Phytophthora lateralis* resides in the soil, just waiting for the chance to attack a tree. It cannot be eradicated, and infected cedars cannot be treated. With the fungus originating in Asia, and with virtually every cedar log now being shipped to Japan, anyone who wants to talk about the biological perils of globalism need look no further than the Port Orford cedar.

Like viruses causing the common cold and influenza, the deadly fungus infects unrestrainedly if only it can get to where it needs to go. For colds and flu, people are the transit system as they sneeze on one another and shake hands. For the cedar's fatal fungus, the vehicles of opportunity are logging trucks, which hammer up and down the slurried mountain roads that wind for thousands of miles, the combined maze looking like a plateful of wet spaghetti thrown onto the map. More specifically, the fungus is spread by mud stuck in the trucks' tires. Once deposited in an area, it can spread through flowing water.

With the rapid rate at which logging roads were bladed into the woods during the 1980s and early 1990s, the showcase cedars faced near-extinction. Up to 20 percent are now infected, victims to the muddy tires that come to haul the current generation of cedars away and inadvertently doom their offspring before they ever have much of a shot at life.

Regulations require drivers to hose down the tires of their logging trucks, but everyone knows how difficult it is simply to clean mud out of the treads in a pair of sneakers. And, seriously, does anyone really expect loggers to be out there with a hose and a scrub brush, their heads crooked up beneath dripping brown wheel wells, during their six-pack hour at the end of the day? Or, for that matter, during the middle of the day, in the middle of the woods, just after they've passed through one of the invisible but ubiquitous fungus zones? How could such a rule be enforced? Purging mud from the treaded crevices of a fourteen-wheel vehicle, on an endless network of bulldozed roads where it rains up to one hundred inches per year and doesn't dry out for months and months at a time — all this hints of a good intention at best but more likely a bone thrown to botanists concerned about cedar extinction. Fortunately, the fungus does not spread by wind. So the effective way to arrest the deadly epidemic is by halting new road construction and closing some of the roads to nowhere that have already been built on public forestlands for the logging companies.

From the flanks of Vulcan Peak, our view extended into northern California and spanned the most diverse conifer forest in North America. This heart of the Siskiyou Mountains was recommended by pioneering conservationist Bob Marshall in 1936 as part of a million-acre wilderness park, a breathtaking vision that now represents the path not taken. In 1964 Congress safeguarded some of the area as the Kalmiopsis Wilderness, and in 1978 it expanded the wilderness to 180,000 acres, but that included a lot of high country and peridotite. Only 5 percent supported low-elevation old growth. Farther inland, southeast of Ashland, President Clinton later designated 52,000 acres at Soda Mountain, where the Siskiyou Mountains and the Cascade Range converge, as a national monument.

The snow from the previous night's storm deepened as we climbed to a ridge and then to the Vulcan summit. Jagged rock tapered down to the northeast until it plunged suddenly into the Chetco River canyon, resolutely wild from our view but containing more than met the eye.

Down there along the river, deep in the supposedly protected wilderness area, a crusty prospector named Darryll Brown had some years ago filed mining claims on twenty-two hundred acres of public land. To prove he had a valid claim, he pushed dirt around with his bulldozer, dug pits and trenches, and set off mountain-crumbling explosives. His claim on the national forest wilderness, otherwise off limits to logging, motor vehicles, and even bicyclists, depended on the Mining Law of 1872, which gives miners free access to public domain, license to damage public land and water, and encouragement to sell the payloads of dug-up rock without offering a dime in royalties to the taxpayers. While the Forest Service charges you and me $5.00 a night to camp in a remote location with no facilities, it's required to sell land in fee simple to miners for $2.50 an acre. Two dollars and fifty cents! Not to sleep for a night but to buy the place! The miners can, and do, then resell, sometimes for windfalls of thousands of dollars an acre. An anachronism from frontier days, the miners' privileged status on public land survives only because the industry gives suitcases of cash to the political campaigns of western politicians.

With all that injustice as a given, Phil Wallin of the Western Rivers Conservancy discovered the only way to avert an environmental catastrophe just waiting to happen along the pristine Chetco. He negotiated for seven years with Brown to buy out the mine for $2.5 million. Though it was a high price to pay simply to save some property that you and I already owned, this is the only option until Congress changes the mining law.

Our high and windy view extended beyond the Wallin-saved canyon of the Chetco to Pearsoll Peak, at 5,093 feet one of the highest among Oregon's coastal mountains (Brandy Peak, at 5,298 feet, rises above the Rogue River; the eastern Siskiyous rise higher and include Grayback Mountain, at 7,055 feet, near the California border). Hidden in a supremely rugged chasm just hinted at from our view, the Illinois River churned with big rapids to the north, the wildest and most beautiful river of the entire Coast Range this side of Canada.

Turning away from that heart of southern Oregon's mountain estate, I faced west from Vulcan Peak, where nearly a vertical mile below us the land made its fabulous end, the ocean its mysterious beginning.

At Oregon's Pacific edge the mountains literally emerge from salt water. Many appear as pointed islands, some of these scarcely visible offshore, some accessible only when the tide ebbs, some stepping directly up to the mainland and the flanks of higher peaks. One sea stack we saw resembled an obelisk, another a windy dome, yet another a flowerpot spilling trees out the top. Some of these first little westernmost peaks of the Coast Range are shaped like shark fins knifing toward shore, their surf side eroded vertically by waves, their landward side more inclined. Many of Oregon's 1,477 islands appear to be direct extensions of mainland ridgelines that dive into the sea and resurface only at their high points before finally submerging for good to the fathoms. Many stacks just seem to pop up out of the sea at random. They are formed by the landward erosion of the surf, which eats away the surrounding softer rock and ultimately leaves the stacks in various stages of isolation.

Getting the biggest bang for the buck in climbing an oceanfront peak, I bushwhacked through poison oak and then hefted myself up with some dicey steep-slope exposure on a miniature Grand Teton — a four-hundred-foot summit called Lookout Rock. From there I watched the ocean foam in full glory directly below; I could have dropped a stone into the water from that osprey's-eye view. Volcanic sea stacks rose to the north and south. Big, translucent rollers that might have traveled nonstop from the Aleutian Islands swelled offshore and nailed the rocks below me with a force that made my knife-edge perch seem uncertain.

Vanning our way northward, we pulled over often before crossing the estuary of the Rogue River, and then stopped frequently beyond it, and I soon began to think of this southern Oregon coast as the Big Sur of the Pacific Northwest. The weather is not as sunny, the ocean-edge mountains not as high or wild, the Pacific not as blue. But it still has the rugged beauty that goes with steep slope and surf. It has difficult-to-reach beaches that ensure your solitude once you've bushwhacked and down-climbed to get there.

The sea stacks and mainland mountains both have their genesis in a volcanic archipelago that collided with North America twenty or thirty million years ago — another stellar episode in mountain building and one of the more recent in the formation of the greater Coast Range. The more interior Klamath Mountains, in comparison, docked ashore as a series of accreted terranes and batholiths beginning about 120 million years ago.

Sandwiched as a sizable anomaly between the North American Plate and the Pacific Plate — the latter still out there in the ocean and creeping toward Alaska, just as it does south of Cape Mendocino — the Juan de Fuca Plate docks ashore here as part of the Cascadia Subduction Zone. Its origins lie in a volcanic rift three hundred miles off the West Coast. One of the active volcanoes out there is called Axial, which rises 3,630 feet and counting from the ocean floor, looking much like the Hawaiian Islands must have before their emergence above sea level. Axial and its wet cohorts are drifting eastward on the undersea Juan de Fuca Plate and eventually encounter the larger, more buoyant North American Plate. The point of collision lies not at the coastline, which would be a good intuitive guess, but rather between 60 and 150 miles offshore. Most of the dense volcanic rocks are driven under in the subduction zone, but secondary effects of this new geologic world order push up the Coast Range mountains. In addition to the puréed shale and sandstone and the greenish metamorphics characteristic of the erodible Franciscan Formation, evident along much of the California coast, the Oregon coast shows ample brown basalt formed by volcanism.

Geologic evidence indicates that exceptionally large earthquakes and tidal waves occur here at intervals of 300 to 1,000 years. The last massive earthquake was in 1700, which means that another could happen at any time now. Even more ominous, recent studies of the rift zone indicate that prehistoric earthquakes along the northwestern coast may have reached magnitude 9 on the Richter scale—a whopper that would make the San Francisco disaster of 1906 look like the Little One rather than the dreaded Big One.

A WOODED trail up the shapely 1,756-foot Humbug Mountain filled a delightful afternoon with views from one of Oregon's highest direct rises out of the sea. Then Highway 101 eventually delivered us to Coos Bay, the largest sawmill town in Oregon's Coast Range and a port for log-laden freighters. Industrial to its blue-collar core, the town sports mills in various stages of use and abandonment, mountains of sawdust, fuel tanks big enough for city water supplies, bleached boneyards of the millwright's refuse, railroad spurs for pickups and deliveries, and adjacent hillsides buzzcut in a starkly unabashed way that reminded me of the defoliated forest above a zinc smelter back where I grew up. With enough deferred maintenance to meet the definition of a rust belt, some mills lay dead but not interred; others limped along with a fraction of their parking-lot spaces filled by the daily commute of pickup trucks arriving from modest neighborhoods and trailer parks.

Whenever I arrive at a town like this, it evokes memories and complicated feelings because it is so much like the place where I grew up. In western Pennsylvania, the communities of my youth centered on steel production. The effects of that industry, in both the positive sense of jobs and the negative sense of smoky skies, toxic water, and ruined land, are more extreme than, but not all that different from, what I saw in Coos Bay. The local people in both places put all their eggs into one economic basket — one that ultimately lets them down.

Along with this heritage, I have a deep appreciation for both fine wood products and the forests that produce the wood, and so the plight of Coos Bay and similar places has interested me for years. I've read about the subject in countless books and articles, interviewed people, and written elsewhere about the fate of our forests, and here is some of what I've learned.

The main reason for the relative quiet of Coos Bay is that the largest trees are gone, having been cut down far more rapidly than they could ever regrow. Another is mechanization of the remaining mills, which eliminated thirty thousand jobs in the Pacific Northwest in the 1980s alone even while logging rates soared and industrial profits broke through the roof. And another reason for Coos Bay's sleepiness was graphically portrayed by an unambiguous sign atop a warehouse I saw sitting next to a city-sized freighter. While giant claws of cranes stacked logs and roughcut boards onto the moored ship, the sign on the warehouse said "Products for Japan."

Why this enterprise advertised the export trade so prominently was beyond me; local workers would have three times the number of jobs if the timber companies milled the logs here at home. And Coos Bay is no isolated case; from industry-owned lands the timber companies export virtually all the good boles of quality clear grain to Asia before milling.

A congressional bill sponsored by Oregon representative Peter DeFazio would have banned raw log exports and given back to Pacific Northwest workers nineteen thousand mill jobs now gone to Asia. The measure was beaten by timber lobbyists and industrial campaign contributors, a corporate group that sweet-talked its blue-collar workers by day but paid western congressmen by night to undermine American jobs. The corporations and their errand-boy politicians maintained the United States' status as the only nation in the whole Pacific Rim that doesn't protect its own workers from the export of raw wood.

But owing to a monumentally successful public relations effort by the companies and other right-wing interests, the laid-off workers think environmentalists are to blame. This fact was evident in local bumper stickers, in the acceptance of falsehoods spread by hate-mongers such as Rush Limbaugh who frequent local radio waves, and in casual conversations I had and overheard. The woods wars are a good example of people's adherence to cultural lines: conflict is likely if for no other reason than that the greenies are outsiders who look, live, and talk differently from the locals. The sawyers, planers, jointers, sanders, finishers, furniture makers, accountants, coffee shop waitresses, and truck drivers still blame the tree huggers, who might have stopped the final 1 percent of old trees from feeding the mills for a few months, but one of the big reasons for job losses is announced clearly on the exporter's own warehouse: "Products for Japan."

Reedsport, the next town north, looked similarly depressed, though I remembered it as thriving, with enough wood smoke for a valley-wide barbecue, when I last visited, in 1977.

Before heading on north, Ann and I pulled off along the lower Umpqua River, intending to stop for a short break. But then we decided to take advantage of the quiet spot and cook an early dinner. With a few minutes to spare between my chopping and dicing duties, I strolled down to the water, where twenty years before I had ended a memorable canoe trip. Once again standing at the edge of the river, sniffing the same aroma in brackish water, I could almost feel the hand of the past reaching up from the deep to pull me back.

It wasn't so long ago, I thought, as I fought the stark reality that it *was* long ago, that I was much older this time. A lot had happened since then, yet how quickly the years had slipped by. I stood there on the bank with old scenes of the Umpqua playing over again in my mind: crisp October mornings, the smell of matted leaves on the ground, the rush of unknown rapids, the people who came down to the rainy, muddy shores.

After dinner, when I dialed the seven digits in a Reedsport phone booth, I didn't know what to expect. Tom Richmond's number in fact appeared in the local directory, but after two decades I wondered if he was still there on his homestead across the lower Umpqua from Highway 38. I wondered if he would remember me, even in the fuzziest recesses of his brain. His phone rang twice.

"Hello."

"Hi. I'm Tim Palmer." I hesitated. "Is this the same Tom Richmond I met twenty years ago when I canoed the Umpqua River?" The silence at the other end of the wire was total but brief.

"The same man? No. That was a long time ago. Tim! How have you been?"

It was in 1977, with my former wife, that I canoed the Umpqua from near Roseburg, at the base of the Cascade Mountains, to Reedsport, one hundred thirty miles through the Coast Range. On the last evening of the weeklong voyage we faced a damp and rainy ordeal upon entering tidal waters that stretch sixteen miles up from the sea — the closest thing to a fjord south of Puget Sound and the largest incision in the Coast Range between the Klamath and Columbia Rivers. Steep slopes climbed from the zone of tidal surge, and mist swirled about the remaining crowns of fir, hemlock, and cedar. Seals poked their heads up through the silvery surface and twitched their whiskers as they watched us paddle toward their sea.

Needing a place to camp, and unable to wait any longer with darkness dropping, we hauled out on a muddy shore, quickly popped up the tent after kicking away a few cow pies, and scraped together a fire on which to cook our spaghetti. It wasn't ten minutes after my plume of punky smoke had scented the air that I heard footsteps behind me.

A bearded man, deeply hooded in a drab rain slicker, surveyed my scene of canoe, tent, fire, food, wife. I stood up. "How's it going?" he quickly inquired.

"Not bad," I offered through the rain, relieved at his friendliness. After a few minutes of chat, he said, "When you're done eating, come on up to the old farmhouse. You can warm up, dry out, and have some dessert. My sister and a few of her friends are there, too."

Thus began a friendship, like many in my traveling life, of one single day. But Tom and the way he lived lingered in my mind through the turbulent though promising seventies, and the vision of him there in these mountains jogged my mind every now and then through the heavily logged eighties and the cultural collisions of the nineties. When I stood by the Umpqua once again that evening, there on the estuary cooking dinner with Ann, I decided to see what had become of my friend.

"Yes, I'm still here," Tom answered on the phone. "But I have a new boat." His tiny skiff had been unsuitable for the biblical-scale floods that poured off the cutover land and sent battering rams of stray logs downriver. "Come on up. You remember the parking spot? Look for my 1964 Mercedes. The same one. When you pull in, I'll boat over and get you."

A while later, in early evening light, Tom piloted Ann and me across the two-hundred-yard width of the Umpqua, Oregon's fifth-largest river, running full beneath the boat. He had aged, of course, but still had a tall and trim look, squared off and straight, as he stood steering the boat in another drab old raincoat. His hair was shorter and thinner, his beard shaved off, his mustache gray. His movements had a slight stiffness, perhaps owing to a lot of hard labor, but the body language, the cadence of speech, the demeanor were all familiar. He *was* the same Tom Richmond, and I was the same Tim Palmer, each of us simmered in the stew of life for twenty years since we last met and neither of us having suffered too badly from an occasional rolling boil.

After tying up at his dock, Tom said, "I have to take care of a sick cow, but if you want to come along, we can talk while I'm doing it."

Tom's great-grandmother, an Indian from the Tututni Tribe, had lived in the coastal mountains near the Rogue River. She married a white man who landed there in 1820 from a Russian whaler, and Tom's mixed blood may have had something to do with the path he had taken. Though he grew up in Colorado, he always felt as if he had this place in his bones. During childhood visits with relatives he had bonded with the green pastures on the Umpqua-gifted floodplain, the neck-craning rise of the mountains, the silvery depths of tidal waters once fertile with salmon, steelhead, and sturgeon. "I always wanted to return," he explained to me.

A back-to-lander of the 1970s when I first met him on that gray, rainy night, Tom had already settled comfortably into his riverfront site. He raised a few cows, cut alder trees for firewood, gardened, shot deer in season, fished for sturgeon and sold the eggs, which are caviar, and did carpentry for cash.

Since that time, Tom had driven a Greyhound bus for sixteen years from Coos Bay to Eureka. "I loved it," he now said of his peripatetic tenure in gray uniform. "Every day my job was the most beautiful drive on earth. And I met some nice people, some who made a difference in my life. One of them, a Yurok Indian woman with a Ph.D. degree in anthropology, got me active in recovering some of the culture of my great-grandmother. The ways of her people had almost been lost. But I started digging, found an elder, Gilbert Towner, still living, and also located a few other people who are interested in reviving some of our roots. If we want to reclaim any of that culture, we have to take what's left and go from where we are. As old Gilbert says, we have to fill in the blanks the best we can and create what seems to fit. We're working on building a cultural center on the lower Rogue River. We'd like to bring back some of the Indian food and crops, start an apothecary using native medicinal plants, and revive traditional basketry with the materials our ancestors used."

After Tom drove the coastal bus route a few thousand times, the Greyhound drivers went on strike, a contentious ordeal of three years. "I soon figured I'd never be going back," he said of this segue into other lives. "For a while I drove bus for educational field trips all over the state. The best was with a geology professor. He was the scientist; I was the people person. But together we'd get everybody singing and having a fun time. We made a good team. Then he suddenly died of a heart attack, a very young man."

"Did that end your driving?"

"No. It just ended a really nice phase of life — you know, students, people, traveling. Then I started delivering half-million-dollar motor homes from a factory in Eugene. These ships were all decked out, painted up, carpeted, tiled, the works. Once I was driving to Raleigh, North Carolina, and this man got on the CB. 'Whose motor home is that?' he wanted to know. 'Sir,' I answered, 'this is Dolly Parton's motor home.' It was just bullshit, of course. But he said, 'Can you put Dolly on the radio?' I said, 'Listen, Mister, Dolly will be a very unhappy woman if I wake her up from her afternoon nap.'"

We laughed. "How about a woman of your own, Tom?" So far I hadn't noticed any signs around his farm.

"It's hard to find a woman who's willing to wade around in rubber boots in the winter, though summers are paradise."

"Not just anybody would want to live on the other side of the river."

"The boat ride, in the dark, in the rain, in the floods — it all eliminates some of the prospects, you might say that, yes."

And then there was the cow. To call her sick was a bit of an understatement. The otherwise prime Jersey milker had pinched a nerve while giving birth, and now her rear legs were paralyzed. But perhaps only temporarily. Tom had slung her rear end in a hoist borrowed from his vet and suspended from an A-frame cleverly bolted onto the back of an old truck. Her rear end bulged with exposed tissue. Tom gently swabbed the animal's membranes, fed her well, and watered her with care. "I might have to get rid of her. A little more time will tell. I'll keep her if I can. But you know, I'd like to get out of the cattle business. Having a good milk cow is one thing, but the price for beef is less than it was twenty years ago. All the cattle do is keep the grass mowed and give us something to eat."

"So how *are* you making money these days, Tom?"

"Oh, listen, I have a nine-to-five job. Actually a one-to-nine job. This just happens to be my night off. I collect weather data at the North Bend airport for the National Weather Service. I enjoy it. I get home late, which is a bummer in the wintertime, but I have my mornings free. Mornings are the best time to fly."

"To fly?"

"Yes. I got my pilot's license a few years ago. I love to fly. The big changes around here have nothing to do with me driving bus or nursing cows. If you really want to see what has happened in the past twenty years, come on up in the air with me."

"You can take me for a plane ride? Over the Coast Range?" My excitement at the idea of seeing the beauty of the mountains from the air was palpable.

"Tomorrow morning. All it will cost is the price of gas, and I'll pay half."

WITH LITTLE effort we manually pushed the tiny Cessna Skyhawk 172 into position on the North Bend runway near Reedsport. Tom proceeded to inspect the wings, rudder, propeller, and wheels.

"Better safe than sorry," I aphorized.

"Taking off is an option," Tom added in that vein, "but landing is a requirement."

We climbed in, snapped our belts shut, and plugged our ears with headsets so we could talk to each other without having to yell above the engine noise. Tom kicked over the motor, taxied, revved up the windy rpm's, and then gunned his little vessel until that miraculous instant when we became lighter than air.

We lifted off and the earth receded below as we crossed the inlet of Coos Bay. Within seconds we soared like Lindbergh over the ocean. "Right there, check it out," Tom advised, turning the plane on its wingtip and banking us into a three-sixty, though I think my stomach kept going straight ahead. I gripped the armrests hard and strained to see a whale as it surfaced, spouted, and dove beneath the blue, its baby alongside. "We saw them down in Baja," I commented without enthusiasm, not wanting to encourage Tom to continue the acrobatics.

"What? Do you recognize the barnacles?" he asked me, a playful glint in his eye as he straightened the trajectory and pointed out the location of my barf bag in case I needed it.

The sandy mounds of the Oregon Dunes National Recreation Area rippled out below, the largest coastal sandhills complex in America, stretching for forty miles. Scores of lakes mirrored the sun's glare like tin roofs—water pockets trapped amid the migrating tonnages of sand that had their genesis in the coastal mountains. The sand is carried to the sea by rivers, then returned once again to shore by heavy surf, and finally piled up and massaged into shape by wind.

Immediately east of the dunes lay Highway 101 on its north–south track, constantly encroached upon by the dunes' windward migration of up to fifteen feet per year.

Just on the other side of Highway 101, I could see where the clearcuts began. They are nominally hidden from ground-level travelers by a paper-thin beauty strip of trees. This way Oregonians are less troubled by the fact that their birthright of a rainforest has been chainsawed to oblivion. Seen unobstructed from the air, the clearcuts lay like bad cubist art, receding to the Coast Range crest and no doubt beyond. For the whole distance the mountains lay checkered with dirt-brown patches of recently stripped vegetation. The pale green of new growth gained a toehold on some steep slopes, and darker shades of forest struggled as adolescent stands of pole-sized timber. Those young forest patches had greened up enough to ease my squint, but greenness alone does not constitute forest health.

From having walked through those kinds of forests and talked to foresters such as Wally Mack, I knew that the even-aged woods were biological deserts. They lacked the old, rotting logs that nourish new trees. They lacked the decomposing cellulose that provides a home for bacteria, moss, and insects at the vital base of the food chain. They lacked the microbes of fungi that build up in old-growth soil and symbiotically support the trees in vital ways by adding to their intake of water, nutrients, and minerals. The even-aged forest lacked snag-topped nesting sites for birds that prey on insects harmful to the forest. It lacked sunlit openings. It lacked the refuge of upended root balls that result when big trees fall after a life long lived.

Below us now, the Smith River of central Oregon wound with sinuous grace from its mountain vastness, but its basin had been clearcut to the hilt. Some of the cutover acreage was national forest land. A lot was owned by the forest industry, its condition typical. Throughout Oregon's Coast Range, 96 percent of all the land has been logged. The lonely remaining 4 percent lies in the Kalmiopsis, Grassy Knob, Rock Creek, Cummins Creek, and Drift Creek Wilderness Areas of Siskiyou and Siuslaw National Forests, along with thirty-five lesser groves on federal land and in state parks. None of those small, lonely tokens of old growth appeared in our wide-angled view.

I had read about northwestern forests and their problems, but now, with the view out of Tom's airplane, I realized that discovering something by seeing it firsthand is a far more powerful experience than just learning about it. Even from two thousand feet in the air the effect was shocking, as if I had stumbled upon a large animal that had been skinned, its bloody, human-like muscles exposed. "What a pathetic place Oregonians have let their state become," I said to Tom, who took no offense but only nodded grimly. I knew that cut and pillage had been the way of life a hundred years ago, in the era of the robber barons. Well, it still is.

At a westbound bend in the Umpqua River we saw Tom's property and a respectable second-growth tract of Siuslaw National Forest adjoining a tributary basin to the north. "They want that, too," Tom announced through the headset, his choler scarcely more hidden than when he had told me about his beloved border collie who had been torn to bits by feral dogs a few years back.

"Coho salmon still find their way up there to spawn," Tom said of the creek. "But they're so rare that scientists come here to study them." Coho are the salmon species most adapted to the coastal rivers and creeks, and they are threatened, endangered, or extinct throughout their range in Oregon and northern California. The principal cause is heedless logging, which causes silted spawning beds, low flows, and high water temperatures.

Along this line Tom added, "Everyone I knew who made his living by commercial fishing is now out of work." Before such widespread forest destruction, fishing for salmon accounted for sixty thousand jobs in the Pacific Northwest, an industry comparable to wood products.

While the timber companies expounded on their thin porridge of economic justification based on "jobs versus owls," much of the fishing enterprise was allowed to die a heartless and avoidable death. The practitioners of that great, age-old trade went to Alaska for salmon-fishing's final hurrah. Or they retrained for new jobs that they didn't want. Or they went on welfare, which they wanted even less. After taking down the fishing industry, many loggers are now on the dole as well.

South of the Umpqua River, Tom pointed out the Elliott State Forest and adjacent industrial land, both so riddled with convoluted logging roads that the scene looked like an outlined diagram of brain tissue. The tree-sheared spaces between the roads could have been bombed. The ongoing erosion from the slopes was extreme, evident even from our height. This view of Oregon was more reminiscent of a napalmed battlefield in Vietnam thirty years earlier than of a rainforest signifying Oregon's true nature.

Swinging upstream from his land, Tom pointed down to a yellow-dirt landslide beginning like the source of a spotlight, its beam fanning out to engulf the slope and everything in its path below. "That's where my neighbor lived. His house was nearly destroyed by a slide coming off a logged slope. His homeowners' policy wouldn't pay for the losses, so he's suing the insurance company." I knew that people have been killed in slides below clearcut areas.

"Shouldn't he be suing the logging company?"

"They're gone."

While reforms improved logging practices on federal land during Bill Clinton's presidency and put many of the remaining old groves off limits to cutting, private land is still being clearcut with abandon. Here in the central Pacific forest, considered "globally outstanding" and "endangered" by ecologists who rated the threats to America's landscape, three-quarters of the total coastal forest south of Canada is privately owned, and most of it is being cut aggressively. State regulations apply, but they are weak and ineffectual in preventing the kinds of results now seen, big as life in our view from the air.

"The logging used to happen slower," Tom said, "and the steepest slopes were spared. But not now. They take it all, and they take it right away. Now I believe what my grandfather said when I was a kid: 'In your lifetime there won't be a stick of timber left in this country.' The corporate timber barons in their offices in Portland or San Francisco never have to look at this, never have to live with it." I took pictures through the open window and fantasized about showing them in the corporate boardrooms.

"The loggers," Tom said, "overrun anything in their way, and unfortunately that includes the system of forest health that's needed to make the forest regrow. Look at that down there. Without soil, how are you ever going to grow trees?"

I was pushing myself to remember about balance, or compromise, or even the necessary sacrifice for essential roof joists and toilet paper. I was trying to think about how reasonable the industrial spokesmen sound when they come on the radio or get quoted in the newspaper. But what Tom showed me from the air was the most widespread and total destruction of a mountain landscape I could imagine. And it's still going on, day after day.

Along some of the roads, Ann and I had seen signs announcing when the forest had been cut and replanted, signs that claimed renewability. But in fifty years, when trees might have managed to regrow into pole stands capable of nominally yielding logs for a sawmill, the forest will be cut again, each cycle further depleting the soil and the land's ability to produce the next batch of trees until ultimately the regenerating ability will be gone. On many serpentine soils of the Siskiyous and the Pacific coast, even the first generation doesn't grow back. Some forest watchers believe that long-term depletion will be starkly evident after four rotations of careless cutting. The captains of industry must think it's even worse than that because they are closing northwestern mills and moving operations to the southeastern United States, Asia, and Siberia.

There is hope for the public forest, if not the private industrial land. Supervisor Jim Furnish of Siuslaw National Forest in the late 1990s reduced timber sales from 360 million board feet in one year to almost none and vowed to close 80 percent of the roads that had inflicted such damage during the logging spree of the Ronald Reagan years. And then, in 1999, Forest Service chief Mike Dombeck took the courageous stand of banning new roads and most logging in wild areas where roads have not yet encroached. It was a historic turning point for the agency. After assuming the presidency, George W. Bush promptly tried to rescind these reforms, and how they will withstand the test of time remains to be seen.

There would always be more to see, but the time to punch in at the weather station was approaching, so Tom banked the plane homeward.

I rejoined Ann, and later that evening we all returned to the Richmond plot of sacred Oregon ground, arriving as the moon rose over the mountains.

"Do you remember what you served up for dessert that night when I camped along your riverfront?" I asked as we paused there together at day's end.

"Whatever it was, I'll bet we put fresh cream on it."

"Yes, exactly! We had home-canned peaches with real cream on them. It was so good I'll never forget it."

"That was a good time in my life," Tom reflected. "Milking the cow was a meditation. You just sat there doing this thing that people have been doing ever since cows were domesticated, and everything else disappeared. I still milk the cow, but back then people shared more. Now it seems everybody's into their artificial little worlds. They're concerned about their car, their house, their computer. Me, I'm happy to walk across the ground, to feel the earth under my feet. Down here, on this land, in this valley, I feel like I'm safe. But I'm not. Is anyplace safe today?"

A MORE personal form of safety became the topic of conversation soon after I met another Tom — Tom Ireland — back at the Harbor Light Family Restaurant in Reedsport, where Ann and I had stopped for breakfast, once again naively thinking we were on our way out of town.

We sat at a booth next to the logger, his profession evident from the gray pinstripe shirt called a Hickory, the red suspenders, the steel-toed, deeply treaded, high-laced boots, and the yellow full-brim hard hat, which for some reason fell from its resting place on the seat and hit the floor with a resounding clunk that could hardly be ignored. "Don't go losing that," I said good-naturedly as he reached to pick it up.

"You're right," the big logger agreed. "Without that lid I'd be out of a job. Or just watch, that's the day I'd get smacked in the head for sure. But, you know, mainly I'd be out of fun. I just gotta have that yellow hard hat."

After a few pleasantries about how good the weather had been,

Tom Ireland returned to his original theme. "I like being a logger. That's why we do it. There's all this stuff about using wood—we all use wood—and about the economy—we need the timber jobs. That's all true, but you can't get around the fact that loggers like to log. I could make more money doing other things. It's hard work, but it's also like being a kid. We're outside, fooling with cables, saws, and axes, driving big machines, and all around us are mountains."

"It sounds great. But what about the hard-hat part? What are the chances of having an accident?"

"There's always that chance, but I don't go to work every day thinking I might get hurt. It's not like it was fifteen or twenty years ago. If someone got hurt back then, you logged over them. Now, if someone's new or injury-prone, guys on the crew will say, 'Hey, you're in the wrong place.' If we can't train a guy to be safe, we send him on his way. He'll end up getting a job with some unsafe company. You can still find a few of those."

With wrinkles under his eyes, gray streaking at his temples, a gold wedding band fitting tight enough to pop out the skin on his finger, and expanding midribs, this logging boss appeared to have stood the test of safety for a couple of decades in the woods. I said, "I suspect the presence of danger adds to the fun—that's the nature of adventure—but do you think about your kids, and what will happen to them if you get hurt?"

"It's funny you mention that. Not long ago I was on a Cat, fighting a canyon fire above Interstate 5. Suddenly the engine went out. I started sliding backwards without power, without brakes, on a steep mountainside, nothing but that freeway down below. I set the blade, but it's made for plowing forward and only threw dirt and rocks up in the air. I kept drifting backwards, and you know how the seconds pass slowly in times like that? What I thought of was my kids. I wondered, What will happen to my kids?"

"Couldn't you jump off?"

"No." Tom shook his head emphatically. "Anybody who jumps dies. You can't get clear. One truck driver I knew lost his brakes in the mountains. He jumped and got run over by his own trailer. Then the truck stopped in two hundred feet. You gotta stay on."

"So what happened?"

"Well, fortunately the 'dozer ran up on a big old root ball and stopped. I sat there sweating and looking down on Interstate 5, the fire burning up above me."

Through the picture window of the café we saw a log truck bulging with a stack of small-diameter trees and snorting through the intersection. "That's a load of alder," Tom interpreted for me, though I had recognized the gray-barked tree of streamsides and wet slopes. "It used to be nothing but a weed tree. Now there's quite a bit of alder being cut, though you can't take it just anyplace. The mills are now so specialized. Some logs go two hundred miles. Trucking is a big part of logging today. We'll take logs to one mill, sort them, and then take half of them to another mill. Some mills take large logs, some small. But we don't cut alder for the mills we deliver to."

"Do you cut Port Orford cedar?"

"Oh, yeah. They used to leave it behind. Now you get three thousand dollars a thousand—that's a fortune for a thousand board feet. For that price we're hauling up logs that were left in the woods twenty years ago. Being cedar, they're still good."

"What about the fungus that's killing the cedars? It's spread by log trucks, isn't it?"

Tom nodded. "We wash off the tires at the end of the day." As if to prove the effectiveness of hosing down at the maintenance yard in Roseburg, he added, "It's a breach of contract if we don't." With this cedar-and-fungus discussion, Tom now knew that I knew something —that I wasn't just a tourist in Oregon for some disappointing steelhead fishing or a noisy jet-boat ride on the Rogue River.

He added, "People think that loggers are heathens, and that's true some of the time, but a lot of us are doing what we can to make logging better. We like to fish and hunt; it's all part of being here. That's why we live here. So we do what we can. We avoid digging up the land. My company used yarders with sky-lines even before we had to. It's better for the land that way. No doubt environmental interests have driven the changes. They pushed the concerns, and that was good; improvements were made."

"Don't let me hold you up if you have to get back to work," I said, mainly to give Tom a graceful out for my next question. "But, do you have any of the old-growth debate up here like they have down in the redwood country?"

"Don't worry about holding me up," Tom said. "I can have another cup of coffee. I'm the boss! But, no. There really wasn't much old growth out here. The coastal mountains have burned through the years. You might have heard of the Tillamook fire. There is old growth up in the Cascades, to the east. And the limits they've put on logging up there have pushed us back this way — back out here to the Coast Range. If anything, there's now more logging out here than there ever was. It's like the 1950s again. Out here, the trees grow fast. Trees that were planted when I was a kid, in 1958, are now two and three feet in diameter, good for cutting. It rains a lot here and there's fog in summer, so these trees never lack for water. When I was a kid, everybody hated what Weyerhaeuser did to its land, cutting everything down and reseeding by helicopter. But now they're already recutting that forest. And it's a beautiful forest."

With this outgoing, forthcoming logger, who obviously knew his job well, I suppressed a subscript blinking up in my mind. There once *was* old growth. The bits that remain are still being fought over by people like forest activist Julie Norman and hundreds of others. . . . The Tillamook fire was big, 311,000 acres, but not much compared with the whole coastal mountain complex. . . . And, come on, hosing off the trucks is not stopping the Port Orford cedar's fungus, any more than free hypodermic needles have stopped AIDS in the ghettos. . . . And, sure, the regrowing forest, cut on forty- or sixty-year rotations, is beautiful when seen as a vigorous young crop of arrow-straight logs. But it's not a forest. Biologists are quite clear, in fact, that the adolescent forest between twenty and one hundred years of age is the least productive for wildlife.

Nonetheless, this logger's perspective was valuable and interesting. Furthermore, I liked the guy. I wanted to hear him out. And I knew, from small-scale experience cutting firewood and building log cabins, that logging really *is* fun.

"You should come out and see what we're doing. Come see for yourself," Tom insisted, giving me directions to his job site.

THE ROAD to the logging operation climbed alongside a small stream running off from a universe of clearcuts, some in neatly regrowing twenty-foot trees, some whiskered in a bristly cover of seedlings, some still in the skinhead phase that had wiped the slate of nature clean. Switching back and forth up a steep and erosive slope — landslides evident wherever water had collected — the road eventually mounted a narrow ridgeline where the legacy of unrestrained logging was as obvious as it had been from Tom Richmond's Skyhawk. Sometimes no more than ten or twenty feet wide, the ridges had been stripped bare and bulldozed flat for roads. Slopes steeper than those negotiated by the finest skiers I know had been denuded. I was curious to see what a current logging operation, run by a conscientious and outdoors-loving foreman like Tom Ireland, was doing differently.

At a saddle in the narrow ridgeline, I came to a bulldozer, semi-permanently parked, that Tom had mentioned in his directions. The Cat's front end was cabled to a thirty-foot vertical steel pole, which was also guy-wired amply to the ground so it could support one end of a stationary cable yawning out into space and sagging under the terrific weight of logs being airlifted off the mountainside below. A yarder, or super-powerful winch, reeled in a thousand feet of movable cable that was linked to the stationary cable. The other end of the cable had been wrapped around logs by three choke-setters down in "the hole"— the bottom of the hill, where the last trees of the sale had been cut by fallers, tidied up by limbers, and bucked into truck-length logs with chip-spewing industrial chainsaws.

At the top, one man operated the yarder inside a glass console, but no one else was around, so I walked to the periphery of the job and began to pick my way down the mountainside toward the bottom, four hundred feet below. Workers down there shouted directions and warnings to one another. I looked for Tom to get an expert description of the scene.

Almost too steep for footing, the hillside had been completely cut except for some currant bushes, to which I clung for self-arrest. As Tom had said, they hadn't zigzagged the precipitous slope with roads to haul the logs out, and they hadn't dragged them like plows across the ground, which would have caused erosive gullies in the gouged-out tracks. By hitching the logs to the cable, suspended in the air, they caused less scarring of the soil. But on the trip up hill, the logs were not entirely airborne; some of them dangled down and dragged against the ground part of the way, especially near the top, where the slope steepened even more in a concave climax ending at the bulldozed loading dock and command center.

Halfway down the mountain I met Tom and the chief faller, a ruddy-faced man named Ken, both of them puffing on their way back up. "So you made it," Tom greeted me, a bit surprised to see me halfway down the hole.

"This place keeps you on your toes," I commented about the steepness. "Or maybe I should say it keeps your heels dug in."

"Nothing's too steep to cut," Tom answered. "But if this were much steeper," he acknowledged, "it would be a cliff." Stopping for a breather, he added, "Hey, check out those buffers along the stream." Obviously proud of the job, he added, "We didn't touch it." The stream itself, for now, appeared unmarred. But only alders grew along its banks. The hemlocks and cedars were gone. State regulations forbade clearcutting up to the edge of a stream with fish in it but allowed selective logging of commercial trees. And if there were no fish to be found, the rules didn't apply.

I commented on two cedars, six inches in diameter, the only standing timber on the entire forty-acre grid of land that had been mowed. "So how come those trees don't get to go to the mill?" I asked.

"I think maybe the faller got lazy. It must have been Friday afternoon," Tom joked. But he knew what was on my mind. "Sometimes you can select-cut, taking only the largest trees, but not here. Not with a sky-line set up this way. Any standing trees would get in the way."

The three of us gripped at handholds and toeholds as we heaved our way out of the hole, Tom's and Ken's progress impeded by their substantial loads: two chainsaws that made my old firewood-cutting McCullough look like a toy. Meanwhile, the choke-setters down below wrapped another cable around a log they had sawed off. The line-setter attached a cable that hoisted the goods up to the sky-line. The yarder operator threw the switch, and the monstrous big load of biomass swung into the air, swaying like a pendulum. Then it zipped upslope, thudding into the ground now and then, where it splintered limbs as big as Tom Ireland's leg without even slowing down.

True enough, loggers do hard, physical, dangerous work, outdoors in all weather with saws, axes, cables, ropes, big-bladed Cats, and equipment so powerful it pulls a log out of the canyon like a kite on a string. I stood and took in this display of force and cunning and good-spirited work, and I wished above all that no one had to worry about destroying a system of life and a watershed in the process. But I kept my reservations to myself.

"You know," I said to Tom and Ken, "this *does* look like fun. I can see why you guys like being loggers." Catching their breath, they both beamed from under their yellow-brimmed hard hats.

BETWEEN THE Kalmiopsis Wilderness of southern Oregon and Olympic National Park of northern Washington, the largest uncut mountain refuge is a 5,839-acre tract hidden north of the Alsea River, about two-thirds of the way up the coast of the Beaver State. I had to see it, especially after enduring mountain after mountain that had been clearcut to dirt, a quondam forest logged to smithereens from one end of Oregon's Coast Range to the other.

No sign marked the route to this little Shangri-la, a place scarcely identified on my maps. After a low-gear pull followed by decreasing widths of forest road, Ann and I came to a dead end, where a small sign identified the prize: the Drift Creek Wilderness Area. With lunch and a camera, we set off to see the sights.

Almost immediately the second-growth conifers and tan oaks gave way to some large Douglas-firs, western hemlocks, and western red-cedars. Huckleberries sprouted as if in hanging planters from broken-off trunks rotting through the centuries. Licorice ferns grew as whole gardens in the crotches of trees. Salal shrubbed the ground with leathery leaves promising to pump their juices into dark blue berries in the coming months.

We switchbacked down the mountain to Drift Creek, and the descent seemed to go deep into my soul as well. The place felt inexplicably good, with tall trees rising up around us, mountain ridges protecting all that lay below—a refuge showing little sign of the blitzed world beyond this little island. Among meadows, glades, deep canopies, and mossy streamfronts, I realized that Drift Creek was one of the most beautiful places I'd ever seen, and the reason was that it had simply been left alone.

Up the creek we embarked on one of the slowest walks I can imagine, but it wasn't slow enough. As at Sinkyone, each detail was exquisite. Here, the greening leaves of dogwood sharply etched in front of a fir's golden trunk. There, the stream riffling behind the elegantly streaked bark of a cedar, furry like the coat of a mink. A real mink scampered up the shore and imprinted five-toed tracks in wet sand.

The stream performed a musical score through overhanging old growth where blackberries, raspberries, and thimbleberries unfurled new life. If I had spoken, I would have done so quietly, without any gossip or small talk. "How could they just cut trees like these down without at least having a second thought or two?" Ann asked.

She hadn't been with me when I agreed with Tom Ireland and his foreman that logging would be fun. And now I was glad I didn't have to defend that statement. It would be fun in the way that building dams in my backyard stream was fun when I was a kid.

We wandered down Drift Creek until stopped by a barrier of undergrowth and steep walls, and we peered onward to where the current hurried and disappeared. Outside the designated wilderness another six thousand contiguous acres remained uncut and could still be protected. The valley had the look of a remote hinterland before anything on earth had gone haywire, if one can imagine such a time.

"Can you believe those tiny little needles can blot out the whole sky?" Ann asked when we stopped and looked up with reverence. I later did some checking. One fir tree can hold sixty million needles. Even without counting roots or soil, the needles provide an acre of surface area for retaining water and slowing runoff.

Almost anywhere we looked, massive logs, some of them dead

twice as long as Ben Franklin, lay in various stages of rot — just another name for recycling. Their carbon and nitrogen had simply gone to work fueling new arrangements of chromosomes. Organisms had sprung from the compost as if it were consecrated with the ultimate life force, right there in the dirt of an undisturbed Oregon forest.

And how about this for some perspective on our own backyard: in the most productive tropical rainforest, such as the Amazon River basin, 185 tons of plants per acre can be found growing. But in a forest such as the Drift Creek wilderness in the Pacific Northwest, the average is 400 tons per acre. Some redwood groves produce 1,800 tons — the largest such figure on earth.

On that clear spring day, the sky seemed so close, the ocean so near. This hallowed wilderness lay halfway in between. Alders, ferns, dead snags, ancient trees, youthful trees, cedars so durable, hemlocks so flexible, firs with bark as wrinkled and worthy of respect as elders — all of it encircled us, surrounded us. Leaves quivered and birds sang in secret languages. I tried to imagine what this whole mountain range once was — what it someday may be again, some long and troubled reckoning from now.

As we climbed back out of the valley, I thought about a proposal I had seen by visionary conservation biologists. This area could be the heart of a biodiversity plan for Oregon's coastal mountains. The remnants of wildness would be relinked by protected corridors where nature would be allowed to recover. The idea of old forests reblanketing the coastal mountains even in limited corridors appealed to me, but the fact that 57 percent of the Oregon Coast Range was privately owned, much of it by the forest industry, made it difficult to foresee the plan becoming reality anytime soon. Yet groups such as the Western Rivers Conservancy have had some success in buying back a few critical tracts of forestland. Perhaps there was hope.

BACK IN THE van, Ann and I motored north through towns busy with the tourist boom. Since 1973 Oregon has had a progressive land-use law requiring that urban growth boundaries be established to curtail sprawl. But those controls seemed hardly evident amid commercialization strung for miles outside the larger towns. That the town fathers of places such as Lincoln City had somehow managed to comply with a state requirement for urban growth boundaries seemed like a farce. Development sprawled at the fringe of each little burg.

They looked different from when I had first traveled this way, in 1967. That summer I worked as a carpenter and laborer for the National Park Service at Crater Lake and always had weekend hitch-hiking exploits. Back then sawmills dominated the economy. Today the service industries employ seven times as many northwesterners as do timber, agriculture, and fishing combined.

There's an upside to this trend: people want beautiful surroundings for their communities and for recreation.

And there's a downside. When we drove through Newport, the radio announced a request for zoning changes to allow an outlet mall in a wetland. Recreational shopping had come to the Oregon coast, no doubt making old Tom McCall turn in his grave. Oregon's illustrious governor from 1967 to 1974, McCall shepherded pathbreaking laws regarding land use and seacoast conservation that are still on the books. But now a right-wing legislature challenges his legacy on a daily basis. Filling McCall's big shoes, Governor John Kitzhaber in a single year vetoed more than forty bills that would have undermined the environment of his state. But development pressure still runs rampant, and whether Oregon's new sources of wealth will be any more kind to the land than the loggers of the past is a good question.

North of Lincoln City, Ann and I detoured onto a mountain road that wound up dozens of tight bends to the summit of Mount Hebo, at 3,154 feet one of the higher coastal summits north of the Kalmiopsis (Mary's Peak, east of Newport, is the highest, at 4,097 feet). Hebo's top had once been part of an Air Force base, which set the stage for what we now faced: another jungle gym of antennas, sci-fi saucers and spheres, soccer-ball radio receptors, and microwave bouncers junking yet another prominent mountaintop consigned to relaying conversations from cell phones and electronic bleeps off satellites. Wilder country lay on the mountain's flanks, but on the ransacked summit we strolled in a cool drizzle, the ache for something better almost audible between us.

REDEEMING itself once again with remnants of its original nature, Oregon next offered us Cape Lookout, which changed our mood entirely. We walked on a spellbinding woodland trail to steep drop-offs plunging into the ocean, and like Oregon's other great capes — Cape Sebastian, Heceta Head, Cape Perpetua, Cascade Head, Cape Meares, and a dozen more — it offered the finest of the Pacific meeting the coastal mountain front.

And Lookout signified more than that. It happened to lie just a few miles north of a line of classic geographic significance — the forty-fifth parallel of latitude, halfway between the equator and the North Pole. In an amazing coincidence, this was also the midpoint in the northwest-trending mileage of the Coast Range, Baja to Kodiak.

We were now halfway.

There, with Sitka spruce rooted into steep slopes and with a stormy Pacific crashing against ancient rock, the chainsawed clear-cuts seemed suddenly distant, and it occurred to me just how fabulous this entire mountain range really is. I had started our journey thinking it would be interesting, beautiful, and adventurous, though I secretly regarded the coastal mountains as second-hat to ranges such as the Sierra Nevada and the Rockies. But with new wonders at every turn, with its pulsing mix of life and landforms, its rocky peaks and sensuous profiles, its precious remaining forests, its seascapes and snowfields, its rivers, salmon, and glaciers to come — with all this and more, how could anyplace be finer?

Halfway through both the arc of the hemisphere and the mileage of the trip, I was also at a point about halfway through my life. If I'm lucky. Thankful for all I had seen and anticipating much to come, I began to regard the rest of the journey with a greater sense of urgency — an awareness owing partly to the undeniable shortness and uncertainty of all life and partly to fears that the natural world was changing so drastically, so quickly. I wanted to see it all, before it's too late.

Oregon had shown us some of the best of the coastal mountains and some of the worst of what has been done to them. The network of state parks along the shore protects incomparable coastal beauty, though the clearcuts just inland have comprehensively knocked nature down.

Partly satisfied, partly troubled, we moved on, and after a few more stops we came to the Columbia River, the largest we would cross, the largest in the entire American West.

Pausing one last time on Oregon soil, we looked across the Columbia's powerful flow toward the bluff of Cape Disappointment. Rising on the Washington side, a cliff-top lighthouse marked our path to the north.

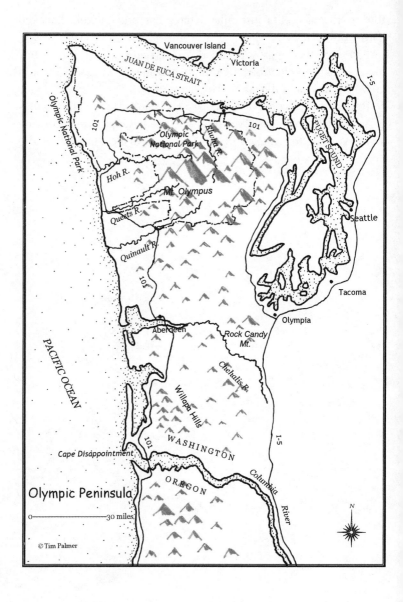

Olympic Peninsula

0 ————————— 30 miles

© Tim Palmer

# 10 | *Olympic Odyssey*

$S$OMEWHERE out there in the great unknown, Mount Olympus connected the earth to the sky, though for now it remained hidden in the fog, the mist, the clouds, the rain, the snow.

By any measure a crowning jewel of the Coast Range, the 7,969-foot monolith is the first glacier-clad peak fronting the Pacific and the highest mountain so close to the ocean south of Canada. It's nearly twice as high as any other summit between southern Oregon and Vancouver Island and centerpiece of the largest national park on the West Coast south of British Columbia, surrounded by the greatest wilderness and largest old-growth forest. Few places had the potential to show in such vivid terms the interactions of nature in the mountains I had come to enjoy and learn about.

I simply had to see Mount Olympus. And more than that, I wanted to climb it, to thrill in the view from the top. But the year of our trip turned out to be the wettest ever in northern Washington. Rainfall topped one hundred ninety-one inches at the Hoh Ranger Station, located at the base of the twenty-mile trek to the big mountain, and the peak itself got far more than that — up to two or three times as much. Though known for its gray skies and raininess, Seattle, in comparison, normally receives thirty-five inches of rain.

In the wet month of April, and especially in *that* year, we would never have made it to the summit. We wouldn't even have seen the summit or, for that matter, anything much at all beyond the metal claws of crampons strapped to our boots for traction on ice. I knew I'd have to return to climb to the home of the gods at some other time. Meanwhile, Ann and I would see what we could at lower elevations in the Olympic Mountains, the heart of a peninsula distinguishing the far northwestern corner of the lower forty-eight, the same peaks that so many people see as the striking western backdrop of Seattle, Tacoma, and Olympia.

Easing into the difficult, wet place, we ventured to the southeastern hills of the peninsula and pulled over to camp along a dirt road, which seemed remote enough for peace and quiet. But late in the night unwelcome company arrived. Grunting aggressively, a pickup truck peeled into the woods and back out again, once, twice, three times. Then it got stuck in there. The engine whined and roared; the tires grated and buzzed; the driver swore and cursed until he finally scored some traction that sent his machine lurching back onto the dirt road. In a violent final escape, it kicked gravel up onto the van. With this introduction to the region, I locked the doors.

The next day we drove to Capitol State Forest, a large tract under care of the Washington State Department of Natural Resources. But that doesn't mean good care. An overgrown logging road served as a path to the top of Rock Candy Mountain, where soil had inexplicably been piled up by a bulldozer and the U.S. Geological Survey's elevation marker vandalized. From the 2,356-foot hillock now growing up in a doghair thicket of Douglas-fir, it was obvious that the lowlands of the peninsula had once been a forest haven and a logger's dream but now represented the aftermath.

Like everything in the Coast Range, the scene resulted from the dual effects of geology and climate. Without much topography in the way, Pacific storms blow freely inland between Saddle Mountain in northern Oregon and the Olympics, allowing rain to soak the lowlying hills of southwestern Washington. As the Coast Range's largest open doorway to maritime weather, these well-watered lowlands extend one hundred seventy miles eastward to the formidable slopes of the Cascade Range. Meandering through the chilly open-air greenhouse, the Chehalis River valley had supported the most wood-packed forest of all. Loggers plucked an extraordinary 1.5 million board feet of lumber per acre from this arboreal Eden (ten thousand board feet can build an average house). Every acre was cut, and most were cut again, and some yet again.

My view from Rock Candy Mountain revealed the state forest and all the land around it as one sprawling serial clearcut, an industrial tree farm now full of timber fit for fence posts or, at most, telephone poles. Logging roads ribboned out in all directions like a funhouse maze done up big. The trees stood in cornfield regularity, not a single old or rotten specimen fit for a woodpecker to be found. Regional essayist Robert Michael Pyle called this, his homeland, "a ravaged land, awaiting the next ravages."

Driving the roads of the peninsula, we were greeted by signs that said "Welcome to the Working Forest." The working forest, as far as we could see, was shaved or in various stages of adolescent struggle, the mathematically organized rows of trees well herbicided, the exotic knapweed, Scotch broom, and yellow clover a plague wherever the soil had been disturbed. Empty beer cans marked every pull-out, with rifle or shotgun casings a midden on the ground even where there was nothing to shoot.

At the southwestern side of the peninsula we paused in the mill town and log-shipping port of Aberdeen, which was brightening up a bit with the current Pacific Northwest economy of service, retirement, and computers—a new regional profile in which logs are scarcely noticed.

Then we pressed on north to the Queets River, which flows from the southern flanks of Mount Olympus itself. Upper reaches of the stream had been safeguarded in Olympic National Park, but the lower miles had been claimed by lumber companies and homesteaders, and the final few bends ran through the Quinault Indian Reservation. Seeking to protect one single American river, from headwaters to sea, in the National Park System, the federal government in the 1930s had bought up the private acreage along the river. As a result, the Queets is the country's only sizable river outside Alaska protected in a national park for nearly its entire length. The acquired corridor, however, is only a mile wide, and the rest of the lower basin has suffered heavy logging.

Also a thin but magnificent corridor, sixty-two oceanfront miles north of the Queets had been folded into Olympic National Park, but only after they, too, were cut. Ann and I walked the trails and beaches, longer than any other wild shoreline north of the Lost Coast of northern California. Though not as mountainous, this oceanfront includes fine unroaded frontage, all of it a mix of remote beaches, fortress-like piles of driftwood, recovering forests, and rocky bluffs gamely meeting the brunt of Pacific storms.

Virtually everywhere but in the national park, the Olympic Mountains are a case study of forests cut down. This might be getting depressing, but I'm just the messenger, and that's the way it is. And grim as it may be to a tree lover, it's the story of everyplace. Nationwide, only 2 to 5 percent of the original old growth remains.

In the Olympics, state ownership of a substantial 365,000 acres made no difference; the Washington State Department of Natural Resources was directed to generate income for schools, and on autopilot for that task, it harvested down to the last stump. Loggers leveled a similar acreage on Indian reservations through contracts that didn't even include reforestation. Completely cut, another 1,750,000 acres belong to private owners, two-thirds of it to timber corporations, the deeds themselves a scam against the public dating to hundreds of straw men who acquired title under the ruse of homesteading and promptly signed their spreads over to the companies for enough money to buy a round of drinks. Even in Olympic National Forest — a 650,000-acre stronghold of public domain — nearly everything was logged except for 90,000 acres of wilderness, most of it at higher elevations. Finally, 900,000 acres of Olympic National Park are off limits to logging, but owing principally to snow and ice, only 27 percent of the park supports old growth.

Always looking for a way to continue the cut for another year or two, the timber industry has persistently tried to open protected land to logging. And it has succeeded. The original Olympic Forest Reserve was reduced by more than 700,000 acres. Then 170,000 acres of lowlands were subtracted from Mount Olympus National Monument in 1915. The next year a law allowed for the salvage logging of dead trees as well as "potential" insect-infested trees within Olympic National Park. Before 1958, loggers removed 100 million board feet of national park timber under the auspices of salvage.

The abundant harvest made logging a way of life for nearly a century, and in the town of Forks the timber culture still hangs on. At this hot spot in the forest conflicts of the 1980s and 1990s, the industry and its supporters successfully resisted efforts to slow the rate of cutting until the ultimate limits were reached—most of the old trees are now gone. Court actions were the only thing that persuaded the Forest Service to reserve some remaining old growth, late in the battle over endangered species such as the northern spotted owl.

In an earlier effort of this type, President Theodore Roosevelt designated Mount Olympus National Monument in 1909 as a refuge for elk, which were being decimated by poachers. Though Congress didn't agree—not unlike its response to the national monument designations by President Bill Clinton nearly a century later—a wilderness reserve of 600,000 acres resulted. In 1938, after visiting the area and drawing a supportive crowd of ten thousand people in the small town of Port Angeles, President Franklin D. Roosevelt signed a congressional bill designating Olympic as a national park. It includes thirty-five peaks higher than seven thousand feet.

Though it represents only the core of what was once a much greater forest, Olympic National Park stands out as an uncommon example of a landscape that politicians set aside in spite of commodity values. Unlike the situation in many parks, where the prerequisite appraisal of the land and trees had to show little with profitable potential, the timber of Olympic was worth a fortune.

One of few radial ranges in America, the Olympics don't pile up in the roughly north–south alignment that characterizes the Appalachian Mountains, the Rocky Mountains, the Basin and Range Province, the Sierra Nevada, the Cascade Range, and most of the Coast Range. Instead, they ramp down in all directions from the central summit of Olympus. Fifteen rivers radiate loosely from high country like spokes on a wheel. This description may make the Olympics sound like an enormous volcano, but they're not. Though much of the rock is igneous, the mountains themselves have seismic origins. The Farallon Plate, which preceded the Juan de Fuca Plate by fifteen million years in its collision with our continent, mostly disappeared beneath the larger North American Plate, but in the process the mountains we now see were piled up like a wedge near the plate-to-plate line of contact.

Adding further definition to the mountains' shape, the peaks above timberline collect more snow than melts, so the annual surplus compacts into dense layers of ice — into glaciers. Though appearing solid, these flex with surprising plasticity and flow as one might imagine a sluggishly viscous river doing. The top of the ice is more brittle than the underbelly, so cracks occurring at stretch marks become crevasses — open slits determined by underlying topography, bedrock, and boulders. The Olympic glaciers rank as America's third most extensive outside Alaska; only Mount Rainier and Mount Baker in Washington, which are far higher peaks, boast larger glacial systems.

The reason it snows so much here is that the Olympics push clouds up to where they are cooled beyond the dew point, producing fog or rain, and then the mountains keep pushing the clouds up beyond the freezing point, producing snow. And there are far more clouds here than anywhere in the Coast Range to the south; the climate in the northern Pacific is wetter, owing to the weakening of the Pacific High weather system. In addition, the mountains retard the storms' movement east, causing rain clouds and snowstorms to pile up against the high country and precipitate in place rather than in passing. All these climatic forces team up to create the wettest place in the contiguous states. Common annual levels of precipitation increase from 100 inches in Oregon to 130 on the Olympic Peninsula, with an estimated 350 to 500 inches falling at higher elevations where no gauges are kept.

Because of ample rainfall, the Olympics at lower elevations serve as an unrivaled nursery for giant trees. Next to redwood country, here is the greatest biomass per acre in the world. The climate is the key, and defining the word *temperate*, the coast of Washington sees fewer freezing nights than northern Louisiana, yet in July it's cooler than in

Minnesota or Maine. Knowing congenial weather when they see it, three-quarters of the birds stay here on the northwestern coast for the winter, compared with one-quarter in the Northeast. The land doesn't even burn very often, which is another reason why the forests live to be emphatically old if they're not cut down.

To see what had been spared, Ann and I drove to the Hoh River trailhead, cloaked up in our best waterproof gear, and hit the trail. The April rain beat steadily on the ancient forest and dripped down on us, and it showed no sign of easing up for days or maybe weeks. While impressive in its life force, the rain dampened and chilled us in just a couple of hours, and it definitely pinned us down to low elevations.

Unseen, yet superlative in so many ways, Olympus was a peak I still had to climb, or at least try, and so Ann and I returned in late August the following year for a shot at the summit during better weather. But because of the danger of disappearing into depthless crevasses, plus the difficulty of finding a route to the summit when rain or snow can blind you at any time, Olympus is not a peak for the inexperienced, ill equipped, or unaccompanied.

My approach to these challenges was to bone up on technique by rereading the classic text *Freedom of the Hills,* to borrow mountaineering gear from an old buddy in Portland, and to invite Ann along with me to see how far we could get. Her approach was to search the Internet, and she ultimately convinced me to call Olympic Mountaineering, an outfitting store and guiding service in Port Angeles, to see what the experts had to say. Over the phone, the hazards seemed real enough, so I arranged to meet Steve Teufert, the only professional guide I'd ever hired except for Trudi Angell in Baja. We would rendezvous at Glacier Meadows, a backcountry campground where forests end and glaciers begin. But just to reach the meadows, Ann and I had to trek for two days up the Hoh River valley.

As THE ultimate American rainforest, the Hoh valley begins on the eastern flank of Olympus and then sweeps around the mountain's northern base before taking a firm westward bead on the Pacific. At every step along the way I could look in ten different directions that each provided a forest scene of captivating beauty: the coppery bark of a tree as wide as our van, the sunlight on clover-like oxalis, a bleached snag of western redcedar that might have died centuries ago, the glassy slip of transparent springwater gurgling from the filter of deep forest duff.

The air, a soothing tonic, penetrated wonderfully deep into my lungs. Clean and moist, blowing in off the Pacific, it was spiced with fragrances of spruce, fir, and smaller woodland wonders. Yellow light beamed in sunlit clearings and through luminous green filters of bigleaf maple leaves, and I concluded that a sunny day in a rainforest is very hard to beat.

Though we had spotted our first Sitka spruce with Nancy Reichard near Arcata, and though this conifer is the dominant sea-level tree the entire way to the Coast Range's outermost sprig, on Kodiak Island, these bushy-limbed, sharp-needled evergreens reach their grandest profile in the Olympics. Here they top 220 feet, while in Alaska they typically reach 165. Growth rings on trees here measure four times the width of their Alaskan brethren. A temperate climate counts.

Giant trees columned up out of the ground with trunks four, six, eight feet in diameter. As we ascended the Hoh valley with heavy packs on our backs, the elder Sitkas yielded space to western redcedar —the girthiest northwestern tree except for the redwood. Douglas-firs stretched more than two hundred feet into the sky. Any one of those lunkers could have germinated in the year 1300, and they very likely measured a foot and a half in diameter when the *Mayflower* landed. The Douglas-firs need sunlight, so they pop out of the ground after a great fire or a blowdown. At the other end of the scale, the western hemlock reigns as the king of shade, the climax tree — meaning that only hemlock seedlings grow well in the shade of a mature hemlock forest. The mature forest keeps on being hemlock until some catastrophe such as a blowdown occurs. Moderating this effect, however, the Sitka spruce maintains a captivating presence because Roosevelt elk graze heavily on young hemlocks, often tipping the balance toward spruce survival. Lightening up the soulful mood of this forest, the starry foliage of vine maples textured every scene with fine lace.

Just as fascinating as the trees on this ultimate arboreal adventure, the mosses and lichens grew in thick, dripping carpets and in living globs on the trunks, branches, rocks, stumps, log rot, and every other available surface. "Do you think it's safe to put our packs on the ground?" Ann asked facetiously. "Or will they be grown over before we finish lunch?"

Probing for depth with a slight sense of unease owing only to fear of the unknown, I stuck my hand six inches deep into a soft cushion of moss that covered low-lying limbs. What else was in there? Plenty: microscopic decomposers by the billions, fungi, mites, springtails, insects, spiders, centipedes, and more.

Lichens had names such as pencil script, beaded bone, antlered perfume, forking tube, fairy barf, lettuce lung, tree flute, freckle pelt, frog pelt, ragbag, bark barnacle, and Methuselah's beard, the latter of which can grow twenty feet long. *Isothecium* grew everywhere in fila-mentous strands, like the Deep South's Spanish moss but without the snakes. On some bigleaf maples, lichens and mosses weigh three times as much as the tree's own leaves. But they don't hurt. In fact, they help the trees and are essential to forest health.

These primitive plants process nutrients and chemicals from the air and share them with their host. They rake moisture out of the fog and deposit it on the tree or in its root zone, and they absorb rain-water and spread its benefits out over time. They even provide natu-ral pesticides that enable the trees to resist attack. Knowing all this, some broadleaf trees such as bigleaf maple actually sink aboveground roots into the masses of epiphytes festooning limbs and trunks.

Back down to earth, there was no letup in botanical delights. Groundcover grew in the most whimsical and artful patterns, the prettiest mixed-green, prewashed salad for elk one could imagine. A dozen herbaceous species might have sprouted at our feet, some leaves shaped like hearts, some like serrated discs, some like mittens, others cutleaf or lanceolate, ovate or elliptical, reniform or lobed, compound, cleft, or dentate. It's as if the forest floor were a labora-tory of every possible shape of leaf and they all turned out to work, or as if children were given shiny green construction paper and the task of creating leaves in every shape their unfettered little minds could grasp. And there we were, with all their artwork on display.

Most of the groundcover, lush and juicy, lacked barbs, spines, and the hard-shell defenses of flora in arid places. Plants here had little need for prickly or scaly adaptations; there was plenty of summertime forage for wildlife, and any defense against evaporative loss of water wouldn't count for much here, where slugs could drown if they weren't careful where they laid their trails of slime. Rather, the need in the rainforest is to gather the most light, and so a winning strategy is to flatten one's leaves to the sky in order to absorb the most rays. This made the ground plants all the more showy because their foliage faced up at our admiring eyes.

Chlorophyll is what enables plants to process sunlight, and it's also what makes leaves green, so it was no coincidence that local species had vivid dark green foliage. They needed the magnum dose of chlorophyll to harvest the limited light leaking down on the forest floor.

In some places mosses carpeted the ground completely, forcing new trees to resort to seeding and rooting on the fallen trunks of earlier generations — literally growing on the backs of their ancestors. Also offering better retention of water, the rotting nurse logs hosted new groves in rows that clearly defined where an old trunk lay. It was free and reliable child care that would last a century or two. The new trees would eventually wrap roots down over the decomposing log and tap into the ground, and by the time the nurse log was completely rotted away, each tree's roots would have filled in to make a stout trunk. All this might require a couple of hundred years. Anything worthwhile takes time, which is an important lesson of the rainforest.

Here among all this life and all this rot one can learn an even more basic lesson: if you want to live, you have to die. It's the most fundamental deal we all make.

And a corollary: the individual dies, but the system of life goes on. I'm reminded of lyrics I once heard Joni Mitchell sing, simply repeated and to the point: "Birth and death and birth and death and birth and death." With little time for mourning, life takes over immediately after death has its moment. The total effect blurs the distinction between the generations of the last millennium and those of tomorrow. It's really all the same. New life thrives on the death of the life beneath it, which earlier thrived on the life beneath it, and so on, down to the gritty surface of rock that thirty million years ago rafted in from the depths of the sea to become the Olympic Mountains.

The effect of the groundcover and the overstory—along with a rainforest of ferns, thickets of berries in multiple delicious species, and elbowing spreads of shrubs as showy as azalea—was a world greener than anything the imagination could conjure on its own. Earlier in our trip I had stood in the Santa Monica Mountains looking out at an ocean so big that I easily understood that the earth is mostly blue. But from here I might conclude that the earth is all green.

This was only the first of seven days we would spend on our trans-Olympic odyssey, first ascending the westbound Hoh valley, then climbing Olympus if we could, and then crossing two major mountain passes to the northeast and exiting via Boulder Creek and the Elwha River.

With much of the very finest in the geographic quartet of mountains, forests, rivers, and seashore, Olympic is one of America's premier national parks. It is mostly wilderness and mostly rainy, but even the more accessible areas are lightly visited compared with Yellowstone or Mount Rainier.

Unique in its biological importance, the park supports a number of plant and animal species that are endemic—found nowhere else—and the reason is ice. The Cordilleran or continental glaciers once flowed down out of British Columbia and buried Seattle three thousand feet deep, isolating the Olympic Peninsula and limiting the species that could migrate to and from this biological island. With the abundant rainfall and mild climate, and with the gradient going from a mile and a half high down to sea level, the mix of species is a taxonomic delight.

Furthermore—and obvious right away in this temperate, well-watered place—the size of plants and animals is extra large. The world's champion western redcedar grows here, twenty feet thick. The bulkiest western hemlock rises in the Quinault River valley. The biggest Douglas-fir dates back a thousand years in the Queets valley. The largest Alaska cedar, silver fir, grand fir, subalpine fir, and vine maple still put on weight here. An elder Sitka spruce bellies out at a girth of forty-two feet and vies with an Oregon tree for champion status.

And it's more than trees. Olympic marmots, for example, are enormous. Propped up on rocks to watch the tourists hike by, these spaniel-sized rodents pose like cute little sphinxes of the high country. The Roosevelt elk — named for T. R. after he saved their habitat — outgrow all other species of elk. Plus, just hiking along, I couldn't help but notice that the blue-flowering larkspur, ankle-high in the Rockies, reached clear to my head. It's even called "tall larkspur." Petals of the king gentian unfold large enough to be noticed in the gaudiest florist's shop. Recognizing the extraordinary biology of the park, the United Nations Educational, Scientific and Cultural Organization proclaimed it an international biosphere reserve and a World Heritage Site.

On our first night, Ann and I camped at Lewis Meadow, where I flattened myself in the grass after enduring spasms of back pain on the hike up. I hoped I wouldn't be too troubled in the demanding days to come.

To avoid the blood-suck of mosquitoes, we lugged our gear down to a breezy gravel bar along the Hoh and fired up dinner while the sun set behind a massy green grove of virgin spruce and hemlock.

With dazzling weather the second day in a row, we pattered up the valley to the High-Hoh Bridge. There we stared, wide-eyed, a hundred feet into a slit-like chasm where water roiled with suspended gray flour that had been pulverized from rocks grated against one another by the creeping glaciers. Higher then, and steeper, the trail wove through silver firs whose glossy green needles flashed white underneath. Higher yet, at its southernmost appearance in the Pacific-front mountains, we entered the zone of mountain hemlock — a tree that needs to be cold to survive.

The trail cut into cliff-like side slopes, where we caught glimpses of the snowy, icy peaks above, and it seemed as if the early romantic Jean-Jacques Rousseau had written about this place from France way back in 1761 when he described what he meant by "beautiful country." He wrote: "A flat stretch of land, though ever so beautiful to some, never seems so in my eyes. I must have torrents, rocks, firs, dark woods, mountains, steep paths hard to climb or descend, with precipices on every side to make me afraid."

No doubt in beautiful country, we arrived at Glacier Meadows and pitched our tent.

That evening we met Steve, the stranger to whom we'd be entrusting our lives. He had just guided a group to the summit, and—always a good sign—everyone seemed to have made it back. Bearded, with long, graying hair thinning on top, he had a hawkish nose and a compact, wiry build and was dressed in a pile jersey and quick-dry leggings with gym shorts overtop. "Be ready at six in the morning," he told us without a lot of fanfare.

A starry, windless night bode well for the next day's weather, but up there you never know. Actually you do know—you know that the odds are for bad weather. And sure enough, by four-thirty, when Ann and I inchwormed out of our toasty sleeping bags, it was cool, cloudy, and breezy. When we met Steve in the dark at six, it began to spit rain.

"So, how goal-oriented are you?" he asked me in our first get-acquainted moment.

To summit Olympus was why we had come. I regarded the climb as essential to my Coast Range explorations. "I'd like to get to the top if we can do it safely."

Steve nodded. He understood. So without comment in the wakening daylight, he rummaged through the cache of essential gear, which had been stowed in a watertight box. A hundred-foot climbing rope, spiked metal crampons to give our boots traction on glaciers, harnesses to buckle around our waists and clip into the safety rope, and ice axes were all placed in a pile and then divvied up.

As daylight leaked out of the heavy overcast, and as we climbed, and throughout the day, I pieced together Steve's story of life on this mountain he calls home. He first summited when he was fifteen. "I lived in Port Angeles, here on the peninsula, but also grew up near Seattle and in Central America."

"That's quite a range of habitat."

"My father died when I was very young," Steve explained. "An uncle in the military raised me, so we moved around a lot." Peripatetic, Steve didn't attend normal schools after grade six. "I had army tutors, exams, and placement tests. Then I got a scholarship to a college in Florida."

"The highest peak there is three hundred forty-five feet above sea level," I commented, having spent some time in Florida myself.

"I summited there," Steve acknowledged with a chuckle. "Yeah, Florida was pretty bad. But in the summers I worked on a ranch in the hills of Georgia. And then when I graduated I hiked the Appalachian Trail." Winding for two thousand miles through the forests of the East, Steve met Jack Ganster of Pennsylvania. Eventually the two hiking buddies started Olympic Mountaineering.

"I love the Olympics," Steve said with unabashed enthusiasm as we zipped our storm parkas against increasing rain. "And Port Angeles, too. It's an old mill town with a lot of the old-style guys — 'Hey, woman, get over here!'— that type of thing, but it's also got a lot of people who have moved in because they like the mountains and the water. It rains a lot, yes, but you deal with that. I'll say to Barb and the kids, "Hey, it's the biggest storm of the year; let's go hike up the Bogachiel River for the day!' Plus, you can get away once in a while. I drive to eastern Washington to rock climb in the dry coulees. On some years the whole family goes to Mexico for a month or two. There's great rock climbing in the mountains of Mexico."

Steve had been climbing regularly in the Olympics for twenty-three years, probably enough to wear an average human body completely out. He runs the store but still guides a hundred thirty days a year, much of it rock climbing but also with frequent summit attempts on Olympus. "We make it to the top or to the false summit about 70 percent of the time," he said. A daughter, twenty-five, and son, thirteen, set him apart from many mountain guides, who tend to be single for occupational reasons.

"You seem to make the unconventional life work," I noted.

"Well, yes. The other life failed for me."

"What do you mean?"

"I once had a job with Eddie Bauer in Seattle. I showed up every day wearing a tie, and I worked in a basement office with no windows. I'm ashamed to say it's the only job I ever walked off of. One day I just knew, right then, that it was killing me. I got out of there as fast as I do when I know an avalanche is coming down."

"Do you ever get tired of climbing Olympus, and the long hike in?"

"Never. There are hard days, yes. It might rain for weeks. But tired of the mountain? No. Of being here? No. And the hike in and out is what I enjoy the most. I do it alone. I get into the Zone, mile after mile through that rainforest. It clears my mind, keeps me healthy and sane. There's nothing like it. I'm not sure how other people get what I get by walking up and down the Hoh River valley."

After a vigorous first-light climb through stunted trees, we topped the steep slope of a lateral moraine — rocky debris pushed into place by the side of the glacier. There, with the final step up to the ridge of rock we had been ascending, and in one startling instant, the world of snow and ice and lofty peaks burst into view. Like a world apart, the blue ice and white slopes lay before us, all in phantasmic harshness. All I could do was stare.

Bringing me back to basics, Steve said, "Last chance for a civilized dump." There on the top of the moraine the Park Service maintained a wind-anchored trash container equipped with a blue plastic bag dispenser. "From here on we shit in a bag and carry it out with us," Steve announced. "Or, you can bag your deposit and leave it right here in the can." I elected to do that, snatching a baggie out of the handy dispenser and scrambling off to a private side of the ridge. When I returned, Steve said, "We have to do everything we can for this mountain. When you climb a popular peak such as Rainier, you see trash and human waste all over the place. But not here. We keep this mountain clean."

At the base of the steep moraine, the Blue Glacier swept down the mountain and carved the landscape even as we watched. With the forest below and the rush of glacial water pounding seaward, the scene was Alaskan in severity, in epic scale, in potential for discomfort.

After scrambling to the foot of the crumbly, steep slope we stepped onto the glacier, and instantly our lives were changed. For starters, the earth no longer lay underfoot. Instead, we stood on water — frozen water sometimes white, with the consistency of packed snow, sometimes as blue as lapis from ages of accumulated freezing. Cracks in the ice — our first crevasses — streaked laterally across the glacier. Mostly they looked easy to step across, but some gaped wide and required us to go around. Rocks had fallen onto the ice through the hundreds of years it had crept down the mountain from its origin high up the slopes, and now those rocks textured the frozen surface like blue-gray candies pressed into the sugar-white frosting of a birthday cake.

"Time to rope up," Steve said, unraveling a blue-and-orange nylon line that looked like an endless caterpillar. Briefly he explained the concept of tying ourselves together for one intertwined fate.

"We'll each clip a carabiner into these figure-eight knots, with me in front. Walk so that most of the slack is out of the rope. If anybody falls into a crevasse or down a steep slope, the other two people self-arrest."

To perform this mandatory feat of heroism, you fall onto the snow facedown and slam your ice ax into the glacier. The ax has a handle about three feet long, and at the T-shaped working end, a small hoe turns out on one side while a sharper pick points out on the other. You dig the pick end into the snow and then hold on for dear life — yours and everyone else's in the party.

"You'll get pulled and tugged and maybe even flopped around a bit," Steve casually warned, "but eventually the ax will hold and we'll stop the other person's descent. Then we'll set up a rescue using snow anchors, prussic lines, and a Z-rig pulley system." This sounded fine in theory. But would it possibly work in real life? "Don't worry," Steve added. "We shouldn't have any trouble."

Steve gave us the option of wearing crampons or not. He didn't wear his, and he appeared comfortable without them. But after a few hundred feet — some of it treacherously slippery where ice mounded up in hummocks between crevasses — Ann and I strapped on those stainless steel traction devices. Immediately I felt like Spiderman, able to walk anywhere, though we had to be careful not to spear our ankles with the sharp points bristling from the opposite foot.

Though the rain blew against us in a fine mist, the sun suddenly poked through the eastern clouds for a minute or two, sparking my hopes. It was clearer to the east, I reasoned, so maybe the clouds were just a whopper of an ocean fog. But the next hour put me somewhere between wishful thinking and gross denial.

The air thickened like a white sauce made by an inexperienced chef, with globs of atmospheric flour lumped here and there. Whole new cloud masses boiled up from the valley while others rolled down from the summit. The wind picked up. And up. We were going to get hammered with whatever the sky could deliver, hammered.

After detouring left to bypass a crevasse, swerving right to miss another one, and giving a wide berth to a whole complex of chasms where the ice scraped against rock walls of the mountain, we stepped off the glacier and onto a snowfield that angled up steeper than escalator steps between rocky outcrops. On a gritty ledge we took a break and I devoured a Clif Bar, thankful for the caloric boost as I felt the first drops penetrate unsealed seams in my rain gear.

"Have you been up that way?" I asked Steve, pointing to an impossible chaos of icefall and freestanding blue-white towers called seracs, where the glacier had fractured apart in the steepness of its pitch down the mountain. I was wondering what the outer limits in the world of glacial mountaineering really were.

"Yes, I've climbed that route once or twice. It's not as hard as it looks."

"Have you been up the mountain in winter?"

Steve smiled. "Back in our testosterone days my friend Shane and I decided we wanted to climb Olympus every month of the year. Eventually we made it. But it meant wading across waist-deep streams on the approach, roped up because the water could sweep you away. And avalanches — now *there's* a definite hazard in the snowy months, and also when it gets warm in the spring. We had some pretty wild times doing the every-month thing."

"This is the best month to climb Olympus, right?" I asked, though you certainly couldn't prove it by the weather at hand.

"Definitely. Winter's hard, and so is spring, with all the fresh snow, and so is fall, with the autumn rains. Other than in late summer, this mountain can be quite a challenge. Even in the best of times, it turns a lot of people away."

"But it's only a four-thousand-foot climb from Glacier Meadows," I said, knowing this is not an unusual gain for a vigorous day of hiking.

"Yes, but it's all mountain. I'll take this climb any day over Rainier." Steve spoke again of the great peak of the Cascades, the criterion mountaineering destination of the Northwest. "You can have every one of its fourteen thousand feet if I can have the eight-thousand-foot summit of Olympus. There's great climbing over there, don't get me wrong. But the dog route up Rainier is far easier than what we're doing here, with the challenge of crevasses, bad weather, route finding, and the final rocky pitch up the summit face."

Still having all that to look forward to, we got back to business, kicking steps into a steep and narrow couloir, and emerged on a dreamy rounded slope called the Snow Dome. Zigzagging, Steve led us to the top, where we were blessed with a break in the clouds and a truly astonishing view of the glaciers and peaks surrounding Olympus, almost but not quite revealing the summit itself. Dark, petrous masses of ancient undersea terrane now bit like underjaw fangs up into the clouds. Below them the snow and ice began immediately, sloping off the summits and ridges and then tumbling in the concave slopes of headwalls. Below those, blocks of ice looked as if whole cities of skyscrapers had been knocked down by Godzilla and then frozen in some wickedly polar epoch. Farther down, the glaciers flowed in sweeping, sinuous curves usually seen only in geology textbooks.

"This is why we do what we do," Steve said, gesturing to the severely spectacular view in front of us. "We just want to turn people on to mountains, and bringing them up here is the way to do that. Some guys charge $700 per person to guide here. We charge $150 if people get a small group together. We like making this climb possible to anybody fit enough to come."

With clouds swirling about and rain fuzzing everything within sight and totally obscuring the rest, the scene was a classic Coast Range experience of mountain, ice, and rock, with the weather as a powerful player for keeps.

Next, our route traversed a vast glacial plain with the sharp blue scribing of crevasses left and right. Parts of Olympus' East, Middle, and West Peaks jutted up in the background, but unclearly, as if we were looking through frosted goggles. Starkly black-and-white, but mostly white, the scene lacked detail for scale and perspective, and I couldn't tell if we had yards or miles to go. The crunch of crampons in snow and the static noise of raindrops on my storm parka drowned out other sounds, just as the clouds mystified the further recesses of our mountain. During one pause, Steve noted the deepening tones of gray layering everything above us. "We're going to hike up there into nothing," he announced.

Now and then I turned to look back at Ann, who was always doing fine, and at the void of space below. The world we had known receded and then disappeared as completely as if we had been catapulted in one abrupt fling to someplace like Baffin Island.

We climbed on in our roped line, Steve fading to gray ahead of me and misting out in the cloud and in the rain that blew between us. Only our umbilical cord of braided stretchable rope connected us to one another, but it felt almost as good as a handshake. With mere whiffs of visibility now between gusts of the storm, route finding would have been impossible had Steve not known the way.

At a flat and featureless spot he waited and motioned Ann and me forward. He had something important to report, I could tell. I was afraid he might suggest we go down.

But instead he warned: "Pretty soon we come to Crystal Pass. This is the crux of the climb. We have to cross some deep crevasses on snow bridges. One of these days they're going to collapse, and we don't want to be on them when they go. It's a long way down. So we'll need to keep moving."

"Hey, no problem here."

We could see the first bridge up ahead, a weighty wedge of crust that lingered between two crevasses aligned head to toe. Had Ann and I come alone, our enthusiasm would have been seriously deflated at this point by doubts regarding life expectancy.

The dicey move bent around the end of the first crevasse and the beginning of the second. No garden-variety gaps, these openings yawned quickly out to ten-foot widths and depthless black pits, tapering thin and then opening again into whole rooms of underground caverns that could at any time be jammed shut by the clapping hands of moving ice.

Then, way more frightening, we approached a skinny snow bridge spanning another, wider crevasse. What held the bridge in place was not evident. Where we would fall if the bridge collapsed was not evident, either. We could see only, say, fifty feet down. If Ann and I had been climbing alone, this was definitely where we would have hung it all up and gone home.

"There are eight people in there," Steve later told us, recapping the tragic story of the latest among many accidents. An experienced mountaineer had summited with his grandchildren. Glissading down — skiing in his boots — the man arrived unexpectedly at the great crevasse. He slid right in. Days later — it can take that long to get word out — Steve was helicoptered in by the Park Service. Nobody had much hope for a rescue at that point. Steve rappelled two hundred feet down inside the crevasse. Two hundred feet is the equivalent of twenty stories down the side of a skyscraper. Or — more akin to Steve's experience — it's like twenty stories down the black unlit elevator shaft inside a skyscraper. All done on a half-inch rope. Inside the ice. Ice that moves whenever it wants to.

"It was creepy," Steve admitted. "The inside of the glacier at that depth was completely black. With my headlamp I could see the man's legs, still far below me. I'm sure he had been dead a long time. We left the body there."

Steve began crossing the skinny bridge. I tried to position myself to self-arrest in case the bridge caved in, and I wondered what would really be required to stop our guide's fall. An earlier path, kicked into the snow by other climbers, had crumbled away. A new path skirted higher than the old one and then teetered on the apex of the snow bridge, which sloped down on either side like the crest of a roof — a roof that would have fit a doghouse without much overhang. Steve crossed, took up the slack in the rope, and planted his ice ax in a boot-belay position that would presumably enable him to catch my fall in quick order. I walked through as light-footedly as I could, climbed up the slope a bit, and planted my ax in the snow so that if Ann plunged into the depths, I could arrest. Theoretically. She crossed with careful steps.

"Some people come and climb this mountain without any protection," Steve said. "They could fall into a pit like that. If you're not roped up, there's nothing anybody else can do. The victim can die of exposure, if he hasn't broken his back in the fall. I hate to see people come here who don't take the precautions they should."

Two more pitches of steep snow slope and a few more detours around crevasses brought us to an upright bread loaf of rock, with nothing else visible above it. In increased wind and rain we scrambled to the top. "This is the false summit," Steve announced, a little less than victoriously. "We're just a hundred feet lower than the real summit, which is over there." He pointed to the void ahead of us.

Through a patchy blend of opaque and translucent atmosphere, I saw a ghostly dark form jutting into the sky. With a bit more clearing it came almost into focus but then disappeared, a black wall of rock, point-blank in front of us but separated by a shallow saddle, a steep snowfield, and a very thick atmosphere.

"Sorry about the weather today," Steve apologized as a particularly sleetish gust of wind wire-brushed our faces, "but that's the Olympics."

"We'll take it like it is," Ann said, of course having no choice with the weather but still having the full range of choices in how to regard the moment.

"We can go up if you want," Steve offered, referring to the phantom-like summit in front of us. "It's wet. It's slippery. It's rotten rock. The visibility is poor and getting worse. And it's a tricky Class 5 climb to begin with. We can go, but I don't recommend it."

My big disappointment wasn't in failing to tackle the final pitch. It was in not seeing the glaciers grinding toward timberline below us. I missed the Switzerland of peaks that surely stood all around us. I was blinded to the velvety folds of ancient forest, to the clearcut checkerboards that angle down to the coastal fringe, to the distant volcanoes of Rainier and Baker, to the Pacific Ocean, to Canada, no less. Fundamentally, I came to *see*, not to climb. If our reaching the summit would have caused the clouds to part, I would have gone up. But of course we would have seen no better from there. Probably worse.

I also realized that, blinded or not, I had come for the real essence of Olympus — for whatever the mountain truly is. Whatever it had to show. And this was it.

"Let's just have a snack and head back to camp," Ann said.

Taking a chill inside my sweaty pullover and dripping parka, I readily agreed.

Though sticky with the damp cold, we slept well that night. The next morning, as the sun tried to poke through a fickle sky, Ann and I packed up our still-dripping gear, broke camp, and walked back down to the Hoh valley. The woodland air fizzed with the pungent scents that only fresh rains deliver. Joyous to be alive, I proclaimed the rain worthwhile if for nothing but the fragrance it releases in the plants it touches.

While the challenging climb was behind us, half the hike still lay ahead.

That evening we camped again along the braided Hoh. We sat on a gravel bar while stars popped into the nighttime sky. We listened to the lyrics of the river as it rushed from Olympus to the Pacific, and now we had a better feeling for what it meant to do this — to go from mountaintop to sea. Life in the Olympics was all so fine, so very fine.

But where were the great rafts of salmon that once brimmed in that river? Only depleted runs survived. And a century ago, we would have heard the howl of wolves. I felt sad that they were both gone. But there was some chance of recovery. The Portland-based Western Rivers Conservancy hoped to buy the lower twenty miles of Hoh River frontage from timber companies and restore salmon habitat. Also, the great canines might have another chance; Park Service biologists have said that the Olympics can support wolves and that the ecosystem would benefit from their presence. Reintroduction plans were being studied with an eye to recent successful efforts in Yellowstone National Park.

Early the next morning, drops of water pelleted against the tent roof. Waking up to the sound, Ann said, "Tim, let's go! Let's break camp before everything gets wet." We shifted into high gear to avoid carrying a heavy, dripping tent all day. The drops proved to be not the front edge of the next storm but rather the drip of fog that had been raked out of the air by the foliage above our camp. Firsthand, we now knew the competence of fog drip in watering the great northwestern forests.

Climbing four thousand feet out of the Hoh valley, we passed in and out of clouds repeatedly, as if moving in slow motion on a jetliner turboing up through mixed atmosphere.

As much as we had wanted to climb to the summit of Olympus, we now simply wanted to see the mountain. But cloud caps still held it securely in grip. We traversed a thousand acres that had burned in 1978, dead snags stark against a backdrop of ominously darkening sky. Red huckleberries glistened at eye level, and we lingered a dozen times to gobble the juicy, sweet fruit, each delay giving the storm clouds a chance to gain on us. After watching their drift, Ann asked, "What do you think?"

"Let's live dangerously," I answered, and we stalled longer, enjoying the delicious berries.

Cresting the shoulder of Bogachiel Peak, we trailed out the High Divide, an alpine ridge with the most vividly colored wildflowers we had seen, the startling magenta of smallflower paintbrush next to the piercing blue of arctic lupine. Being governed by the depths of snow, which is blown completely away here and into thirty-foot drifts there, timberline in the Olympics is highly variable, and with this condition comes a fascinating pattern of alpine-level trees growing in clumps and in isolated but crowded communities.

Above it all, the weather quickly deteriorated. Olympus remained invisible, and then the lower peaks ducked behind the great white curtain as well. Heavier winds brought purplish clouds, then rain, then flakes of wet slush, then snow — real snow bombarding us, with an early-winter sting in it.

Bailing off the exposed ridge, where there was no chance of finding a campsite with even a hint of shelter from the storm, we scrambled cross-country and steeply downhill toward Lake Eight. Bad as the weather had been when we were there, I was glad we weren't trying to summit Mount Olympus today.

Going too fast, I slipped on the coarse, enameled stems of white heather and took a nasty fall, my right leg shooting forward while the weight of my pack slammed me down, my left leg still underneath me — not just a little plop onto my butt but the kind of dive that can twist a knee, sprain an ankle, break a leg. I once broke my leg in just this way. I was only three years old but clearly remember the slip, the split, the fall, the pain.

As I humbly rolled over beneath the load of my turtle-shell, my tumble served as one more reminder of the thin line between competence and helplessness in the wilderness. Here and elsewhere, life can be going so well, so easily, but then in one second everything can fall apart. The mix of possibilities is endless, controlled only by your skills and knowledge and good fortune, if you call that any kind of control. I've grown more cautious with the passing of years, which I'm sure is why I've been able to stick around to see the years pass. Yet the chance occurrence, for better and for worse, is just around every corner. And I guess that made life all the more precious as I gathered my feet underneath me and set off again looking for shelter from the storm.

At the lake, a tuft of mountain hemlocks and the weeping foliage of an Alaska cedar only suggested the function of shelter, but we pitched the tent, cooked dinner, commenced shivering, and crawled into bed. Our sleeping bags, our pillows of damp clothing, our skin — all of it set a new standard for the word *clammy.*

Thus far denied the joy of eyeballing Olympus — even during our climb to its sub-summit, a mere hundred feet from the top — we dearly wanted to see the peak in all its glory. So when I poked my head out the tent door at dawn and saw some blue up above, it was my turn to say, "Annie, let's go!"

We packed quickly to seize what might be a narrow window of good weather. We pumped our legs back up the steep slope to High Divide. There, where yesterday's paintbrush and lupine had popped in brilliant color, all the blooms lay iced in a glaucous mantle, a million candied flowers.

In the background, across the dizzying depth of the Hoh River canyon, finally free of clouds, Olympus stood tall, accented in rock and lacquered in ice. We dropped our packs and stood in awe at the hard-earned sight. We placed its landmarks and traced our crampon route to the sub-summit. Then, frequently glancing back up at the mesmerizing sight, we cooked our oatmeal and boiled our tea. As we sipped and ate we admired the Blue Glacier in its sweeping curves off Olympus. Then the summit, wisped by moisture, began to fade behind cloudy curtains again.

While the sun still shone generously on us, the mist of the valley arose—the local atmosphere a perpetual watering machine. As we had seen, heavy cloud cover releases its rain, but even if the sun comes out the next day, radiant heat immediately evaporates the moisture that has just fallen, and so new clouds arise from the ground. This moisture shrouds the valleys again and expands upslope as the new clouds grow, puffing out into bigger spaces the way gases always do.

While we did the dishes, sturdy fronts of moisture replaced the gauzy ones and completely took away Olympus, one of the more chronically invisible monoliths of rock and ice in America.

From that perspective it was powerfully evident how connected all the mountain systems are. The peaks squeezed moisture out of the clouds, the tumult of snow-formed glaciers carved the land into swales and valleys, and the forests sucked up the rainwater and snowmelt and then greened the slopes. The rivers merged together as lifelines for remaining salmon that spawn at the headwaters, swim to sea, and return to the same headwaters, their life cycle physically and symbolically linking mountain, forest, river, and ocean as one place, one life.

Near the end of our hike two days later, we came to a set of hot springs, the thermals nourishing a hallucinogenic algal garden of slimy black licorice next to shockingly green crème de menthe. Mystified but not repulsed by whatever the chemistry entailed, we undressed and slipped into a lower pool of clear water. Relaxing to a new height of comfort, we soaked in luxury above the rush of Boulder Creek, the mountain-heated runoff flowing out of the rock and onto our resting bodies.

Silverthrone Mt.

N

Mt. Waddington

Cadwellder Range

Port Hardy

Port McNeill

VANCOUVER ISLAND

Nimpkish R.

PACIFIC OCEAN

CLAYOQUOT SOUND

Strathcona Park

Campbell River

Golden Hinde

Mt. Myra

STRAIT OF GEORGIA

Tofino

Port Alberni

Vancouver

Nanaimo

JUAN DE FUCA STRAIT

14

Victoria

San Juan Islands

## Vancouver Island and
## Southern British Columbia

0————— 34 miles

© Tim Palmer

WASHINGTON

# 11 | The Island of a Different Nation

W HEN I WAS young, I worked in the summers and
on weekends for a neighbor. Retired then, he gardened on the scale
of a truck farmer and kept up an orchard, a strawberry patch, and a
broad sweep of lawn beneath the shade of silver maples. The old man
and I worked steadily but also enjoyed each other's company. Several
years into the job, he surprised me by mentioning a brother. Knowing
that *my* brother was in the bunk bed below me every night, I asked,
"Where *is* your brother?"

"He went to British Columbia and never returned."

*He went to British Columbia and never returned!*

The words conjured up visions of adventure and the frontier, of
bald eagles, brown bears, Indians dip-netting for salmon, and above
all, tall forests in valleys enlivened by rivers and shrouded by mountains larger than anything I thought possible.

I always wondered if the province I had imagined really existed. I
knew it once did; I had seen pictures as proof. But were the forests
still there? Were the mountains really so beautiful, so untouched?
Were the backgrounds as snowy, even in summertime, as the postcards showed? And as I grew older and learned more, I wondered
how the Canadians treated their land. Facing the imperatives to cut

their woods later than we did in the United States, were they doing anything differently? And just who *were* those Canadians, anyway? They lived so close, yet they *were* in a different country. They *were* a different people, or at least they had been up until recently.

British Columbia now lay dead ahead. A new land on the horizon, its cloud-piercing peaks and misty valleys lured us onward. The sea guarded it all, looking like blue molasses, the swells shiny and soft and unhampered by roughening winds. Vancouver Island, where we were about to land, is the largest island off the western coast of the Americas.

Canada is far larger than the United States but has one-tenth the number of people, its whole population from Atlantic to Pacific to Arctic Oceans less than that of California. Even with a lot of land up there, most Canadians live within a hundred miles of the border, leaving large parts of the country empty, even by the standards of Maine or Montana.

In the years since I heard that my boss' brother never came back from British Columbia, I'd learned that Canadians are a friendly, traditional, predictable people compared with Americans. Less rebellious, they have greater regard for government, law, and order. They have far less violence in their communities. While American law enforcement officers confront an unflattering lack of respect, plenty of Canadians still revere the Royal Canadian Mounted Police. A picture of the Queen of England still hangs maternally in Canadian post offices and schools.

You can't help but sense that nature figures more prominently in the lives of Canadians than in the lives of Americans. The Canadian flag lacks nationalistic symbols but rather presents to the world a maple leaf. The coins and bills of our northern neighbors are decorated with artful engravings of birds and animals, while Americans use currency with the steely stares of Washington, Lincoln, and the cold-blooded Indian exterminator Andrew Jackson.

Canadians are taxed as heavily as Americans but get health care instead of a large army, nuclear warheads, and a bankrupting Star Wars missile system. Of course, they need not fear a foreign invasion because they know that if Canada is threatened, America is threatened, and so the U.S. military will protect them from anything. Except, of course, from the big invasion—the insidious advancing line of American culture and economy itself, sometimes ingeniously imperceptible, sometimes a blitzkrieg.

Canadian logging towns, even after mills have been shut down, remain pleasant communities, swept and gardened with pride, unlike the burned-out mill towns of the American Northwest or the has-been mining hollows of Appalachia.

A labor crew on a Canadian railroad might include a college graduate who majored in philosophy, an older man who goes back to England to see relatives every year, and a crewcut young laborer who habitually ends sentences with "Eh?" In keeping with this egalitarian society, more women seem to work in jobs such as ferryboat tender, gas station attendant, and firefighter.

Ideologues have less sway among our sensible northern neighbors. For example, in defending strict laws regulating handgun ownership, Canadians are unwilling to listen to the National Rifle Association argue that if they restrict ownership of flamethrowers today, their most cherished liberties will automatically be flushed down the toilet tomorrow. And here's another example: the United Nations, a while back, suggested that 12 percent of the land of every country be set aside and protected as natural areas. In neighboring Montana, the idea would have rallied a scourge of self-appointed militia, bogus but armed, and the governor of that state might appear to be cut from the same piece of cloth. But the British Columbia government, under Premier Mike Harcourt, did not see the recommendation as a subversive liberal plot to topple his province. Rather, he understood 12 percent to be a reasonable standard, adopted it, and proceeded to set aside land, with public support for his foresight. His successors continued the program, and now B.C. has set aside 12 percent, though this alone is surely not enough to rescue the extraordinary nature of the province.

Related to this line of world-conscious behavior, weather reports in Canada include the temperatures of American and other cities. Even at such an elementary level, Canadians see themselves as citizens of the earth, while Americans are Americans, feeling little need to look further for anything except maybe a cheap and unregulated labor force. Canadians, as journalist Andrew Malcolm wrote, are maliciously well informed about Americans, while Americans are benignly ignorant of Canadians.

These northern people are generally not troublemakers. This virtue, which delivers an ordered, peaceable, predictable society, might be carried to a fault when citizens refuse to question those in power or the greedily corrupt choices their leaders are not immune from making. For many years, Canadians who did make waves lacked the legal safeguards and paths of access taken for granted in America —the Freedom of Information Act, environmental impact disclosures, and the right to sue the government. Much of this has changed recently. Historically, however, few people have bucked the system. On the other hand, Canadian corporations, as well as foreign corporations doing business in Canada, have had few qualms about suing citizens who had the gumption to block progress on something like oil drilling in high-country wilderness.

WITH THE entire length of coastal British Columbia lying ahead of us, I revved our van off the ferryboat and into Victoria, the capital city on Vancouver Island, directly across the Strait of Juan de Fuca from Port Angeles. I could immediately see why people come here and never go back. The provincial capital is a sweet, flowered, cultured town, the waterfront an adventurous face to the world, the downtown a beehive with cosmopolitan flair, the neighborhoods trim and homey, the parks spacious enough to go shake yourself loose in. Yet, like every place so blessed, it faces the ache of acute growthitis. Outskirts of sprawl had surged since my first visit, as a hitchhiker in 1967, back when afternoon tea in this most British enclave in the Americas meant more than a staged-up twelve-dollar splurge for tourists at the Empress Hotel.

Many Canadians dream of living in this city boasting northwestern sunshine and a civilized bearing on life. "We never expected to live here on the island," said Richard Bocking, who with his wife, Winnie, had moved from the east after an illustrious career producing films for the Canadian Broadcasting Corporation. I had met Richard several years before, and now Ann and I stopped by to say hello and fish for some travel tips.

"We came to visit friends in Victoria," Richard explained. "Almost in jest, we told them to let us know if anything good came up for sale. A few months later they called, and we flew out, and the next day we bought this place."

The Bocking home overlooks the Strait of Juan de Fuca, allowing full view of the Olympic Mountains when they are not enclouded. Those high peaks help to cast a rain shadow over the southeastern terminus of Vancouver Island and leave it with a banana belt, so sunny that we saw the Pacific madrone, a tree more common in the hot coastal forests of northern California than in the drippier, cooler Northwest.

Leaving the gracious Bockings and their dream home behind, Ann and I rolled northward on Vancouver Island, a two-hundred-eighty-mile-long cigar shape of both contradictions and consistencies, not to be confused with the city of Vancouver, which lies on the mainland to the east. That booming metropolis at the mouth of B.C.'s largest river, the Fraser, clearly ranks as the most beautiful city on the continent, a cleaner San Francisco with more mountains and more public waterfront, plus a fabulous forested park abutting the downtown, countless new immigrants from Hong Kong, and all those pleasant Canadians.

But island-bound for a month, Ann and I tooled on northward where the road followed the eastern shore and offered views of the Gulf Islands—the Canadian continuation of Washington's picturesque and artsy San Juan Islands chain.

Quite unlike Victoria, with its engaging legacy of the past, the city of Nanaimo, sixty miles to the north, foreshadows the future. It describes exactly what my Canadian friends fear with the free-trade movement: a mishmash of McDonald's, Wal-Mart, Taco Time, Blockbuster Video, A&W, Best Western, Midas, Subway, Firestone, Chevron, Toys "R" Us, and Kentucky Fried Chicken establishments, just for starters, all in their fully glaring, fully asphalted, fully American glory.

Through most of history, Canada has looked different from the United States, in part because Canadians wanted it that way. They liked it being Canadian. From my own perspective as a traveler, going to Canada has, in the most positive sense, been like going back fifty years to a countryside with haystacks, to cities that function in commonsense ways, and to small towns with real service and no American chain stores. But as Richard Bocking had warned us, "with the trade barriers coming down, we're seeing the ascendance of big corporate powers and the last of the democratic influence in the economy." Hence a Nanaimo, B.C., that looks like the outskirts of Toledo, Sacramento, or wherever.

Striving to leave the commercial incursions behind, Ann and I detoured west at Parksville and began to cross the width of the island. Other than a short highway from Victoria along the southwestern shore to Pacific Rim National Park Reserve, and the highway to Gold River farther north, our current route was the only paved road to the western side—the wild side.

In several hours of driving since leaving Victoria, we hadn't seen a single old-growth tree, let alone any sizable tracts reminiscent of real forests. But at MacMillan Provincial Park we pulled off to stroll through redcedar and Douglas-fir that reached for the sky and cast shade enough for slugs to skid on their slime-belts all summer long.

Lest we become too charmed by this aberration of uncut nature, a sign at the beginning of the trail pointed out that the old trees here suffered "butt rot." This message explained that the fungus *Phaeolus schweinitzii* eats holes in and ultimately debilitates the trees, even the ones that appeared so grand to us today. As good as the old growth looked, the hidden text here was "Why not just cut the old trees down and put them out of their misery?" I questioned not how many years but how many centuries it would take for butt rot to administer its sinister curse. Ignoring my question, a boosterish illustration put up by the province's parks ministry showed a family backpacking into a greened-up woods that had just been cut, the ax men still at work cleaning up the edges. Around the margin of the poster, shiny log trucks toted their cargo to mill, and tugboats colorfully herded log rafts as they do at Port Alberni, a town that lay just ahead.

We drove on, climbing Sutton Pass, and then tilted down the Pacific slope toward Clayoquot (pronounced *Clay*-o-kwot) Sound.

I had been hearing about the place for years. Many of the Sound's

650,000 acres had already been clearcut. But what remained consti-
tuted the largest undamaged forest on Vancouver Island.

The Sound itself is a lineup of glacier-gouged inlets, embayments,
and fjords where seawater fingers into a forested domain like the
work of an artist wielding a wide brush dipped into plenty of blue
and green paint. Rich with salmon, whales, dolphins, seabirds, oys-
ters, bears, eagles, and a wild menagerie of related fish and wildlife,
Clayoquot became the rallying point as the Canadian forest protection movement in the 1990s drew worldwide attention to the nettle-
some issue of sustainable forestry.

The road runs north on the Esowista Peninsula, providing flashing
glimpses of what has been done and what remains at stake. Appearing a lot like the aftermath of General Sherman's march to the other
sea a century and a half ago, the logging of recent years stands for all
to contemplate. The land is scraped clean and scarred deep by multiple roads that now bleed silt and soil into bays once squirming with
salmon and alive with orcas. But unlike in the once-great forests of
California, Oregon, and Washington, here large tracts of hoary old
growth survive on other slopes and ridges, the two-hundred-foot-tall
conifers flattening in the distance to a velvet of biomass reaching
from tidal splash up to where snow lingers against woody boles for
many months. From the road, you know it's all out there. But to really
see the country, you have to go by boat.

We just happened to have four boats with us on the van, and
though we didn't have an oceangoing kayak—the craft of choice—
we figured our larger canoe would do if launched in the protected
waters near Tofino.

This budding little postcard community struck me as the way
Carmel might have looked when the first California tourists pulled
up to the beach in Model T's. From town we could see mountains
that rose from inlets and wore a cloak of eight-hundred-year-old forest. Behind these loomed a freshly accreted terrain of conical or
jagged peaks, snowy even into June. Monuments to one of my chief
passions—backcountry skiing—those high mountains whetted my
appetite and made me think that maybe I'd still get in a lick or two of
telemark turning before the summer melted away the last of the
snowpack.

But unlike Carmel, Tofino soaks in rain. In 1995 Clayoquot ranked as the wettest place in North America where measurements happened to be taken, with two hundred fifty-six inches of free water falling out of the sky. No matter when you schedule your visit, it might pour day in and day out. Ann and I were lucky, with some of the sunniest weather locals could remember.

Checking in at the Tofino Sea Kayaking Company, we chatted with the old salt Mike Mullen and picked up a few tips on where to go and how to get there safely. We bought a nautical chart and plotted our route to Meares Island.

A few years back at that bastion of old growth, Indians had faced off with the multinational logging companies. After trying to talk it out, the natives commandeered the local boat dock. From there they welcomed the lumbermen into their ancestors' and children's garden but insisted that the chainsaws be left on the boat. Indian — or First Nations, as they say in Canada — and provincial action eventually banned most cutting on the island.

As we headed across the blue depths in our canoe toward that still-green Indian-saved forest, Ann and I didn't know much about tides, estuarine currents, and shoals. We didn't even know how to read the nautical chart, but we learned fast. We had consulted the tide tables, added or subtracted for our specific location, and gauged the distances we had to clock between points of land, all the while estimating how the wind would skew us on the way. Trying to plan so that we'd be paddling with the tides, we cautiously plotted to avoid open exposure to the west. "The bottom line," Ann emphasized, "is we don't want to be swept out to sea."

Black-robed cormorants flocked on the water, and we saw loons, ravens, gulls, and bald eagles winging high, all their respective eyeballs peeled for fish, living or dead. Slinking in the shallows off a rocky peninsula, we spied on underwater crabs bigger than the fan of our outstretched fingers. A school of four-inch-long fish speeded toward us and veered away in unison at the last instant, their means of communication a wonder.

After paddling several miles from town, we camped at a modest clearing that had a surprising feel of remoteness, given the short distance we had come. Redcedars stood above the shore in gnarled dress. Wind-blasted, fork-topped, as wide as the length of our boat, they sported bark-fringed buttresses shoring up their sides like the corners of a great cathedral.

Beyond the diminutive clearing, our world became a high-latitude jungle, the understory impenetrably garbed in salal, red and evergreen huckleberries, thimbleberries, and salmonberries, which grow thumb-sized fruit just like blackberries but orange, appearing unripe even when sweet. Labrador tea, red alder, and cascara were rooted among fallen logs. Skunk cabbages lushed out with leaves two feet long, tropically exotic to the eye though perfectly native. With just a quick appraisal of the neighborhood, it was easy to believe that six hundred species of moss grow in coastal B.C. and Alaska. And here, devil's club replicates the chain-link cholla of Baja with hypodermic capability. Thorns radiate all around its stems and even on the undersides of its leaves, a formidable threat to anyone who even thinks about bushwhacking, though deer and elk see it differently, nibbling with relish on the leaves and shoots.

Pacific silver fir had scattered itself among other evergreens, including the western yew—a small tree once annoying to loggers but now valued for its precious bark, which contains taxol, a rainforest cure for breast cancer. It just goes to show, we never know when some obscure species found in nature will serve our most urgent needs.

The combined trees put forth a chaos of limbs, roots, and logs, a three-dimensional woodiness that's hard to imagine until you're wide-eyed in its midst. The girthiest cedar on the island measured sixty feet around—about the same as a very large redwood—no doubt infected with butt rot for the past half millennium but looking none the worse for the wear. Each mature Sitka spruce and western hemlock fills a large space in the forest. In a deeper sense, it fills a large slot of time, running back as many as a thousand years. When a tree of that age is hauled away, it leaves a gap not only in the space it filled but also in the time represented by all its accumulated biomass. For centuries it had been organizing itself into habitat useful for hundreds of species and billions of individuals, microbe to grizzly bear.

The tree's loss will mean homelessness to a large community for a long time.

As we tried to walk through the jumble, we saw that rocks here and there had been unearthed by uprooted giants. When those trees fell, they didn't just make a noise in the woods; they altered a whole landscape. Now a part of the topography, a six-foot-diameter trunk ran out a hundred feet or more, its broken branches splayed all around. "These trees are the whales of the forest," Ann said, climbing up on the fallen fir.

While the old forests at Big Basin, Sinkyone, Prairie Creek, Drift Creek, and the Olympics were exquisite in their ancient beauty and complexity, the wetness, matted moss, and girthiness of ancient cedars here—especially in the dim light of evening—conveyed a deeper sense of the wild. Without being paranoid, I could imagine an eight-foot-tall bear appearing out of nowhere to claim his territory or protect her young. In fact, bear tracks and mounds of tarrish scat large enough to overtop a clodhopper covered the paths. Owls no doubt spied on us with binocular eyes, though we only heard their hoots. This woods was lovely, dark, and deep, as poet Robert Frost said, and, I might add, as primitive as anything I have seen.

We cooked dinner while sunlight faded and sea grasses swayed on the vagaries of tides. As if condensing from thin air, tiny flies suddenly took to life at the surface of shoreline waters and from the interstices in everything. Pesky, biting, maddening, they drove us, fanning and swatting, into the refuge of our tent.

We wanted to climb Lone Cone Mountain on a trail beginning at the other side of the island, so the next day Ann and I paddled several miles around, carefully ticking off the landmarks as we went. At Opitsat, a First Nations village, houses lined the shore above the usual storm tides. Just past another headland we found the correct inlet and piloted the canoe to shore on a small beach. After hiding our boat in the woods, we walked up a path, past an abandoned sweat lodge, and into the old village of Kakawis, a collection of boxy wood homes along dirt streets. Because the Indians own Meares Island, we sought permission to climb Lone Cone from the Nuu-chah-nulth people.

"Hi," I said to a young man pacing on the porch of his home, his black hair buzzcut but ponytail-length in the back. He rocked a infant in his arms. "It's a beautiful day," I added.

"Really," he said, nodding, with another bounce of the baby.

"We'd like to hike up Lone Cone. Do you know who we should see for permission?"

"Yes. Louise. She lives that way." He helpfully pointed to the next group of houses.

As we walked past a row of trailer homes with decks and roofs of cedar, a young Indian woman happened to open her door and step onto the porch for a squinting appraisal of Sunday morning, her bare legs mostly unconcealed beneath a long tee shirt. I'm sure she hadn't expected to have us come strolling by. I hesitated to speak. "Excuse me," Ann intervened, "do you know where Louise lives?"

"Yes," the young woman answered with a smile. "Go that way." She pointed in yet another direction.

We found two older Indian women drinking Cokes on the porch of a house with a shrine to the Virgin Mary out front. "Excuse me, do you know where Louise lives?" Ann asked.

"Yes. She's down *there*." One of the women pointed to a pair of houses. "I think she's home. Just go down and yell, 'Louise!'"

Doing so, I found a serious, competent woman in her forties at the door, businesslike but friendly with her permission to hike, apprecia-tive of us for asking. From her we learned that the people of Kakawis, in fact, did not live there. The current residents were visitors, Indian people who were either enrolled or working in a drug and alcohol rehabilitation program.

"I have to run over to the office for an emergency now," Louise said calmly, "but if you want to talk to somebody about the program, see Rose, in the house over *there*."

An elder Salish woman, Rose lived in Nanaimo and spent two weeks each summer here. Whether she regarded this as her time off or time on, I couldn't tell.

"I listen to the kids," she explained of her duties. "They have a lot of issues to work out. I'm not a counselor. I just listen." I sensed that there was something inherently Indian in this approach — in simply having an elder on hand.

Rose implored: "Have a seat. Let me get you a soda."

She reappeared with two cold ginger ales.

"We'd like to climb your beautiful mountain," Ann said, as an explanation of our presence seemed to be in order.

"Ah, you'll see our island well," Rose replied. "It's beautiful here. The water, the mountains, Lone Cone. And the trees. We talk to the trees. We're thankful for what they do. They hold the water back. They make shade. They are home to animals. The logging, it's awful. It's as if they don't think about the future, or the future generations. All they see are dollar signs." Rose paused, as if to crook her ear and listen. Then she added, "There are wolves here, too."

"Do you hear them howl?"

"Not always. But you know they are here. You just know. I see a pair of them sometimes." Rose paused, then added more lightly, "And you two, you are a pair. Are you enjoying your stay?"

We eventually told Rose, the designated village listener, and a real pro, I might add, that we were writers.

"But you're not writing about Indians, are you?"

While I paused, wondering how to deal with this temporary setback, Rose added: "Once a woman anthropologist came and stayed with us Indians. She was supposed to be studying and writing about us. *We* should have been writing about *her!* She chased my son around until he ran up into the attic."

"Well," I said, "I'll tell you what, Rose. I won't write about you very much."

"Oh, God help us, another writer!" and she laughed with an infectious sense of hilarity at my profession. Then she added, "I'm only teasing you. You two have a nice time here on our island. It's beautiful up there. You'll see."

ANXIOUS to go, Ann and I returned to the canoe to gather our lunch, camera gear, and water bottles for the rigorous climb, but a woman's shout from up above interrupted us. "What's she yelling?" I asked Ann.

It was Louise, and with the tables turned now, she was having difficulty finding us. I ran up to meet her, wondering what could have gone wrong.

"We like to give people a CB radio in case they have any problems," she offered. "It's back at the office. Come over and pick it up before you leave." We felt no need for a radio but didn't want to appear unappreciative.

Years before, Ann had used a citizens band radio while working in Canyonlands National Park, and I had used one while working on forest fires, so we required little training, and we soon set off in earnest. The trail began in the woods and crossed a wetland corduroyed by half-sunken logs. Then we began to climb.

The entire mountain was dressed in virgin forest — cedars, firs, spruces, and pines, two, four, six feet in diameter, their root masses like a dense net thrown over the soil and bound tightly into place as if the mountain were a bale of garden mulch packed into a fine-mesh bag. In places we grasped for roots that webbed the ground above us while we toed onto root-ribbed mini-steps at our feet. If I hadn't ever dug in the dirt and generally known what is there, I might have thought that the entire mountain here was wholly composed of roots.

From that perspective it was easy to imagine what would happen to these slopes if the net of roots were to rot away after logging. The mountain would collapse, like a sack of flour left out in the October rain until the paper bag turns soggy and formless and spills its contents all over the place.

Climbing the hill was a lot like climbing the trees. First, picture us as tiny humans next to the base of a giant spruce. From there we puffed upward on a two-to-one slope, steeper than any stairway, and after quite a bit of climbing we gazed point-blank into the crown of the same great tree. Then it receded below us. But of course other great trees always rose up above us, so we climbed to the height of a tall cedar and then to the top of a hemlock. "I've never seen such big trees on such steep slopes," Ann said. I agreed. After an hour and a half of this we looked up at yet more needles, more limbs, more trunks.

Finally, through the foliage, we saw the sky, just one more tree height above us — so close now, as if the blue itself were almost reachable. Then a saddle near the top of Lone Cone ramped up to the summit, 2,395 feet above our hidden canoe.

On a rocky outcrop like a big buck tooth grinning above the forest, a view to the whole Clayoquot Sound awaited us. The ocean reflected as blue as the sky on that stellar day. The green of the forest was startling in its richness of organic texture, the trees catching sunlight on one side and shadow on the other, a fabulous rhythmic monotony to the two-hundred-foot-thick biomass adhering to the mountains like fur on the skin of an otter. Dozens of hilly islands dotted the sea below, each landmass with a healthy scalp. Vargas Island was shaped like a stout little Africa to our immediate west. Tofino represented a node of civilization to our distant south. At Clayoquot Sound, green and blue were the colors of the world.

SEEKING TO keep it that way, Valerie Langer, forest campaigner for the Friends of Clayoquot Sound, greeted me at her Tofino office, the unpretentious nerve center for protecting this extraordinary place. Posters and maps clung to the walls. Papers and reports layered the desks and tables in the converted little house.

"I came here for two weeks as a tree planter," Valerie explained about her direct path of arrival from Ontario. "Immediately I met people who were active in the logging issue. You come here, and it's so beautiful. You can *see* it. It's not like a toxics issue in eastern Canada or poisoned groundwater that you have to be told about. You can *see* it, all around you — both the forest and what used to be forest. After I got here, I couldn't leave the place. I got a job teaching literacy and math. My two-week trip has turned into a decade and a half."

Wearing jeans and a bulky wool pullover that gave her a real coastal B.C. look, Valerie had dark hair that splayed out around her face like a bit of the wildness she sought to save on the land. Her voice floated out even and smooth, revealing of harsh and difficult forces, yet unalarming in tone.

To begin the history of conflict between logging and not logging the trees that remained in Clayoquot Sound, Valerie said, "The United Nations World Commission on Environment and Development had just issued a report on sustainable development, and in the 1980s we were hopeful that people could agree on what was sustainable *here*. We tried to hammer that out for years, in three separate processes. Through the town, we had initiated the work, but we needed more information, and we had to have government and industry participate. So the province came up with funds for planning. But then they hijacked the process. We called it 'talk-and-log.' We talked and they logged. All the negotiation efforts failed. The basic problem was that we could not get others to address the long-term future. For fourteen years we tried to protect what was left uncut, and for fourteen years the rate of cutting increased."

With reference to colorful but grimly informative maps on the wall, Valerie pointed out that one-quarter of the Sound had been logged, much of it with heavily roaded clearcuts that I already knew looked like bulldozer practice by voc-tech freshmen. What was left, even with the losses to date, was no less than the largest uncut low-elevation and low-latitude rainforest remaining in North America. Differing in growth rates and species composition from that on the coast of central and northern B.C., the forest from Vancouver Island south rates first for productivity and diversity of habitat, making it critical to the natural world as we know it.

Throughout Vancouver Island, 75 percent of the old forests had been shaved off. Each year from 1972 to 1990, loggers felled sixty thousand acres. Only 12 of 170 large watersheds remained uncut, and half of those were at Clayoquot. Quietly negotiated in the 1950s, contracts had virtually given away B.C.'s public forests to corporations, which enjoyed unregulated chainsaw privileges until legislation in 1994 finally set nominal requirements for corporate conduct on public land.

Because Clayoquot Sound was the best of a dwindling ecosystem, it became the place at which Canadian forest protectors would stand and fight. Even under the new forestry rule—best described as minimum standards—and even with designation of new parklands, three-quarters of the Sound's remaining original rainforest was allocated to the forest industry. And island-wide, provincial plans slated all the unprotected forest for liquidation by the year 2022.

"Things didn't begin to turn around until we worked with the international markets for wood products," Valerie continued, introducing the concept of ultimate persuasion in the corporate model for the earth. Much of the ancient forest in B.C., it turned out, was ground up for pulp. And 90 percent of the newsprint produced by MacMillan Bloedel—the company doing the most logging—was exported (over citizen opposition in Canada, this company was later bought by the American industrial giant Weyerhaeuser). Seeking to strike a sensitive nerve abroad, since they had not been able to do so at home, the Clayoquot guardians flew to Europe with photographs in hand. They talked their way into fancy boardrooms, where they showed the paper buyers the consequences of their purchase, all the gory details abundantly revealed.

Valerie and others who hit the European circuit found that businessmen didn't want to buy paper that came from such an irreplaceable and rare forest. The buyers began to cancel contracts with Mac-Millan Bloedel. Lucrative contracts.

"While talk of sustainability had gone on for years, this new twist created a panic in B.C.," Valerie recalled. "The logging companies, of course, rushed their own people overseas to reassure the buyers, but the Europeans had seen pictures of the cutting—pictures that no one could really argue about—and so they believed us. They canceled more than $5 million worth of contracts in England, and at least as many in Germany. We were called 'traitors' by company executives and provincial officials. Over a period of five years the government spent $49 million in public relations efforts against us."

The phrase *Valerie and Goliath* came to mind.

The reason for the pro-cutting complicity goes back through decades of cozy relationships between government and business, which can be summarized fairly simply: in the midst of the old-growth debate, the province spent $50 million buying MacMillan Bloedel stock. With authoritarian gall that's beyond the pale in the U.S., a legislator proposed a bill forbidding the Friends of Clayoqout Sound to travel abroad and speak about the forest economy of B.C. Of course, this could not legally be done; if nothing else, the Canadian Federal Charter of Rights and Freedoms would prohibit such action. But avoiding this frightening brush with fascism, other lawmakers opposed the bill and easily killed it.

Valerie continued: "As effective as our show-and-tell efforts in

Europe had been, the real economic bite of what we were doing hadn't yet been felt, and the cutting continued. So when we came back, we started the blockades of 1993."

Now the story really got thick. Upping the public relations ante, armies of protestors from all over Canada converged on Clayoquot Sound and sat down on roads and at logging sites. For their peaceful civil disobedience, eight hundred thirty people were arrested and subjected to the largest mass trial in Canadian history. Stiff sentences with fines of up to three thousand dollars and imprisonment of sixty days were given to the tree huggers. Nonetheless, protesters camped at one site all winter.

The maple-leaf nation's long-lived tendency toward compliance made the arrests and protests remarkable — history-making, really. It was a sign of changing times that Canadians acted with such boldness to protect their natural heritage.

The blockades delayed the cutting. Provincial plans had called for protection of one-third of the Sound's forests, and then related restrictions limited total cutting to half the trees. But unwilling to give up half when Vancouver Island had already been halved again and again, protesters continued their opposition to the timber company–government cabal.

In a critical turning point, the province appointed a science advisory panel, which narrowly escaped control of the corporations and drafted stringent guidelines on how logging could be done without causing damage to watersheds, fisheries, and wildlife. The panel's recipe for management sharply restricted new cutting. Timber company executives, now feeling the pain of the canceled contracts from Europe as well as Japan and the United States, eventually adopted the guidelines. The actual amount of logging was reduced from 20,000 truckloads in 1992 to 5,000 in 1996. The tide had been turned.

"Why do you do this work?" I asked Valerie, who had labored without pay for some years and had been rewarded for her concern for Canada's future by being called a traitor and a pariah to the government she sought to improve — the government she *did* improve.

"I do it because our society is in the process of converting complex biological and social systems into simple industrial systems. We're taking everything in one generation, and nobody has the right to do that. There is beauty and worth in the diversity of life on earth. If we industrialize and simplify, we will lose. Humanity will lose."

With hope, Valerie added, "I think we'll be successful in saving most of the unlogged watersheds in Clayoquot Sound, but how the rest of this turns out is up to the First Nations. They control some large areas. I don't envy them. Some of their people want to log and some don't. I think they are committed to the guidelines of the scientific panel, which means the logging won't be as bad as in the past. They're trying to maintain their culture, which depends on the native forest, but they're also in social disarray because of poverty. It's a daunting task for them to enter the industrial economy without losing their culture."

Culture, of course, is like roots in the soil of Lone Cone Mountain. Without it, the world falls apart; it collapses like that sack of wet flour.

I wanted to talk to Indian people about these cultural, ecological, and economic connections while I was there. "I don't think you'll be able to do that," Valerie said. "A twelve-year-old boy just committed suicide in the village, and they will be in mourning for some time."

MORE ACCESSIBLE, a forest industry representative was available to tell me his side of the story. Dean Wanless worked as the area manager for International Forest Products (Interfor), one of the big companies headquartered in a new building on the outskirts of Tofino. A middle-aged, physically fit, articulate man willing to talk and share his point of view, he pinned his case—after all that had transpired since the 1980s—on the industry's willingness to compromise and log responsibly. Preferring to use the term *wilderness* rather than Valerie's *biological diversity,* he began by saying, "The issue is about society's need for wilderness, and it's about forest practices."

He pointed out the window to a butchered clearcut done by some other company twenty years earlier and admitted, "There are some sorry-looking mountains out there, eroding roadcuts and plantations of Douglas-fir that didn't grow because this isn't the place for Douglas-fir. We can do better than that. We're changing the way we work, based on the recommendations of the scientific panel. We think we can still log in this area. Under the new guidelines, we're down to 33 percent of the land base. If you took out the remaining pristine watersheds, it would be another big reduction. Instead, we feel that we should practice forestry on the land that's left, and do it sustainably, and in ways that are socially acceptable. This province was built on the forest resource. If the land is not going to generate forest products or employment in the timber industry, that will be a cost. And if we don't do a good job, the public will ask us to leave. We'll follow the guidelines of the scientific panel, and if that doesn't work, I'll sell my house and get out of the business."

I had little doubt that this man's concern was genuine, his response honest. But the current news was troublesome: fined for faulty road-building practices, Interfor had asked to have charges dropped. The Friends of Clayquot Sound reported that a logging access road had turned into a sea of mud, sinking trucks toward their axles and prompting a stop-work order by the provincial forest service. The defense of a corporate spokesman was that an unexpected rainstorm —in one of the predictably rainiest months, October—had caused the mud and the erosion. In other words, God himself did the damage. Interfor did not get off with that argument, but the penalty was reduced from $10,000 to $7,500, an amount scarcely detectable on the corporate ledger.

In the aftermath of all this activity, the parties all finally began talking together in earnest, and a Clayquot Sound agreement was eventually reached to spare the remaining pristine valleys in return for lifting the international campaign against sales of rainforest products —one more testament to the effectiveness of the boycott approach.

So far Ann and I had seen only the mountainous edge of this great island. Wanting to explore the elusive backbone, we returned to the eastern side, headed farther north, and then entered Strathcona Provincial Park. A sizable green triangle on the map denotes 518,700 acres that constitute this first provincial park in British Columbia— the province's Yellowstone, so to speak. And it could have been one of the great parks of the continent if the government hadn't made a century's worth of compromises allowing whole valleys to be stolen from protected status.

High country still lay deep in snow, and partly because of that, I wanted to see this mountainous heart of Vancouver Island. Having spent January in Baja, February in southern California, and so forth on up the line, I hadn't gotten to ski all year. Ironically, in the summery advance of late May, my chance now awaited.

After a long drive skirting the mud line of Buttle Reservoir, which years before had terminally flooded a once-timbered and boggy valley at the core of the park, we followed huge-bucketed trucks to a mining site incongruously centered in Strathcona. We parked, and I packed for a three-day ski trip to the high country of Mount Myra. Ann, who was coming down to the wire on her wetlands book, would lodge at a local campground and once again labor in the van while I was out having fun.

"At least I'm done with the manuscript," she said as she sharpened her pencils for the illustrations that would accompany each chapter opening. The sketches promised to be fun in their own way, and Ann, a fine amateur artist, looked forward to the opportunity for another form of creative expression.

While trucks battered the road with tires that pulverized the dirt and kicked up clouds of asthma-inducing dust at the wilderness trailhead, I arranged my gear and food. "You can't write about this park and not talk about the mine," Ann said, appalled at the bite that had been taken from Strathcona.

"Yes, well, later," I promised, determined now to enjoy my long-awaited ski trip.

Under a burdensome load of sixty-five pounds — avalanche shovel, winter gear, and all — I kissed my wife goodbye and set off down a forested lane. I soon spotted a grown-over bulldozer track curving up the mountain, my only access to Mount Myra. The old Cat track soon deteriorated into an eroded trail, then just rocks washed seasonally by water, then water itself flowing on the remains of the trail, then rocks, water, and an exasperating thicket of alder branches that snagged at my skis, which I had strapped upright on the sides of my pack. Now I really understood something that a local mountain guide, Chris Lawrence, had told me a few days before: one reason why the park has little backcountry use is that the high country is so difficult to reach. Farther uphill, the rocks were covered by snow, and I got my hopes up for easier travel on skis.

But nothing is easy. For a while the snow and rock patches alternated, making skis a poor option, yet the snow had rotted enough that not skiing also made a poor option. I broke through into deep pits. The rigors of post-holing eventually forced me to put my boards on, even though I would have to take them off in another fifty yards when encountering rocks again.

No sooner had I set up a modest rhythm of progress on this sorry excuse for a trail than I encountered a footbridge. But its metal deck had been mangled by high water and twisted like a pretzel above the terrifying deluge of springtime flood. To climb through the steel wreckage would be risky and difficult with a full pack, the consequence of error severe. Instead, I pressed on, trailless, hoping to cross the stream on a natural snow bridge at a higher elevation.

I entered an impressive forest of western hemlock, the coarsely barked trunks wallpapered in olive green lichens. The roots of those trees seemed to care nothing about mountain gradient, but facing the radical steepness, I again had to remove my skis in order to kick steps into firm snow. Cliffs eventually called an end even to this painstaking gait and forced me to turn to an open ravine that lay free of trees because avalanches had bulldozed their way downhill there every winter.

I wasn't concerned about triggering an avalanche in that low-elevation runout zone, paved with chunky snowballs that had been hurled forcefully from up above. Confidently I strode forward on my skis, into the ravine.

I made it halfway across.

Then, so quickly I didn't know what had happened, my footing fell out from under me and I dropped straight down through a rotted break in the rubble of avalanche debris. In a split second I stood not on top of the snow but down to my shoulders in an unsuspected slit in the earth, as if a fissure of San Andreas proportions had opened up and pulled me in by the ankles. I had come to rest, as it turned out, on the fallen trunk of a large buried tree.

Would I fall farther? Would the lumpy snow around me tumble

down and embed me there? Could I climb out without triggering a dangerous cave-in? I couldn't answer these questions. Suddenly the routine crossing of a ravine took on precarious overtones in the unfolding of adventure.

With great care I slipped out of my heavy pack and set it on the surface, flat on the ground so it wouldn't roll down the steep slope and splash into a stream that surfaced far below. A stream! That was the first time I recognized the snowy ravine for what it really was — a buried watercourse, a tributary to the deluge that had destroyed the bridge down below. Perspiring a little at this fact, I tried to remove my skis, but the left one pointed downward, and heavy snow pinned it in. I bent over and dug my way to the binding of the entombed ski. Snowballs that I knocked loose fell beyond the log at my feet, and icy chunks rattled down through cavities beneath the log. Perhaps they fell clear to the streambed carrying water an unknown distance below me.

I had been bitten off by the mountain and swallowed — a Jonah in the belly of the whale — and the process of digestion could soon begin if I made the wrong move.

After releasing my left ski, I had to dig and pry the tip loose. Impatient to return to the surface of the earth, I wanted to pull hard on the ski, though I knew I shouldn't tug to the breaking point. After gaining some confidence that I could stay standing on the buried log, I eventually exhumed both skis, set the poles flat on the rotted snow at face level, and gingerly climbed out of my hole.

Now having time to think instead of just act, I grew shaky with visions of how my situation could have deteriorated. Had I stayed beneath the snow, what would have happened to Ann? How would she ever know what had happened to me?

Though my risk had largely been unpredictable, I vowed not to take chances in the future. Life seemed to be a matter of becoming ever more careful, and hung over at that moment from my close call, I found the concept of carefulness far less repugnant than ever before.

After a short climb out of the ravine I entered friendly meadowlands ringed by firs and cedars like silent choirs standing robed and ready for concerts here and there. Mount Myra, my destination, arose to the east, and when I saw it, my enthusiasm for adventure rekindled. From a white and windswept bald ridge high on the mountain, long alpine ridges swept down, tantalizing me with skiing possibilities for tomorrow. I camped in the lee of subalpine fir trees while a balmy wind buffeted the tent. After dinner I put the skis back on to tour the neighborhood and scout my approach to the summit.

What had looked like a doable ramp on the map was in fact a ramp with a steep band of rock in the middle. The rock had heated in the warm afternoon sun, causing snow to slump off when the meltwater percolated down to ground level. This can cause a wet-snow avalanche of heavy debris that sets up around its victim like cement. I could climb to Myra in the morning while the snow surface remained firm from its nighttime freeze. But what would I encounter on my way down?

Already the lure of the summit was tempting me to take the kind of chance that only a few hours before I had resolved to avoid. I finally concluded that it was unsafe to push for the summit. Tomorrow I would need to content myself with skiing around the bowls and forests of the lower slopes.

The next morning, with plans to tour only the flanks of Myra, I packed a hearty lunch and overnight survival gear, just in case. I always take this kit when skiing alone in the backcountry: an Ensolite pad, bivy sack, down parka, and extra hat, mittens, and socks. Always I take rain gear.

I began on the route I had planned to follow to the summit. A joy of a climb, it went so well that I kept going, just to see how far I could go.

The route steepened, and I could see the way up. But I wasn't sure how much steeper the climb would be at its crux, where I would have to step up through the belt of outcropping rock before reaching the seductively gentler slopes swelling toward the summit.

After gaining substantial elevation and confidence, I faced an abrupt rise with no way around. Even my climbing skins—plastic traction devices strapped to the bottoms of my skis—now failed to provide adequate bite, so I carefully took the skis off and strapped them to the sides of my pack. Now I kicked steps into the mountainside, compacting the soft and relenting snow and then rising up on it, one short step after another. Striving for three-point traction at all times, I stabbed both ski poles into the crust securely before I lifted either foot off the snow.

Above me the bands of dark volcanic rock jutted out. Catching the rising morning sun, the snow granules liquefied as I watched, preparing chunky slabs to slump off the steepest rocks. If I fell, the slope might be too steep for self-arrest. Like a plow aimed downhill, my sliding body could trigger an avalanche of heavy, wet snow.

I knew I was entering dangerous territory. If the threats didn't diminish in ten steps, I reasoned, I would turn around and start down. But in ten steps my situation was neither better nor worse. I stood for the longest time weighing the siren call of the summit against my security. More fundamentally, I weighed my desire for intensity in life against my desire to simply live. I thought about Ann. Then I turned around.

Though my security was ensured, my disappointment was overwhelming. I had wanted to be up there, looking down, not down here, looking up. As an exercise in living for the moment, I reminded myself of the beauty of the snowfields and alpine meadows all around me. If I hadn't expected to see the view from the summit, I'd be happy now. Time and again, it seems, expectations are the root of unhappiness.

Somewhere in the distance a grouse introduced himself with a throaty "Galoop," making his life force known to the opposite sex. He had the right idea. Simple life is the main thing. Making it to the summit is secondary.

Hearing the hiss of a waterfall, I skied toward it and discovered a jet of a stream emerging full force from a snowbank and spraying off the mountain slope as if it had a running start. The falling water splattered the cliffs on its hundred-foot plunge down into a snowdrift, where it disappeared in shadowy silence as fast as it had been born into light, here and then gone, a fleeting, momentary, brilliant life above ground.

Back at my tent by midafternoon, I was pleased to have nothing to do. I sat and stared at what was around me, dredged up my pasts, speculated on the future, and then remembered to enjoy each and every present moment. After a few nodding jerks, with the feeling that I was falling off the top of the hundred-foot waterfall I had just seen, I fell asleep. I awoke looking at the clouds, a view that some-how linked me to the mysteries of my youth when, as a boy, I lay on my back in the sunshine of a Pennsylvania summer, staring up at the sky. Delighted then and now by the shapes of clouds, I smiled, happy to be alive, in love with the earth.

Heavy, airy vapor soon blocked the sun and cooled me. But then, finding a hole in the clouds, a ray of light flashed on me and quickly kept going, scanning the land like a spotlight. As the wind blew the cruising clouds across the face of the sun, this illuminating beam slid across the slope until it shone on the elusive summit of Myra herself. Then the dancing light was gone, so transient. Once again the Coast Range became the cloud-mountains, buried by gray masses of mois-ture so formidable that it seemed the birds up there would have to swim rather than fly.

The atmosphere was so thick that I could easily imagine it as an outer shell of the earth, slipping past an inner shell of snow, which in turn was just an ephemeral covering of a rocky crust, which in turn was just the veneer of a continental plate sliding across the viscous interior of the earth. Each of these layers shifted with constant motion, constant change.

In the evening I skied up to a mounded rise at the top of the bowl and found a fine lookout to the Golden Hinde — not a reference to anatomy, as are the Tetons of Wyoming, but rather to the sailing ship of Sir Francis Drake, the knighted captain and pirate. At 7,218 feet — almost equaling Mount Olympus in Washington — the Hinde is the highest mountain on Vancouver Island.

Setting now, the sun knifed through a slit in the clouds in a magnificent final flash of orange light before the atmosphere con-gealed again and began to shed water like a wet blanket wrung out in the heavens.

With this show of light and clouds and rain, I once again had the overpowering sense that the mountains are the source of so much in life. The mountains catch the moist winds and recirculate the evaporative upper layer of the sea. The soil of the mountains is recycled from rocks that once lay at the bottom of the sea. When the snow in front of me melted, it would pick up that soil in solution and suspension and redeposit it on lower ground, and it's by this mountain-shed water and soil that life down below is able to live. In all respects, the mountains work so well.

In the blue-gray fade of twilight I skied back to the safety of my camp and the dryness of my tent, and the next day I skied out.

DOWN BELOW, once again, I was faced with Westmin Resources' copper and zinc mine, the extracted donut hole of Strathcona Provincial Park. The mining company had been awarded the use of two and a half by six miles of land, including the head of Buttle Reservoir, the summit of Mount Myra—thus far untouched—and dozens of streams. Some of these coursed directly through the rejected tailings, alongside the berm of gravel freeways, and past yawning pits that collected rainfall and concentrated pollution that looked like pastel Easter-egg dye tinted at a Brobdingnagian scale.

Founders of Strathcona in 1911 thought it could be another Banff—a mountain refuge of world-class stature. And surely it could have been. But three legislative acts and multiple administrative cave-ins granted one compromise after another, amputating an arm here, a leg there, some would say removing the heart and castrating other vital organs. Five dams flooded many miles of cedar bogs and wild rivers. Clearcutting swept through five valleys, ostensibly given away by the government to keep timber companies from logging public land elsewhere, as if that were a good deal for the Canadian citizenry, who already owned both of the forests in question.

Serving the Westmin mine, scores of ore trucks dominated traffic by pounding the park roads daily. Until 1980 the company dumped tailings directly into Buttle Reservoir, a practice that killed fish and threatened city water supplies, not to mention the salmon waters immortalized by Roderick Haig-Brown, the great angling bard who lived along the stream near the town of Campbell River.

Tailings ponds now require $1 million a year for upkeep, and what follows came as a shock to me: simply maintaining these treatment facilities is now regarded as a rationale for indefinite expansion of the mine. In other words, so much damage has been done that the province needs the miners to keep the treatment plants operating. This guarantees them a lifetime pass to Strathcona. But, as compliant as the government is and as conscientious as the corporate powers might be, this mine, like all others, will someday close, and then the accumulating chickens will come home to roost in the public's lap. My interviews with good-natured representatives of the mine only served to confirm this disturbing news.

The losses at Strathcona might be regarded as now-unconscionable acts of historical negligence, but not so long ago another corporation proposed yet another mine inside the park at Cream Lake. This high-country gem, however, was blessed with Marlene Smith as its guardian angel.

STILL CARRYING her Dutch accent, Marlene greeted us at her home. Calloused hands marked this athletic woman of forty-seven as an avid gardener. Thick bangs and a healthy crop of amber-blonde hair going gray accentuated the bright dance in her eyes. A veterinarian for livelihood and mountain climber by avocation, she had once frequented the Alps and wound up here after meeting Steve Smith, a rock-solid, broad-shouldered, curly-haired mountaineer who taught at the Strathcona Lodge, a premier outdoor skills center at the edge of the park. Marlene and Steve's home burst with flowers, a rainforest regrowing around them, their skis propped in the mudroom, their canoe nosing out of the woodshed.

"Jim Boulding was the conscience of the park," Marlene began. "He and his wife, Myrna, had started Strathcona Lodge as an outdoor school, and he worked tirelessly for better care of these mountains. He had a powerful spirit, and on his deathbed, in 1986, he put his hand on mine, took a deep breath, and said, 'Marlene, will you take over the fight against the Cream Lake mine?' What could I say?"

At the height of land, a corporation had proposed another extensive mine, complete with roads, tailings, and acid-bearing waste — a death warrant to southern Strathcona. Comparable to the Republican Party in the United States, the Social Credit Party of B.C. was in power, poised to give the site over to mining by demoting the province's oldest park to the status of "recreation area." Recalling this linguistic sleight of hand, Marlene said, "When I studied English, I learned that recreation means things like hiking and canoeing. Now the B.C. government was redefining the term to mean logging and mining. But this was supposed to be a park! Not only were the politicians going to give it away, but we were all going to *pay* to give it away with a lot of subsidies for the miners."

Marlene was getting worked up just talking about this outrageous level of largesse. "We took television crews out to see the lake, and we got the papers to publish articles, and we lobbied, but still the mining exploration went ahead. Yet we knew the people of B.C. would not agree if they just understood what was going on. The bulldozers were ready to roll. With no choice left, we organized civil disobedience workshops."

"So you trained yourselves and came up with a plan?"

"Well, yes and no. One of our people happened to be there hiking when the drilling rigs arrived. He saw the yellow equipment rolling in, big and loud. He drove straight to a telephone and called me. We had to start the blockade right away. 'Can you do it?' I asked over the phone. His elderly parents were with him, but he said yes, and the three of them sat down in front of the bulldozers. I got on the telephone, and the next day we had a large group of people there. We stayed for three months, even into the winter, when it dipped to ten below. Sixty-four people were arrested and carried off singing the national anthem, "O Canada." On television. This shocked citizens all over the country. We delayed the mine, and then the New Democratic Party came to power in 1989 with Premier Mike Harcourt, and we got a moratorium on the mine and on further explorations. The company made one last effort to delete the Bedwell River valley from the park, and though we lost some land to logging in a compromise, we kept Strathcona mostly intact. Now the protection's going to last. People won't let it be lost."

I asked Marlene the big question: "Why did you do it?"

"Once you start taking care of a piece of land, it adopts you. I love the land and it loves me back. When I go there I really sense this, as if I belong to that place. When I look at the map now, it's a nice feeling. I see a park, and not a park with another big hole in it. And it will be that way all my life. Then I'll pass the responsibility on to some other poor sucker, the way Jim Boulding did to me."

When we drove away, Ann reflected on our own lives, itinerant and nomadic, drawn to the places we care about, but so often drawn to different and new places. We live in stark contrast to Marlene and Steve, who have adopted their home with a possessive vengeance against those who would ruin the land. "Someday I want to do that," Ann said. "I want to work for the protection of a place that means a lot to me." In the truest sense, Marlene was an inspiration.

As SOON as we left Strathcona, we once again encountered the universe of clearcuts. Trees had been chopped everywhere as we drove west to the Gold River and then north to the Nimpkish, the largest stream on the island. We couldn't resist the pull of those whitewater rivers and so spent an afternoon on each, me in my canoe, Ann in her kayak.

Later, at Port McNeill, we couldn't resist the pull of a milkshake and sundae, so we stopped at an ice cream store. There, on the wall, a poster showed a group of mustached loggers posing in the unsmiling demeanor of a nineteenth-century daguerreotype, except that all these men clutched chainsaws. Somebody had written across the bottom, "Share the forest. Don't let your love of wilderness blind you to the needs of your fellow men." More subtly, more cryptically, more cynically, another person had penciled in, "Share the stumps."

To share, as the poster said, may be the key issue. But how about sharing with the rest of the community of life and with the generations to come?

With the dueling poster captions summarizing much of what we had seen so far, the rest of British Columbia's coastline lay ahead, an edge of mountains far more remote, far less touched, than anything we had seen. I couldn't help but wonder, How would the balance between wholesale cutting and protection be struck there?

At Port Hardy, in a drizzle of warm rain, we boarded a ferryboat that would take us to the greatest of all mountain forests.

Northern Coast
of British Columbia

0————30 miles

© Tim Palmer

# 12 | *Northward by Boat*

AS WE CRUISED northward on the ferryboat, the Coast Range rose unseen beneath us, its western limits flooded by the ocean. To the east, tiers of larger mountains ramped up out of the water.

The coastal uplift in British Columbia follows a double track, each by turn more enticing than the other. Vancouver, Haida Gwaii, and many other islands compose the seaward front, pushed up by the Queen Charlotte Fault, which takes over where the Cascadia Subduction Zone ends, at Vancouver Island. The second track of the Coast Range lies on the mainland and presents a continuous barrier of glacial peaks, crevassed icefields, and timbered slopes, a two-hundred-mile-wide swath of geographic extremism, more rugged than any land we had yet seen.

Our ferryboat followed the Inside Passage, a trough that is God's gift to mariners between the two tracks of the greater Coast Range. The mountainous islands offer reliable shelter from rough seas, yet the channels are immensely grooved and navigable to deep-draft utility ships as well as tiny ocean kayaks, to the cedar dugouts used by Indians millennia ago and to the big-bellied diesel we now rode.

Unlike the comparatively smooth-sliced coast of the United States up through the Olympic Mountains, the British Columbia ocean-front is shredded with inlets, embayments, fjords, and low-lying river valleys, which had been drenched with salt water after ice-age glaciers depressed the landscape here by sheer weight and then boosted sea level by four hundred feet when the ice melted. B.C.'s airline distance of 530 coastal miles becomes a whopping 16,000 if you follow the edge of water in and out and around each freestanding mountaintop peeking up from the sea.

While the topography of Vancouver Island had been spectacular, the mainland range was the big time — a monolith of trees, rock, and ice, its granite-intruded peaks silhouetted in the arrow-light rays of sunrise as our boat accelerated from Port Hardy with a belch of oily fumes.

John Muir had come this way by boat as well, and in 1879 he wrote, "I know of no excursion in any part of our vast country where so much is unfolded in so short a time and at so little cost. Without leaving the steamer from Victoria, one is moving silently and almost without wave motion through the finest and freshest landscape poetry on the face of the globe."

Along the mainland of B.C. north of the city of Vancouver, only five roads transect the Coast Range — only two of them paved. If transposed onto a map of California, this scarcely visited territory would run from San Francisco to San Diego, and it adjoins even wilder country in Alaska.

Capping off the high terrain, Mount Waddington rose to our east, the highest mountain entirely within British Columbia. I had seen Waddington's sharp top and mantle of ice from an overlook back on Vancouver Island. This peak and others in the Cadwellder Range now fulfilled my fantasy of witnessing the Coast Range stair-stepped against interior country as tall as the Rocky Mountains. Here the full vertical relief rises from zero to 13,177 in one fell swoop.

When seen from the air, the region appears to be blessed with endless peaks, glaciers, rivers, forests, and fjords — mountains everywhere. Sayre Rodman, a climber who pioneered first ascents here in the 1950s and 1960s, bemoaned the growing worldwide accessibility of remote peaks but still admitted that there are "a hundred years of fun" left in coastal British Columbia.

All that fun would remain just a glimmer in the eye to me. Here, as in Alaska, the Coast Range includes some of the hardest-to-reach mountains in North America, isolated from the rest of the world by an impenetrable forest, by foul weather forever spewing rain or snow, and by remoteness from highways. These conditions are all trademarks of B.C. and Alaska, but they reminded me that the Coast Range has an element of inaccessibility throughout. Aridity and the spiny cacti of Baja made those mountains a challenge to explore. The thick tangles of chaparral in California blocked travel as soon as I stepped off the byways and trails. Then, in the Northwest, the rainforest did its job of filling every available space with biomass, leaving little room for footsteps. That's the way it was here, only more so, with the thorny devil's club conscientiously guarding the gates of the backcountry. Like John Muir, Ann and I for now contented ourselves with looking out at the grand sweep of geography surfing past our wake. We spyglassed the ocean for whales, porpoises, eagles, and seafaring birds.

The capacious boat toted a fleet of cars, vans, motor homes, and even semis ballasting its underdeck. On the upper levels, Ann and I met a varied cast of travelers, including John Stebbins, in his wheelchair. At an unexpected instant some years ago his spine had been severed in a car collision. Before that, he was an avid canoeist. "I finally got to raft the Salmon River last year," he said with fond memories and what must have been a bittersweet mix of appreciation for what he can do and disappointment at what he can't.

"You're still seeing the world," I commented with respect and admiration, wondering if I would have the will to do the same.

"It's an adjustment," John said, gesturing to the wheels beneath him. "But doing this is far better than the alternatives that were facing me."

We met Ted and Molly Hawkley, of Cleethorpes, Humberside, England, who leavened the conversation with amiable smiles and soft laughter. "Touring British Columbia and Alaska by ferryboat is becoming quite the thing for the English," Ted said. "We islanders are fascinated by this area. The whole U.K. would fit into one valley or two out here." A retired social worker, he had spent a career aiding people after their near-death experiences in hospitals. Following his retirement but before he met the charming Molly, he took passage again and again as a volunteer host on a palatial cruise ship. One of his obligations was to dance in the evenings with unattached older women.

"Women do love to dance," I commented.

"Oh, most definitely," Ted agreed. "Even those who are quite up in years."

Reflecting further on the package-tour format, he added, "You stop here and there to see the sights. But you always have to keep your eye on your watch because the boat is moving on. You don't see the places, really. On this trip, we're going slower."

"We are, too," Ann said.

A snowy peak had muscled its way up through cloud cover, and I added, "but not slow enough."

The leather-jacketed Aaron Beckord and Kari Downey had parked their Harley-Davidson downstairs, lost like a black bug among a herd of motor homes. Talk about time constraints: New Zealander Kari was visiting North America on a six-month visa. "I hope to renew it," the pretty Kiwi said with a fond glance at Aaron.

He lived in the roughcut logging town of Forks, Washington. "When I'm gone," he confessed, "my worst fear is that somebody will steal my trees."

"Your lumber?" I asked, a bit puzzled.

"No. My trees. People come in and cut them down, right off your property. Even a small Douglas-fir is worth a lot of money. When I go back and pull into the driveway, I might be saying, 'Hey, who took my trees?'"

In seventeen hours of daylight on the ferryboat we saw unstolen trees, salt water, ice-furrowed inlets, snow-weighted mountains, bedrocked shores, two villages, one very small town, and a single lighthouse keeper waving valiantly, no doubt a victim of social deficit. It rained about half the time, the sea taking on the matte finish of skated-up ice, the mountains diving into the brine at forty-five-degree angles, their above-water hues of gray-green fading to lighter grays in the distance, up to ten layers of subtly colored landmasses stacked behind one another like color paper cutouts. Those layers went on far enough to give a hint of the once-untouched plenty of this coast. Enough of it remained to keep the myth of abundance alive and to let all the people I talked to feel the vigor and fullness of a natural globe, round and full — an undamaged world that seemed to run on forever.

But of course it didn't. Much remained hidden and unknown from our boat-top view, and I itched to somehow ply the fjords and mountain passages to see what was back there in the recesses of the Cadwellders.

Not so forbidding to the logging companies now that they've run out of old trees closer to the mills, this section of B.C., called the Great Bear Rainforest, amounts to eight million acres along three hundred miles of ocean frontage. It holds the largest remaining tracts of uncut ancient temperate forest anywhere and will be the battlefront of protection-versus-logging debates in the decades to come. Some areas have already been scythed, including plenty of oceanfront mountainsides behind the beauty strip of uncut slopes fronting the tourists' ferryboat route. As evidence of the cutting, we saw impressive barges motoring their way from cut-down forest to pulp mill. They carried logs stacked to toppling heights, like a zillion toothpicks on a butter dish, all speaking volumes of the mowed mountainsides that lay hidden from our chamber-of-commerce tourism-committee view.

After detailed analysis using the latest satellite technology, the Sierra Club of British Columbia had revealed that, unlike on Vancouver Island, where most of the forest had been cut, 40 percent of the Great Bear Rainforest survived intact, a resource considered by ecologists to be globally outstanding but vulnerable. The province had protected only 6 percent from logging, the remainder diminishing even as we admired it.

Untouched watersheds awaited their turn to be sawed, including K'lskwatsta Creek, though the Forest Action Network and other groups were fighting to keep it intact. Groups lobbied to save the pristine Klaskish River, home of eagles, salmon, and wolves. After a ten-year battle, the provincial government had set aside the greatest mother lode of grizzly bears on the B.C. coast when it made the

Khutzeymateen Valley a provincial park. In another hopeful sign —
revolutionary in its way — MacMillan Bloedel had announced it
would phase out clearcutting. This corporate giant was responding to
public pressure but perhaps more to canceled newsprint contracts in
Europe. Ironically, while America's best timber goes to Asia, half the
B.C. timber is exported to the U.S. Boycotts in the States, such as
one supported by the company Home Depot, could be effective in
encouraging reform of old-growth logging.

After a day and night of augering northward, Ann and I jumped
back into our van and clanked across the metal gangplank into Prince
Rupert, the only sizable town in several days of travel between Port
Hardy and Juneau. Wide streets carved up the hillside on which the
bustling burg sat. Boxish hotels and stores seemed to be thrown into
the mix of shops and homes, all of it netted down by overhead wires,
the whole amalgam a trucking depot that links the sea to the interior.
It has some good sides to match the banal, but we set off at once up
the valley of the Skeena River, a wide and braided conduit pushing
water by the megaton out to sea, once incredibly rich in salmon, as
were all the B.C. coastal rivers.

The whirlpooling Skeena is the province's second-largest river. In
its background, waterfalls spouted off mountainsides in streaks a
thousand feet long. Clouds huddled thick enough to decapitate glac-
iered peaks, and detached wisps of moisture smoked the ground here
and there, making little mysteries out of everyplace. We drove in and
out of fog, clouds, drizzle, and opaque curtains of rain. Water everywhere was vaporized, flowing, ponded, or iced to the summits. Any
state of water — you name it, we saw it.

At Terrace, whose highway frontage might have been laid out as an
exhibit of the boneyards of extractive industries, we turned south and
drove another hour to Kitimat, a grimly efficient company town circa
1955. Its sterile purposefulness reminded me of Los Alamos, New
Mexico, built by the U.S. government for assembling the atomic
bomb. Three-story apartment buildings and rows of ranch houses
with tidy lawns and clipped hedges tapped into wide streets. Plumes
from both an aluminum smelter and a paper mill puffed a disgusting
atmospheric entrée across town — sulfuric fumes like the intestinal

gas of a large creature that ate the industrial equivalent of beans, boatloads of them. Even more, the smoke drifted across the inlet to our next destination.

We rolled another six miles to the distinctly spelled Kitamaat, a village of First Nations people. Where we eased into town, the windows of a school faced the water — a saltwater channel probing back a hundred miles from the open Pacific to here. Modest 1960s-style ranch houses lined a main street and a grid of gravel roads. Incongruous high-tension wires arced over the village. Those power lines originated to the east, at the Kemano hydroelectric plant, part of a sprawling scheme that diverts a biologically significant portion of the Nechako River — a giant Fraser River tributary draining the interior Coast Range — and pipes it westward through a tunnel in the mountains to spin turbines for the energy-hungry smelter at Kitimat. The adjacent pulp mill had been built to consume excess power, and now the formidable fumes from both industries teamed up and wafted through the Indian village while electricity crackled like a big bug-zapper from wires sagging overhead. Slopes around the inlet had been punk-cut and their deceased cellulose hauled to the pulp mill for shredding, cooking, and chlorine bleaching.

I arrived at the office of the Nanakila Institute, wondering what the name meant in English. I asked for Ken Margolis. A young native man said that Ken was gone. "You can wait for him here if you like. Or outside." Ann and I decided to stretch our van-weary legs on the streets of the village.

Indian kids, for all we knew, could not detect the presence of white people. We were completely ignored. The eyes of one teenage boy walking past flickered up at the last instant. I smiled, but he looked away.

Eventually Ken, a white man, arrived at his office and invited us in, apologizing about unexpected emergencies. A boat owned by the Institute had sunk but was recovered. Usually a resident of Portland, Oregon, Ken had started out in theater arts but then changed paths and opened The Nature Conservancy's first Pacific Northwest office. Later he and a partner, Spencer Beebe, co-founded Conservation International, laboring for protection of tropical rainforests. But three years into the job, the two decided that the rainforests of home deserved their attention just as much as those in any tropical clime. They passed the Southern Hemisphere off to others and founded Ecotrust, dedicated to helping communities along the Northwest coast develop in ecologically sustainable ways. The premise is that conservation can serve people, and people's needs must be satisfied if we are to make lasting progress in protecting land and water.

"We started with a survey," Ken reflected, "and we were shocked with the findings. There were no large pristine watersheds left in the coastal rainforests of the lower forty-eight. The largest temperate rainforest system still intact anywhere was the Kitlope River drainage south of Kitamaat. We stood there looking at the map, its message clear to anyone who could see, and Spencer said, 'We have to work on this.'"

The 900,000 acres amounted to one-fourth of the ancestral homeland of natives called the Haisla Indians. Checking in with these people would clearly be the first step in any effort to protect the forest. The Indians met with the Ecotrust staff and embarked on a cooperative program of study for their land. However, the West Fraser Timber Company had long ago secured a tree-farm license from provincial bureaucrats and planned in no uncertain terms to cut the area, mountaintop to seashore, sawdusting their way through the whole thing in a few short years. They deigned to share their plans with the Indians who had been living there for ten millennia, maybe more.

At a village meeting, the company promised jobs, always a strong hand to play. When the tricolored bar-graph presentation petered out and the corporate cards lay on the table, and a stony silence settled in the room, the outcome could have been anyone's guess. The Indians needed jobs, everyone knew.

Rising slowly from his chair, villager Morris Amos was the first to speak.

"You don't understand," he began in response to the timber man. "This is not about jobs. This is about our heritage."

One by one — each in his and her own way — the Haisla villagers repeated that message. After a while, disgusted with the way things had gone, the corporate representative picked up his papers to leave.

But a tenth-grade Indian girl stopped him cold with the point of her finger. "You sit back down," she said, nearly losing her cool. "We've listened to your company tell us what to do for too long. Now you are going to hear what we have to say."

The man sat down.

More native people spoke of their customs, their salmon, their bears, their homeland, their determination to face a troubled future without losing their culture, without losing their land, without losing their lives. Up against a wall of continuing resistance, the company later dropped its plans to chainsaw eight hundred thousand acres. The province subsequently protected the watershed as the Kitlope Heritage Conservancy Protected Area.

Key in its location, the Kitlope has headwaters that back up against Tweedsmuir Provincial Park, the largest park in British Columbia though viciously compromised by the Nechako Reservoir, built in 1952 as a cornerstone to the Kemano power scheme. On the opposite side of the Kitlope, the Fiordland Recreation Area had already been protected, and the adjacent Princess Royal Island remained mostly uncut. There one might see the spirit bear, a race of black bear known for having white offspring 10 percent of the time. In all, the Tweedsmuir–Kitlope–Princess Royal ecosystem ranks as one of true global importance. And it could be linked with other parks in a network of even more sweeping significance throughout British Columbia's coastal mountains.

But still to be logged in the Kitlope area were the basins of the Barrie and Kowesas Rivers. The Haisla people relinquished Barrie, recognizing they could not save everything. But like the Sioux at the Little Bighorn, the Indians took a stand at Kowesas.

"I had been working with the Haisla through Ecotrust," Ken recapped. "To manage the Kitlope and to plan for the Kowesas, the tribe formed an institute called Nanakila. That means 'The one who watches over.' The idea was to promote cultural and environmental values apart from village politics. The Haisla brought me on board to help get things started."

Seasoned in such efforts, Ken still had to make adjustments to a new culture. "People here carefully respect each other's right to speak," he said as one illustration. "Interrupting might be the only way to get a word in edgewise among a group of white people, but here it's different. When a person stops talking, I count slowly to ten, just to make sure they're done."

Remembering all too well an irksome mistake he had made, Ken explained, "Once I acted as a spokesman for the tribe when I shouldn't have. This was a serious breach of etiquette. To make amends, I had to follow tradition: I bought a beautiful wool blanket and at a public event presented it to the people I had offended. Then everything was okay."

Ken arranged training for a staff of Haisla people to work as wardens for the Kitlope, shipping some of the village's more promising young men off to law enforcement school. He co-authored a watershed assessment that made the scientific, economic, and cultural case for not cutting down the trees in the Kowesas basin. "From this larger perspective," he said, "the timber values paled in comparison with ecological and cultural values. The damages inherent in logging — erosion, depleted salmon, a crippled way of life — were all too much, no matter how valuable the timber. But proving that alone might not be enough, so the Haisla decided to build a lodge."

Though First Nations people had been using the Kowesas basin for thousands of years, they had never built much there. They just lived there, leaving few signs of their presence. To lay claim on the watershed in a way white people might understand, the tribe decided to construct a lodge at the mouth of the river. "It's also a way to train some of the young people in construction," Ken explained. "Plus, the lodge will be a center for ecotourism benefiting the Haisla, and if the plans to log move forward, it will be a base for blockades to keep the forest companies out of the Kowesas."

"The lodge is way back up in the fjords, isn't it?" I asked.

"A two-hour motorboat ride from here. Would you like to see it?"

EARLY THE next morning, Cecil Paul, the son of a Haisla chief by the same name, and another young Indian loaded plywood, pipe, and gasoline onto a twenty-foot aluminum motorboat and welcomed Ann and me aboard. They untied the lines and turned over the engine, and soon we were zooming southward through Devastation Channel. Gray-blue rocks at the shore yielded quickly to forests. Cliffs ascended to wet domes. Waterfalls danced off the mountainsides — four, six, ten waterfalls in view at once. A gray sky streaked above it all. At one outcrop of surf-weathered rocks Cecil said, "We call this the seal hotel," and sure enough, a flesh-pile of harbor seals lounged and barked at the tide line.

Now in his twenties, Cecil had grown up in Kitamaat Village. "My father has been taking me out on the water and into these mountains ever since I can remember," he said. "In March of each year, for example, we set up camp to catch eulachon. It's a small fish we boil down for oil, and its preparation is an important tradition."

"It must be good to have those roots here," I suggested, obvious as it was.

"Lots of roots."

Cecil hesitated. Then he decided to go on with his story. "I went away for a while. I got a job working at a helicopter logging site on Vancouver Island. I didn't always like it, but I needed a job. The pay was good. I got promoted within a week. Then I met a girl. But I had to leave when a guy there threatened to kill me."

I could scarcely quell my curiosity about this sequence of promotion, girl, and death threat, and no doubt there were some blanks that Cecil left in the story, but I did not press for details because it would have been impolite and pushy. I simply said, "Coming home to Kitamaat must have looked pretty good then."

"I think most young people would like to stay. But there's no more room in the village. People have to live outside, in Kitimat — the smelter town. Or move away."

"Would you want to get a job logging here?"

"No way. This area hasn't been touched, and it should stay that way. Even the Haisla people don't come up here very much. Most don't camp out. My girlfriend's that way. She'll come up for the day but not for overnight. Yet most people don't want it to be logged. There would be blockades if West Fraser tried to cut it."

At that point the other young Haisla man, who did not want his name to be revealed, piped up: "Maybe they shouldn't log it, but look,

I'm not an environmentalist. I'm not going to chain myself to any tree. I've got a career in law enforcement to think of. And I'm not necessarily opposed to what has happened around here. Take Alcan — the aluminum smelter. I owe a lot of my well-being to that company. My father worked there for years. When I see that smoke, I see money."

This brief divergence of view reminded me of Valerie Langer's comment about how difficult it is for First Nations people to plot their future in starkly contrasting worlds.

An hour and a half of motoring south and east through fjords led us deeper, deeper into the mountain womb of coastal British Columbia, which I had seen only from a distance on the ferryboat. Now we admired three peaks rising on the horizon, snowfields still frosting their summits in early summer. The hard-pack of avalanches persisted in ravines that funneled down to green water at sea level. Then, in the cusp of the bay, I saw a helical curl of smoke and the yellowish log structure of Kowesas Lodge.

After we tied up at the dock, Ann and I got the proud carpenter's tour from Mark Downing, a white man who built high-end homes in the Portland area. "A few years ago," he said, "I decided to spend two weeks every summer using my skills for conservation purposes — building things for groups like The Nature Conservancy. That way, I can do some good and maybe assuage some guilt about building large houses out of wood." Mark smiled, I think presuming I would regard his counter-career as somehow inadequate. Yet the issue needed no further explaining. What he was doing was admirable, and inconsistencies accompany all our lives.

"On one of those projects I met Ken Margolis, and I found out about Kowesas." Mark had volunteered as building supervisor the previous summer, when construction began. This year Nanakila found some money to pay him to supervise the work for several months, and rather than build another million-dollar house for an executive in the computer industry, the master builder came here.

I commented on the absence of electricity, the attenuated supply line, and the dire consequences of injuries way back in the fjords. "Unique challenges definitely come with this project, and I like them," Mark said. "Power tools or not, if it involves wood, I do it. You can see that we're milling this timber right at the building site. We snag the logs out in the water and tow them here by boat. Then we use this turfer to lift them into place." The turfer — a pulley system with a hundred feet of cable attached — was anchored in standing trees at the periphery of the site and allowed two men to do the work of a hydraulic crane. It was just one of many adaptations Mark and his Haisla coworkers had made to the wilderness. Eighteen- by eighteen-inch beams had been turfered into place and then inter-locked with other beams by mortise-and-tenon joints and pegs tamped through holes. Almost at the lap of high tide, the lodge looked out over the water to a granite dome across the channel.

Feeling a bit like a fifth wheel when the men turned to a discussion of the materials being delivered and others unavailable or soon to be needed, Ann and I followed Mark's advice to take a walk out back and get a feel for the place.

We picked our way through the rainforest to a stream that descended the mountainside. It split into two branches, each leaping over separate waterfalls, flinging jewel-like drops into space. The two channels reunited on the rocks below in a garden greened with ferns, seedlings, and mattresses of moss. Through a final grove of primeval cedar, hemlock, and Sitka spruce the fresh water whooshed out to the tidal inlet to renew its long oceanic phase.

Like other enclaves of the Coast Range, this one spoke of timeless beauty and the unfathomable workings of nature in rock, soil, forest, stream, and sea. Unlike most others, this place was still the home of a people who fiercely defended it from unwanted change, people who belonged here and knew their place in the world.

Back at the lodge, we reboarded for the long ride out, zipping up against a wind-driven rain. Motoring away from the bay, I tried to imagine the arrival of boatloads of loggers, the docking of butter-dish barges like those I had seen plying the inland passage between the cutting fields and pulp mills, and the transformation of the Kowesas River basin from Haisla sanctuary to industrial forest. I could imagine all this because I had seen so much of it elsewhere, from the red-woods of northern California through the tortured topography of coastal Oregon, through mile upon mile of scrubby tree farms on Vancouver Island. But here, I could also imagine a completed Kowesas Lodge and the loggers' landing platform occupied by the

Haisla people — grandmothers with babies in their arms, angry young men with clenched fists, and bowlegged elders, all standing stoically together at the water's edge, where the hard-hatted timber cutters would have to disembark if they insisted on taking Indian land with the sharpened tools of their trade.

I asked myself, Which side would win?

SEEKING THE answers to related questions back at Kitamaat Village, I found Ken Hall at the docks, installing new seats in his boat with a calm, deliberate sense of workmanship. Also known as Chaqueekash, Ken is the hereditary chief of the Kowesas, a tribe called the Snow People. Quietly and thoughtfully he responded to my questions, out of which his story slowly emerged.

He skipped most of the first ten thousand years and began when his people were nearly wiped out by diseases brought here by Europeans. The survivors moved from the hidden, but not hidden enough, recesses of the Kowesas basin to Kitamaat and joined the Haisla people.

"We used to have four million acres," Ken explained. "But three-quarters of that has been damaged by logging. Indians did not speak up enough when this was happening. You see, our elders taught us to respect others, and that is what held us back from speaking up sooner. But at the Kitlope and the Kowesas, we had to take a stand. The mountains and the forests there are the source of our water. Each family has always had an area for their harvest of berries and for trapping and hunting. I remember living up there as a kid. I enjoyed it. Nothing bothered us. We had freedom. There were half a dozen families. While few people depend on it completely anymore, subsistence by hunting, fishing, and gathering is still important to us, and so the health of this land is important. We could not allow it to be logged." Ken paused.

I looked across the water and counted to eight.

"For thousands of years life went on here. Now, the pace of change is so fast. In the past forty years so much trouble has been created, and I don't know if we can recover. There's dioxin in our fish now. All our food sources are affected. Where do you go from there? You see the smoke from the mill and the smelter, you see the logging and the landslides that follow it, you see the loss of wildlife, the disappearing salmon. These losses hurt everyone, but we will suffer more than others."

He pointed across the bay to the plumes of pollution. "Some of the people over there don't care about their environment as long as they get a paycheck. I asked them, 'What's for your grandchildren? What's for the future?' They couldn't answer. But I know the answer. They will move on while my people will stay."

My eyes became stuck on the smelter smoke for a while. It puffed up, spread out, drifted east, fell down on us. "Is there hope?" I asked.

"Hope? I don't know about that," the graying Chaqueekash answered. "So much has been lost. How can we get it back? I don't know. It will be difficult. But what we have done here at the Kitlope may give others hope. Other First Nations don't realize what is at stake. Some are blinded by the money. I argue with them. I say that without our forests we are headed for poverty regardless of whether the logging jobs are here this year or not. I argue that poverty will be worse if we destroy the whole country. Other nations come to see what we've done. Maybe some of what we've done will rub off."

NEXT, I sought out Louise Barbetti, a Haisla woman whom Ken Margolis had recommended, noting that her father had been the highest hereditary chief of the Haisla. She and Ann and I met in her living room, which was beautifully furnished and decorated with Northwest Indian art.

With a serious, strong look in her eyes and black hair cut medium length, Louise wore a sweatshirt brightly colored with totem figures on the front. "The Kitimat and these other rivers had always been the breadbasket of the Haisla," Louise began. "Here at the village we were protected from the elements, from the north wind and the big storms. Our creeks didn't dry up in the summer. The fish right here in these waters were our food source. And then came a lot of change." She paused long enough that I thought she had finished, though I failed to count to ten.

"What do you think of the change?" I asked, wanting to know this before she moved on with her story.

"I absolutely hate it. When Eurocan polluted our water, we took them to court. We won some money and improvements, but our fish are still poisoned. The logging has devastated our valley here. We are a poor country. But when the West Fraser Timber Company came to cut down the forests of the Kitlope, our elders said that too much has been lost. Now we must fight."

Louise glanced at Ann and me, and then she said: "One thing that must be understood is this: when the land does not survive, we will not survive. When I step out and look at these mountains, I feel that I *need* them to survive. I can safely say that nearly all our people feel that way."

"But your people must have lost control of your land, of your lives, of everything."

"Everything. Even our families. A big problem was that for years the government hauled our children away to boarding schools. They tore children away from their families and banned our language, religion, and customs. Some of the children were horribly abused. In the name of assimilation the schools broke the back of our culture. They created a lost generation that had no idea how to live. It has left us a handicapped people, and we're just now beginning to recover from it. But here's the thing: some of us didn't go to the schools. I had a strong father and mother. I heard my father say to the official who came to get us, 'If any one of my children goes, you're a dead man.' We stayed home to learn from our parents and from people in the village."

"You were lucky to have parents with such courage," Ann said.

"Yes. A few of us were spared the awful things they did in the schools, and a little of our land has been spared, too. The Kitlope is a very spiritual place. I can't explain it, but once people go there, they come back knowing we need to save it. It doesn't belong to us. It belongs to the children of the world, and it's our responsibility to see that they have it."

I asked, "How is it that the Haisla are successful in saving their forest, but other Indians are not?" I thought of the cut-and-run logging on Indian land of the Olympic Peninsula, of the First Nations' dilemma in Clayoquot Sound, and of land held by native corporations in Alaska, where some of the worst logging in North America has occurred.

"I think it's because here we are united as one people. At other reservations, five or six different tribes might be thrown together on the land. Being different people, they disagree about many things, as they have done for centuries. Also, some of the First Nations have lost their cultural roots and don't see value in the land anymore. Many lands were lost a long time ago. But here, and especially on the Kitlope, we are more isolated, our land is less damaged, and we look at our future as one people."

"Louise, what do you see happening to your people?"

"My vision is that we will once again be a strong, capable people, the way we always were, healthy and wealthy in our ways. One day we will walk as tall as our Haisla ancestors. We've already come a long way, battling drugs and alcohol. For centuries we had none of those things. Those problems were learned. That is what we learned from some of the good Christian people."

"And how can your people regain their strength?"

Louise paused, and I sensed that she was looking back into the deep, reflective waters of her own life, waters we could only skim in this conversation. "I worked for the school district twenty years ago. I was appalled at the racism in the schools. But what could I do? I was one person. Where could I start? Well, I spent a lot of time watching the kids. I noticed that one thing making a difference in their confidence was their teeth. Yes, their teeth. Many First Nations children had no front teeth. So twenty years ago I started with dental care. Then I moved on to general health, and then to emotional health. To deal with physical, emotional, and sexual abuse is very difficult, but we're doing that. It's the beginning of a healthy community. People's minds and bodies and souls are like a braid, all intertwined, and no less than that, the health of a community is tied to the health of the land. We have to remind all First Nations people that they can be proud of who they are. If you don't believe in your heart that you are valuable, then nothing that anyone can say will help. To have that sense of value, we need an awareness of our roots, and for that, we need our land."

AIMING TO reestablish roots in the land, Karen Nyce was the director of Rediscovery, a Haisla program to take First Nations kids out into the wilderness that was the home of their ancestors. In her twenties, she had the long raven hair of her people. Her dark eyes shone with hope. She bubbled with excitement about her work.

"From scratch, we recently built a traditional longhouse," Karen said. "They are made with cedar and were the place where people lived and held ceremonies. Building a lodge with a bunch of kids can be a challenge when it rains for twelve days straight. But it was a good experience for everybody. Just to get to the camp took a day. Fifteen of us motorboated up the inlet and then walked ten kilometers up the Kitlope River. We worked hard on the house, but we also played games to get to know one another. Some of the kids came from far away — a few were white and a few were even Inuit, from the far North — people who had never mixed with First Nations down here. We all got up in the morning, stretched, ran, cooked, and did some of the chores that our people used to do all the time. About halfway through the week, the students went out on solo — off by themselves for twenty-four hours with nothing but matches and a potato. Spending time like that alone helps them see important things about themselves. We learned about fishing and cooking. We picked lots of blueberries in our spare time. Being up on the Kitlope, where the land hasn't been logged, is magical and healing. Just being there, you can feel it. It's a force that's hard to explain. But the students definitely felt it."

Karen looked upward, picturing the scene in her mind. "Up there," she continued, "the students gained control over their lives. To do it, they had to work together, which is a powerful thing." This young Indian woman held her hands wide apart and said, "They went out there like this. Then they came home like this," and she clasped her hands together, her fingers intertwined.

"Up on the Kitlope, we got to see what our people used to do, how they lived. We got to see how *strong* they were. It moved us all. The environment is a part of Haisla culture. The land, animals, plants, river, ocean, and food are all tied together. Respect for the whole thing — for yourself, for one another, and for the environment — it was all one thing, and now we're trying to reconnect those bonds."

I asked if she could give me an example of how the experience affected a child.

"Okay. One kid had been abused. He trusted nobody. He was violent, a terror to everyone around him. But out there, he opened up. He smiled. Being there made him stronger inside, and the bond with the other kids helped. He will still have trouble, but I think that being there started him on the right path."

"It sounds as if everyone was putting down new roots."

"Roots, yes. Elders came out with us and taught the Haisla language and stories. We learned that every mountain and stream has a story that goes with it. We drank the water from the lake, and it was much better than the water here. The mountains are the source of that water and of so much of what we use. The mountains show us that we are very small, and with that awareness comes humbleness and respect. All that is important to our culture."

As ANN and I drove back down the Skeena River valley toward Prince Rupert, we thought of the Indian groups we had seen from the deserts of Baja to here: small reservations in southern California, the Yurok Indians at the mouth of the Klamath, the Nuu-chah-nulth people of Clayoquot Sound. The challenges facing all those people were enormous. But here on the coast of British Columbia, the Haisla were showing that the needs of the individual, the culture, and the landscape can all be met when they take good care of their place.

In later action affecting the entire Great Bear Rainforest, an agreement was reached between First Nations people, environmentalists, logging companies, and local communities to protect another 1.5 million acres, to defer logging on an additional 2.2 million acres, and to adopt ecosystem-based planning for all forests. Whether or not the agreement will survive changes in B.C. politics remained to be seen.

Boarding another ferryboat, Ann and I set our sights on what the natives call the Great Land. Alaska lay just ahead.

Southeast Alaska

0————————100 miles

© Tim Palmer

# 13 | *Glaciers to the Sea*

A̲s we crossed the invisible boundary between British Columbia and Alaska, puffed masses of moisture overhung the higher mountains to the east, where granite peaks knifed their way skyward through the fog and the damp. Among the gray-green lower-elevation mountains, streaks of mist angled up from unnamed valleys. To the west, clouds hovered like layers of rolled-up rugs over broad waters and enticing little islands.

Chugging along at twenty miles per hour, which seems fast on a boat, the blunt-nosed ferry cut Revillagigedo Channel like a rubber spatula drawn across frosting. We cruised so stably on the quiet seas that from my perch at the front deck, the impression — after a long, hypnotizing stare into the water — was that the boat was standing still and the earth rotating toward us. The horizon line minutely turned upward to our approach, revealing more water, more forest, more world to see.

All around us — toward the continent and away from it — mountains floated up out of the ocean. Those summits of islands — a thousand of them in the Alexander Archipelago — represented scraps of floating plates that geologists call exotic terranes, smaller versions of the Juan de Fuca Plate, whose remains we had seen from central

Oregon through Vancouver Island. The terranes had inched their way up here by continental drift from as far away as the Southern Hemisphere, perhaps even Peru. Collectively called Wrangellia, they had collided with the North American Plate fifty million years ago, crumpling into the earthy wreckage we saw here oceanside in southeast Alaska.

Off the coast of Oregon, the Juan de Fuca Plate shouldered its way in between the Pacific and North American Plates, but here the two big ones again grated against each other as they did in California. Rock-against-rock friction at the Queen Charlotte Fault, which now took the place of the San Andreas, had cultivated the ground and piled up mountains like multiple mud pies squished together into one big pan.

Here we began touring the final of the four American states in our Coast Range odyssey and by far the largest, wildest, highest. Alaska contains one-fifth of the land of the United States and one-third of its coastline. Seven of the country's twenty largest rivers flow here, and fifteen peaks reach higher than any in the other states.

In what might be pictured as an extension of the Cascade Mountains of the inland Pacific Northwest, the Alaska Range arcs across a southern interior swath of the state, throws up the 20,320-foot Mount McKinley as the loftiest summit on the continent, and then continues southwestward to become the Aleutian Islands, a chain of eighty volcanic islands dotting the ocean and extending toward Siberia.

South of that mountain mass, the Coast Range arcs the whole way westward from British Columbia to Kodiak Island, where the land finally ends. The peaks in this complex exceed those of any other oceanfront mountains in the world. Not counting the contiguous, steep front of British Columbia, this supremely rugged topographic wall runs for 1,130 miles. Overlain on the rest of the country, the span of Alaska's coastal mountains, even without counting the additional 1,400 miles of the Aleutian Range, would reach from Canada to Texas.

Into Alaska, hour after hour, our boat hummed northward, a shipful of strangers on various personal and professional missions. In my eye the passengers fell into five categories: young adventurers, older people on motor home trips, Indians, white working-class men, and, on this particular boat, Australians enjoying a package tour. I met mostly the young and older tourists, as they roamed the decks and loafed in social places while the others mostly didn't.

Sharing space along the railing with Ann and me, Tony and Kate came from Great Britain but had settled in Beijing. Dorothy, in her fifties or so, traveled alone and told us about her lifelong ambition to journey to the Last Frontier state from her native Indiana, where she worked in a nursing home. "I finally realized that if I was going to do it, I'd have to do it alone," she said of her difficult but rewarding plunge into a new world that so wholly embodies what Indiana is not.

During a lap around the deck for exercise, I adjusted my pace for a while to that of stiff-legged Bill, according to the scripted name on his ball cap. He also sported flashy red suspenders that said "Wrangell" on them. Remembering that Alaska island town as the takeout for a Stikine River trip I had made ten years before, I asked Bill if he'd spent much time there. I thought my question was open-ended enough.

"Hell, I *live* in Wrangell," he replied, a bit miffed to have his local identity in doubt on this ship of fools.

More talkative, Ron, from suburban Boston, was a reluctant architect. "You wouldn't believe how fast land there is developing," he said. "And I was a part of it. I hated my job. So I quit and came on this trip to Alaska."

"Will you go back?" I asked, thinking of the inevitable reckoning, as when you throw a ball up in the air and know it has to come down.

"Yes, Mary Ann and I will have to go back, but only when we run out of money. When that time comes, I want to do something else. I'm trying to decide what that is."

Dan Moss, a tall young man with a friendly smile and Tennessee drawl, was on his way to band birds at Tetlin National Wildlife Refuge. "I used to be pretty far-left-leaning," he confessed of his political views. "But then I went to graduate school in wildlife biology and hung out with a lot of hunters and conservative academics, and I shifted to the right. But then I came to Alaska last summer and quickly jumped back again to the other side. This place shows you that we need to do all we can, as fast as we can, to protect what's left. To take the usual middle road here would be a waste."

In wind, fog, and drizzle, a lone group of us remained on the deck, glued to the view even with parkas zipped up and hoods clutched tightly at our necks.

By midafternoon it had brightened up, and our captain ruddered us into the port of Ketchikan. While we waited for the deck tender to tie up his fat braided rope and for the traffic to come and go, David Berg, from the Bronx, counted seventy bald eagles in the trees. A fine naturalist, David had spotted marbled murrelets, pigeon guillemots, and other cryptically mottled seabirds as we cruised north. With Audubon New York he ran a metropolitan environmental program that organized volunteers to reclaim vestiges of nature such as wetlands in Long Island Sound. "Those are important remnants," he said, "but now it's good to see a place that's still whole."

After the short layover, I met a man who had just boarded, wearing a blue jacket with lettering that said "Rudy's Wild Game Dinner."

"It must be quite a feed," I surmised, pointing to the inscription that the man apparently advertises on his back wherever he goes.

"Most any kind of wild game you can think of, people bring it to Rudy and he cooks it up."

"Sounds great. How's life in Ketchikan otherwise?" I asked, grabbing at this chance to chat with a working-class man after my earlier pitfall with the Wrangellian.

"It's hell," the man said, immediately turning grumpy in disposition. "The pulp mill closed. A thousand eight hundred jobs are gone. Lots of houses up for sale. You wanna buy a house?"

"Come on, don't tempt me. Where are the people going?"

"I don't know. All over."

"Why did the mill close?"

"It's all political. Al Gore and his stuff. LP couldn't get a contract to cut national forest timber."

"Why not?"

"I don't know. People from the outside, they all think Alaska should be a park. That's fine, but what will the people who live here do? They need to work, too."

I later talked to a lot of people about the forests and the logging industry of southeast Alaska. I learned that the Louisiana-Pacific Corporation's pulp mill at Ketchikan and another mill at Sitka had repeatedly been found guilty of violating pollution laws and degrading the waters and fishery around them. Both mills faced heavy fines and cleanup costs, and both closed down. But the cleanup wasn't the real problem.

Those mills had been able to operate in the first place only because Congress guaranteed the industry a $40 million minimum annual subsidy for roads and cheap trees from national forest land. Timber appraised at $1,000 a thousand board feet was sold to the mills for $1.22. For the price I paid the Forest Service for a pocket-sized paper map, Louisiana Pacific could get enough lumber to load a large pickup truck to the gills — loaded with the finest lumber money can buy.

Not only was the natural wealth of the best land relinquished without a war, but we taxpayers all paid lavishly for this insult with subsidies that typically topped $60 million a year, ostensibly to keep a couple of thousand southeast Alaska mill workers — like the man who attended Rudy's Wild Game Dinner — employed. Campaign contributions, rather than jobs, probably had more to do with the real political motivation.

Not only was the cutting subsidized, but also, under exemptions from export rules that apply to national forests elsewhere, virtually all the Alaskan logs were shipped to Japan and a few other Asian countries.

I couldn't help thinking about this when I later viewed an exhibit of the hard-fought battle of Attu in the Second World War. Here in Alaska, the only battle fought on American soil claimed the lives of 549 American soldiers and wounded 1,148. Looking at photographs of the grim and storm-swept war zone, I was struck by the irony that blood had been shed over that distant island of barren rock and grass, unimaginably distant in a stormy Pacific a thousand miles even beyond the western coast of the Alaska mainland. And then, only a few decades later, some of the most valuable natural assets in our country, coming from one of the rarest ecosystems in the world, were being cut down, the land scarred, and the forest handicapped for centuries in order to ship the timber to Japan. Of course, the issue of military invasion makes Attu a whole different ball of wax, but just the same, Americans of my father's generation died for an island of rock, only to have Alaska's politicians turn around and give away the very best.

Under this model of profit for somebody but poverty for the public, half a million acres of the finest commercial timber of the country's largest national forest—the Tongass, spanning all of southeast Alaska—has been cut since 1954. Another half million acres fell victim to logging by Alaska native corporations, which impose even fewer environmental safeguards. This occurred through the 1980s and 1990s as a direct result of the Alaska Native Claims Settlement Act. The law called on the Indians to form profit-making corporations, and then it set those corporations loose with irresistible incentives to liquidate their resources. Bypassing both existing tribal governments and the leadership of elders, who with their ancestors had mentored life in Indian communities for thousands of years, the corporate model flew in the face of traditional wisdom that still resides with many native people. Now the selling of natural assets has flooded selected villages with short-term cash but torn tribes apart politically, socially, and culturally. The outcome in Alaska stands in stark contrast to that on Haisla lands, where heritage-oriented views prevailed.

The maze of logging roads and leveled forest on Indian land and national forest alike put the rich biology of southeast Alaska at great peril. Some of the last healthy populations of deep-wilderness animals—brown bears, bald eagles, northern wolves, king salmon, and a host of other species—suffer in this area, which represents 29 percent of the world's temperate rainforest and one of few remaining enclaves with large tracts of giant trees. After intense lobbying on both sides, Congress passed the Tongass Timber Reform Act in 1991, protecting some important wild areas. Other subsidies survived, but the $40 million guarantee was terminated.

While much remains to be done, the Tongass reform act stands as one of the great conservation victories in American history. Not two but twelve pulp mills had been proposed when the guaranteed subsidy went into effect in the 1950s. The Forest Service had once called for the cutting of 95 percent of the Tongass' commercial timber. That number has dropped to 40 percent, most of which is already gone.

Much of the success can be credited to the Southeast Alaska Conservation Council's nationalizing the plight of the Tongass and motivating people all over the country to press their congressional representatives for change. Fortunately, this effort was concluded before the 1994 Republican Party takeover of Congress, which rewarded Alaska's retrograde politicians with committee chairmanships. Also important, conservationists organized in Alaska communities, where fishing accounted for more jobs than any other sector in the state except government. Their arguments to reduce logging appealed to Indians who were still using their homeland for hunting and to smaller-scale loggers, who benefited from the reduction of subsidies to corporate giants.

As the rain picked up on our cruise northward, Ann and I ducked inside to dry off while attending an onboard lecture by a Forest Service volunteer, a gray-haired man in uniform. We often learn a lot in these interpretive programs. But without justification, the man staunchly defended the clearcuts that blanket Tongass lowlands such as Prince of Wales Island—one single island shredded with thirty-five hundred miles of logging roads. Most passengers were oblivious to the ratty look of that rugged island and many other mountainsides because the view from the ferries remained pleasantly uncut, the systematic felling of timber obscured behind a thin curtain of unlogged trees.

The uniformed man went as far as to say that the clearcuts benefited wildlife. According to him, cutting down all the trees was the best thing that could be done for the woods. The seated rows of tourists took all this in with blank TV-stares or with uncritical nods of the head.

"Can you believe he's saying this?" Ann whispered to me. Biologists conclude that beyond the temporary boon to deer that feed on shrubs for a few years, the clearcuts are devastating to wildlife.

While I was clearing my throat and trying to think of a diplomatic way to deal with what I regarded as gross misinformation, David Berg piped up. "How about the salmon streams that get ruined? How about the deer that need old growth when it snows? How about the pole-sized forest that takes two centuries to mature and be any good at all for wildlife?"

Trying to pretend that the New Yorker's attack had not occurred, the speaker called on an Alaskan, who said that he had sold a log he found drifting near his dock for $3,000. Faced with "Ooohs" and "Ahhs" and amazed appreciation at how far one log might go in a place like Wal-Mart, I couldn't resist backing up David.

"Why," I asked, "with prices like that, why does our government sell two-hundred-foot-tall trees for $7 apiece? That's less than we pay for one lousy little board at the lumberyard."

"It's outrageous," piped up Tony the Brit, sounding a lot like the commentators we hear on British Broadcasting Corporation newscasts — the guys who mince no words about American politics being so corporate.

Scrambling in bureaucratese, the retiree was rescued by a woman who said, "Aw, come on, I'm sick of political stuff." And with those words, the beauty-strip blackout of information survived with only a hint of exposure from a New Yorker, a guy drying out in yellow rainsuit overalls, and an Englishman.

I later discussed the logging issue with Forest Service deputy regional chief Jim Caplan. Perhaps embarrassed by the old subsidies, he made no excuses for bad resource management in years past. I suspect he knew that no explanation would be adequate. Rather, he itemized improvements made in the new forest plan. It increased buffer zones at waterfronts. It protected sensitive areas. It represented an enormous reform when compared with what had seemed inevitable just a few years back. Still, he recognized it was not truly an ecosystem-based approach, desirable as that was. "We're working in that direction," Caplan said, "but it might take ten years."

As the ferryboat approached Wrangell, we crossed the silty edge of the Stikine River outflow, which looked like a giant cup of creamy coffee spilled on a blue-green kitchen counter. On the seaward side, the water shone icy clear; on the landward side, it swirled with rock dust that had been washed down from glaciers high above and carried three hundred forty miles down this second-longest river crossing of the entire coastal mountain chain.

From the deck we could now see the LeConte and Shakes Glaciers —the southernmost American ice masses that still scrape their way down to sea level. Above them, at the Coast Range crest, Kate's Needle and Devil's Thumb rose, with granite spires and walls, 10,023 and 9,077 feet, respectively. The whole picture, in low evening light, reminded me of a note written by John Muir during his trip in 1879: "Never before this had I been embosomed in scenery so hopelessly beyond description." Muir traveled this way twice, paddling with natives in the raw, rainy chill of October, climbing peaks scarcely considered approachable today, and leaping crevasses that split ice-blue glaciers. He was able to strip away barriers to the natural world and immerse himself in everything the land had to offer. He did not restrict himself with fear, convenience, or convention. One hundred years later, he remained an inspiration for us to see, to do, to live! "I just can't wait to get *out* there myself," Ann said as we inhaled the tantalizing view.

During a quick stop at Wrangell, Ann and I hurriedly walked the town with David Berg and our tightening little group of deckside characters, having bonded simply by nature of what we had seen together from the prow of the ship. Beckoned back by a belch from the craft's foghorn, we reboarded, and our captain soon propellered us into the constriction of Wrangell Narrows. The steep slopes of Mitkof Island rose on our right, Kupreanof Island on our left. The approaching nighttime at eleven P.M. disappointed all us deckhands, the silhouettes of mountains darkening above us like canyon walls in the desert.

Ultimately alone, I stared over the rail into the black and swirling waters of our wake. Though scintillating in the lights of the ship, the sea looked so huge, so mysterious, so subconscious, so final. A creepy chill caused me to grip the rail a little harder and then abandon my edgy perch altogether.

Ann and I sought out a nesting place away from the crowded sleeping deck, where quite an assortment of vagabonds snoozed chockablock on chaise longues. We pitched our tent under a smaller overhang at the back of the boat, and a spattering rain dampened our waterproof fly.

Just five hours later the morning light found us approaching Kake, an Indian village with homes clustered above high tide. Beyond them, a cutover rainforest sought to recover its old-time status, and on a few remaining snags bald eagles roosted like robins.

As we watched from the deck, I noticed an Indian child boarding the boat with his mother. He held tight to a stuffed toy eagle, worn bare in spots from many nights in the little boy's grip. It struck me: how fun, how real. What if every child had a beloved toy that represented something authentic about his or her place? It might be a stretch to say that hugging a toy bald eagle was a step toward this boy's sense of belonging to a local community of life, but given the options of blue trolls or E.T. or pink teddy bears, I had to smile and wish for every child a stuffed toy totem like the little boy's eagle.

Had I been at the helm instead of the schedule-conscious captain, we would have detoured up an icy fjord to the Sumdum Glacier, which sweeps boldly toward salt water. Then we would have plied the waters of Tracy Arm Fjord, which penetrates north and then east to its origin at the face of two grand glaciers. These shed icebergs as small as refrigerator cubes and as large as ships, 90 percent of their icy mass lurking beneath the surface of the water. Now we could see Volkswagen-sized bergs that had drifted out into the main channel of Stephens Passage, and surely I wasn't the only one to think, *Titanic!*

To the east lay the hundred-mile-long Admiralty Island, the largest mostly uncut woods in the Tongass and thereby the largest protected refuge in the temperate rainforest of the United States, comparable to the Kitlope and Kowesas watershed in British Columbia. The Indians know Admiralty more graphically as Kootznoowoo, Fortress of the Bears. The density of brown bears — a nine-foot-tall coastal variety of the grizzly — is higher here than anywhere. Seventeen hundred of the salmon eaters occupy about one square mile apiece. Fully fifteen hundred square miles once lay on the loggers' chopping block, which raised the obvious question: What would happen to the fifteen hundred forest-dwelling bears who needed that woods? The Sierra Club sued in 1970 to prevent the cutting and bought some time. Then President Jimmy Carter finally designated Admiralty a national monument, affording it protection comparable to that of a national park.

When the boat eased into the ferry terminal north of Juneau, Ann and I scrambled under the deck with the other passengers and sighed comfortably, as we always do when returning to our compact little home. I kicked over the engine, and we drove into a most interesting city, unique among all Coast Range settlements.

SQUEEZED between salt water and glacier, Juneau clings to the western front of the mountains, most of the town existing on alluvial fans that have built up where the Coast Range tips into the sea. Cozy homes and flowery, terraced gardens front abruptly on narrow streets that climb heart-attack pitches and terminate in stairways that bump up to the next level of street. Born as a mining site, the town reflects the tent-sized lots and two-story wood-frame style of nineteenth-century gold-digger settlements all over the West. We visited an onion-domed Russian Orthodox church, which spoke to the heritage of early Russian settlement there.

The state capitol in this unlikely town six hundred airline miles from Anchorage — which happens to house ten times Juneau's population — is a boxy structure a few stories high. Alaskans voted in 1976 to move the capitol to a more central and accessible location; poor visibility often closes the Juneau airport, and no roads venture into or out of this virtual island amid glacial mountains. But citizens reversed their vote after planners tallied a moving tab of $2.8 billion, enough to nix the coveted cash stipend each Alaskan gets annually from oil-export revenues.

Near the center of things, the Baranof Hotel, taller and classier than most, has long served as a social hub. Otherwise, the downtown of narrow, curved streets has been dense with shops and a lot of trinketry since cruise ships started docking in Juneau.

Though harbored for only a night or two at a time, the ships now claim architectural dominance, seven stories of Royal Caribbean or Holland America dwarfing everything else in downtown Juneau put together, including whatever people actually come to see. Except, of course, for the mountains. An inner-city population of a few thousand swells to ten thousand each time a few of the spit-shined white palaces tie up. When the gangplanks come down, money washes ashore — income for some local people but a consumer tsunami for others. Not the least of local concerns is the oil, garbage, paint, plastic, ballast, and food waste the ships have dumped into Alaska waters: many of the cruise lines have been found guilty of Clean Water Act violations.

The Juneau waterfront still maintains some of its old style, with seaplanes buzzing in and out and heavily netted fishing boats creaking at their moorings. Trollers, trawlers, long-liners, and seiners jockey for space, as do sailboats, small freighters, and oceangoing tugs that pull barges stacked with cargo from the lower forty-eight — a world lumped together and locally called the "outside." As polyglot as can be, the Juneau melting pot, especially near the wharf, includes Asian seamen, Filipino immigrants, Mexican working-class men, sourdough Alaskans with years of salty crust about them, and the full range of tourists, from athletic ocean kayakers to heavyset Americans to Europeans toting shoulder bags. They all take in the sights and search for a decent place to eat.

Though I stood among the crowds amid the multilingual chatter, my destination was the mountains, and big mountains lie closer to Juneau than to any other city in America. Often you can't see them because of the rain and clouds, but they're there, right out the door.

One of the many accommodations Juneau has made to the booming tourist trade is a tram that hoists people up the flank of Mount Roberts and plunks them down in alpine terrain. Choosing instead to examine the details and to sense the elevation gain in my feet as well as my gut, I walked to the end of Sixth Street and hit a trail that switchbacked through Sitka spruce and crossed bubbling rivulets.

The forest there grew thick and lush, and after an hour of solitude I emerged, somewhat culture-shocked, beneath the deck of a restaurant that towered fifty feet overhead. Taut steel cables of the tram hummed their industrious tune; the Erector set towers reached for the sky and supported whole busloads of multinational pilgrims. In a huddle of puffing sightseers for a while, I strode on up through meadowlands toward several visible summits. Once above the congested area, I ran into a couple from Switzerland, not surprising up in that alpine zone.

I lucked out with a spectacular day for Juneau, where some fifty-six inches of rain and ninety-two inches of snow come down on three hundred precipitating days a year. Hardly a cloud could be seen on that cheery afternoon. The sun shines the most here in May and June; the heaviest rains come in October and November, after the Pacific High retreats southward. Thankful we had made the difficult compromises earlier in our Coast Range journey in order to be here now, I basked in summer sun, the balmy comfort thrilling in a region so habitually damp. I snacked on a bagel and stretched out in the heather. Soon the Swiss couple returned from their hike.

"Beyond this peak, there are many other peaks," the man reported, struggling a bit with his English. "I think it is a never-ending walk."

Indeed it is. Rested and inspired now to go far, I topped the first shoulder-like summit, where marmots scampered among the grasses. Whistling warnings back and forth, they waddled to lookout posts above their holes and then stood on their haunches with their noses confidently in the air until I neared.

Without difficulty I topped another rounded summit. But beyond it, a snowfield slanted sharply down from a high peak. To continue, I would have to cross the slippery, white pitch.

Steep enough to give me pause, the top tilted at forty-five degrees. The gradient eased for a space, but then the slope curved down in a frightening convex drop-off to a horizon beyond which the fall presumably accelerated even more, a truly scary prospect. But I was prepared.

I extracted the businesslike ice ax from my pack and kicked a few steps into the soft upper six inches of snow. With each stride I held

the ax ready for self-arrest, keeping my eyes fixed on the snow's surface for balance because the terrain was disorientingly steep. I
looked for cracks or irregularities in the snow ahead of me and listened for the deep-diaphragm "Whoomp" of snow settling into air
space against the ground—an adjustment that can trigger an avalanche. In a few hundred steps I had crossed the snowfield, and I
happily smudged my slushy boots onto the dry grit of rocks. Then I
pressed upward to Mount Roberts' 3,819-foot summit.

From my view on the highest point around, everything I saw was
big, big. The blue water of multiple fjords lay so far below that I
couldn't see boats, but only the long lines of their wakes behind fly-
specks of gray. The islands of Admiralty and Chichagof lay to the
south and west, incised by dozens of hazy inlets. Landmasses rose up
through green timber zones to whole Colorados of mountain peaks
on just the islands alone. Northward, the white wilderness of the
Chilkat Range marched off to the interior of Alaska, British Columbia, and Yukon Territory.

Only a distant convoy of helicopters marred the scene. Sometimes
three or four in a squad, they paraded customers over the icefields. A
business of 2,000 trips in 1984 had grown to 60,000 ten years later and
was expected to quickly double again. What this escalation means to
everybody else's experience and to wildlife is a good question. Loud
and intrusive to wilderness travel, the helicopters hover atop summits, causing animals such as mountain goats to become stressed
and run from the noise. The incessant "Chop-chop-chop-chop" noise
was the reason residents of Haines fought a helicopter company's
request to set up business in that town. In the world of helicopter
travel, respect for place and even minimal preparation or effort become irrelevant. Veteran Alaska guide John Svenson lamented: "Helicopters can go anywhere, drop people off anywhere. It's a climber's
worst nightmare, to complete an ascent and have a bunch of people
arrive in a noisy helicopter, pull out their cell phones, call home, and
then get back in and fly off to some other summit."

The choppers passed, the quiet returned, and the utterly awesome
scene from my vantage lay inland—eastward. There, the heather and

rock of my summit yielded to an unknown depth of snow that dropped into a canyon but then ramped up again into the 770,000-acre Juneau Icefield, now enormous in my view. Crevassed glaciers and smooth white veneers passed for a Pleistocene geography spotted with pyramidal nunataks. These sharp summits of rock protruded above the baseline of white as if a whole mountain range had been flooded almost to its uppermost peaks by ice, which is precisely what happened. They looked a lot like monumentally outsized versions of the gray, rocky, pointed sea stacks in the ocean off the shores of Oregon.

Beyond the sprinkling of nunataks lay the backbone of the mainland Coast Range. Unlike many mountains and islands of the Pacific edge that are composed of erodible sedimentary and volcanic rocks, the mountains here are granite, like a whole Sierra Nevada still under glaciation in the North. Too windy and steep to hold snow, too high to be decked in glaciers, the uppermost peaks challenged the sky with an unforgiving sharpness. Far to the north lay Mount Ogilvie, but Devil's Paw made the real highlight, a four-pronged granite skyscraper reaching to 8,584 feet at the international border, thirty-four miles away.

Never before had a view appeared so big to me, so spaciously wild, so beautiful in its grand arrangement of ice-age power. And I knew I was seeing just a sample of the hundreds of miles of glaciated coastal uplift.

Though only at their edge, I felt as if I were finally within grasp of those northern mountains. I longed to go farther, to set off on skis across the white wonderland before me, to really experience the icefields and see if I could reach one of the nunataks that rose from the stunning sea of solid water.

The Taku River fjord lay below, drawing ample flows from high country to the east and pulling my eyes in that direction. One of few rivers to completely transect the Coast Range in this region, the Taku begins in the Atlin Lake area of the interior, where miners proposed a new gold mine. The B.C. government hastened to approve and subsidize this venture, just twelve miles upstream of the U.S. border and threatening to pollute the Taku with acid mine drainage. Canadian and American conservation groups were fighting the plan because, like the Stikine River to the south, the Taku is one of the largest unprotected but largely wilderness watersheds on the West Coast, with one of the finest remaining salmon fisheries.

Two bald eagles now soared over a mountain-edge thermal, one of them only ten feet off the ground, making me wonder if I needed to duck.

Then, as I walked farther along the skinny, snow-free ridge, a sizable furriness ahead of me began to move. Perpetually alert for bears, even up there, where there shouldn't be any, I sighed with relief at the creamy fleece of a mountain goat, huge in the belly, no doubt pregnant and ready to drop her kid at any time. I stood still behind a rock. She stared back with dark eyes, curious yet cautious. I sat down, and she relaxed, grazing on flowers and then slowly wandering along.

Later I spotted her watching me from the edge of a more distant snowfield. In my imagination—just a harmless little fantasy—she accepted me as a member of the mountain community. And with fond feelings for her, I wanted to camp up there for a month and flip off the helicopters if necessary to drive them away from her and her baby.

Loath to leave, I needed to make it out by dark. Just in time, I caught the last tram down, at ten o'clock.

ANN AND I celebrated the next day. Her manuscript was done, the artwork finished, the maps drafted, the photos labeled. With the whole package sealed and addressed to Island Press, we walked to the post office.

"It feels good, doesn't it?" I suggestively asked Ann.

"Yes, but I think maybe I should have edited the final chapter once more."

"Oh, come on. It's great. This is the time to feel good about a job well done."

Ann smiled, unconvinced. "I guess I'll have a chance to make corrections when it's copyedited." Then a glimmer sparked in her eyes. "The best part is that I'm finally free to be *here*."

"And now we're going to have fun."

In fact, a tantalizing series of adventures awaited on our docket. For starters, four friends trickled into Juneau during the next two days. First, Kaz Thea took two weeks off from her job with the U.S. Fish and Wildlife Service in Idaho to join us. Mike Medberry, a twenty-year veteran of conservation work, arrived from Seattle, where he was finishing a master's degree in creative writing. Terry and Thomas Halleran, father and son, flew in from Connecticut. Terry and his wife, Alice, had been Ann's most beloved high school teachers. With the curiosity of a scientist, Terry had wanted to come to Alaska for a long time. Seventeen-year-old Thomas was eager, with boundless energy, to see the world.

They all came to sea kayak in the renowned Glacier Bay, sixty airline miles west of Juneau. Though most people go there to see whales and ocean-edge glaciers, I wanted to see the mountains, but the only way to reach them in this supremely rugged, completely unroaded territory is by boat. Even John Muir, during his trips in 1879 and 1880, explored mostly by water.

Though we had all paddled on rivers, only Kazzie excelled in ocean kayaking. She had once led trips in the cold coastal waters of Maine, so we all counted on her to rescue us if necessary.

Planning cautiously, we chose a route that lacked long crossings of open water and treacherous tidal bores. The East Arm of Glacier Bay, also called Muir Inlet, seemed perfect. The skyscraper tour ships, which tend to dominate in the way an elephant would do even in a large room, are not allowed there. Brown bears can be a problem anywhere in Glacier Bay—a few years back a lone traveler had photographed the horrific sequence of a bear charging, right up to the fatal bite—but the reputation of Muir Inlet was not as frightening as that of the West Arm.

When I had planned my first Alaska river trips, twenty years before, I consulted with a friend, the famed bear biologist Frank Craighead. He told me that when he traveled in country where he expected to encounter grizzlies, he generally carried a shotgun loaded with slugs. These are heavy single bullets rather than a shotgun's usual wad of beebees, and they provide the best stopping power for a bear at very close range. Thus informed, I always carried a twelve-gauge double-barrel that once belonged to my grandfather. With this serviceable antique I lacked the ability to fire more than two times without reloading—an advantage afforded by modern weapons with pump action. But balancing that out, I could say with confidence that the old family heirloom of straightforward design had never once misfired in eighty years of service.

The other defense, in a can the size of a ketchup bottle, is pressurized capsicum spray. When fired point-blank, this aerosol of cayenne pepper stings bears' eyes and repels most attacks. Though many Alaskans never set foot in the bush without a gun, others now consider bear spray a better option. A gun, after all, can get you into big trouble if you shoot a bear unnecessarily or wound a bear that would otherwise go away. Even worse, a gun can embolden its carrier so much that he stumbles into dicey situations otherwise avoided.

Having had plenty of troubles with black bears over the years, and after being regaled with stories of close calls by a friend who once guided sea kayaking trips in Glacier Bay, I regarded some form of defense as critical. So when Ann and I learned that regulations banned guns in the national park, we bought a bear spray canister for each member of our group.

But, on checking in with our charter air service, we now learned that rules forbade bear spray on airplanes. At the same time, they told us our aircraft was grounded because clouds and rain had socked in the airstrip at our destination, Gustavus.

With Glacier Bay's history of bear attacks, we might not have gone there at all had we known we would be denied the nominal defense of capsicum. Ann quickly checked on the alternative of catching a boat across the strait, but no passage could be arranged. Surely we could buy new bear spray at Gustavus. But a phone call revealed that it was out of stock. A woman on the line shrugged off our predicament in pure Alaskan style. "Just put the bear spray in a Nalgene water bottle and close the lid."

I hung up and said, "Excuse me," to Ann and our party. "I have to run and get something I forgot."

I took my largest waterproof duffel bag to the van. From the depths of the storage compartment there I dug out my army surplus ammunition can—standard gear for rafters, who use these indestructible waterproof steel containers for valuables on whitewater river trips. Into the can I placed our assortment of bear sprays. I clamped the lid shut. Then I wrapped the can in extra clothing and buried the entire suite in the middle of my duffel. I couldn't imagine that safer packaging had ever been devised for bear spray.

At eight o'clock that evening a hole cleared in the patchy skies over Gustavus, and we took off. Once beyond the suburbs and shopping centers north of Juneau, we winged high above the blue water of Stephens Passage. The pilot, who looked like a teenager, pointed out a spouting whale below and said, "We could circle to get a better view, but I think we'd better try to hit the hole over Gustavus while it lasts."

As we approached Glacier Bay, Icy Strait flattened westward toward the open Pacific. Rain peppered the windshield, and cloud cover thickened in mottled masses that threatened to cotton us out. But a donut hole in the atmosphere remained, and into it we flew, dropping like a dive-bomber groundward. A runway suddenly materialized out of nowhere. We hadn't been up for long, but on an evening like that it felt good to step onto terra firma once again.

For fifty dollars a bush cabbie in a battered van drove us and our formidable stash of gear via puddled dirt roads to the Glacier Bay Lodge on Bartlett Cove, where we had reserved oceangoing kayaks and accessories. Even so late in the day, a woman named Tanya received us with a warm welcome, rounded up our rental equipment, and showed us where to camp for the night and where to meet the tour boat in the morning. At seven A.M. a sizable cruiser would haul us and our kayaks twenty-two miles north to Sebree Island, at the junction of the East and West Arms of Glacier Bay, where the paddling would begin.

Under a steady rain, everything took agonizingly longer than it should have. Just in the nick of time I caught the harbormaster, who sold me a gallon of white gas for our stoves, an essential item I had known was forbidden on airplanes. Then we loaded the food into bearproof canisters, easier said than done. With six people to feed for seven days, the menu amounted to one hundred twenty-six meals bought by Ann and me in a Juneau grocery store, and its reconfiguration into the stubby little conga-drum barrels took some work. Then, while the rest of the group packed their personal gear into waterproof bags, Ann and I headed off to the campsite, half a mile away, toting overnight essentials via wheelbarrow. In persistent rain we strung a tarp and fired up dinner. By the time we all hit the sack, it was one A.M. Projecting similar delays for the morning, I figured we should get up at four-thirty.

"Why even go to bed?" Ann wondered aloud, still wired from all the setup for the trip. But the cool, damp chill—if nothing else—drove us into our sleeping bags.

I must have mis-set the clock because I awoke at five without any help. "Holy smokes!" I said, shaking Ann. "We have to get moving!" I rousted the others, who, to a person, groaned at my fatherly wake-up call. We wheelbarrowed everything out to the dock where we had paddled the kayaks the night before, and then we faced the sobering reality of cramming our gear into the two-seater craft to see if it all would fit. Halfway through this difficult exercise, our ship arrived, in a light drizzle.

A hundred tourists boarded while we hefted our kayaks and yard-sale of equipment onto the deck. At seven sharp the captain set off on a speedy drone to Sebree. Kazzie surveyed the scene of our group in head-to-toe rain gear complete with high, black rubber boots, muddy from the slogging we had done below tide line. Many of the tourists —a lot of them in small groups of retirees—wore spotless pastels. "Okay," Kazzie said. "This is a quiz. Which group is different?"

Kaz befriended about half the people on the boat, including a German woman returning to the West Arm to resume a trip that had been inconveniently interrupted. With a pained expression on her face, Kazzie motioned us over to hear the story. In accented English the woman told us that a brown bear had invaded her camp, rolled one food canister into the ocean, smashed two kayaks, and slit a tent, top to bottom, with the casual rake of a paw. The woman and her partner paddled the remaining kayak out to a fishing boat, radioed for help, caught a ride to Gustavus, and resupplied themselves with gear, food, and two new boats. Now they were returning to rescue their party and resume their trip. Without a lot of comment we all took the story in, sparing one another our own private fears.

While cruising up the bay we eyed clown-faced puffins and spouting whales. When the boat nosed onto the cobbled beach at Sebree, we hustled quickly, as we had been advised. As soon as the deckhands had passed the third kayak down to us, the first mate shouted, "Do you have everything?"

I did not take this as a rhetorical question and proceeded to count people and boats. Then I intended to itemize paddles and finally tick off the major stashes of gear. But before I had even finished with the paddles the captain threw his ship into reverse and gunned the engine.

"Bye," the cheery mate yelled from the rail.

"Ah, you know, I think I left the food bags on board," Terry kidded.

"Seaweed's quite nutritious," Ann responded to her former science teacher.

Our mother craft receded rapidly into the gray sea, with dozens of people waving farewells to Kazzie and snapping pictures as if we were about to disappear into the Congo for an indeterminate period of time.

Within seconds it was quiet; just the pelt of raindrops ticked on my rubberized overalls and hooded raincoat. Now we faced the big question we had tried to tackle earlier: Would all our gear fit into the kayaks?

Most of it did, though we had to cram essentials even into the space between our legs, with lunch or camera bags on our laps but still under the spray-skirts. While an outgoing tide and miniature chop broke ashore, we lugged our loaded boats into the sea, squirmed inside the cockpits, and stroked away.

With the rain and clouds so low they passed for a pea soup of fog, everything lay monochromed in soundless gray, the world's largest sensory deprivation chamber, animated only by the synchronized paddling of our friends in the other two kayaks. Eventually we would need to cross the three-mile-wide Muir Inlet, but we elected not to begin the trip with a blind compass crossing against an outgoing tide that could push us an unknown distance toward open seas. Instead, we sneaked up the western side of Muir Inlet, giving the weather a chance to improve.

Slowly coming into focus under the heavy atmosphere, another kayaker appeared. As he passed a hundred feet away, I could see he paddled a sleek touring boat, unlike the broad-beamed Beluga kayaks we handled, which were capable as freighters but inefficient for seriously cutting water. The lone paddler, a deeply tanned Asian with long black hair, responded to us with only a stoic hint of a smile.

Coming out of the mist as he did, with such a timeless visage, he called to mind the tradition of Eskimo kayaking in northern waters and the earliest Americans who migrated from northeastern Asia. Archaeologists have long thought that the first Americans came to this continent about twelve thousand years ago. But Dennis Stanford, chairman of the anthropology department at the Smithsonian Institution, counts himself among a growing number of experts who believe that Asians might have come to America earlier. Some may have worked their way by boat down the West Coast rather than hazard the ice-free walking route through central Alaska and down east of the Rocky Mountains. The new theory suggests that the earliest Americans could have been Coast Range dwellers who traveled, in a sense, as we now did.

When the rain stopped and the ceiling lifted a bit, we still couldn't see the skyscraper mountains that our topographic maps promised, but at least we could see the opposite side of Muir Inlet, so we ruddered out into the big water and dug our paddles into the three-mile passage. Sitting on the floor of that kayak, with only a quarter inch of fiberglass separating me from the numbing waters of the North Pacific, I felt a new sense of vulnerability—a frailty never felt when boating on rivers where the shore awaits only a short, though perhaps turbulent, swim away.

We camped on the other side, and on the next day we paddled farther up the inlet. Just beyond the McBride Glacier, within earshot of the booming collapse of icebergs but beyond the reach of waves thrown up when they hit the water, we pitched our tents, cached our gear, and in a dampening drizzle strung the kitchen tarp deliberately within the reach of incoming tide. That way, the scent of our cooking, along with any crumbs dropped on the ground, would be washed away at eleven-hour intervals and not attract bears. But we had to be ready to move the tarp and the entire kitchen as the tide encroached.

We unscrewed the food canisters, and Ann soon had the Glacier Bay Café hopping. Thomas sliced vegetables. Mike tended one stove while Terry monitored the other. Kazzie rummaged for the necessary ingredients, and I hustled as the chef's right-hand man, moving the pots and skillets to where they needed to go. While we sizzled vegetables, boiled pasta, and grated cheese, an iceberg the size of a golf cart drifted by on the incoming tide, and atop this freely moving perch sat a bald eagle, eyeing us with stern disapproval. I wondered if he saw us as competitors for food. "You guys better not be fishing"— I could almost hear his reproach.

Giving us less warning, the bears could definitely regard us as competitors for space, and even more fundamentally for the coveted top spot in the pecking order, so we took extreme precautions. First, before committing to the campsite, we'd scoured the beach for brown bear tracks—far larger than a black bear's, with formidable jagged claw marks and, most diagnostically, with the toes aligned in a relatively straight line rather than in a curved arc. A black bear can be a redoubtable pest as well, but we thought we might be able to chase one of those away. We tried not to walk in brush, but when we did, we made lots of noise so we wouldn't surprise a bear, especially a sow with a cub, because she would do anything to protect her baby from even the most faintly perceived danger. We kept a spotless camp and avoided wiping food-scented hands on our clothing. We kept our bear spray handy and closed the food canisters as soon as we could.

At night we cached the food apart from other gear, tucked it under a tarp, and finally sprinkled a few drops of Lysol around the perimeter while invoking some reverent words to the bear: "O great bear, we honor you and the land you inhabit. . . . " and so forth. The whole nightly ceremony harkened back to my Catholic heritage. Though certainly not holy water, but not so unlike incense, the Lysol had been recommended to me by an old Alaskan guide whose food had never once been bothered by a bear. Call his success coincidence if you want, but it made sense. "Look at it this way," Mike suggested, perhaps just to humor me in my stratagem. "If you were a bear, would you want to eat something that smelled like Lysol?"

On the next day, in full sunshine, we took a layover for hiking. I wanted to get as much elevation as possible and hoped to summit McConnell Ridge, a four-mile-long promontory of rock and pioneering forest surrounded by ice and water. The McBride Glacier gouges past its south face, and the Riggs Glacier constantly reduces the ridge's northern slope. The route to this high island of rock seemed like a good plan to the others as well.

We began by walking up the inlet to the ice of McBride. From the top of a lateral moraine we soaked in a grand view of the glacier and its spectacle of blue crevasses and pinnacled seracs. From there we could also better see the terrain of our hike. While rocks outlined the top of McConnell Ridge, the lower slopes presented a scrubby thicket of Sitka alder and some of the challenges of walking cross-country in a place like Borneo.

We selected the likeliest route, but even so, the trees lashed us in the face as we fought our way through. In some places the alders were so thick we walked directly on the bent-over branches and springy, stick-sized trunks, never setting foot on the ground. We clapped our hands and talked loudly to the bears in more casual terms than at our before-bed ceremony: "Hey, bear, whatcha doin'? It's only us people," and so on. We also called out to keep the group together.

"Hey, Thomas, slow down!"

"Annie, Kazzie — where are you two?" They were right *there*, but I couldn't see them.

The thicker the brush got, the worse the pesky flies became. When the going got steep, we tried to follow a drainage until Kazzie announced, "Hey, you guys, we're damaging this stream too much by walking here." So we tried a higher line, but it soon crumbled across a rock outcrop that pushed our balancing talents to their limits.

Thomas was ready for anything, his teenage energy overflowing, which was fun to see. But the rock jutted up too steeply for some of us; the bugs and the bear threats were a legitimate concern of others. Terry was running out of steam, but I discouraged him from throwing in the towel because the best precaution against bears — by far — is to travel in a group. I was about to give up myself on what could quickly degenerate into a lot of discontent for our tight little party. At that point Ann suggested we retreat to a ridgeline down below, along the side of the glacier. I surrendered my high-country ambitions, but not without disappointment.

The lower route, however, proved to be spectacular. Easy walking in the recently glaciated zone just above the blue walls took us to one rocky dome after another, the slow cadence of erosion by ice and water clearly evident all around us. A solid river of white curved up into the icefields and down into the blue-green waters of the inlet.

When the testy Captain George Vancouver explored here in 1794, he found Icy Strait choked with ice way down beyond the mouth of Glacier Bay. When John Muir visited in 1879, the ice had retreated more than forty miles but still extended thirty miles farther than it does now. I tried to imagine a glacier covering all that area now filled with water and a pioneering forest. And why stop there? Imagine the continental glaciers smothering the entire Northeast and upper Midwest in ice thousands of feet thick. My native Pennsylvania and Ann's Connecticut went through their own alder phases much like this when the glacial ice melted and a new forest evolved.

Even though it was a temporary feature on the landscape, the glacier directly below now rumbled with crevasses whose cerulean blue darkened to an aquamarine cobalt and then obsidian black as the fissures deepened. Rifle-like claps announced the movement of the glacier as chunks of ice broke. Lured on farther and farther, we wanted to see more of this primal landscape, and I felt like keeping an eye peeled for woolly mammoths. Eventually, with hunger beginning to growl in the pits of our stomachs and a darkening sky threatening to growl overhead, we knew we had to turn around and return to camp.

As we approached our tents in dusky light, the rain hit hard. To cook dinner, we strung the tarp near the water, but an incoming tide soon forced us to flee to higher ground. While the tidal fluctuation along many seacoasts might total three vertical feet in a six-hour cycle, twenty-five was common here, and we saw it happening before our very eyes. For a while there in mid-tide, each wave lapped up an additional horizontal foot—far more than we had anticipated.

Again, then again, the incoming salt water threatened to flood our stir-fry dinner. We had to split into a cooking crew and a full-time moving crew. And the tide was not the only natural phenomenon that would have us guessing.

Early the next morning I sat on the ground, straight across the water from the fifteen-hundred-foot vertical face of White Thunder Ridge, which was obviously the result of some powerful seismic and glacial forces. I jotted notes, and a short distance across the gravel bar Mike was doing some writing as well. Everything was quiet.

Suddenly and without warning the earth moved. Imagine sitting in a car and having a heavy man step up on the bumper. For a few seconds I heard what sounded like a distant railroad train. "Hey, Mike," I yelled over when the deep roar stopped, "if we were in California again I'd say this was an earthquake."

"So what would you call it in Alaska?" he shouted back.

Southern Alaska, it turns out, has more earthquakes than anyplace in North America. Clear across the arc of the Coast Range they're happening virtually every day. The seismic equivalent of the 1994 Northridge quake—the costliest disaster in U.S. history—could occur here almost any time. Even sizable tremors don't make the news because there are no cities to be leveled.

Here at the seismic hot spot of the continent, massive adjustments and displacements continue to build the coastal mountains. Glacial rebound is also a regular seismic sideshow, and this was probably what we experienced. At the height of the Pleistocene epoch, the weight of ice had depressed the land, sinking it like a big man boarding a small boat. Now that the glaciers were receding, the land was buoying back up by an inch and a half a year. These increments add up: so far the total rebound is more than three hundred feet. Terraces far up the mountainside had once been hammered by surf.

"You think we'll get a tidal wave out of this?" I asked Mike.

"We'll soon know," he casually answered. We both stared out at the water for a while, and then, without going to the extent of declaring ourselves safe, but seeing no indication of the sea draining outward the way it would if its volume were being sucked into a wave of great dimensions, we returned to our writing.

After breakfast we secured our base camp at McBride and then wiggled into our kayaks for a day trip as far up the inlet as we could go. For our first digression we beached and walked across a sandbar to the snout of the Riggs Glacier, two hundred feet high and just a wave lap from high tide. A whole river issued from the cavernous bowels of ice at a pumped-up pressure of eight hundred cubic feet per second and then roared, silty gray, through a rapid formed by grounded icebergs the size of cars. Then it tongued into the sea, the whole waterway no longer than a hundred yards, no doubt one of America's shortest rivers. Of course, it had run much farther under the ice, most likely beginning on mountain slopes near the head of the glacier, some miles away.

We marveled at the river, the delta, and the sea as it corroded icebergs where they lay like beached whales that didn't stink. Terry examined zebra-striped rocks that had been metamorphosed underground long ago but delivered just recently by the ice. "The earth is still being formed and reformed in truly astonishing ways," he said, referring to all the dynamism around us.

We paddled on up the inlet, spotted scoters and gulls, admired the featherlight flight of arctic terns, and laughed at the comical wooden strutting of oystercatchers, with their bright orange beaks and eye rings, a stiffly moving, masculine-looking bird but flaunting pink-stockinged feet as if in drag. Eagles gathered on a gravel bar and took turns pecking at a slimy glop of long-dead, unidentifiable offal, to our bias a disgusting diet for the national bird.

Waterfalls ripped down treeless slopes as we entered the only-yesterday-glaciated upper inlet. We beached again and walked up rocky slopes with glorious views to the Muir Glacier, so different from the old man's other namesake, the deep redwood shade of Muir Woods, back near San Francisco. We could have strolled for miles on grassy balds not yet claimed by the most incipient of forest, Sitka alder, if only we'd had more time, more time. On every day and every month of this entire trip, we needed more time!

The next evening rolled around before we knew it, and we retraced the three-mile crossing to Sebree Island. As we eased ashore for the last time, the sun dipped low behind the towering Fairweather Range to the west, surreal in its icy mantle, the sea a pudding of satiny swells. Breaking that enormous quiet, whales spouted and respired with great, spraying hydrants of water. Softly Ann said, "Remember that magical night in Baja when we heard the whales breathing?"

The next day, and right on schedule as we expected, knowing first-hand about the captain's discipline in avoiding delay, the tour boat plucked us off Sebree Island, and our trip back to civilization included a tour of the West Arm — an odd adjustment for us, motorized now amid such a crowd. Then we had one final night of ocean camping at Bartlett Cove.

The mosquitoes whined and bit as only the born bloodthirsty can do, so we stoked a fire and lounged around its smoky edge while chatting about our lives and days together. Terry and Thomas led us in singing a few songs, and we all toyed with plans for seeing one another again — a ritual at the end of good trips. But also, we hoped, more than that.

Eventually a dusky light marked the darkest hour of a midsummer's night in the North. But the tide was still coming in, so we waited until its lapping waves trickled up the beach to where our fire burned. First the water hissed against underlying hot rocks and coals. Then the rising Pacific extinguished the last of the flame and snuffed the smoke with an oceanic chill, and we all said good night.

BACK AT Juneau we warmly parted company. Our friends returned south, and Ann and I boarded our last northbound ferryboat on the Inside Passage. We cruised up the Lynn Canal, an inapt name for that twenty-four-hundred-foot-deep waterway, not a canal at all in the sense of the Erie Canal, but rather the deepest and most imposing natural fjord on the continent.

Timberline descended under the immutable rules of geography as we migrated northward. While trees yield to rock and ice at 7,200 feet in northern California, the level drops to 5,000 in southern British Columbia, 2,000 here in southern Alaska, and 500 farther north, in Prince William Sound. It's a curious irony that in Baja, the trees don't end but rather begin at high elevations because there, you have to go up to get enough water. The bending, blending rules of climate and topography never cease to fascinate me.

I stood at the boat's rail, gazing at Alaska's timberless mountain balds, wondering how I might get up there myself, and right about then an Indian happened by. I said hi, and he stopped to stare at the same mountain that had caught my eye.

"My grandfather used to bring me up here by boat from Juneau," he began without looking at me. "We'd stop right over there — at the base of Lion's Head Mountain. Early in the winter, with snow nearly at sea level, the mountain goats would come down, and we'd go out to hunt them in order to have some fresh meat along with the late-season salmon. Mountain goat is pretty good. We'd scramble up there as far as we could go." I smiled in appreciation of his tale. He continued.

"Once I shot a goat, and while I was carrying it out I slipped on a ledge above a stream. I fell into the water, on my back, and all the weight of that goat held me down. Its fur filled up with water and made it even heavier. I was pretty wet. Could have drowned, I suppose. I rolled over and finally got out. After I carried the goat to the boat, I changed my clothes. It was cold, you know. Now a man has to go a lot farther up to get a goat. Now you have to be a physical fitness guy." We both looked at the mountainside, he with a perspective I will never know.

After a moment of quiet, I said, "I hunted with my grandfather, too. He lived next door, up a little path from our house." I hesitated and then added, "We hunted rabbits."

"Rabbits are pretty good," the Indian acknowledged with an agreeable nod. Then he continued.

"My grandfather, he had a place between Haines and Klukwan where people would pull over for coffee. A woman who stopped by now and then once said, 'How about I build a restaurant here?' My grandfather said, 'Sure, fine.' She built her restaurant, which was okay, but then she got a patent on the land, and we lost it."

That was the end of the story. The man left as quietly as he had arrived.

Speak of building something and thereby losing something, I stared again at the eastern-shore wilderness and wondered what it would look like with a highway sliced into the cliff-bound mountainside where the Indian had gone goat hunting. In fact, the state's Department of Transportation wanted to build a new road along that untouched shoreline from Juneau to Skagway—the town where miners embarked on their 1898 quest to Yukon gold fields. Among other things, the highway would connect Juneau to the continental road system. At stake was one of the wildest, least accessible enclaves on the west-facing coast of America. The ninety-five-mile road would cost $232 million, according to the DOT's hopeful estimates, plus another $4.3 million every year for maintenance, including the clearing of snow and debris from fifty-eight avalanche chutes. It would be the most avalanche-prone road in America, if not the world. I couldn't help but think of the Big Sur highway where annual maintenance costs in today's dollars now exceed the original construction cost on a frequent basis.

Haines—on the western side of the canal—would be connected to the highway by a short ferryboat hop, but town residents and businesspeople there had turned out in force to say no. They argued that the ferries already offered a completely flat, ice-free, avalanche-free highway. If people want easier access, they said, the DOT should upgrade the ferry service. It would be cheaper and safer. The road was stopped, though the proposal wasn't dead.

Happy that we couldn't just drive up from Juneau the way you do from San Diego to LA, Ann and I enjoyed the ferryboat venue, staring into the water and watching the mountains ease by. All too soon we rolled off the deck at Haines, a town with homes clustered above blue seas and beneath icy mountains. It may be the most beautiful town site on the West Coast of America. Here we would prepare for our travels across southern Alaska.

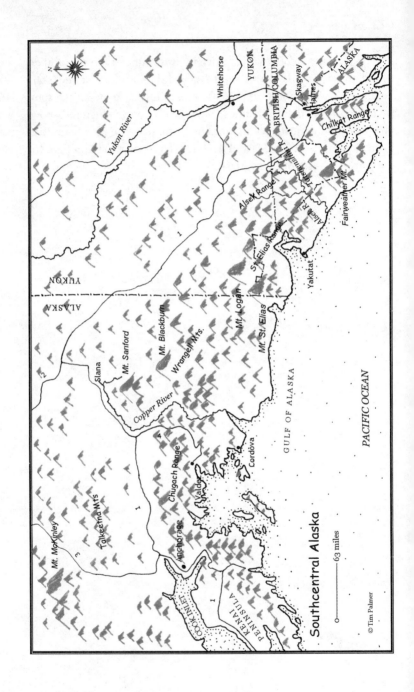

Southcentral Alaska

0 ———— 63 miles

© Tim Palmer

# 14 | *The Ultimate Mountains*

From a rocky outpost on Mount Ripinski, above
Haines, I struggled to grasp the enormity of what still lay ahead.
There at the northern end of the Alaska Panhandle, the continental
shoreline that so far had led us northwest arced more sharply west
and continued in that direction for six hundred thirty mountainous
miles, to the end of Kenai Peninsula. And beyond that lay Kodiak
Island — our final destination.

The Chilkat Range lay across the braided inlet of a powerful river
where three thousand bald eagles come to feast on late-season
salmon runs in the fall. Farther west, the Alsek Range intertwines
with the Saint Elias, the greatest range in North America. Even with
Mount McKinley in the Alaska Range, the mountains here in coastal
Alaska and adjacent British Columbia and Yukon Territory exceed all
others on the continent in terms of continuous high peaks spread
over a long distance. Northwest of the Saint Elias, the Wrangell
Mountains form a skyscraping series of volcanoes, and immediately
west and south of those lie the Chugach Mountains, no less a fanta-
sia of lightning-rod peaks and grinding glaciers, which extend to
Cook Inlet and the neighborhoods of Anchorage.

Between here and there, this panoply of ranges creates a nearly impassable barrier of rock, river, and ice. From Haines, no roads slice through this mountain belt for three hundred fifty miles westward — the distance from Los Angeles to San Francisco. Then, from Valdez to Anchorage, it's another hundred twenty miles devoid of roads and all that roads bring. The inaccessibility and scale of it all presented no small challenge to our efforts to see and experience the coastal mountains in any comprehensive way.

This south-facing slope of Alaska is the culmination of the entire Pacific Coast Range, the grand climax. This is where the long seismic journey of the Pacific Plate ends up — the final episode of earthquake slippage, shear-line faulting, and Richter scale bulldozing that has been going on since desert peaks first buckled up at the tropical end of Baja. All along the way, that plate has been creeping northward, its edge often scraping against the North American mainland, pushing up accretions and island topography. Yet all that land building is really just a sideshow to the big train wreck to come. Here the bulk of Alaska arcs decisively westward at a right angle to the incoming Pacific Plate, whose head-on crash with North America guarantees the proverbial contest between an irresistible force and an immovable object. And here, both behemoths maintain their status quite well. The Pacific Plate keeps moving. The North American Plate does not yield. But something has to give, and the final result is that mountains — really big mountains — buckle up into the sky.

Being denser than the rock that composes Alaska, the northward-pushing plate is first forced under the lighter mass of the continent, in a process we had seen repeatedly since Cape Mendocino. Here the Pacific Plate initially dives into the yawning undersea depth of the thousand-mile-long Aleutian Trench, one of the deepest on the earth, bottoming out at twenty thousand feet. But the downward-plunging plate is eventually heated by the earth's interior into molten explosives that resurface with a vengeance farther inland, where volcanoes and igneous extrusions push skyward.

This extreme demonstration of fiery volcanism is coupled with some of the world's most extreme seismic rupture. The largest earthquake recorded in North American history occurred just north of the Alsek River's mouth in 1899, measuring 8.6 on the Richter scale, significantly larger than the infamous San Francisco quake. The 1964 Alaska earthquake also scored 8.6.

The mountains of the far northern Coast Range are literally new land, fresh out of the sea or the inner earth, still rising, still being shaped in extraordinary ways — not gradually, as in the ancient weathering of the Appalachians or even the Rockies, but radically, day by day. Here, in the final chapters of our journey, the land itself lacked a certain refinement that the settling of age brings. The mountains rose in sharp and craggy profiles rather than rounded visages. The drainages lacked the articulation that eons of erosion bring. Instead, the streams flowed one way and then another, or they dropped precipitously and then didn't drop at all but pooled up in backwaters of lakes.

It's new land in an absolute sense, and it's new to non-native people as well. The mountains here show few signs of civilization. From the Baja Peninsula, which was occupied by Spanish missionaries as early as the 1500s, we'd come north to a land largely unsettled still. Though Indians had inhabited the coast for thousands of years, they had avoided many of these mountainous areas entirely. The absence of people here meant that the rest of nature had prospered, with few of the setbacks seen in the overgrazed desert of Baja, the smog-filled basin of Los Angeles, or the clearcut valleys of Oregon. Biologists evaluating all of North America rated these coastal mountains as one of very few relatively intact ecosystems in the United States. Another was the adjacent Kodiak Island.

Try as I might from Mount Ripinski, I couldn't see the truly high peaks. In search of them, Ann and I drove north of Haines, where Highway 7 climbs as one of the most beautiful mountain routes we've ever driven. From a pull-out we hiked to a summit at the Nadahini River headwaters and saw a lot of rugged country clothed in tundra grasses, wildflowers, and dwarf birch. But we couldn't make out the Alsek Range or the Saint Elias, let alone the far distant Wrangell or Chugach Mountains. They all lay hidden to the west, shielded by countless intermediary peaks that alone compare to the Continental Divide in Colorado.

But I *had* to see those mountains. The Saint Elias Range alone boasts three of the continent's four highest peaks. Mount Logan, in Yukon Territory, rises 19,850 feet — scarcely shorter than Mount McKinley. It's the highest point in Canada. Mount Saint Elias, at 18,008 feet, offers the greatest vertical rise from mountain base to summit in the world — 5,000 feet more than Mount Everest, which happens to sit on a three-mile-high plateau. Once thought to be the highest peak in North America, Saint Elias had been summited by only twenty parties. The weather rarely permits anyone to see the mountain at all, let alone set foot on top and marvel at the three-hundred-mile view. One recent climbing party enjoyed one two-hour window of clear weather in fourteen days. Another stalled out when faced with thirty feet of new snow and hundred-mile-per-hour winds, a wicked combination for drifting and avalanches. When I asked Alaska guide Karen Jettmar about these mountains, she said, "If you want to climb the peaks of the Coast Range, the required mountaineering skills are the least of your problems."

To see the icy mountains that lie beyond a foreground of endless fastness, there are three ways. First, you can be delivered to a remote site by helicopter. But I dislike helicopters and prefer to leave mountains unvisited rather than visit them in that way. Second, you can wage a mountaineering expedition, fly in on a ski plane, cache food and supplies, tote climbing gear, and commit yourself to weeks in the approach and the climb — all requiring expertise, an unlikely share of good luck with the weather, and a lot of money. Third, you can follow the rivers.

No surprise, we chose to explore this grandest of all North American mountain landscapes by boat.

Two rivers completely transect Alaska's central Coast Range, carving from interior headwaters and pushing out to sea. Feeling competent with thirty years of rafting experience between us, Ann and I planned to run them both. First we would float the Alsek River by way of its tributary, the Tatshenshini River, right through the heart of the Alsek–Saint Elias Range complex. This route follows a one-hundred-sixty-five-mile reach beginning in Yukon Territory, then flowing through the northwestern corner of British Columbia, and finally disgorging into Dry Bay, Alaska. Then, two weeks later, we would descend the Copper River—the longest river transection in the entire Coast Range—as it flows past the western base of the Wrangells and out to sea through a dramatic severing of the Chugach.

We looked forward to river travel in a mountainous land, not only because it's the easiest way to go but also because there is something magical about the way rivers reveal the soul of a place. Poet Gary Snyder wrote that mountains and waters are a dyad that "make wholeness possible." Indeed, on our entire trip since Baja, water and mountains together had been inextricable, defining and highlighting so much of what we had seen and done. So here, *on* the rivers, *in* the mountains, I looked forward to the ultimate blending of everything that counts.

Though I much prefer spontaneity, these trips required planning. For starters, it took two years to secure a permit to navigate the Tatshenshini and Alsek Rivers. Plus, we wanted some friends to come along, and tangling our lives with those of other people demanded foresight.

We staged up at the home of Peter and Linda Enticknap, generous friends I had met on an earlier trip to Alaska. Tall, bespectacled, with a square-cropped mustache and outgoing manner, Peter could be taken as a successful businessman, which indeed he had been, directing E. F. Hutton's real estate office in San Diego. But after some years he'd had enough of that.

"Linda and I decided to leave California," Peter explained of their unlikely arrival in this corner of the Coast Range. "We didn't want to just do the Oregon or Washington thing. So we looked at Alaska. As a child, I remembered having a map of the state on my bedroom wall. I always wanted to go there. When we got to Haines, we liked what we saw. This house was for sale, and we made an offer, just on a whim. They took it, and here we are." Linda—tall, beautiful, and gracious as well—gardened with impressive success so far north. Semi-retired, Peter and Linda together still did some real estate work from their home.

During the following days I repeatedly drove down to the ferry terminal or the airport to pick up friends who would be joining Peter, Ann, and me on the trip. Jamie and Florence Williams arrived from Helena, Montana, where Jamie headed the Montana Nature Conservancy and Florence was a freelance writer for national magazines. They had been college friends of Ann's, and we had shared other river expeditions. Sandra Brown, from Arcata, worked as a hydrologist. I had met her thirteen years before, when we both guided a whitewater trip on the Tuolumne River for the California conservation group Friends of the River. Tom Lotina had led river trips for Outward Bound in Utah and Colorado, connecting with Ann and me in that past era of our lives. Dorrie Brownell, an experienced river runner and gonzo skier, made her living as a cartographer for Ecotrust in Portland, lately mapping an atlas of Pacific coast salmon stocks. Glenn Oakley and Kathy Jones, both professional photographers, came from Boise, where I had met them while writing a book about the Snake River.

We would all travel in rafts: my own fourteen-foot Avon Adventurer, a larger Avon rented from outfitter Stan Boer, who just happened to live next to Peter, and a third boat shipped north for Glenn and Kathy's use by its manufacturer, which expected some promotional pictures in exchange.

We hired Stan to shuttle our gear three hours' drive north in his flatbed truck, and while I rode with him, we chatted about his first venture down the Tatshenshini, in 1976. At that time only a few people —unknown to Stan and his friends—had run this river. "It was my best trip ever," Stan fondly recalled. "We didn't know what we'd see. It was a very beautiful place, and we were learning as we went."

Ah, yes, so it is with adventure. And now Ann and I and our eight friends were launching an adventure of our own. Stan and a few thousand others had passed this way before, but it was all new for us, and that was what counted.

At the put-in near Dalton Post we inflated the boats, packed our gear, and kicked off decisively from shore. Open mountain country there on the interior side of the Coast Range soon funneled into a canyon of agitated flow, with balsam poplar and white spruce whizzing by on the shores. Cliffs rose up from the edge, and within the river the water beat like a high-pressure fire hose against exposed rocks. The river poured over large chunks of stone, which caused the current to gouge holes in the water below the obstructions. I opted for conservative lines, not wanting to risk a flip in that resoundingly remote country and reluctant even to get damp from the frigid splash. A quickening, untamed thing, the Tatshenshini required us to pull constantly on the oars to evade both the biting teeth of bedrock and the swallowing power of the holes.

From what Stan had told me, I knew we must be nearing the key hazard of the upper river. A ten-foot-wide jet of angry runoff cascades over a giant rock there, but not by much, thereby creating M&M Falls and a nasty hole directly beneath. This steep drop could over-turn a raft or easily catapult a passenger into the drink.

At the same place, a logjam bristled on the left side of the river, and I saw the logs before I saw the hole. Logs are a worse problem than rocks because water flows through rather than around them. This dramatically increases the deadly risk of entrapment. Needless to say, I obsessively avoid logs and logjams. This particular one posed no real hazard, being up against the shore, but I couldn't tell that from my vantage point upstream, and as I kept my distance from the derelict logs, I inadvertently set myself dead center on the line of M&M.

Suddenly, there it was! With no chance of evading the pour-over, I pivoted with my oars to hit the big water squarely—head-on—and then I pushed on the oars to drive us through the stopping power of the monstrous hole, which had the potential to scrub us clean. The raft wrinkled as the river spit us unceremoniously into its Maytag-pit, but flotation is a wonderful thing, and we buoyed up again and floated onward, no worse for the wear.

In the rental raft behind me, Ann had not seen M&M because my perfectly mispositioned boat had blocked her view, so she followed my pitiful line right into the pour-over. Making the best of the river's surprise, she, too, salvaged the moment in good form. Glenn and Tom were still shaking down the rigging of the third raft but managed to miss the hole and ace the rapid in spite of an oar that kept popping out of its lock at inopportune times.

We all counted our blessings from the river gods and swished onward, the canyon drawing us unequivocally into the narrow gap that the Tatshenshini and then the Alsek Rivers create through the continent's greatest mountains. Camping at the mouth of Silver Creek, we pitched tents between patches of *Dryas*—a fleecy, fuzzy wildflower that pioneers on well-drained gravel bars and guarantees, as we joked, a dry ass.

Carving its way through the Coast Range, the river was our only trail. Of course, we could see the mountains all around us, but to walk or climb on them was nearly out of the question. Undergrowth guarded the valley bottom and the lower flanks, not only making it difficult to walk but also exposing us to the temperamental nature of brown bears, which lounge in the brush.

The one place we could hike was on a trail above Sediments Creek, so we camped there the second night, with ambitious plans to climb the next day. Leaving the rafts behind in the morning, we forded the silty stream in our knee-high rubber boots—Alaskan sneakers, as they say. Then, with the goal of reaching the highest point possible, we switched to running shoes and climbed up and up on a path worn by other travelers. After two thousand vertical feet, we emerged in meadows cloaked with grasses, sedges, wildflowers, and dwarf willows—tundra that ramped skyward like an alpine prairie. Eagles soared below us, and white-crowned sparrows and Wilson's warblers darted between tufts of mooseberry. Lupine, paintbrush, gentian, and fireweed speckled their purple, red, and blue in the sea of green that undulated up to a mosaic of tumbled-down rock. Surrounding ridges angled to summits far beyond our day-hiking endurance.

Aiming for a canyon rim to the east, we teetered out to a sheer drop-off far above Sediments Creek. I followed the view down to where the creek joined the Tatshenshini and then saw the river pulsing southward. Way off in the distance, I could see where we were headed. Icefields and glaciers clung to summits and unreachable slopes. The heavily whitened Alsek Range lay twenty or forty or sixty miles away—it was difficult to tell in that expansive landscape, so Alaskan, so Yukon, in scale.

In most wildernesses, I'd been able to walk out to civilization, or at least imagine walking out, even if it took a week. Here I could not. Our frail boats of cloth and air, buoyed on that artery of mountain runoff, were essential for our survival, a fact astoundingly clear from my high and vantageous perch.

Suddenly, across the Sediments Creek canyon, something moving caught my eye. I strained to see what I thought at first might be the white breasts of birds, perhaps a flock of ptarmigans with some residual winter plumage. But as soon as I pointed them out to Ann and Tom, I realized they were not feathered creatures at all. They were mountain goats, four ewes and four kids. How could I mistake a goat for a bird? Well, they were farther away than I thought. I felt like quite the tyro, but the lack of perspective can trouble anyone. The great wildlife biologist Adolph Murie once mistook a marmot for a grizzly bear because scale is so difficult to gauge in the spacious, undetailed landscape of the North.

We spent three hours descending what had taken six to go up, returning to camp tired and sweaty but with a few good hours of late Alaska daylight left. Knowing what we needed, the whole gritty gang took a bathing dip in the river, an icy flow that made us cringe. But then the low-angled warmth of the evening sun felt exquisite.

On day four the current rushed us forward in an onslaught of ever siltier and ever more determined meltwater. Yet the river was full of inconsistencies, depending on the whims of hydrology and the unscheduled bulk deliveries of silt and rock by tributaries. At one point the boiling Tatshenshini split into braids, then subdivided again and again until, ironically, despite all that swelling runoff, we scarcely had the modest three inches of water needed to float our boat. I was forced to choose from another left or right channel — one choice too many — and we entered a willow-choked path where our escape was in doubt. To run aground is bad enough. But in a boat of air, nothing could be worse than washing up against a splintery old log blocking your progress, so I jumped off the raft and held it while Ann jogged ahead in her Alaskan sneakers to scout. After a critical appraisal she gave the all clear sign by patting the top of her head with her right palm. I disengaged the oars in order to pole from bush to bush, shoved off the pebbly shoal, and rattled down the shallow channel. As if catching a slow-moving freight train, Ann jumped back aboard before we burst into the grabby flow again.

Not far downstream, the opposite thing happened. Disparate currents joined in a vortex of diagonal waves that sucked us into the largest rapid on the river. We soared high on muddy waves and then foamed down in a thrill of big water as if we were in the Grand Canyon.

Before long our whole world was much, much bigger. The O'Connor River entered on our left, doubling the already powerful Tatshenshini. New runoff there joined in multiple outlets across a gravel bar that ran for two miles alongside the main channel, a desert rockscape but brilliant in places with the magenta blooms of broadleaf willow herb.

At the O'Connor, a proposed mining road would have come down from the east, crossed the Tatshenshini on a bridge, and opened this resoundingly primitive wilderness to the forces of a world economy. The fight against this mine marked one of the most significant conservation battles in British Columbia and Alaska history, and our friend Peter Enticknap labored at the center of it all. That evening he told the tale of this epic battle between a giant Canadian mining corporation and a band of river runners, salmon fishermen, and nature lovers who created an international conservation campaign and carried it to the highest levels of government.

To extract copper in the middle of one of the largest wilderness areas on the planet, Geddes Resources would have built its road into the heart of the Tatshenshini, excavated a mountain aptly called Windy Craggy, heaped toxic tailings behind an earthfill dam in the most active seismic zone on the continent, run thousands of ore trucks per day through the Alaska Chilkat Bald Eagle Preserve near Haines, and constructed a harbor on the storm-swept waters of Lynn Canal. Glacier Bay National Park and one of the finest runs of salmon would have been endangered by acid effluent and the high likelihood of the dam's rupture over the course of the next few decades, let alone the thousands of years the waste would remain toxic.

Canadians organized under the leadership of Ric Careless and his organization, Tatshenshini Wild, while Peter Enticknap, Tom Cassidy of American Rivers, and others worked the U.S. side, securing the support of Vice President Al Gore. Building on a series of progressive environmental reforms, Premier Mike Harcourt ultimately declared the 2.5-million-acre wedge of northwestern British Columbia as Tatshenshini Alsek Provincial Park. Nestled between Kluane National Park in the Yukon and Wrangell–Saint Elias National Park and Preserve and Glacier Bay National Park in the United States, the resulting protected land is now the largest park complex in the world, 23 million acres altogether.

"Thanks for doing all that," Kathy offered as a bit of an understatement from all of us when Peter's story wound down.

"It was a special time," he reflected. "Helping to protect the Tatshenshini and Alsek stands out as the best thing I've ever done. Those years were a major turning point in my life, when I became clearly aware of a change in values. I already knew the environment was important, but when the threats to it became a real thing, I saw that I had to act or lose something. Without people becoming involved, a corporation would have run roughshod over this place. I'm pleased that the bears and wolves still have a place to live, in an ecosystem that's large enough to sustain them. The hard part was the infighting of environmental politics, and the time it all took. Suddenly I turned around and my son Ben was grown up. I'd like to have spent more time with him." At this we all fell quiet for a moment. What could we have said?

I think I understood Peter's midlife sense of satisfaction and regret all at once. In other regards, I have had similar conflicts about the paths I've taken and not taken. For example, I used to live in a place I loved perhaps as much as Peter loves his new homeland. I left there to adopt the mountains and rivers of North America as my home. I abandoned the stewardship battles of local life for the more diffuse mission of reporting on many places. I abandoned steady friendships for sporadic ones subject to distance and nourished intermittently at best. Within the wide world I had adopted — Baja to Kodiak in this year alone — I could not possibly gain the satisfaction Peter enjoys in the one treasured place he worked to save. Like Marlene Smith's inspiration to Ann back on Vancouver Island, Peter was an inspiration to all of us to be responsible for the places where we live.

And while Peter regretted that his family life had suffered, my own take, after visiting with the Enticknaps for a couple of weeks, was that he and his son had far more going on together than most families. And whatever the time constraints had been, young Ben had turned out great. He — and certainly the world — might even be better off for the model Peter provided in taking responsibility for his homeland.

I couldn't help but think about the necessity of people adopting similar public roles on the earth. In an age of privatism — from the gated communities of southern California to the politicians' abandonment of libraries and parks to the blind eye that so many in the "me generation" cast toward the unfortunate — it was refreshing to see that Peter had recognized his public role and carried it out unselfishly.

"Thanks, Peter," Kathy again offered, breaking the quiet and bringing me back from my own thoughts.

THE NEXT day, the Tatshenshini River below the O'Connor took a quantum leap in scale, the current unrelenting. What appeared to be rock shelves along the opposite shore turned out to be cliffs a hundred feet tall. What appeared to be stubby hills knobbing up behind a foreground of bogs and forests were mountains thousands of feet high.

Mile by mile, as inevitably as we dropped toward sea level, the river took us back in time. I mean deep time. Back toward the ice ages. The history of glaciers gouging out the valley was apparent from the U shape of its cross section. I easily envisioned a few thousand feet of ice packed in there ten millennia ago.

The wind picked up on day five as we left behind the drier, more open terrain of the interior and passed beneath mountains bulging up higher, their surfaces grated coarsely by ongoing glaciers. Large ice masses looked like spreads of smooth frosting, while small ones resembled enamel fillings in the molars and canines of the Coast Range, all the cracks, indents, and cavities packed full with white ice. Here big peaks and marine weather took stronger control of the landscape, the climate, the vegetation, and the lives of all us puny boaters.

We camped on the alluvial fan of Towagh Creek, where a spattering of rain sent us scrambling for our kitchen tarp. Picking up force, the first serious downpour of the trip raised the possibility of double jeopardy: a rising river could flood our site on one side, while a swelling tributary could spill over on the other. Though it rained all night, we saw little change in either stream, which spoke to the abundance of water they carried on a regular basis.

While the river speeded into a broad set of S bends with the added force of accumulating tributaries — too many to name — the current whisked us along like little chunks of wood in a tempestuous sea.

Before I expected it, we entered the spacious basin marking the confluence of the Tatshenshini with the Alsek — an even larger river. The two giants converge at a mile-and-a-half width of gravel bars studded with islands that could be created and destroyed by the forces of this water in a day. I knew it was a long way across to the other side, but when Ann rested her oars and pointed out another party of rafters drifting near the far shore, I was shocked. I could hardly pick them out among the waves. To be in such a grand place was truly humbling. We could see and feel the raw forces of the earth at work, and it was satisfying to see nature, rather than people, with such power.

Below the confluence I turned to gaze back upstream at the breadth of breaking water and at the Noisy Range of mountains — a subset of the Alsek Range, which climbed to craggy heights above the confluence. The scene truly captured me for reasons at first unknown, almost like déjà vu. Then I recognized how kindred those mountains looked, with their rock walls and ice-sculpted summits, to the Teton Range of Wyoming, where Ann and I had lived in recent winters. I was struck at how similar the river and its benchlands looked to the Snake River as it courses through Jackson Hole at the base of the Tetons — except that here, the river was twenty times as large.

At that moment I realized that the Alsek today is like the Snake was ten thousand years ago, when ice-age glaciers melted from half a dozen ranges surrounding Jackson Hole and engorged the Snake River with a flow that would have looked a lot like this.

At camp that night, on a sandbar separated from the mainland by a narrow slough, tracks of wolves, moose, and brown bears with claw-tipped paws as long as my forearm had been imprinted on the sandy shores and muddy backwaters. Clearly we were not at the top of the food chain here.

We wanted to see a bear, yet we didn't want to see a bear. My tendency was to keep my pepper spray as handy as a gunfighter's pistol. Meanwhile, Jamie — a fine naturalist who didn't want to miss the king of the mountains in this part of the country — joked about slathering honey in his hair to draw one of the teethy bruins in for a view. But regardless of our wishes, the bears eluded us. Yet we knew they were there.

Wandering behind the kitchen area, Ann found perfectly imprinted brown bear tracks with holes in the ground pricked by claw tips three inches beyond the ends of the toes. She made a plaster cast that came out like a piece of art. We all admired her work with implicit admiration for the bear, and without talking about it we upped our precautions. To eat our sloppy burritos, we lined up and leaned over the river's edge, dripping excess salsa directly into the water rather than on the land where we needed to sleep.

The next day the Alsek carved straight through the heart of the Coast Range where the Saint Elias Mountains cross. The river flowed almost to the face of the Walker Glacier, where we pitched our tents in a refrigerated downdraft. After gobbling down lunch, we all set out for the ice.

Unusually flat and accessible, the lower end of the glacier invited us to tramp across its rough and scarred surface, some places covered with rocks that had fallen onto the ice as it sculpted its way down out of the mountains and some places slick with the blue sheen of frozen water. We peered into aquamarine crevasses. I threw a rock into one and listened to it chatter against the sides, bounce from one wall to the other, and then fall silently for slow seconds until it finally ker-plunked into deep water. Ann and I looked at each other. "No slipping allowed here," she said.

We walked on a steepening grade of crunchy ice and gritty hitch-hiking rock to where a two-hundred-foot headwall, deeply cracked and fractured with seracs and sculpted cavities, stopped us. I stood there in awe at the vertical edge of glaciation—the cutting edge, quite literally, of this great shaper of the earth. On the way back to camp, Ann stopped to paint with her miniature kit of watercolors, turning out fresh likenesses of the blue-and-white scene.

Our camp lay only a few hundred yards in front of the glacier and only a dozen yards behind the river. On this narrow refuge, in the middle of the night, a thumping noise sent me scurrying for the tent door to see if a bear had ripped into our food cache. But it was just the settling of ice. The booms, cracks, and thuds awoke me again and again. The ice was alive.

At five in the morning, I heard a drizzle that sounded like fine grains of sand dusted against the tent. By six, a gusting wind delivered steady rain. By seven, sheets of rain splattered against our waterproof fly, dousing it with potent cold drops. At eight, the rain seemed horizontal, a threat to even the best-built shelter and the most impervious creature.

Simply breaking camp in heavy rain invokes what I call the 10 percent factor: just pulling the tent and packing up means you get 10 percent wet. And with a storm of this intensity, we would surely lose another 10 percent through the day, with water running down our faces and necks, trickling up our forearms when we lifted the oars to row, leaking through unsealed seams in our rain gear, and falling on every single item we might take out during the day—lunch, map, toilet paper. Then another few percent would get wet when we made camp again in the evening, all in order to sit on a soaking boat and see nothing but clouds around our heads all day long.

"How about a tent day?" I asked the group when we convened

under the flapping, billowing tarp for breakfast. Everybody agreed, and we all headed back to sequester ourselves.

The time flew by. Ann and I read books in our capable shelter — not the tiny backpacking model we take hiking but a roomy version that offers enough square footage to sleep four good friends in a pinch. In front of a river of ice, next to that river of runoff, and within a river of rain and low-lying clouds, conditions in the tent offered such utter contrast to the outdoors that I couldn't help but chuckle at our good fortune amid these elements as different as solid, liquid, and gas, yet all of a piece, all the same element, all intersecting here, where we had come to rest for the day.

We read, slept, pulled on our yellow slickers for lunch under the tarp, and then read, napped, identified plants, and wrote in our journals. Suddenly it was dinnertime. We would never have chosen to spend a whole day inside our tent, but a mandatory rest felt good.

The next morning dawned partly clear, so we loaded up and embarked again, the lower flanks of mountains visible but the tops still in the clutches of clouds. With tributaries pulsing in flushes of snowmelt, creamy glacial runoff, and turbid storm water, I guessed the flow of the Alsek to be about 60,000 cubic feet per second — a lot of water by any standard. The Colorado River in the Grand Canyon, for comparison, often flows in the range of 15,000 cubic feet per second.

For a change of pace that day, all five women crowded onto our little raft, where Ann gave everyone a turn at the oars. Judging from the laughter, they had way more fun than we guys did on the other two big boats.

It wasn't long before we came to the mouth of the Novatak River, where we camped again on a great gravel plain. Jamie, Florence, Ann, and I hiked up the valley with rapt fascination through a whole afternoon spent in the Pleistocene. We set our destination at the terminus of several glaciers where the Novatak was born. There, in a sizable instantaneous flow, icebergs bobbed in a swirly surface that could have been gray paint, it was so opaque with rock dust and silt.

Walking along the shore in this landscape glaciated only recently, Jamie spotted a jet of water forced like a small geyser into the air. "Let's check that out," he suggested, picking up the pace.

Little gradient existed in the river channel, so the spray was not caused by a rapid. Rather, it appeared to come from some oddly artesian source within the river itself. Gingerly we edged up to a steep and crumbly gravel bank to investigate this provocative feature.

From the remains of rock and ice all around us we deduced that the glacier had pushed down from the mountain at a ninety-degree angle to the river and completely crossed the channel we now saw, forcing the water out into the broad plain of gravel and willows behind us. Water always wins these battles, given enough time, and the river in fact had eroded back through the ice, though not entirely. Enough ice remained to create a ponded surface of water behind it, and a significant flow was still forced around and even under a remnant of the frozen glacial dam. The spray jet we saw was the result of water being pushed up through a hole in the residual ice dam.

In miniature, the Novatak blockage resembled those once extant at a far vaster scale, when ice-age glaciers dammed rivers as significant as the Saint Lawrence and Columbia. Enormous ice dams there forced their backed-up waters temporarily down the Hudson River and the Channeled Scablands of central Washington until the thawing dams fractured to pieces, much as this one in front of us was now in the final process of doing. Small as it was, the ice dam on the Novatak enabled me to vividly picture the glacial cataclysms that had shaped other lands so dramatically in the past. Once again I was reminded of how young this land is, and how our journey extending the length of the Coast Range had been one of going from the old and settled to the new and wild.

In the pond formed by the remaining ice, a businesslike beaver swam back and forth, now dragging a willow branch cut in the thicket where the rerouted river once flowed. The farsighted, bucktoothed rodent took the sprig to his lodge for storage as part of next winter's food supply. Years from now, in the dried-out, rotten remains of that lodge, a fox might make its den, and on the soil formed from the decomposing willow branches a new forest might begin to grow, eventually with balsam poplars tall enough for an eagle's nest. Already on this brand-new landscape the beaver was laying in the building blocks of a new ecosystem.

Leaving Jamie and Florence to kick back at the glacial dam, Ann and I walked onto moraines that curved like giant mole mounds into the willow thicket. On sandy soil there we saw cute little baby bear tracks, no larger than Ann's fist. We might have been closer to the cub than to the mother; her tracks were nowhere to be found. With this notion sinking in, we abruptly about-faced and returned to the wide-open corridor along the river.

Early the next morning, when I crawled out of the tent I saw Mount Fairweather rising in snow-cone glory to the distant south, celestial on a horizon serrated with other glacial mountains. Comparable to Mount Saint Elias itself, this was the sky-peak of our trip, at 15,318 feet. No other mountain in the world rises higher in a direct uphill shot from sea level. It stood above multiple layers of lower slopes that grew whiter from bottom to top. When I cropped a vertical column of view from the larger scene, it was like a totem pole of landscape, the riparian foreground rising to alder-greened hills, to gray, rocky mountains, and then to snowy ridge after ridge after ridge. By the time we loaded the rafts, the misnamed Fairweather had disappeared into the clouds, never to reemerge. We were lucky to have seen it at all.

On the water again, we were pushed by the ever growing, ever colder glacial melt, the chill suffusing everything around us now, with humid air that cut to the bone even though we wore three times the amount of clothes we wear when skiing in the dead of winter. We stopped on a gravel bar to warm up, following Florence in an African dance step — hopping and jumping forward, back, forward, back, arms waving, knees lifting, blood moving once again. And then, on a river two miles wide with breaking waves the whole way across, without any warning of a darkening sky, without a wisp of wind, it began to rain, the splatter of cold drops right away meaning business.

Fortunately, we were close to our destination for the day, the lower end of a sandy peninsula that separates Alsek Lake from the river, a place of major consequence because of its unique alignment of geography. At the bottom of the three-mile-long peninsula, the main flow of the river spills through a channel to the left and enters the lake.

This unusual lacustrine feature floods up against the mouths of twenty-mile-long glaciers that push down from the highest peaks. A fortress-like wall of ice a hundred feet thick forms the eastern shore of the lake, and from it icebergs break loose and float in sizes as small as our raft and as large as the ferryboat we had caught in Juneau. From this spot the Alsek would carry solid as well as liquid runoff.

Where the river first spills into the lake, an island a few hundred feet high called Gateway Knob splits the flow. The bulk of the Alsek goes left into the lake, while a much smaller channel shortcuts down the right side of the island and bypasses the main body of the lake. One of the highlights of rafting the Alsek is to float left of the island and through the lake, where from a safe distance one can admire the bergs and the imposing wall of ice calving into the water.

But—and here's the catch—the icebergs sometimes get blown over to the near end of the lake and create a jam that completely blocks the passage. Ending up in this situation is not a matter of just sitting in a lake into which some ice has been plunked. Rather, imagine the full force of the Alsek pushing your frail little raft up against all that ice—frozen-water wreckage representing all the accumulated force of the Pleistocene. The icebergs routinely flop over as melting shifts their centers of gravity, and when they do, you don't want to be anywhere near them. And if that isn't enough, once you're in the lake the wind can blow you hopelessly against the wall of the glaciers themselves, especially if you had to detour in that direction to get away from floating icebergs.

All this boiled down to a mandatory scout of the lake's inlet. If the passage was blocked by ice, we would have to avoid the lake altogether by pulling to the right channel of the river and floating down the right side of Gateway Knob.

Now, as we floated through increasing rain toward this intimidating complex, the knob appeared to be perhaps a mile away, though I saw no ptarmigan-colored mountain goats or other details to judge scale by. Not wanting to chance being closer, we pulled over to camp on the peninsula that separates the river from the lake.

Dripping wet, we strung the tarp, and Tom offered to make hot quesadillas for lunch. While we wolfed these down, Dorrie shouted, "A bear! It's a bear!" Sure enough, swimming across the wide and hard-flowing river was a black bear. Its trajectory, given the stiff current, would land him somewhere between our boats and our quesadilla stand. But with more swimming strength than I'd imagined, the sopping bruin, which must have carried thirty pounds of water in his fur, docked just above our boats and ambled into the brush without giving us so much as a glance. Jamie called this champion swimmer the consolation prize because it was smaller and less fearsome than the brown bear he had hoped to see. But by and large, most of us did not feel deprived by the lack of a grizzly in that limited space, and we were thankful that the bear had no appetite for Mexican food.

Just to familiarize ourselves with the neighborhood, we all took a short walk to the lake side of the peninsula, making a lot of noise to alert the bears. The rain picked up, and through the thickening atmosphere we saw a lot of icebergs, but even with binoculars we couldn't tell from that distance whether or not they clogged the route shut. Behind the still life of floating ice, white on blue, the glaciers curved from the peaks, their stepped-down elevations evident only piecemeal between layer-cake wisps of cloud and fog, the sum total wrapped in a gauze of rain.

Quickly becoming wet, we hustled back to camp through a thicket of pea-podded vetch, delicate white saxifrage, startling blue gentian, and paintbrushes crossbred in yellow, pink, and orange, each and every bloom varnished with a fresh spray of water.

By now our crew was a finely tuned team, and together we assembled one tent at a time under the dryness of the kitchen tarp and then ran each fully erect structure out to the site where its owners had chosen to sleep. Once cover for everyone was ensured, we all climbed in to let the storm rake its way across that skinny, sandy, flower-covered, bear-owned peninsula.

The storm, however, didn't seem to go anywhere. Pounding and pummeling, it stayed and stayed, in just the way the Aleutian Low storm masses off the Gulf of Alaska are driven into the mountains only to stall there at the obstruction of high peaks. It rained all night and continued with no letup, so we hunkered down in our tents the next day as well. At lunchtime we couldn't even see across the river, which beneath a semi-liquid atmosphere seemed doubly cold, silty, and hostile, swirling in icy brown depths.

Then, suddenly, above the splatter of raindrops bombarding the wind-flapped tarp, I heard an airplane engine, loud and raspy. Surprised that any but the most desperate pilot would be out in such supremely foul conditions, I looked into the storm to see a two-engine plane winging upriver fifty feet above the ground. Its propellers set the wet branches of alder trees whipping back and forth. Aviation law in Alaska requires pilots to maintain visual contact with the ground. This pilot did so by minimizing the air cushion beneath him, windy, wet, and unpredictable as the afternoon weather was. It all seemed foolhardy to my untrained but survival-conscious eye.

We, too, would be flying back to Haines from our takeout at Dry Bay, scheduled for tomorrow. Weather permitting. I hoped our pilot would not consider this kind of weather permissible and wondered if I'd have the will to refuse the flight if it looked this bad.

My stomach now churned at the prospect. I had lost my inevitable boyhood romance for bush planes. They are the only way to get to most of Alaska, and many backpackers, river runners, hunters, and fishermen depend on them. All these people routinely trust intrepid pilots who glide pontoon planes onto choppy lakes or alight on cobbled gravel bars with the forgiving bounce of balloon tires. But the more time I spent in Alaska, the more bad bush-plane stories I heard. The superb pilot who had flown me to the Sheenjek River headwaters six years before was now dead. He had crashed. Along that river, I had witnessed another plane in the process of emergency landing, though I didn't know it at the time. It flew low over my camp and disappeared around the bend. The next day, from my raft, I spotted the plane sitting with a broken strut along the riverbank. The people were all gone. Another pilot I met in the Alaska town of Palmer had recently quit flying, complaining of too many foul-weather flights. Since his retirement, four of his buddies had crashed and died.

So now I approached these flights with a sense of dread. Though I still looked forward to the bird's-eye view of the land, the carefree sense of adventure was gone. I just hoped for clear weather during our flight back to Haines.

At dinner, which began and ended with hot drinks, Peter noted that this wasn't the typical July storm but more like the monsoons that started in August and intensified into the cold, drenching gales of September and October. We wondered, When would it end?

The next morning, after leaving four inches of water in the bottom of a plastic bucket left upright in my boat, the rain finally stopped. We bailed out the rafts and packed up our wet gear. Then we took the mandatory scouting walk down the peninsula to where the Alsek River cuts left into Alsek Lake, approaching much closer than we had in the rain two days before.

Sure enough, the ice was packed in solid. It extended in a line from the shore of Gateway Knob out across the lake, with not a sliver of water between the bergs, let alone enough gap for us to chance the vagaries of that ineluctable flow pushing us into the jam wherever it chose to do so. We would have to row to the opposite side of the river and catch the right-hand channel around Gateway Knob.

Back at the boats, we watched the Alsek flowing hard—ninety thousand cubic feet per second, I later learned. Complicating the crossing, the river bent to the left, making the ferry angle—the angle the boater strikes against the current—much trickier and sharper than a simple straight-across pull. The three rowers—Jamie, Glenn, and I—discussed what to do if we didn't make the cut. We decided we should keep rowing and aim for the shore of the island, where we might, with difficulty, catch a sandbar on Gateway Knob and line our boat back upriver to the right-side channel. The wall of ice was to be avoided at all costs.

Jamie went first, in the big rental boat, with Florence and Peter and Kathy paddling double-time for extra power. Glenn launched second, with Ann and Sandra aboard, and pulled fiercely in his spiffy self-bailing raft, which skated well across the water owing to its highly inflated stiffness. I went third, immediately planting my oars with a hard tug as Tom and Dorrie pushed me offshore and jumped aboard. I rowed as fast as I could, rising up slightly out of my seat at the end of each pull. In twenty strokes, I was already panting for air. In thirty strokes, I could tell the shore we had left was farther away, but when I glanced behind me, the shore I aimed for seemed no closer at all. Any progress I made seemed incidental, a spit in the ocean. Downstream, the enormous flow of the Alsek curved left toward the lake and toward the ice. I pulled harder, harder, cheered on by Tom and Dorrie.

But I had seriously underestimated the length of river required to make the pull across the current. I had underestimated the power of the flow and the aggravating force of the left bend. I had underestimated the hazard of the ice and the consequences of this behemoth river pushing me and my trusting friends into the face of an ice jam. I knew then that however hard I had ever rowed, I now had to row harder. There was no fallback, no safety net.

To cross a river, I would normally point the back of the raft at the opposite shore but slightly upstream. This decreases the downriver distance otherwise claimed by the current. But here, the force of water was so overpowering that any upstream slant would have doomed us in lost time, so I angled slightly downriver, pulling for the opposite shore, that sweet right-hand shore where we would find safety.

Still, no matter how hard I rowed, the current pushed harder. It seemed to be winning, a steadily approaching doom against which all my efforts seemed trivial. "How are the others doing?" I asked, out of breath.

"They're working, too," Tom answered. "Just keep pulling, Tim."

I could tell my passengers were worried. On and on I pulled, eyeing the right channel downstream, which was finally looking nearer. Was I far enough right to catch it? Maybe, yes, soon, but not yet. We could still be pushed either way. This was one of those moments that really count.

I pulled on, wondering how much my strokes had weakened, wondering when my grip on the oars would become exhausted. And then I felt the resistance of the river soften. At last I had crossed the subtle but great divide where the river split. Now the flow ran to the right side of the island. I breathed deeply with relief and heard my friends in all three boats cheering, each at their own deliverance.

WITH ALSEK LAKE behind us, the lower river speeded beneath our boats, and it seemed we had entered another world. As we approached sea level, the mountains wore such a full cloak of alder green that they looked Hawaiian. But reminding us of the glacial landscape we'd left behind, icebergs tumbled in the current and plowed into depthless holes, which we easily avoided in the broad channel.

At Dry Bay, where a commercial fish camp, gravel airstrip, and ranger station shared the same little lobe of trembling land, we tied up for the last time. The ranger told us that our flight had been canceled by bad weather in the mountains. So we derigged with leisure and camped.

It rained again the next morning, but then it stopped, and at ten o'clock two planes arrived from Yakutat, a city fifty miles west along the coast. Eyeballing our gear and counting heads, the pilots determined that we couldn't all fit. One person would have to stay behind and defend a stash of gear in case a bear showed up. Clouds were still packed around the mountains, and Ann and I wanted almost desperately to fly together, but we also had the most flexible schedules, so I volunteered to stay.

"We'll be back to get you when we can," the older pilot assured me, "but it'll depend on the weather." I kissed Ann goodbye with an especially long hug, a tear in her eye causing a pain deep in my heart.

With cloud masses hovering above and a mortal chill in my bones, I counted the minutes — only about sixty — until the planes should have arrived safely in Haines. I didn't mind waiting, even another day or two, but I longed for certainty that Ann was safe and that I'd make it out myself without crashing into a mountainside. After all, I wanted only to write about the Coast Range; I didn't want to be buried there. Not yet, anyway.

When adventure becomes dependent on machines and technology and people I don't even know, it's not fun for me anymore. When the possibility arises, however remote, of dying without being able to plot and scramble and claw for my own survival — to do it myself — I don't like it. I would have been a poor astronaut, cooped up with all those buttons, blinking lights, and voices from mission control.

Glad that we could fly from Dry Bay but still disgruntled to be relying so fully on technology at the moment, I waited in the tent alone, the rain pattering on the roof and bear spray at my side because the ranger had warned us about scavenging grizzlies.

Clouds darkened and the rhythm of rain quickened, not good conditions for flying. I resigned myself to waiting out the day and managed to read a bit. Then I heard the drone of an engine. Growing quickly louder, the plane landed on the gravel strip and within seconds taxied up to my camp. "Let's go quick, while we can," the pilot said.

I struck the tent and packed my gear in a rush. Though it was a tight fit, the gray-haired, crewcut pilot and I crammed the remaining raft, frames, and bags into the cargo bin. Then I stepped in. The girthy-necked, broad-bellied man grunted as he weighed into his seat, the left wing of the plane dipping noticeably. We buckled ourselves in securely and took off into the wind with a brain-rattling roar.

He had been flying a long time and described these bush-plane adventures as his retirement. With some mild prying I learned that he used to fly fighter jets.

"In Vietnam?" I asked.

"Yes," he said.

"How many missions?"

"Hundred sixty."

"In four years?"

"In one year."

"Bet you were happy to get home."

"It's been so long I don't even think about it." I took that to mean he didn't talk about it, either.

From the air, the river and the mountains looked magnificent, first in vague hints of terrain through the gray-out of fog and low-lying moisture, then through scattered holes in the Swiss-cheese cloud cover. I soon spotted the floating icebergs of Alsek Lake, looking like bits of broken china from that elevation. Silty outflows of glaciers that had been invisible from our raft-bound view lay within a mile or two of the river. The clouds began to dissipate as we winged upstream toward the drier climate of the interior.

"Up there's the moment of truth," the pilot announced over the noise of the straining engine, pointing to a high-country pass significantly above us still, making our approach feel like a ramp of air. "If it's clear, we go on. If it's not, we go back."

"Fine with me," I said, meaning I didn't mind returning to that clammy, bear-infested gravel bar if there was the slightest doubt about being airborne.

At the pass we burst into sunlight. Mountain goats toyed with steep slopes high in the O'Connor River basin, where we flew beneath peaks on either side, two hundred feet from wingtip to goat perch, which unfortunately sent the furry mountaineers scurrying. Then we slipped over a rock-clad shoulder and into greener open country that flowed down toward the Chilkat River and Haines, lovely Haines.

After we taxied to a stop on the paved airstrip and stiffly stepped out, the pilot cocked a critical eye at the wheel on the tail of his craft, as if the rear of the plane had failed some kind of test quietly proctored by pilots wherever they go. As it turned out, without people inside, that wheel was not supposed to be dragging on the ground. The big man grabbed a bulging, dry bag and said, "Come on, let's get this stuff out of there before anyone sees our load."

Back at Peter's house that evening, Linda welcomed all us weatherworn adventurers with a delicious salmon dinner, wild fish caught locally by Peter. We easily made the transition from cold eats under a dripping tarp to an elegant meal in the comfort of the Enticknaps' home. We toasted to our return, to our friendships, and to a wild Tatshenshini River.

After two days of cleaning gear, packing, and seeing our friends off, Ann and I headed northwest, reentering Canada where the highway sliced across a stellar mountain corner of Yukon Territory.

At Kluane National Park we finally saw the long-awaited grizzly bear. He was grazing his way through blood-red buffalo berries, harvesting a path down the side of the highway like a six-hundred-pound organic combine, advancing, harvesting, eating, and even crapping as he went, one completely integrated process as the young bruin lumbered closer and closer to where we had pulled over on the berm. I climbed on top of the van for a bird's-eye view while Ann sat ready to rev the engine for our escape. Big claws and saber teeth shone like ivory from the bear's distance of ten feet. He never even looked at us, and it would have been easy to regard his disposition as harmless — a berry-picking Teddy, a speechless, no-nonsense Yogi.

The long drive across Alaska's eastern interior spoke of vastness — mountains everywhere. For the first time on our entire Coast Range trip, we were forced to bend far inland, at one point two hundred twenty miles from the sea, with no roads anywhere out there. What a great feeling it was, knowing that such a large place was virtually untouched, a home of garbage-free bears, airplane-free mountain goats, and dam-free salmon.

Skirting the western edge of the Wrangell Mountains, we drove through the upper Copper River valley, which was decked out in forest and sprinkled with rural homes one might liken to a boreal Appalachia. Houses stood half finished, bare plywood warping in the pitilessly wet climate. Junk cars sprouted brush, and rusty steel cables barred driveways cut raw by the scrapes of bulldozers. It was all very Alaskan.

Just as in the pot-growing belt of northern California, signs curtly ordered, "Keep Out." As in Baja, an inordinate number of buildings had been partially built and then abandoned. And as in Baja — only at the opposite time of year — strings of motor homes driven by gray-haired husbands with little dogs on their laps convoyed on the highway, with strength in numbers.

Beyond the Copper valley, the one-hundred-twenty-mile dead-end road to coastal Valdez is one of the most stunning mountain roads anywhere, even outdoing the Haines Highway. It bridges wild rivers, peeks at glaciers, and tops out at Thompson Pass, where I spent a day hiking to a rockbound, ice-bordered summit. From there I looked longingly into the Chugach Mountains, which rumpled westward farther than I could either see or imagine.

Weather permitting, this pass offers the finest high-mountain, road-accessible hiking in the entire Coast Range, with an extravagance of lichen-colored meadows, walkable rock, and ice. Unlike so much of the coastal mountain chain from Mexico north, this land was free of the brushy undergrowth that often prevents foot travel except on trails. Here above timberline everything lay wide open, allowing free-form wandering, at least up to the edges of cliffs and ice. But only in the short sweetness of summer. Snowfall here has set the Alaskan annual record of eighty-one feet. I could believe this even in August because I counted forty glaciers in one sweep of the eye. Throughout the coastal mountains we never escaped the immediate influence of the hydrologic cycle, and now a dark bank of clouds wafted in from the sea and sent me scrambling for cover.

We drove down to Valdez, an ugly incarnation of tasteless architecture sprawled across a plain gridded by wide streets still being paved. But the site of Valdez—what town builders started out with—is one of the most spectacular coastal and mountain locations imaginable. Snowy peaks rise from a deep blue inlet of sea. Valdez was reborn after the Alaska earthquake of 1964, when a thirty-foot tsunami rolling landward at a hundred miles per hour obliterated the old town. The relocated and larger version now sits mostly above the tidal-wave zone.

Being America's northernmost ice-free port, Valdez marks the terminus of the eight-hundred-mile trans-Alaska pipeline. The tanker depot sits directly across the bay from town on scraped-out terraces that put quite a dent in the mountain over there. The crude oil is pumped into ships as infamous as the *Exxon Valdez*, which ran aground not far out on Bligh Reef. If the deadly oil slick could have been picked up as one big slimeball and spilled on California's shores instead, it would have blackened beaches from the Golden Gate to Mexico.

Even though the Copper River does not flow to Valdez, Ann and I based our next raft trip from the pipeline town. First, at the ferry terminal, we picked up Mary and Greg Bettencourt — my mountain biking companions from Cayucos, who happily joined us. For the multi-legged shuttle we first hired a driver to drop us off at the put-in, a good seven hours away. After we floated two hundred seventy miles down to sea level near Cordova, which is located on a peninsula isolated from the state road system, we would schlep our gear onto a ferryboat and cruise half a day back to Valdez and the nearest road.

As a memorable two weeks of my life, the Copper trip ranked right up there with the Tatshenshini and Alsek trip, the river growing from a couple of thousand cubic feet per second where we put in to an unfathomable 200,000. We boated the border of Wrangell–Saint Elias National Park and Preserve, at 13.2 million acres the largest national park in the United States, six times the size of Yellowstone and home to nine of the country's sixteen highest peaks. From the river we glimpsed the distant volcanic giants Mount Sanford, at 16,237 feet, and Mount Blackburn, at 16,390. Eyes wide, we floated right through the Chugach Range, where Spirit Mountain soared seven thousand feet up and where the Childs Glacier pushed its blue ice against our constricted current for two utterly unique miles of river running.

A heavy-breathing highlight of this adventure was Abercrombie Rapids. Here the lower Copper funneled from the width of a mile into a choked-off outlet several hundred yards wide. We couldn't see what was to come because the river dropped off suspensefully beneath a horizon line, but I had it from good sources that the rapid was easily runnable. Yet, taking less and less comfort in that information as we got closer and closer to really knowing, I could see disconcerting sprays of angry water shooting high in the air. The resonant roar set butterflies loose in my stomach. I didn't know it then, but the flow we were riding was much higher than normal.

Swells at the rapid's entrance rolled six feet high, bobbing our raft like a toy in the Pacific. Then the waves gathered in a chaos of breaking tops and sloppy, rollicking collisions. Because we were alone in a single boat, a flip would have presented a serious problem.

While I strained to keep the raft pointed straight into the waves, something strangely disturbing caught my eye. Down near the end of the rapid it looked as though logs were being tossed end over end in the translucent waves, really scaring me for an instant. "Annie, what's that down at the end of the rapid?" I shouted over the rush of water as I pivoted on the top of a wave.

"It looks like logs—but wait a second." She hung on tight and stood up. "I think they're seals!" We had never encountered seals in the middle of a rapid we were running. But as we approached, the cadence of the waves smoothed, and sure enough, they were harbor seals that had swum thirty-five miles upriver to fish.

Two days later we took out at the Copper River Delta, one of the largest wetlands in America, where sixteen million shorebirds summer over. From the mouth of the river, as prearranged, we caught a school bus back to the town of Cordova, where I learned that local people were fighting plans of a native development corporation to build a fifty-mile-long road, log eight thousand acres of rainforest, and allow a Korean company to mine and export coal, the burning of which would send acid rain back to us across the Pacific. Even in such a remote place there is no escape.

AFTER RETURNING to Valdez and parting with Mary and Greg, Ann and I set off alone again, our Coast Range agenda shortening and summer rolling toward its close. But we knew we had saved some of the best until last.

We skirted the northern front of the Chugach Mountains, where palisades of glaciers cropped up in the distance. Then Anchorage offered both the amenities and banalities of a planlessly growing city, the largest city we had navigated since San Francisco. We found delightful bikeways along Cook Inlet and mountain trails that stairstepped directly from neighborhoods, but also miles and miles of commercial strips and subdivisions.

On our first morning there, traffic on the four-lane was blocked to a standstill by a moose, standing calmly on mucky hooves while people in idling cars waited, the signs for gas stations and mini-marts cluttering the background. The scene signified change, poignantly evident here in Alaska in ways that are forgotten in places where urban sprawl displaced the wildlife long ago.

Turning south for one more great fling before the Coast Range heads terminally out toward sea, we wound over mountain passes of the Kenai Peninsula to the appealing, compact little town of Seward. Nearby, the Harding Icefield — the largest icefield entirely within the United States — spreads out across the top of the Kenai Mountains.

There I hoped to travel by foot and by ski, not just at the edge of ice, as we had done at Muir Inlet and along the Alsek River, but across the glaciers themselves, up where whole ranges still lay buried in the frozen depths of the ice age.

N

Anchorage

COOK INLET

KENAI
PENINSULA

1

Kenai Mts.

Exit Glacier

Seward

Harding
Icefield

1

Homer

Aleutian Range

GULF OF ALASKA

Kenai Peninsula

Kodiak Island

0 ——————————— 100 miles

PACIFIC OCEAN

© Tim Palmer

# 15 | *Across the Icefield*

I f it was foolhardy, I didn't want to go. So I checked in with Mike Tetreau at the Kenai Fjords National Park office in Seward. An experienced glacier traveler, ranger Mike filled me in on details about the Harding Icefield and assured me that the crevasses, this late in the year, were plainly visible for the most part. But he said I would definitely need crampons for traction on the ice at the beginning of my outing, and he offered to loan me his own pair. "I haven't been up there in a while," he added, "so stop by here or at the house after your trip and let me know how it goes."

Among all the icefields from southern British Columbia to the northwestern end of the Coast Range, I chose to explore Harding because a trail leads to its edge, making it possible to reach without the bug-ridden, bear-infested ordeal of bushwhacking through alders and a thorny hell of devil's club, without the danger of glacier climbing, and especially without the use of helicopters.

Along with mountains, it's the weather that makes the icefields and glaciers what they are, and for the weather we respectfully had to wait. Parked in the van along the flooding Resurrection River, we sat rain-bound for two days, our noses in books when we weren't watching logs float by. Ann was still thrilled to be done with her manuscript and spent hours writing overdue letters to friends. With her compact sewing kit she stitched together a stuffed fish for one college mate whose baby was due. About midafternoon of the second day we wondered if we should wait for the sun or just suit up and go anyway. But our break came the next morning with a partly cloudy, late-August dawn, and we were out of there, gear loaded, skis strapped on the sides of my pack, poles in hand, and real vigor in our step because it felt so great to be moving again.

"We're out! We're out!" Ann exclaimed as we entered the stream-bottom woods.

Black cottonwoods along the river won the grand arboreal prize. We'd seen them growing in Baja, throughout California, in the Pacific Northwest, and now here. This fragrant, water-loving hardwood has the longest range of all the trees in the coastal mountains and had accompanied us nearly the whole way.

The trail climbed for three thousand vertical feet on the scraped-off terrain bordering the Exit Glacier, a steeply dropping jumble of seracs and crevasses, impossible to travel on when not covered by a winter's depth of fresh snow. After several hours of sweating and deep breathing we emerged in rock fields, where wildflowers pioneered new ground, at the top of the glacier. There, in a convex transition zone where the cracked ice looked like wrinkled white skin on the back of an old elephant, the glacier transformed itself from the relatively narrow canyonful of white to a gently sloped icefield. Far more vast than the glacier, this blanketed the whole interior of the Kenai Mountains — our next-to-last subset of the coastal mountains. One might think of the icefield as a solid lake up in the high country and the glacier as a solid river draining the lake over frozen waterfalls into the valley below.

When we topped the last rise in the trail, the view took our breath away. It reminded me of the fog we'd seen eight months before in the southern California valley nestled beneath the Laguna Mountains. Down there, opaque water vapor had flooded the country up to its armpits but left the higher flanks, ridges, and summits in the clear and exposed to the sun. Here it was not fog but snow that had inundated the land spread out before us. Then it had compacted into ice and filled the interior mountain basin. Only the tops of distant peaks remained exposed as nunataks — starkly black and vertical within the gravity-flattened white ice all around them. Ann and I pitched our tent on a micro-bench just above the glacier, enjoyed dinner, and sighed with excited appreciation of the view.

All it takes for an icefield and glacier to be born is annual snow-fall that exceeds melt-off. That had definitely happened here. Tent-bound, Mike Tetreau once endured a single storm that brought eight feet of snow, not an uncommon occurrence. In its publications, the National Park Service conservatively lists the annual snowfall here at an impressive 400–600 inches, but no one actually collects weather data across the icefield, so nobody knows how much snow really falls. Agency researcher Bud Rice speculated that the real amount could possibly be as much as 2,000 inches a year in some places. A hundred sixty feet! I couldn't imagine such a climate. For comparison, Mount Rainier holds the official North American record of 1,000 inches a year, though the icefields on Mount Baker, Mount Olympus, and the peaks of southern Alaska certainly get more.

Ann and I hoped we could avoid the everyday expectation of storms while we camped at the icefield. But, embarking just after one deluge had passed, we recognized that our weather-based fate was nothing but a crapshoot with poor odds.

Nobody knows how deep the ice really is up there, either. So, while we could see the nunataks poking their rocky, pyramidal summits up out of the frozen sea, we had no idea how deep the interior valleys of the icefield went in a blacked-out landscape no doubt replete with canyons, hillocks, knobs, and meadows-to-be.

We speak of the ice age as if the great sheets advanced down the mountains and down the latitudes only once, but in a million years the earth has seen nine major ice ages. Some glaciologists subdivide the number to nineteen. When people say "the ice age," they usually mean the last one, which reached its zenith about eighteen thousand years ago, when it buried 30 percent of the earth's surface, most of it in the polar regions and northern North America.

Climatologists now believe the glacial epochs are governed by Milankovitch cycles, named for the astronomer who discovered them. The earth's orbit around the sun periodically takes a more oblong trajectory, increasing the throw from our heat source and causing the weather to cool. This can be reinforced by variations in the tilt of the earth's axis and by sunspots that reduce radiation. Glacial advances have typically lasted about 100,000 years each, with the interglacial warm periods running 10,000 to 40,000 years. The glaciologists emphasize that we are still in an ice age—just a warmer phase of it. After all, glaciers cover one-tenth of the land—the same amount as farms.

But, by burning fossil fuels, we are now altering the climate faster than nature ever began to do and far faster than any natural counter-cycle might cancel out the human-made heat. Each year, at most ice-fields, more land becomes exposed to daylight by the accelerating melt. The glaciers are receding in the frighteningly warming climate of our time.

Of course, the meltwater has to go someplace, so sea level rises. If all the earth's ice melted, half the world's major cities would be flooded, and some part of this scenario is now inevitable with the reality of global warming, a phenomenon that will also bring about intensified tropical storms, increased aridity in midlatitude drylands such as the Great Plains, 80 percent less snowpack available as water supply in California, and northward expansion of warm-climate dis-eases such as malaria. The United Nations' Intergovernmental Panel on Climate Change predicted a sea-level rise of four inches to four feet during the twenty-first century. Other scientists predict more, but even the conservative estimates predict flooding of enormous urban areas and severely eroded beaches and shorelines. In this unexpected way, the highest recesses of the northern Coast Range are linked with the lowest, most populated cities to the south, Seattle, Los Angeles, and San Diego among them.

At dawn, a foggy haze yielded to blue sky and sunshine that burned off moisture in the air, bringing the icefield slowly into focus. Emerging in my view was a wide, white pathway, gleaming, unearthly, enticing.

We had only one pair of crampons, so I would strike out alone. I packed lunch, water, and survival gear, promised to be home by dark, kissed Ann goodbye, and descended the rock pile of the moraine to the ice. It didn't begin with a finely tapered edge, like water at the beach, but rather with an abrupt front, a stretch-step up. Though not nearly as forbidding as the severely crevassed face of the glacier we had hiked alongside, the final slope leading up to the icefield was steep and riddled with cracks in the elephant-skin texture. So right away I strapped on the crampons to keep from falling, sliding, and disappearing into the blue jaws of Harding.

Though awkward for a while, the metal spikes on my feet made it possible for me to grip securely on steep surfaces as hard as the block of ice you can buy at the store. Because my feet crunched along without even a tentative slip, I soon fell into a cocky sense of indomitability, fun but dangerous because, feeling so capable, I could easily get myself into trouble.

At first I avoided all crevasses, walking along their edges until they tapered shut and allowed me to pass. I regarded even small cracks with critical suspicion. Would the edges crumble when I stepped near? Could I slip, fall in, and be trapped? Would I see all the fissures easily, or would some lurk beneath a disguise of broken snow or rotted ice? But soon I routinely stepped across chasms two feet wide; then I took little jumps across larger gaps; and then I trusted broad and sturdy-looking ice bridges that spanned some of the crevasses and passed the test of my poking a ski pole at them. When I planned the day's trip, I didn't think I'd have crevasses to cross at all, but now they lay everywhere, demanding that I keep my eyes at my toes as if I were in rattlesnake country. I detoured widely around a yawning gulf that was blue-black, with drips of water echoing beneath as if hell were wet and cold.

When I topped the steep rise to the icefield, the gradient flattened out and the possibilities seemed endless. The surface became more like crunchy snow than hard ice, and the crevasses narrower, so I packed up the crampons, unsheathed my cross-country skis, and strapped on their climbing skins because the gradient continued gently and steadily up. Still, every thirty feet or so I crossed a crevasse, usually less than a foot wide. I simply skied straight overtop, scarcely giving the little chasms more attention than I would to a rutted ski track. The cracks occurred at right angles to the direction of the ice's flow, which was fortunately at right angles to my route as well. Keeping an eye peeled for any negative space big enough to swallow me, I zipped over hundreds of small crevasses during the next few hours.

All the time I wondered what lay underneath me—what dark magnificence of canyons and valleys? What kinds of waterfalls and subglacial rivers tore through glassy-walled caverns down there? Whole hidden netherlands could one day become meadows and forests where people might play as they now do in the once-glaciated Yosemite Valley or, for that matter, downtown Vancouver and Seattle.

Like the remains of some lost world—flooded not by water, on the Atlantis model, but rather by ice, on what I call the Polaris model— the multiple summits of the nunataks stood stark and barren, numinous in quality. Heat waves reflected off the sun-warmed snow in front of me and looked like an uncolored flame running across the foreground—visible waves of air shimmering against the backdrop of the blackened peaks. This strange dance of atmosphere heightened the icefield's powerful sense of otherworldliness—except that this really *was* my world. This really *was* the Coast Range, in an essential phase of its evolution.

Once in a while I heard a muffled "Whoomp" as ice settled around me—scary because the same sound heralds an avalanche on steep mountain slopes. But nothing ever seemed to happen on my nearly flat and temporarily solid platform.

Otherwise, the place was utterly silent. Extending thirty-five by twenty miles, the icefield stretched an amazing distance to be as quiet as a cave. Two gray-crowned rosy finches flittered past, and then all lay silent again, the eeriness inveigling me onward.

I tried to imagine crossing the whole expanse. Every year or so a party of glacier travelers might try to do this. They ski in the springtime, when the crevasses on the approach routes up and down the glaciers are still covered with snow. They take twice the food they expect to need, and the weather always socks them in with whiteouts that immobilize everyone for days under fierce extremes of climate. I lucked out on this sunny late-summer morning. But I was also wary of change because I had already learned that the North Pacific storms blow up quickly, with a vengeance of wind, rain, or snow at any time.

The fair weather of the Pacific High finally comes to a complete end here in a mixing zone called the polar outbreak, guaranteeing radically variable winds and severely unpredictable weather. Here the warm, moist air of temperate latitudes confronts the cold polar air of the far North. Being lighter, the warm air rises rapidly and is cooled to its dew point, causing fog, rain, and snow. This is the Aleutian Low weather system, a storm-spewing breeder of some of the foulest weather on earth.

I had begun with the ambition to ski to the nearest nunatak. But after three hours of steady travel, kicking along at a snappy pace, the charismatic landmass had hardly grown any larger or more textured. Each dark pyramid still lay surrounded by snow, now more separate, more monumental, in its piercing of the icefield. The nunataks remained surreal, enchanted in my eye, literally capstones of the entire Coast Range, emerging as they did from the ice.

By afternoon I had to admit that the mountaintops lay beyond my grasp, unreachable. But I breathed with deep satisfaction. I had made it to this icefield, and skiing across those wide-open spaces made a grand culmination of my year of travel. Still rising beyond me, those outliers of rock would remain unknown.

I like the idea that much remains unknown. But I also like the idea of knowing things, of knowing places. After all, that's what this whole trip was about. I like the idea of understanding life fully, from the moment of creation through the physical processes, into the ecological web, and on to the social response, the political manipulation, and the unavoidable effects on me and on what other people think, do, and feel. But the more you know about anything, the more you realize that it's not really possible to know it all. And here the nunataks presented me with that message. I could try to see them, to know them, but I never really would. This left me wanting more, so I hungered for what tomorrow would bring. And for that matter, today was not nearly over.

I had gained enough elevation to see out the sides; the icefield overflowed through gaps and valleys leading north to the Skilak

Glacier, west down the Tustumena Glacier, and south down many fingers that reached directly to sea level in Kenai Fjords National Park. Altogether, thirty-two glaciers radiated from this single icefield — in effect thirty-two places where the ice leaked out of the high mountain basin.

Stopping to stand in awe of it all, I detected the first cool breeze from the south. Because the low-pressure storms travel from west to east in cyclones — circles of air spinning inward and rotating counter-clockwise — the advancing edge of a storm often arrives from the south. A faint band of clouds was now building up in the southwest. The weather was changing. It was two o'clock anyway, and to make it back by dark I had to turn around. I removed the climbing skins so I could slide freely on the skis.

Before long the clouds blotted out the sun, and then they blanked out the southern and western horizons. I stepped up my already hustling pace, breathing deeply in a continuous aerobic workout. Now looking back over my shoulder, I saw that puffed-up clouds had devoured the nunataks. Then a gray fuzz of atmosphere clipped off the tops of nearer peaks at the sides of the icefield. A damper atmosphere billowed up behind surrounding ridges of the Kenai Mountains and slowly poured through gaps onto the icefield. The clouds were catching up, blowing in much faster than I was skiing out.

In the dark, thickening skies, I sensed I was witnessing the onslaught of an Aleutian Low in fine form. Quickening my pace, I checked the compass bearing on our camp next to the Exit Glacier in case the clouds obliterated all the landmarks signposting my way. At any moment I could be left with nothing to lead me home but white ice and water vapor.

But the edgy weather held off, its buildup a protracted affair, and at six o'clock I rejoined Ann, though none too soon to witness the storm's final, theatrical approach. A dark sky of earnest intent moved toward us — a cloud mass of enormous proportions eating the near peaks and staged to inevitably overtake us. A rippled tint of pink arced across the western horizon and added a freakish overlay of color — less a hue of creation, more a hint of apocalypse.

After I was greeted warmly by Ann, who had spent a wonderful day there painting and writing among the wildflowers, the rising wind chilled me to the core, so I quickly changed from my sweaty ski out-fit into dry wool. I smelled like a wet dog but felt much better.

Weighing the option of tenting in a howler of a rainstorm versus retreating back down the trail to an emergency shelter we had seen, we took the sensible approach.

We packed hurriedly and fled, and like a man pursued, I kept look-ing over my shoulder at the storm. It gained on us by the minute. Stinging drops began to plug us in the back about the time the shelter came into view. Woven cables on taut turnbuckles belted the little wooden hut to bedrock, and the steel strapping was not a contrived flourish of design. As we would see, it was needed to hold the shelter to the earth.

Our backs now soaked, we burst through the front door, stepped into the dry little haven the size of our van, and broke into laughter at our good fortune.

The wind picked up, whistled against the eaves, ripped at the roof like a hurricane, and rattled the stoutly hinged door so much that I jammed a sock against the latch so I could sleep. The pounding of rain, splattering against the outside walls, shook me awake again and again, but each time, my internal alarm quickly melted to cozy com-fort. I cradled Ann in my arms and fell back to sleep again. As morn-ing approached, the storm blew itself out and we awoke dry and con-tent, already wondering what our final exploration of the coastal mountains would bring.

Homer

Kenai Mts.

Barren Islands

Mt. Douglas

Afognak Island

ALASKA PENINSULA

Three Sisters

Kodiak

Center Mt.

KODIAK ISLAND

Narrow Cape

UGAK BAY

PACIFIC OCEAN

Kodiak Island

0 ———————— 50 miles

© Tim Palmer

# 16 To the Ends of the Earth

A PITCHING boat called the *Tustumena* pushed a wide path into Kachemak Bay, and the town of Homer receded from view. Situated as far west in the Coast Range and in Alaska as the continental road system goes, this winsome little community faces out across the bay to the far side of the Kenai Mountains. Where we left our van behind, we had come not only 2,600 miles due north from Baja but also 1,600 miles west. It was like driving to Hawaii. In fact, a line drawn south from Homer crosses the Pacific only two hundred miles east of Honolulu.

The charm of Homer was not easily resisted. Just staying there would have been a pleasure. It's the sunniest place in coastal Alaska, and now the drenching rains of autumn could be expected out where we were headed. But the Coast Range carries on, and so we carried on as well, the end in sight, figuratively if not yet literally speaking.

The Kenai Mountains, which I had seen all around me from the Harding Icefield, now exited across the Pacific, disappearing underwater for forty-three miles. But then more mountains emerged again, as the Coast Range's grand finale, in a set of rugged islands. This archipelago's largest uplift is called the Emerald Isle by tourism promoters, the Rock by its residents, and Kodiak Island by the rest of us.

Without the van we felt surprisingly free. We had stashed all the essentials in our packs, which were strapped up as sizable append-ages to our bodies, ready to go wherever we went. Without worries about parking, breakdown, or rip-off, we suddenly realized it was a joy to be so independent of our vehicle and all those other possessions.

Without the protection of the van, our lives also promised to be more vivid, more vulnerable to the world. Our choices would be more consequential. Leaving our turtle shell behind, we would be more public as we exposed ourselves in new ways, hitching rides here and there. Living in the van no doubt gives us these same intensifying qualities compared with living in a house. But now, with just our back-packs, and despite whatever risk or inconvenience might arise, Ann and I agreed that this purer, simpler, stripped-down level of vaga-bonding was going to be fun. Even more than before, we believed we could live out Thoreau's admonition to have the night overtake us "everywhere at home."

The winter, spring, and summer of our journey had vanished, and the coming of autumn was upon us, so soon, so inevitably. The sea-sons in the Coast Range are not distinctive as they are in New Eng-land, for example, or the Rockies. With the moderating influence of the sea, the coastal mountains lack the piercing cold of winter, the sizzling heat of summer. Here the changes come more subtly, but the weather still swings seasonally, with variation in temperature and, especially, in rainfall.

In the far North in September, the warm days and lower-angled sun grew all the more precious for their increasing scarcity. The leaves had picked up a tinge of color, ready to explode in yellows on the cottonwood and aspen, reds on the fireweed and huckleberry. The stirring scent of fermenting dead leaves announced another cycle of life completed, another year waning toward its close, another mountain journey soon to end. Time was running out before the wind-driven rains would begin to batter us regularly and force us back to the south.

The flame of autumn's color never fails to give me a sharper view of the world. The ominous threat of winter — here taking the form of unrelenting wetness — hung in the air, and that breath of consequence heightened my awareness of each day as a special opportunity to live. Since the easy days could now be numbered on two hands — if we were lucky — I strove harder to live each rotation of Mother Earth to the fullest.

Whatever hazards we had encountered in our travels from Baja to here paled against the danger of wasting precious time. Autumn always shows me how scarce and valuable time really is, and each passing fall reminds me that I will not have the chance to live that year again. "Make it count," I say quietly to myself, knowing Ann agrees but also knowing that — being younger than me — she would not feel the sense of urgency that I cannot repress.

As with any adventure, facing the autumn made me more alert, somehow more alive at the edge of discomfort and scarcity and danger. In the fall, everything begins to matter more — for example, whether I'm sitting in the sun or the shade. Greater significance comes with the passing of each daylight hour. After all, there are fewer of them. The inevitability of change — and, let's face it, of loss — makes the earth even sweeter. Is a year like a lifetime, evolving from the springtime of youth, maturing to middle age, and then speeding toward its end in late autumn? This metaphor has survived the ages because it rings so true. And now I wondered, Is a journey also like a lifetime, going from initial sensations that thrill and amaze to a greater depth of knowledge and understanding and, finally, to serenity and feelings of completion? These kinds of thoughts floated up when I so much as sniffed the sweet rot of autumn leaves falling from the alders, and especially after undertaking a nine-month journey across the seasons as well as the land.

But for now, out there on the boat, it was the fresh dampness of the Pacific I smelled, the brine splashing beyond the deck and up to the rail as we entered the open sea and the *Tustumena,* or *Tusty,* as local people say, hit full stride on its one-hundred-thirty-mile voyage. The increasing swells pitched the boat and rocked Ann to the greenish brink of seasickness for several long hours.

Murres and a few puffins winged in and out of our path. Sea otters floated playfully on their backs, their whiskered faces glancing up at us. Then they dove under the opaque reflection, which was all I could see of the ocean, unknown to me but home to them. With chilling effect, a fog bank quickly enveloped us, blotting out the sun and lending extra mystery to this section of the Gulf of Alaska, which would take us most of the day to cross.

After tucking my jacket around Ann where she half lay and half sat — her eyes partly closed in anti-nausea determination and partly open to key on the rising-falling sea — I set my binoculars aside and chatted with strangers for a while.

A young man named Sean wanted to study at Humboldt State University in Arcata but in the meantime had landed a volunteer position at Fort Abercrombie State Historical Park on the island. "I don't know what I'll see or what I'll do," he said. "But, hey, that's life. The main thing for now is that I'm going to Kodiak."

"It sounds like a great adventure," I offered, remembering my own summertime jobs in the West during college.

Jerry drove a truck, his semi heavily packed with building supplies in the hold down below. Like many men I talked with across southern Alaska, he used to work as a commercial fisherman. "I'd rather be doing that today," he admitted, "but you have to make a living." A lot of fishing still goes on, but the boom years of the industry, when men raked in a few hundred thousand dollars in a few months and thus worked harder and harder to catch more and more fish and attracted more fishermen to do ever more of the same, have turned to bust. "The fish have gone somewhere else," was Jerry's take on the problem. It's precisely what people said about the passenger pigeons.

"Or the lion's share has been caught," I said, not a novel suggestion. The fisherman-turned-trucker shrugged his shoulders. But I knew from reading accounts of ocean fisheries that denial seems to be an occupational trait of many commercial fishermen. If it weren't for nominal regulations, they would compete until the last fish was gone in this ongoing tragedy of the commons.

Next I met Paul, who guided hunters on Kodiak Island. He had first gone there when his father bought him a one-way ticket as a graduation gift. The one-way part remained unexplained, but Paul had stayed seventeen years without begrudging his old man. "People come to hunt for game they've never hunted before, brown bears especially, but also sea ducks such as eider. Now I'm getting a lot of photographers who just want to take pictures. Those trips are the most fun. There's a lot less baggage to them, and I don't just mean fewer guns."

"Ann and I are going hiking in the mountains," I said. "Are we likely to encounter bears there?"

"There are three thousand bears on the island, but this time of year they're all down eating salmon at the mouths of the streams. Kodiak's known for its bears, but up where you're going you probably won't see even one."

Another man, traveling with his wife and four kids, had just taken a job as a school principal on the Rock.

"Interesting," I commented. "Being so isolated, Kodiak must avoid many of the problems affecting other schools today."

"There's no escape," the educator said. "Not unlike in Los Angeles, a fair number of the kids don't speak English. And the isolation breeds its own set of difficulties." Indeed, Filipinos, Mexicans, Japanese, whites, and others came to work in a fishing industry that had made Kodiak the second most productive commercial seafood port in America, but it was also a bit of an island-wide laboratory of social problems. Even during the boom, when fathers were often out at sea and by necessity away from their kids, hard work was interspersed with months of unemployment, when addictions ran rampant.

After the brief interval of fog, the skies cleared and our route skirted the starkly uplifted Barren Islands. Then we passed Afognak Island, its forested slopes in tatters where native development corporations logged mercilessly at the Sitka spruce. The former trees had not so long ago colonized this land in the wake of the ice ages. Using reparation money from the *Exxon Valdez* oil spill, the state and federal governments bought some of the cutover native property to protect as parkland, where the next forest of the future can grow.

Ann and I stood bellies to the rail as the boat finally approached Kodiak, which seemed dreamy from a wave-ribboned distance that admittedly obscured the details of drugs, alcoholism, overfishing, and a whole confessional of human complications seen almost anywhere up and down this long mountain chain. But now, sweet with evening sunshine on its shoulders, the isle rose hospitably from a blue sea, its emerald slopes steep, rounded, and backed by larger mountains on the horizon.

"Look at those hills, Tim," Ann called out, pointing to three tree-less cones furred in grasses of blue-green, purple-green, yellow-green. They just begged to be climbed. "Let's go there first," she said, and I agreed at the enticing prospect of walking in those wide mountain spaces, a big-sky country here in the far North.

We lucked out because Claire Holland waited at the ferry landing to greet us. I had spoken with her only once, on the phone, a conversation she concluded by saying she'd meet us at the boat if she could, though she had another commitment that Friday night. The district ranger for state parks, Claire had responsibility for six sites, ranging from criterion wilderness to Fort Abercrombie, on the edge of town. She had risen through the ranks of the agency and loved her job. "The island is an amazing place to work," she said, "and I have a lot of latitude in making decisions. I'm the chief of maintenance, law enforcement, and planning. I'm the one who answers to the public. I don't know if I could function where there are deep bureaucratic channels to wade through." Yes, I thought, remote islands do have their advantages.

Not the usual park superintendent, Claire looked as if she was in her mid-thirties, and she had earned an interesting athletic credential. She and a fifty-three-year-old woman friend had recently placed third in a classic Alaskan race — the one-hundred-forty-mile, point-to-point cross-country route from Hope to Homer. They walked forty-five miles the first day. They carried thirty-two-pound packs, one of which held a raft used for running a river on their five-day wilderness trek.

Friends in Juneau had given me Claire's name as someone who could orient us to Kodiak, and we didn't have to prompt her. "The vegetation here is interesting," she said with unabashed enthusiasm for her adopted homeland. "We have a coniferous forest of one species — Sitka spruce. Wiped clean during the last ice age, we're now isolated from seed sources, but the trees are recolonizing from the direction of the mainland at a rate of one mile per century. Though Afognak Island is forested, only the northern tip of Kodiak has tree cover. From sea level up to a thousand feet you can find brush, with lots of delicious berries at this time of year, but above that it's an open country of grasses, forbs, and lichens."

"So where do people go hiking and skiing?" I asked.

"Most people *don't* go hiking and skiing. Fish and bears are what bring people here. I should say fishing and bear hunting. Now bear *watching* is getting to be a business. But the commercial fleet is the big economic engine of the island. The weather's pretty bad for anyone not involved with what Kodiak uniquely has to offer. You see, the island gets eighty to a hundred inches of rain a year, a lot of it as fine mist that lasts for weeks, and a lot as big storms that can blow you away."

We stopped at the state park office, where I bought maps to help us plot our explorations. Spreading out the charts on the table, we did a quick reconnaissance of the island, two-thirds of it a national wildlife refuge. "Nearly every square foot is mountainous," I reported, scanning the maze of contour lines denoting rugged country rimmed by sea and bays that probed deep into the glaciated canyons.

"Look at this, right here," Ann pointed out to Claire. "From the boat, Tim and I saw these three hills north of town and thought they'd be a good place to start."

"The Three Sisters. Sure. That's a great place to start. I'll give you a lift out there right now if you want."

AFTER A night camped on a brushy, bearish streamside near the foot of the Sisters, Ann and I hung our food high in a tree, cached our packs under the weeping arms of a Sitka spruce, and set out for the summits that had looked so alluring from the boat. Through fruited berry thickets we clapped and sang and spoke loudly. The brown bears on Kodiak are touted as the largest terrestrial carnivores in the world, though they are really omnivores — they'll eat almost anything. They love berries, for example. But feasting on salmon is what really bulks them up. While grizzlies of the interior might weigh a perfectly respectable 900 pounds, the Kodiak browns—just a big version of the same species—can top 1,500, a knife-clawed, saber-toothed, temperamental creature bigger than a buffalo.

The thicket soon gave way to grass and wildflowers. This was not the grass of the California savanna, or of any lawn anywhere. This tangled scalp of green grew three feet tall and so thick we had to lift our feet high. The slope curved up in a concave fashion, and the climbing escalated from the realm of uphill walking to stair-stepping to grabbing fistfuls of deeply rooted grass and forcibly pulling ourselves so that our feet didn't slip. What would happen, we wondered, if we were to fall onto that bed of slick, grassy blades and start sliding?

"This is so unusual," Ann said as we stood for a breather, clutching grass to brace our stance and gazing out at the foreground of green and background of blue.

"It's not the prairie of Nebraska, that's for sure."

A potent wind animated the place but also made it difficult to hear, to speak, to relax. Soon it plastered our clothes against our bodies and drowned our voices completely. I never knew that the whistle of air on grass blades could be so loud. We doubly tightened our caps against the wind. It caused the grass to flow in all directions, with swirls bending one way, then the other. Then the blow became a bit more steady and moved the grass in waves rippling up the hillside.

When we neared a sub-summit of the first Sister, the gusts of air intensified into blasts, and as I stepped onto the ridge I knew I could not remain there long. The wind, reflecting the differential between high- and low-pressure zones in the big scheme of Kodiak's weather, felt as if it would snatch me up and launch me like a kite into the stratosphere. I crouched low and scooted off to the micro-shelter of an eroded wrinkle in the ridgeline. Coming up behind me, Ann instinctively threw herself over the ridge back and crawled into the sheltered area. While we ate lunch, with minimal relief from the gale, small clouds flew by like floats in a fast-motion parade, and their shade caused us to zip up tight.

Our view northward showed the emerging Sitka spruce forest of limby evergreens pioneering the isle in a many-fingered, opportunistic pattern. We saw quite literally the front line of the forest's advance following the last ice age, much as the forest of Maine or Michigan had once advanced after continental glaciation. The Pacific coastal coniferous forest—which began with Jeffrey and Coulter pines on the highest peaks of Baja, which featured redwoods from Big Sur to southern Oregon, and which grew into the greatest temperate rainforest on earth from Washington through British Columbia and up into southern Alaska—ended here on Kodiak. The rest of the island was covered with grass, wildflowers, shrubs, rock, snow, and ice, but no more trees. This spot marked the abrupt end of our Coast Range arboreal adventure.

On the other side of the ridge, the town of Kodiak showed in little glints of white and red and blue, but the overall mark of this eight-thousand-person community lay light on the land. Mainly what we saw below the dizzying slope of grass was the endless blue water of the Pacific, with nothing else to the south but Antarctica, nearly a globe's length away.

To the west, mountains stacked out to the horizon, a high sphere of lichen, rock, and snow—the great, final uprising of the Coast Range, irresistible.

WE HITCHED back to town for one more social call before heading off to the ends of the earth.

Stacy Studebaker and Mike Sirofchuck lived on a quiet street, where our considerate driver asked, "Are you sure this is the place?" We knew that Claire Holland would not have erred in her directions, and when we knocked, Stacy welcomed us in. It happened to be Mike's birthday, and they were stepping out to the Mexican restaurant for dinner. "You want to come?" Mike offered, not even knowing us.

Some years ago their winding paths through life had led them both here, to become entangled in the workings of Kodiak. The bright-eyed Stacy recalled: "When I was working at Yosemite National Park, I went into the library one rainy day and read John Muir's *Travels in Alaska*. Right away I knew that I just had to come. So first I kayaked from Vancouver Island to Glacier Bay."

"Wow—the whole way?"

"Yes. I wanted to do what John Muir had done. It was wonderful. Then I got a job with the National Park Service in Glacier Bay National Park for six summers, and then in Katmai National Park and Preserve for two years. After that I guided trips for a wilderness tour company. But in that business, with complaints about the coffee being either too strong or too weak, the routine got old pretty quickly. I decided that if I got a teaching credential, I could work almost anywhere in Alaska. So then, given the choice, I came out here, out to the end of the line."

At Kodiak High School, Stacy had taught biology ever since, doing what she could to help kids make the connection between themselves and the rest of life. "I can't imagine a better place to teach earth and life sciences," she offered with enthusiasm. "Here we are, at the edge of the Pacific and North American Plates. We have volcanoes and wild animals. We can go out the door and down to the beach or up to the mountains."

Stacy explained what really motivates her: "I get to help these kids understand what kind of place we really live in. It's important to know and understand our home. And while we're doing it, we have a good time." She also produced a radio show that Ann and I had heard on public radio stations during our van time driving north. In five-minute vignettes as "Lila Liverwort," Stacy revealed the biology of "bears to birds to the bottom of the sea."

Mike, on the other hand, came here following a girlfriend who had worked as a Vista volunteer, something of a role reversal in this state dominated by men who migrate north for unusual job opportunities. "It didn't work out," Mike said of the relationship, "but it did pull me away from my teaching job in Ohio."

After working awhile as an electrician, Mike scored a teaching post near Anchorage, which set him up to meet Stacy. They spent a summer kayaking together and married in 1987. Fortunately, Mike then landed a job at Kodiak High as well, teaching English.

Aware that many Alaskans get fed up with the weather and the darkness, and after twenty years bail out for the southern states, I asked, "Will you stay?"

"Stay? Of course," Stacy said. "We love it here."

I could tell I was talking with true Kodiak enthusiasts. "So what makes Kodiak so special?"

"Number one," Stacy began, "you can't drive here. It's an island. From a biological point of view, that makes the plant distribution fascinating. I really enjoy going out and looking for new plants. After all these years I still find one now and then. It's the kind of endless search I enjoy."

"People are not pretentious," Mike added. "Some of the fishermen have made millions, but they all look the same. It's an interesting, divided community. Many people are conservative, some of them veterans of the World War II navy occupation here. And then there's the ethnic mix, plus a fair number of people who enjoy the outdoor opportunities — people who really appreciate the island."

Mike continued: "Mainly what's special here is the land. I'm not so much a marine person as a mountain person. Here I can put my backpack on and go up almost anywhere. I love to climb high and sit there looking at the world. I've really become quite good at sitting and looking. It's probably like someone else watching TV; we go out and stare at the mountains. And the weather — the weather is definitely special here."

"You mean the rain?"

"Yes. Rain like many people have never seen before. Not just rain, but rain, sleet, snow, fog, cold rain, warmer rain, harder rain. You get the picture."

"I must say," Stacy added, "the lack of sunlight through the winter does affect me. Once March rolls around, I think, 'Ahh, we've made it.'"

Mike added: "In other places they say they have hurricanes. Here they just call it wind. They say, 'Well, it's going to be pretty windy, so we'd better go out and tie down the boat.' And then it blows eighty miles an hour."

"Oh, look!" Stacy interrupted. "There's a hummingbird! We don't have a lot of hummingbirds out here. Even robins are just starting to come here."

We all checked out the hovering, flittering flight. "And what other changes do you see on the way?" I asked.

"Well, there's one we hope not to see," Mike offered.

"The rocket launch," Stacy filled in grimly.

"Rocket launch? As in Cape Canaveral north?"

"They built Cape Canaveral where they did for good reasons," Mike answered. "And Kodiak Island is about as opposite from Cape Canaveral as you can get."

Here, in the foulest weather system America has to offer, in a place inaccessible by road and often unreachable by plane, chronically prone to tidal waves and earthquakes, the plan was to build the Kodiak Launch Complex, a $20 million rocket launch facility on Narrow Cape, in the Gulf of Alaska southwest of town. The U.S. Air Force said it would launch two rockets from the site. Two. Then it would turn the investment over to the Alaska Aerospace Development Corporation, an entity created by the "build-it"-crazed state legislature to promote private business in the northland.

Undeterred by a vacuous documentation of need, oblivious to the implications that huge amounts of public money would be laundered into private hands, Senator Ted Stevens — a master of pork barrel for military funding — inserted a rider in a law otherwise about interstate commerce. His provision guaranteed that no environmental impact statement would be required for a rocket launch facility on the doorstep of America's premier national wildlife refuge, at the edge of America's finest ocean fishery, and at ground zero in the grand seismic finale of the continent's entire coastal mountain chain. The senator then added $20 million to the defense budget with the tacit agreement that the money would be funneled away from any initiatives actually critical to national defense and into the Kodiak rocket launch.

"The chamber of commerce supports this boondoggle with the usual line about jobs," Mike said, "as if a little temporary payroll for construction workers were worth risking timeless employment in the fishing industry. We've been leading the fight against the rocket launch, which has been a pretty lonely excursion, but now the spending issue has finally got people stirred up. The facility would be a continual drain on taxpayers' money, and I have little doubt we'd be left with the costly cleanup of an abandoned site. Or maybe it would become a nuclear warhead base if there were another big buildup, making us a bull's-eye on the map. Who knows what we'd be stuck with before this is over."

Stacy added: "The whole thing is a violation of what Kodiak Island *is*. If Ted Stevens and the military want to spend money here, why don't they clean up the seventeen Superfund toxic waste sites we still have left over from World War II?"

I thought it was a good question.

Rocket launch? Superfund? I realized, once again, that you can't get away from it. The Japanese trawlers scrape the Gulf of California bare. A Texas tycoon chainsaws the redwoods to oblivion. The automakers promote their sport utility vehicles and rake in the profits by smogging Los Angeles and killing ponderosa pines. The real estate developers plaster up mansions in fire zones and on mudslide slopes, replacing the charcoaled remains of one millionaire's house with another one twice the size and just waiting to be burned again. The Canadian timber corporations mow what remains of the greatest temperate rainforest on earth and try to get their hands on the Indians' land at Kowesas. The miners plan to convert the Tatshenshini into a river of acid in order sell copper to a market oversupplied with it.

From the ferryboat, Kodiak had seemed like a world apart. But it wasn't. Even there on the Emerald Isle — on the Rock, on the final water-rimmed uplift of the coastal mountains, where salmon and bears survived in their ultimate stronghold — even there, Kodiak Island was not really an island at all but inescapably part of the cultural continent.

Exhausted by the awesomely idiotic notion of tearing up even one cape on this island to launch two military rockets, and outraged at a system that so easily devalues the land and all the essential good the land stands for, my own internal self-preservation mechanism kicked in to lower my blood pressure, and I just felt thankful that Stacy and Mike were there. They were seeking not simply to survive on this rock in the ocean, not simply to make money off Kodiak, but to leave a better place behind them. With these two people as schoolteachers, maybe there was hope for the future.

Stacy spotted another hummingbird, a delicate creature buzzing from flower to flower, so uncharacteristic of this weather-beaten, green-blanketed rock far out in the stormy North Pacific. She pointed and smiled, thrilled to see the tiny bird. She started to tell me about the flowers the bird would search out. I didn't hear the words, but only the feeling.

In love — this woman was hopelessly in love with this place she had adopted as home, this place where she and Mike were striving for the grand and essential goal of stewardship on the earth. Like Trudi Angell in Baja, like Larry Orman in San Francisco, like Valerie Langer in Clayoquot Sound, and like so many others I had been fortunate to meet, these two people on this remote island were showing the rest of us the way. They were taking responsibility for what we all do and fail to do. They were living lives of purpose that recognized other people were yet to come. They were blazing a path to a new citizenship, to a new patriotism that truly recognizes the value of our country, our land, our home, our mountains. Stacy sighed after listing the plants the hummingbird would pollinate, and then she exclaimed, "You know, there's only one Kodiak Island."

To this Mike added, "And only one earth."

WITH OUR own sense that the coastal mountains were like one island on one earth throughout all the miles we'd come since Baja, Ann and I set out on a final journey. With loaded backpacks and rain suits ready on top, we hitched a ride to the southern cusp of Woman Bay. Then, one more time, we began to climb.

Much as the shortening days of autumn make life itself seem more precious, the last hike in the Coast Range seemed less like a walk in the mountains and more like a pilgrimage capping off everything I had seen and every place I had visited.

We followed a crudely hewn all-terrain-vehicle trail up a heart-thumping slope, brushing our arms and legs against salmonberries for a few hundred yards and then breaking free from all that bear cover and into grass and wildflowers. Some colors brightened and others faded to autumn's call.

Because we'd started late, we needed to camp soon. As darkness fell, we luckily found a flat site near a rivulet of fresh water where moss and crowberries lay in a luxurious, spongy thickness, eight inches deep and rooted in loose, light ash that had blanketed Kodiak after volcanic eruptions on the mainland in 1912. Looking north, I saw scattered houses of the town's fringe, the day's last sunlight blinking on tin rooftops. At a quarry to the west, a pump hammered away, draining water from the pit, and at a rifle range to the east, hunters triggered off ammo rounds until dark, no doubt calibrating their sights for the upcoming deer season. Farther north, with the charm of the miniature, the town of Kodiak turned on its lights. In the morning we would leave all those signs of civilization behind.

Setting out early, we walked on narrowing paths into higher country and then roamed free-form across the ascending slopes. While the broad-brush view of the meadows was simply green, the richness of plants living on those treeless mountains made for a botanist's holiday. Blueberry yielded to large-leaved avens, hawkweed, geranium, aster, lupine, leatherleaf saxifrage, burnet, Siberian aster, harebell, paintbrush, gentian, white bog orchid, nagoonberry, cranberry, bunchberry, variegated willow, grass, sedge, and lichen. Many flowers still bloomed in curvilinear mosaics, purple patches lobed with orange and yellow, each with leaves of subtly different greens. In the lee of a rock we found a cluster of Kamchatka rhododendron; it colonizes not from the mainland of Alaska but from Siberia. We were that far out.

Gaining a ridgetop, we followed its bony spine to the south, winding with the vagaries of mountain morphology, dipping down to step around little bogs and then climbing higher. Center Mountain was our destination, and by the second night we could see it clearly. Last winter's snow radiated in tentacles from the summit down through ravines where drifts and shadows had conspired to build a year-round base of white.

After dinner we strolled pack-free along a secondary ridge to the north, reveling in an evening charmed with no rain, no bugs, no wind. All year long the big question had been, How will we deal with the rain on Kodiak Island? Will we even see the mountains at all? I had never expected to find the finest of all hiking days here, with full sun, in such an open, exuberant landscape.

To the north, across the water, the high country of the Alaska Peninsula lay in the glowing serenity that only great distance brings to great peaks. Mount Douglas, a glaciated giant, rose nearly a hundred miles away. From there, a bending chain of summits over six thousand feet high trailed out toward the Pacific to become the Aleutian Islands. Though undeniably coastal, the Aleutians geologically extend from the Alaska Range. The Coast Range ends here with Kodiak.

Now, after so much had come together in our journey, the journey was nearly over. But as I had seen in the fatalism of Baja, in the seeds sprouting after chaparral fires, in the carbon cycles of the rainforest — as I had seen in storms strong enough to produce apocalyptic floods yet nourishing life every moment as they blew past — I knew that rebirth accompanies the loss of nearly everything in nature. New life would take over for the old. What kind of life would it be?

Back at the tent, with no reason to expect anything else of the day, we sat on rocks for a while, just watching the overhead dome grow dark, hours sooner than it had been doing only two months before, on the Alsek River. We lingered outside to see a sprinkle of stars fall into the sky as the sunlight faded to nothing. Then the Big Dipper held my eye for the longest time, so bright, so true in pointing to the North Star. Polaris had marked our general direction since the beginning of our Coast Range trip, and now that we had come as far northwest as the mountains go, I considered the journey complete. I was fully satisfied to stargaze on that final night. Nothing else was needed.

But then, off to the side of the dipper, just above the horizon, a ray of white light flashed into the sky. Another beam seemed to spotlight the dark heavens, soon to be joined by another. Then a broader bank of white, rippling light shimmered up from the horizon and across the face of all the stars lying to the north. It was the aurora borealis, the northern lights, the mysterious, luminous fireworks related to the magnetic fields of the earth. An extraordinary show on that rare clear night in early September, the sheen and quiver and curtain-like ripple of white, blue, and green light held us rapt.

Also watching the aurora here on the southern coast of Alaska,

John Muir wrote of the "radiant glory of that midnight sky, as if the foundations were being laid for some fairer world."

In the same 1890 journal entry he added, "In such places standing alone on the mountain-top it is easy to realize that whatever special nests we make—leaves and moss like the marmots and birds, or tents, or piled stones—we all dwell in a house of one room—the world with the firmament for its roof."

THE NEXT morning Ann and I set out, with just our daypacks, for the summit of Center Mountain. Along a narrowing ridge we peered across a canyon at streams that looked like capillaries of snowmelt oxygenating the whole landscape. Six ravens and a bald eagle soared below us.

A number of rounded pre-summits lay in our path, and with each successive crown of uplift, Center Mountain stood more reachable, more real. With timberline long gone now, we strode closer and closer to grassline. The veneer of dwarf herbs blanketing the mountains grew thinner, all the more precious to the life force of that place. Green patches became smaller and smaller, and then the rock took over.

Across a snowfield and up a steep rise we approached the summit. At three thousand feet anywhere else in the Alaskan Coast Range we would have encountered glacial ice or cliffs, but there on temperate Kodiak Island we strolled unchallenged. As we climbed higher, the ocean didn't become smaller with our greater distance but larger and larger as we were able to see farther and farther.

Soon we stood on top, as high as we could get above the Pacific, with lots of ocean and lots of mountain both in view.

Gem-like lakes dotted the country below us, some encircled by barren rock, some hugged by crescents of clean, white snowfield. One of the larger lenses of water still lay two-thirds covered by last winter's ice, one-third turquoise in depth. Emerald slopes folded down in rounded mound after mound to the streams that each year bring the salmon back from the ocean and the bears back to the salmon—just one of the vital chain reactions in these mountains.

Directly west, partway down Center Mountain's steep slope, I could see that the shady chasm of a canyon yawned with green walls dripping in moisture, its edges gullied by water working its way back to sea in a microcosm of the hydrologic cycle.

To the southwest, the fjords called Ugak and Terror notched deep into the body of the island. At the heads of those bays, streams cut Kodiak's wrinkled surface at low elevations, while mountains everywhere reached for the sky, peak after peak, ridge after ridge, some with snowfields, some with glaciers, many with sharpened bare rock. The valleys, plateaus, canyons, summits, alluvial fans, moraines, lakeshores, meadows — every bit of it was wild. Beyond it, as always in our adventures this year, lay the great edge and the Pacific.

Seeing it all out there on the final slope into the sea, I had a feeling of satisfaction that seemed greater than understanding. Through mile after mile for the past nine months I had gone the distance to see what I could see, and now the trip was over. In all those miles I didn't capture anything I could really put my finger on but instead had been captivated myself by the mountains, by the weather, by the play of light on rock, by the timeless waves of an ocean washing onto the timeless uplift of land.

Yet I had no doubt that my sense of connection to all life had grown stronger; my sense of separation had become less. My feeling of gratitude at being alive in such a vibrant landscape had at times overwhelmed me. My sense of outrage at what we are doing to this land had been fueled like an annealing fire, and through people I had met, a sense of hope had also kindled my spirit.

Looking out from the end of the Coast Range to the Pacific, I wanted the moment to last forever. I wanted to stay just a little longer before I said goodbye. I wanted the mountains to work on me so that I would never really leave them, but always have them in my heart, wherever I went. Such beauty, such power, such peace, such adventure, such life. To me, they offered all this at once.

Though the sky was still clear overhead, the breeze felt cool with its moisture, and a thickening ripple of clouds spread from the southern horizon. I knew what was coming.

Though this high peak marked the end of the journey and seemed like the ends of the earth, I thought about the name of Center Mountain, and then I pictured its summit not as the end of anything but as the center of the universe. Everything radiated out in patterns from that place — the mainland of Alaska to the north, the Aleutian Islands to the west, the Pacific all around us. High above it all, leading back to the east and then to the south, the Coast Range showed us the way home.

# Notes

The following citations identify some of the more important and accessible sources of information used in *Pacific High*. This list mainly offers a sampling of the types of books and articles I used and can serve as a reading list for those who want a deeper understanding of the many fields I've touched upon.

PROLOGUE: BETWEEN THE SEA AND THE SKY

xvi.  *"Rise free from care"*: Henry David Thoreau, *The Annotated Walden,* ed. Philip Van Doren Stern (New York: Clarkson N. Potter, 1970), 336.

CHAPTER 1: INTO BAJA

12.  *"future is viewed with fatalism"*: Alan Riding, *Distant Neighbors: A Portrait of the Mexicans* (New York: Vintage Books, 1989), 6.

13.  *Spanish invasion:* Joel Simon, *Endangered Mexico: An Environment on the Edge* (San Francisco: Sierra Club Books, 1997).

17.  *seismic rift:* Wayne Bernhardson and Scott Wayne, *Baja California* (Oakland, Calif.: Lonely Planet Publications, 1994).

18.  *geology:* Deborah R. Harden, *California Geology* (Upper Saddle River, N.J.: Prentice Hall, 1997), 7; Kenneth A. Brown, *Cycles of Rock and Water: At the Pacific Edge* (New York: HarperCollins, 1993).

19.  *latitude of deserts:* Joe Cummings, *Baja Handbook* (Chico, Calif.: Moon Publications, 1994).

19. *swelling of cardón cactus*: Norman C. Roberts, *Baja California Plant Field Guide* (La Jolla, Calif.: Natural History Publishing Company, 1989).

20. *Sierra San Pedro Mártir*: Richard A. Minnich et al., "A Land Above: Protecting Baja California's Sierra San Pedro Mártir Within a Biosphere Reserve," *Journal of the West* 39 (autumn–winter 1997): 613–695.

23. *"commonweal barely exists"*: Riding, *Distant Neighbors*, 9, 370.

24. *Sea of Cortés*: Simon, *Endangered Mexico*.

24. *tortuga nearly extinct*: Cummings, *Baja Handbook*.

CHAPTER 2: THE VOLCÁN AND THE MEXICAN DESERT

37. *"If an excursion agent had planned"*: Henry T. Finck, *The Pacific Coast Scenic Tour* (New York: Charles Scribner's Sons, 1891), ix.

40. *seventeen thousand gray whales*: Stewart T. Schultz, *The Northwest Coast: A Natural History* (Portland, Oreg.: Timber Press, 1990), 71.

40. *salt mine expansion stopped*: Serge Dedina, *Saving the Gray Whale: People, Politics, and Conservation in Baja California* (Tucson: University of Arizona Press, 2000).

43. *destructiveness of highways*: Paul Brooks, "Baja: Emergency and Opportunity," *Audubon*, March 1972, 4.

46. *"neighbors understand each other so little"*: Alan Riding, *Distant Neighbors: A Portrait of the Mexicans* (New York: Vintage Books, 1989), xi.

CHAPTER 3: BORDERLANDS AND REFUGES

51. *birthrate dropped*: Mary Jo McConahay, "A Smaller but Better Future," *Sierra*, July 1999.

51. *up 20 percent*: Terry McCarthy, "The Coyote's Game," *Time*, 11 June 2001, 60.

52. *Border Patrol agents arrested 67,282*: *High Country News*, 23 December 1996.

52. *thousand people arrive in Tijuana each day*: Tom Miller, *On the Border* (Tucson: University of Arizona Press, 1985).

52. *illegal aliens in United States* McCarthy, "Coyote's Game," 60.

52. *grows by 2 million a year*: Joel Simon, *Endangered Mexico: An Environment on the Edge* (San Francisco: Sierra Club Books, 1997).

52. *90 percent seek greater prosperity*: Leon Kolankiewicz and Roy Beck, *Forsaking Fundamentals: The Environmental Establishment Abandons*

*U.S. Population Stabilization* (Washington, D.C.: Center for Immigration Studies, 2001), 33.

56. $50 *billion a year industry:* Tim Padgett and Elaine Shannon, "The Border Monsters," *Time,* 11 June 2001.

57. *take jobs away from American citizens:* Roy Beck, *The Case Against Immigration* (New York: Norton, 1996).

57. *with taxes in mind:* Peter Schrag, *Paradise Lost: California's Experience and America's Future* (New York: New Press, 1998), 58.

57. *population growth in California:* Tim Palmer, "A Great Number of People," in *California's Threatened Environment: Restoring the Dream,* ed. Tim Palmer (Washington, D.C.: Island Press, 1993), 19–32.

58. *1.2 million immigrants settle:* Steven A. Camarota, *Immigrants in the United States—2000* (Washington, D.C.: Center for Immigration Studies, 2001).

58. *Latino birthrate:* Dan Walters, *The New California* (Sacramento: California Journal Press, 1986), 16.

58. *population increase caused by immigration:* "Immigrants: Who and How Many?" *Washington Post,* 19 November 1996.

58. *two-thirds of population increase:* Camarota, *Immigrants in the United States.*

58. *projections underestimated:* Leon Kolankiewicz, *Immigration, Population, and the New Census Bureau Projections* (Washington, D.C.: Center for Immigration Studies, 2000), 3.

58. *high crime rates:* Claude Fischer, *The Urban Experience* (New York: Harcourt Brace Jovanovich, 1980), cited in Tim Palmer, *The Heart of America: Our Landscape, Our Future* (Washington, D.C.: Island Press, 1999), 274.

59. *polls:* Leon F. Bouvier, *Americans Have Spoken* (Washington, D.C.: Negative Population Growth, ca. 1993).

59. *1.2 billion in deep poverty:* Philip Shabecoff, *Earth Rising: American Environmentalism in the 21st Century* (Washington, D.C.: Island Press, 2000), 155.

59. *more than one million a year:* Kolankiewicz and Beck, *Forsaking Fundamentals,* 28.

59. *environmental groups abandoned population goals:* Kolankiewicz and Beck, *Forsaking Fundamentals,* 1.

60. *population growth would flatten:* Kolankiewicz and Beck, *Forsaking Fundamentals,* 29.

61.  *Mediterranean habitats:* Deborah B. Jensen, Margaret S. Torn, and John Harte, *In Our Own Hands* (Berkeley: University of California Press, 1993), 46.

62.  *troubles with cows:* Tim Palmer, "The Native California Landscape," in Palmer, *California's Threatened Environment,* 245–251.

62.  *imperiled oaks:* Tom Griggs, "Valley Oaks: Can They Be Saved?" *Fremontia,* July 1990, 44–47.

63.  *hundred forty pounds of acorns:* Malcolm Margolin, *The Ohlone Way* (Berkeley, Calif.: Heyday Books, 1978).

73.  *communications towers:* John Dillon, "Why Birds Hate Seinfeld," *Audubon,* May 1998, 16.

73.  *health effects of electromagnetic radiation:* Arthur Firstenberg, "Radio Waves: Invisible Danger," *Earth Island Journal,* winter 2000–2001, 25.

73.  *telecommunications towers in national parks:* National Parks and Conservation Association, "Towers Loom on the Horizon," *National Parks,* November 1997, 20; Becky Gillette, "Concerns Linger About Electromagnetic Fields," *E Magazine,* November 2001, 40.

77.  *Beier's lion study:* David Wicinas, *Sagebrush and Cappuccino* (San Francisco: Sierra Club Books, 1995), 156.

78.  *not enough parks:* Pete Dangermond, "Parks and Recreation: Vital to a Way of Life," in Palmer, *California's Threatened Environment,* 219.

79.  *bighorns:* Martin Forstenzer, "Bighorn Sheep Losing Ground, and Lives, to an Old Foe," *New York Times,* 29 September 1998.

CHAPTER 4: RISING ABOVE LOS ANGELES

85.  *private security:* Robert D. Kaplan, *An Empire Wilderness* (New York: Random House, 1998), 86.

86.  *"a gigantic improvisation":* Carey McWilliams, *Southern California: An Island on the Land* (Santa Barbara, Calif.: Peregrine Smith, 1973), 13.

87.  *San Andreas Fault:* Charles C. Plummer, David McGeary, and Diane H. Carlson, *Physical Geology* (New York: McGraw-Hill, 2001), 376; Rick Gore, "Living with California's Faults," *National Geographic,* April 1995.

88.  *federal disaster assistance:* Rutherford H. Platt, *Disasters and Democracy: The Politics of Extreme Natural Events* (Washington, D.C.: Island Press, 1999), 65.

89.  *Big Bend and uplift:* Deborah R. Harden, *California Geology* (Upper Saddle River, N.J.: Prentice Hall, 1997), 383.

90. *floodplain surrounded by mountains:* Allan A. Schoenherr, *A Natural History of California* (Berkeley: University of California Press, 1992), 315.

90. *mudslides:* John McPhee, *The Control of Nature* (New York: Farrar, Straus and Giroux, 1989), 196–265.

92. *Olmsted's plan:* Greg Hise and William F. Deverell, *Eden by Design: The 1930 Olmsted-Bartholomew Plan for the Los Angeles Region* (Berkeley: University of California Press, 2000).

93. *smog:* Schoenherr, *Natural History of California,* 403.

94. *per capita pollution down:* Jane Hall, "The Atmosphere We Breathe," in *California's Threatened Environment: Restoring the Dream,* ed. Tim Palmer (Washington, D.C.: Island Press, 1993), 41.

94. *ponderosa pines:* Charles E. Little, *The Dying of the Trees: The Pandemic in America's Forests* (New York: Viking, 1995), 59.

96. *costs of suburban sprawl:* Urban Land Institute, *The Costs of Alternative Development Patterns* (Washington, D.C.: Urban Land Institute, 1992).

96. *population projections:* Planning and Conservation League, *Land Conservation in California* (Sacramento, Calif.: Planning and Conservation League, 1999), 6 (citing the California Department of Finance).

97. *longest urban–wildland interface:* Mike Davis, *Ecology of Fear* (New York: Metropolitan Books, 1998), 202.

CHAPTER 5: MOUNTAINS AND FIRE

108. *Chase's impression:* J. Smeaton Chase, *California Coast Trails* (Boston: Houghton Mifflin, 1913), 57.

118. *250,000 acres burned:* Rutherford H. Platt, *Disasters and Democracy: The Politics of Extreme Natural Events* (Washington, D.C.: Island Press, 1999), 270.

119. *liability with real estate:* Mike Davis, *Ecology of Fear* (New York: Metropolitan Books, 1998), 145.

121. *soil as insulator:* Paul Henson and Donald J. Usner, *The Natural History of Big Sur* (Berkeley: University of California Press, 1993), 240.

122. *dangerous locations for fire:* U.S. Department of Agriculture, Forest Service; and County of Los Angeles, *A Homeowner's Guide to Fire and Watershed Management at the Chaparral/Urban Interface* (Los Angeles: County of Los Angeles, 1982).

126. *rules relaxed:* Davis, *Ecology of Fear,* 108.

127.   *"lethal mixture":* Stephen J. Pyne, *Fire in America* (Princeton, N.J.: Princeton University Press, 1982), 404–415.

128.   *green line parks:* Charles E. Little, *Hope for the Land* (New Brunswick, N.J.: Rutgers University Press, 1992).

129.   *Santa Monica Mountains:* Randolph Jorgen, *Mountains to Ocean: A Guide to the Santa Monica Mountains National Recreation Area* (Tucson, Ariz.: Southwest Parks and Monuments Association, 1995).

CHAPTER 6: A DREAM OF CONDORS

135.   *Transverse Ranges:* John A. Shimer, *Field Guide to Landforms in the United States* (New York: Macmillan, 1972).

136.   *Fault lines:* Michael Collier, *A Land in Motion: California's San Andreas Fault* (Berkeley: University of California Press, 1999).

138.   *dwindling condor numbers:* Paul Henson and Donald J. Usner, *The Natural History of Big Sur* (Berkeley: University of California Press, 1993), 176.

138.   *lead shot:* Frank Graham Jr., "The Day of the Condor," *Audubon,* January 2000.

138.   *Compound 1080:* David Darlington, *In Condor Country* (New York: Henry Holt, 1987), 193.

139.   *new condor population:* David Wilcove, *The Condor's Shadow* (New York: W. H. Freeman, 1999).

145.   *temperature variation only ten degrees:* Edwin Way Teale, *Autumn Across America* (New York: Dodd, Mead & Company, 1950), 323.

147.   *grizzly bears:* Roderick Peattie, ed., *The Pacific Coast Ranges* (New York: Vanguard Press, 1946).

147.   *volcanism and Morro Rock:* Deborah R. Harden, *California Geology* (Upper Saddle River, N.J.: Prentice Hall, 1997), 276.

148.   *blueprints "mixed up":* Harvey Arden, "East of Eden: California's Mid-Coast," *National Geographic,* April 1984.

152.   *$12 billion:* Planning and Conservation League, *Land Conservation in California* (Sacramento, Calif.: Planning and Conservation League, 1999), with addendum.

156.   *convict labor:* Heather Millar, "The Ups and Downs of Highway 1," *Smithsonian,* June 1999, 55.

157.   *J. P. Burns slide:* Henson and Usner, *Natural History of Big Sur,* 293.

CHAPTER 7: THE PEOPLE'S MOUNTAINS

165. *San Bruno Mountain:* Rasa Gustaitis, "Secrets of San Bruno Mountain," *California Coast and Ocean,* spring 2001.

166. *Oakland Hills fire:* Rutherford H. Platt, *Disasters and Democracy: The Politics of Extreme Natural Events* (Washington, D.C.: Island Press, 1999), 263.

167. *USGS estimate:* U.S. Geological Survey, *The Next Big Earthquake in the Bay Area May Come Sooner Than You Think* (Menlo Park, Calif.: U.S. Geological Survey, n.d.).

167. *Hayward Fault:* Bay Area Regional Earthquake Preparedness Project, "Living on the Fault," brochure (Oakland, Calif.: Bay Area Regional Earthquake Preparedness Project, n.d.).

178. *varied vegetation:* Elna Bakker, *An Island Called California* (Berkeley: University of California Press, 1971).

187. *"How it shines":* John Muir, quoted in Roderick Nash, "Muir Woods and Hetch-Hetchy Valley," in *Green Versus Gold: Sources in California's Environmental History,* ed. Carolyn Merchant (Washington, D.C.: Island Press, 1998).

187. *Pacific High weather system:* Alan Strahler and Arthur Strahler, *Introducing Physical Geography* (New York: Wiley, 1998).

189. *upwelling:* Paul Henson and Donald J. Usner, *The Natural History of Big Sur* (Berkeley: University of California Press, 1993), 35.

190. *Davidson Current:* Stewart T. Schultz, *The Northwest Coast: A Natural History* (Portland, Oreg.: Timber Press, 1990), 30.

190. *El Niño:* Paul D. Komar, *The Pacific Northwest Coast* (Durham, N.C.: Duke University Press, 1997), 118.

191. *El Niño in California:* Peter K. Schoonmaker, Bettina von Hagen, and Edward C. Wolf, eds., *The Rain Forests of Home: Profile of a North American Bioregion* (Washington, D.C.: Island Press, 1997), 38.

191. *El Niño and global warming:* Patrick Mazza, "The Heat Is On," *Cascadia Times,* December 1997; Strahler and Strahler, *Introducing Physical Geography,* 125.

192. *precipitation increase with rise:* Schultz, *Northwest Coast,* 24.

196. *moment magnitude scale:* Charles C. Plummer, David McGeary, and Diane H. Carlson, *Physical Geology* (New York: McGraw-Hill, 2001), 392.

197. *cover-up:* Thurston Clarke, *California Fault: Searching for the Spirit of State Along the San Andreas* (New York: Ballantine Books, 1996), 202.

197.  *emergency response:* Platt, *Disasters and Democracy,* 249, 253.

197.  *quake due:* Plummer, McGeary, and Carlson, *Physical Geology,* 410.

198.  *citizen campaigns:* Martin Griffin, *Saving the Marin-Sonoma Coast* (Healdsburg, Calif.: Sweetwater Springs Press, 1998).

CHAPTER 8: THE NORTH COAST

203.  *"new society":* Ray Raphael, *Cash Crop* (Mendocino, Calif.: Ridge Times Press, 1985).

206.  *Sinkyone tribal council:* William Poole, "Return of the Sinkyone," *Sierra,* November 1996, 55.

210.  *more living mass:* Jon R. Luoma, *The Hidden Forest* (New York: Henry Holt, 1999), 80.

213.  *location of San Andreas Fault:* National Geographic Society, "The Earth's Fractured Surface," *National Geographic,* April 1995, map insert.

213.  *water temperatures:* Stewart T. Schultz, *The Northwest Coast: A Natural History* (Portland, Oreg.: Timber Press, 1990), 30.

218.  *"For children to live":* Thomas Berry, *The Great Work: Our Way into the Future* (New York: Bell Tower, 1999), 82.

225.  *magnitude 8 earthquake:* Rick Gore, "Living with California's Faults," *National Geographic,* April 1995.

225.  *tsunami evacuation:* Paul D. Komar, *The Pacific Northwest Coast* (Durham, N.C.: Duke University Press, 1997), 61.

226.  *rainfall:* Schultz, *Northwest Coast,* 25.

227.  *Mattole salmon:* Freeman House, *Totem Salmon: Life Lessons from Another Species* (Boston: Beacon Press, 1999).

227.  *coho salmon:* Luoma, *Hidden Forest,* 184.

229.  *Mendocino Triple Junction:* Deborah R. Harden, *California Geology* (Upper Saddle River, N.J.: Prentice Hall, 1997), 328.

235.  *redwood seedlings and burls:* Rudolf W. Becking, *Pocket Flora of the Redwood Forest* (Washington, D.C.: Island Press, 1982).

235.  *only 4 percent uncut:* Reed F. Noss, ed., *The Redwood Forest: History, Ecology, and Conservation of the Coast Redwoods* (Washington, D.C.: Island Press, 2000), 89.

237.  *thirty conifer species:* Taylor H. Ricketts et al., *Terrestrial Ecoregions of North America: A Conservation Assessment* (Washington, D.C.: Island Press, 1999), 238.

237.  *Gasquet–Orleans Road:* Peter Matthiessen, "Stop the GO Road," *Audubon,* January 1979.

237. *Clinton's old-growth policy:* Reed Noss, "A Resource Design for the Klamath-Siskiyou Ecoregion," *Wild Earth,* winter 1999–2000.

CHAPTER 9: KALMIOPSIS TO THE COLUMBIA

241. *serpentinite:* David D. Alt and Donald W. Hyndman, *Roadside Geology of Oregon* (Missoula, Mont.: Mountain Press, 1978), 18.

241. *specialty plants:* Verna R. Johnston, *California Forests and Woodlands* (Berkeley: University of California Press, 1994), 187.

241. *Port Orford cedar and fungus:* Defenders of Wildlife, *Oregon's Living Landscape* (Washington, D.C.: Defenders of Wildlife, 1998), 87.

241. *substitute for hinoki cypress:* William L. Sullivan, *Exploring Oregon's Wild Areas* (Seattle: Mountaineers, 1999), 168.

241. *Port Orford cedar shipped to Japan:* Wendell Wood, *Oregon's Ancient Forests* (Portland, Oreg.: Oregon Natural Resources Council, 1991), 110.

243. *Marshall's Siskiyou wilderness proposal:* Roderick Peattie, ed., *The Pacific Coast Ranges* (New York: Vanguard Press, 1946).

243. *mining law:* Tim Palmer, *The Heart of America: Our Landscape, Our Future* (Washington, D.C.: Island Press, 1999), 47.

245. *Juan de Fuca Plate:* R. Monastersky, "Signs of Eruption Found off Oregon Shores," *Science News,* 28 February 1998, 153.

246. *magnitude 9:* Paul D. Komar, *The Pacific Northwest Coast* (Durham, N.C.: Duke University Press, 1997), 11.

247. *mechanization of mills:* Jon R. Luoma, *The Hidden Forest* (New York: Henry Holt, 1999), 157.

247. *export of unmilled logs:* Tim Palmer, *The Columbia: Sustaining a Modern Resource* (Seattle: Mountaineers, 1997), 83.

253. *Oregon Dunes National Recreation Area:* Stewart T. Schultz, *The Northwest Coast: A Natural History* (Portland, Oreg.: Timber Press, 1990), 327.

254. *Oregon's old-growth groves:* Wood, *Oregon's Ancient Forests.*

255. *coho salmon:* Robin A. Abell et al., *Freshwater Ecoregions of North America: A Conservation Assessment* (Washington, D.C.: Island Press, 2000).

255. *sixty thousand fishing jobs:* Peter K. Schoonmaker, Bettina von Hagen, and Edward C. Wolf, eds., *The Rain Forests of Home: Profile of a North American Bioregion* (Washington, D.C.: Island Press, 1997), 214.

255. *forests and fishing industry:* Pacific Rivers Council, *Coastal Salmon and Communities at Risk* (Eugene, Oreg.: Pacific Rivers Council, 1995), 6.

256. *people killed in slides:* Kathie Durbin, "Death and Destruction Ravage Oregon Timber Country," *Cascadia Times,* January 1997.

256. *"globally outstanding":* Taylor H. Ricketts et al., *Terrestrial Ecoregions of North America: A Conservation Assessment* (Washington, D.C.: Island Press, 1999).

257. *regeneration on serpentine soils:* Wood, *Oregon's Ancient Forests,* 114.

257. *depletion after four rotations:* Carl Safina, *Song for the Blue Ocean* (New York: Henry Holt, 1997), 166; Schultz, *Northwest Coast,* 337.

257. *Jim Furnish of Siuslaw National Forest:* Luoma, *Hidden Forest,* 198.

257. *Mike Dombeck's ban on new roads:* Palmer, *Heart of America,* 91.

264. *Drift Creek Wilderness Area unprotected acreage:* Wood, *Oregon's Ancient Forests,* 131.

265. *sixty million needles:* Chris Maser, *Forest Primeval* (San Francisco: Sierra Club Books, 1989).

266. *forest productivity comparison:* Schultz, *Northwest Coast,* 253.

266. *linking protected corridors:* Reed F. Noss, "A Preliminary Biodiversity Plan for the Oregon Coast Range," *Wild Earth,* spring 1993, 73.

267. *sprawl on the coast:* 1000 Friends of Oregon, "The Oregon Coast Under Siege," *Landmark,* September 1997.

267. *legacy of Tom McCall:* Brent Walth, *Fire at Eden's Gate: Tom McCall and the Oregon Story* (Portland: Oregon Historical Society Press, 1994).

CHAPTER 10: OLYMPIC ODYSSEY

271. *thirty-five inches of rain:* Stephen Whitney, *The Pacific Northwest* (San Francisco: Sierra Club Books, 1989), 40.

273. *"a ravaged land":* Robert Michael Pyle, *Wintergreen* (Boston: Houghton Mifflin, 1986), 29.

274. *2 to 5 percent of old growth:* Keith Ervin, *Fragile Majesty* (Seattle: Mountaineers, 1989), 246; John J. Berger, *Understanding Forests* (San Francisco: Sierra Club Books, 1998), 24.

274. *logging on Indian reservations:* Kathie Durbin, "Abusive Logging Batters Quinault Reservation," *Oregonian,* 15 October 1990, 20.

274. *timber corporation landownership:* Tim McNulty, *Olympic National Park: A Natural History Guide* (New York: Houghton Mifflin, 1996), 211.

275. *salvage logging in Olympic National Park:* Carsten Lien, *Olympic Battleground: The Power Politics of Timber Preservation* (Seattle: Mountaineers, 2000).

276. *Farallon Plate:* National Geographic Society, "The Earth's Fractured Surface," *National Geographic,* April 1995, map insert.

276. *wettest place:* Daniel Mathews, *Cascade-Olympic Natural History* (Portland, Oreg.: Portland Audubon Society, 1988), 6.

276. *greatest biomass per acre:* McNulty, *Olympic National Park,* xiii.

276. *temperate climate:* Elliott A. Norse, *Ancient Forests of the Pacific Northwest* (Washington, D.C.: Island Press, 1990), 19.

278. *spruce survival:* Stewart T. Schultz, *The Northwest Coast: A Natural History* (Portland, Oreg.: Timber Press, 1990), 295.

281. *champion trees:* Bruce Brown, *Mountain in the Clouds: A Search for the Wild Salmon* (New York: Simon and Schuster, 1982), 8; John Mitchell, "War in the Woods," *Audubon,* January 1990, 87.

282. *"beautiful country":* Jean-Jacques Rousseau, *La Nouvelle Héloïse,* quoted in Matt Cartmill, *A View to a Death in the Morning* (Cambridge, Mass.: Harvard University Press, 1993).

CHAPTER 11: THE ISLAND OF A DIFFERENT NATION

300. *maliciously well informed:* Andrew H. Malcolm, *The Canadians* (New York: Times Books, 1985).

303. *Clayoquot Sound:* Ecotrust Canada, *Seeing the Ocean Through the Trees* (Vancouver, British Columbia: Ecotrust Canada, 1997).

310. *United Nations report on sustainable development:* United Nations World Commission on Environment and Development, *Our Common Future* (New York: Oxford University Press, 1987).

311. *nominal requirements:* Government of British Columbia, "Protecting Our Natural Heritage," brochure (Victoria, British Columbia, Canada: Office of the Premier, 1994).

311. *liquidation by 2022:* Sierra Club of Western Canada, *Ancient Rainforests at Risk* (Victoria, British Columbia: Sierra Club of Western Canada, ca. 1996), 26, 32.

312. *province bought MacMillan Bloedel stock:* Natural Resources Defense Council, "Campaign to Save Clayoquot Sound," flyer (New York: Natural Resources Defense Council, ca. 1996).

313. *fines and imprisonment:* Ron MacIsaac and Anne Champagne, eds., *Clayoquot Mass Trials* (Gabriola Island, British Columbia, Canada: New Society Publishers, 1994).

313. *logging reduced:* Maryjka Mychajlowycz, "Friends of Clayoquot Sound See Destructive Clearcuts Continue in '96," in *Beautiful Clayoquot*

Sound (Vancouver, British Columbia: Western Canada Wilderness Committee, 1996).

315.   penalty reduced: Valerie Langer, "Interfor: Guilty as Charged!" Friends of Clayoquot Sound, spring 1997, 2.

322.   compromises at Strathcona Provincial Park: Friends of Strathcona Park, Strathcona: B.C.'s First Provincial Park (Vancouver, British Columbia: Western Canada Wilderness Committee, 1987).

CHAPTER 12: NORTHWARD BY BOAT

328.   "freshest landscape poetry": John Muir, in John of the Mountains: The Unpublished Journals of John Muir, ed. Linnie Marsh Wolfe (Boston: Houghton Mifflin, 1938), 261.

331.   Great Bear Rainforest: Taylor H. Ricketts et al., Terrestrial Ecoregions of North America: A Conservation Assessment (Washington, D.C.: Island Press, 1999).

332.   Home Depot: Jo Ostgarden, "Better News Than a Blue Light Special at Kmart," Cascadia Times, September 2000.

332.   British Columbia salmon: Geoff Meggs, Salmon: The Decline of the B.C. Fishery (Vancouver, British Columbia, Canada: Douglas and McIntyre, 1991).

333.   Kemano hydroelectric project: Richard Bocking, Mighty River: A Portrait of the Fraser (Vancouver, British Columbia, Canada: Douglas and McIntyre, 1997).

335.   linkage of mountain ecosystems: M. A. Sanjayan, Richard Jeo, and Dennis Sizemore, "A Conservation Area Design for the Central Coast of British Columbia," Wild Earth, spring 2000, 76.

335.   Kowesas watershed: Interrain Pacific, The Kowesas Watershed Assessment (Portland, Oreg.: Interrain Pacific, 1996).

345.   ecosystem-based planning: Ian Gill, "A New Start for the Great Bear Rainforest," Cascadia Times, March 2001.

CHAPTER 13: GLACIERS TO THE SEA

351.   Tongass and pulp mills: Ted Williams, "Tearing at the Tongass," Audubon, July 1995, 31.

351.   timber sold for $1.22: Robert Glenn Ketchum and Carey D. Ketchum, The Tongass (New York: Aperture Foundation, 1987).

351.   $60 million subsidies: Paul Rauber, "The $64 Million Question," Sierra, July 1993, 55.

352. *Alaska Native Claims Settlement Act:* Jerry Mander, *In the Absence of the Sacred* (San Francisco: Sierra Club Books, 1991).

352. *Tongass campaign:* Chris Finch and Alan Phipps, *Alaska Rainforest Atlas* (Juneau: Southeast Alaska Conservation Council, 1993), 12.

353. *Prince of Wales Island logging roads:* Donald Snow and Carolyn Servid, eds., *The Book of the Tongass* (Minneapolis: Milkweed Editions, 1999), 19.

354. *clearcuts devastating to wildlife:* Rita O' Clair, Robert H. Armstrong, and Richard Carstensen, *The Nature of Southeast Alaska* (Bothell, Wash.: Alaska Northwest Books, 1992), 91.

355. *"embosomed in scenery":* John Muir, *Travels in Alaska* (New York: Houghton Mifflin, 1915).

357. *nixed capitol move:* Alaska Geographic Society, *Southeast Alaska* (Anchorage: Alaska Geographic Society, 1993).

358. *cruise ship pollution:* Gershon Cohen, "A Royal Sewer: Cruise Ships Foul Alaskan Waters," *Cascadia Times,* September 2000.

360. *increasing helicopter flights:* U.S. Department of Agriculture, Forest Service, *The Alaska Region: The Forest Service in Alaska* (Juneau, Alaska: U.S. Department of Agriculture, Forest Service, 1997).

361. *Taku River:* Andrew Romanoff, *Tongass Rivers* (Juneau: Southeast Alaska Conservation Council, 1995).

363. *Glacier Bay:* Jim DuFresne, *Glacier Bay National Park* (Seattle: Mountaineers, 1987).

368. *new migration theory:* Charles W. Petit, "Rediscovering America," *U.S. News and World Report,* 12 October 1998, 57.

CHAPTER 14: THE ULTIMATE MOUNTAINS

380. *Alsek watershed and earthquake:* Ric Careless, *To Save the Wild Earth* (Seattle: Mountaineers, 1997).

381. *earthquakes:* Charles C. Plummer, David McGeary, and Diane H. Carlson, *Physical Geology* (New York: McGraw-Hill, 2001), 391, 402.

381. *one of few intact ecosystems:* Taylor H. Ricketts et al., *Terrestrial Ecoregions of North America: A Conservation Assessment* (Washington, D.C.: Island Press, 1999).

382. *Mount Saint Elias mountaineering:* Bill Sherwonit, *Alaska Ascents* (Seattle: Alaska Northwest Books, 1996), 8.

383. *"make wholeness possible":* Gary Snyder, *The Practice of the Wild: Essays* (San Francisco: North Point Press, 1990).

387. *mistook a marmot:* Adolph Murie, *A Naturalist in Alaska* (New York: Devin-Adair, 1961; reprint, Tucson: University of Arizona Press, 1990).

406. *Exxon Valdez oil spill:* George Laycock, "The Baptism of Prince William Sound," *Audubon,* September 1989.

408. *Copper River Delta:* Chris Finch and Alan Phipps, *Alaska Rainforest Atlas* (Juneau: Southeast Alaska Conservation Council, 1993).

CHAPTER 15: ACROSS THE ICEFIELD

413. *record snowfall:* Daniel Mathews, *Cascade-Olympic Natural History* (Portland, Oreg.: Portland Audubon Society, 1988), 24.

414. *causes of glaciation:* Deborah R. Harden, *California Geology* (Upper Saddle River, N.J.: Prentice Hall, 1997), 184.

414. *global warming:* Intergovernmental Panel on Climate Change, *Climate Change: The IPCC Response Strategies* (Washington, D.C.: Island Press, 1991).

414. *global warming effects:* Bill McKibben, *The End of Nature* (New York: Random House, 1989).

414. *climate and storms:* Stewart T. Schultz, *The Northwest Coast: A Natural History* (Portland, Oreg.: Timber Press, 1990), 23.

CHAPTER 16: TO THE ENDS OF THE EARTH

424. *commercial overfishing:* David Helvarg, *Blue Frontier: Saving America's Living Seas* (New York: W. H. Freeman, 2001); Carl Safina, *Song for the Blue Ocean* (New York: Henry Holt, 1997).

437. *"we all dwell in a house of one room":* John Muir, in *John of the Mountains: The Unpublished Journals of John Muir,* ed. Linnie Marsh Wolfe (Boston: Houghton Mifflin, 1938), 321.

# Acknowledgments

Thanks go first to my wife, Ann Vileisis, who encouraged, discussed, reflected, persuaded, rode, drove, navigated, cooked oatmeal and a thousand unnamed delicacies, walked, paddled, skied, painted, modeled for my pictures, laughed, cried, and loved with me the whole way from Baja to Kodiak and beyond, even while finishing a book of her own. A superb and demanding editor, Ann often put as much care, energy, and dedication into this book as I did.

For financial help while writing, I greatly appreciate the generosity of Jim and Pat Compton and Yvon Chouinard of Patagonia. These benefactors have used their resources to strengthen the forces of good in the world, and I'm honored to be among the many people they've supported. Thanks also to Drummond Pike and the Tides Foundation.

Barbara Dean of Island Press is a blessing to the world. A hopeful person has to think that her life's work in editing and publishing books will make a difference. Laura Carrithers of Island Press also read a draft of the manuscript with uncommon insight and offered encouraging suggestions. The work of Randy Baldini, Sam Dorrance, June Matherly, and the entire staff at Island Press is much appreciated. I can't imagine working with a finer group of people in a publishing house. The gifted work of copy editor Pat Harris made the final mile a good one.

The entire manuscript was helpfully read by Ann, Barbara, Laura, Pat, and also Jerry Meral—for many years director of California's Planning and

Conservation League, a reader I appreciate for his ability to catch inaccuracies and nuances of content and for his interest in words and ideas. Chris Duff, who writes fabulous books of his own about ocean kayaking, also read an early copy.

Chapters or parts of them were read by geologist David Howell, native plant aficionado Ed Grumbine, atmospheric scientist Ben Sayler, writer Thalia Zapatos, Canadian steward and spokesman Mark Angelo, and a number of people who appear in the book: Trudi Angell, Christy Lynch, Greg Bettencourt, Larry Orman, Ronnie James, Nancy Reichard, Richard Bocking, Marlene Smith, Stacy Studebaker, and Mike Sirofchuck. I received help with Spanish from Pat Munoz, Monica Larenas, and Jamie Bettencourt.

The authors of many fine sources are listed separately. The *Cascadia Times,* published by Paul Koberstein in Portland, proved to be an excellent bimonthly dispatch of news about what is happening to the Pacific mountains today, and I would never consider myself informed without it.

Peter and Linda Enticknap opened their home to Ann and me and, after Alaska's bitter cold rainy season began, even turned its care over to us for a while when they were gone. Mary and Greg Bettencourt of Cayucos, California, were likewise boundless in their hospitality and friendship. More than once my sister, Becky Schmitz, her husband, Steve, and their son Steve retrieved needed materials from my files, stacked in a corner of their Charlottesville, Virginia, basement. My mother, Jane Palmer May, forwarded mail from Pennsylvania as she has done for years, also sending regular dispatches of encouragement and love, which she has done for even longer.

All along the way, strangers and friends alike were forthcoming with information, guidance, and kindness. Many of these people were interviewed or mentioned in the book. To them and all others whose paths I crossed along the way, my heartfelt thanks and best wishes.

# About the Author

Tim Palmer is the author of thirteen other books. His recent title *The Heart of America* was named best travel and essay book of the year by the National Association of Independent Publishers. His book *The Columbia* won the National Outdoor Book Award. Also an accomplished photographer, he frequently speaks and gives slide shows to public audiences and college classes nationwide.

# Index